Middle East Tapestry

Middle East Tapestry

ROGER H. GUICHARD JR.

WIPF & STOCK · Eugene, Oregon

MIDDLE EAST TAPESTRY

Copyright © 2021 Roger H. Guichard Jr.. All rights reserved. Except for brief quotations in critical publications or reviews, no part of this book may be reproduced in any manner without prior written permission from the publisher. Write: Permissions, Wipf and Stock Publishers, 199 W. 8th Ave., Suite 3, Eugene, OR 97401.

Wipf & Stock
An Imprint of Wipf and Stock Publishers
199 W. 8th Ave., Suite 3
Eugene, OR 97401

www.wipfandstock.com

PAPERBACK ISBN: 978-1-7252-9834-7
HARDCOVER ISBN: 978-1-7252-9835-4
EBOOK ISBN: 978-1-7252-9836-1

03/02/21

Maps are reproduced under license from Shutterstock

For Laura

Contents

Illustrations | ix
Maps | xi
Preface | xiii

1. Arthur D. Little | 1
2. The Arabists | 26
3. The Magic Kingdom | 69
4. The Farm | 89
5. The Yemen | 97
6. Monte Carlo | 122
7. September Eleventh | 145
8. Morocco | 163
9. The Hejaz Railway | 178
10. The California Zephyr | 188
11. Home | 211
12. Tel al–Shehab and Mudawwara | 213
13. The Jordanians | 236
14. The Bach Festival | 242
15. Feelers | 276
16. The Renegades | 281
17. Nablus | 317
18. Christmas in Jerusalem | 326
19. Ramallah | 336

Illustrations

One of the Accountants | 9
Madam Su'ad | 10
The Hijab | 12
Street Scene, Cairo | 16
Flame Trees, Dokki | 22
Egyptian Desert | 23
T. E. Lawrence | 28
Charles M. Doughty | 31
Richard Burton | 34
Gertrude Bell | 37
Wilfrid Scawen Blunt | 41
Lady Anne Blunt | 42
Carsten Niebuhr | 47
J. L. Burckhardt | 51
Gifford Palgrave | 55
St. John Bridger Philby | 58
D. G. Hogarth | 61
Wilfred Thesiger | 65
Hejaz Mountains | 72
Meda'in Saleh | 73
Roundhouse, Al-Ula | 74

Dunes, Nefud | 78
Ramparts, Diri'ya | 80
Teak Dhow, Qatif | 84
Caves, Hofuf | 85
Jidda Skyline | 89
Arabian Homes | 91
Mashrabiyya, Jidda | 93
Gingerbread House, Sana | 100
Bab Yemen, San'a | 101
Ramlet Sabatain | 103
Sluice Gate, Ma'rib | 104
Guard Ma'rib | 105
Earthfill Dam, Ma'rib | 108
Old City, Ma'rib | 109
Awwam Temple | 110
Mohammed | 112
Escarpment | 113
Ablution, Jibla | 114
Mosque, Tehama | 116
Chewing Qat | 118
Plowman | 119

The *Fair Lady* | 127
The Big Screen | 129
Monte Carlo | 130
Motorized Yachts | 136
Race Day | 140
Highway, Asir | 149
Ape, Asir | 150
Kella, al-Ula | 184
Meda'in Saleh | 185
Amphitheater, Um Qais | 214
Bedouin, Wadi Rum | 217
Wadi Rum | 224
Abdullah | 225
South Mudawwara Station | 231
The Tiergarten | 247
Soviet Tank | 248
Thomaskirche | 251
Leipzig Motif | 253
Bach Statue, Leipzig | 254
The New and the Old, Halle | 262
Michaeliskirche | 270
Typical West Bank Scrub | 320
New Construction | 324
Amman Snowfall | 328
Damascus Gate | 329
Ramallah Real Estate | 336
Ramallah Street Scene | 338
Judaean Hills | 339
Roundabout, Ramallah | 342

Maps

Saudi Arabia | 68

Jordan | 177

The West Bank | 316

Preface

THE BOOK THAT FOLLOWS represents the final installment of my thirty-plus years living and working in the Arab and Muslim Worlds. The previous works, *Masr* and *At the Margins*—also published by Wipf and Stock—covered outlying areas of the region, Egypt, South Asia, and West Africa. This book marks a return to the central lands of Islam: the Arabian Peninsula, including Saudi Arabia and the Yemen, with lengthy excursions into lands to the north, chiefly Jordan and the West Bank. However, it begins with a piece on Egypt since that experience set the tone for nearly everything in the years that followed.

A first question was what to call it. The title, *Middle East Tapestry*, was chosen after careful consideration of several alternatives. At first, I thought of *Oriental Tapestry*, using an imprecise modifier that was once widely used, even in knowledgeable circles, to describe the lands east of Suez. But, at least since the publication of Edward Said's *Orientalism*, the word "Oriental" is considered by some to have outdated, offensive, or even racist connotations. However, I chose the alternative of *Middle East* not from any disinclination to enter into that particular fray, with its freighted connotations in the early twenty-first century. Rather it simply seemed better as a descriptor of the area inhabited by the world's nearly four-hundred million Arab Muslims and makes up in familiarity what it may lack in definitional precision and nuance.

The word *Tapestry*—technically, an elaborate piece of textile work with pictures woven into the warp and weft—was also carefully chosen. It more generally describes "an intricate combination of things or sequence of events, not necessarily related," that seemed to answer to the complexity of the area I am describing. Indeed, there is hardly a thing in the history of the area that is *not* intricate or complex. I first thought of *witness*, but where that word might have carried the implication of control, the word *Tapestry* is intended to remove the sense of agency, "of action or intervention designed to produce a particular effect." It more properly suggests that, rather than controlling events, we only react to them belatedly after they occur.

Egypt makes a brief cameo appearance at the outset as the place where it all began in 1980. It is followed by the Arabian Peninsula, including Saudi Arabia and the Yemen, from 1985 to 1989. Then, there was Jordan from 2000 to 2005 and, and, finally, the West Bank in 2008. As is the case with *Masr* and *At the Margins*, the pieces were written at the time the events they describe occurred. They have not been revised with the benefit of hindsight. This may seem counter-intuitive. But I believe that the value of immediacy, of testimony at the time the events took place, outweighs any consideration of timeliness. And the intractability of the problems in the Middle East means that not much has changed over the years since the pieces were written. The final three pieces reflect a short period of time in the West Bank, once the epicenter of discord in the region and now merely a foreshadowing of a perhaps more widespread and indiscriminate conflict.

Like *Masr* and *At the Margins*, this book consists of themed essays that shed light on particular aspects of the countries in question. More particularly it is a mélange of simple reportage, ruminations on history, literary criticism, thumbnail biography, and, particularly, the region as seen through the eyes of "experts," some originally from the region and others not. The West, particularly the United States and Great Britain, have had a checkered history with this area, in spite of a devotion to monotheism, commitment to private enterprise, and a whole litany of shared values.

It would be unusual if events preceding and following September eleventh, 2001 would not be mentioned. Indeed, it could be argued that the events surrounding that catastrophic event changed matters dramatically. In fact, there was a pre-9/11 and a post-9/11 in the region, not to mention the world, almost as profound as BC and AD, although the change was not obvious to most Americans. As detailed by Dana Priest and William Arkin in the *Washington Post*, there has been a dramatic growth of the national security apparatus in the United States after 9/11. From the role as the ineffectual broker of an elusive two-state solution to the "Arab-Israeli dispute," the United States moved to that of a player, arguably the most consequential, in the region. The series of events that cascaded from the American invasion of Iraq has yet to fully play itself out, although the rise of ISIS—a development that makes Osama bin-Laden appear to be a comparative moderate—the trauma of Iraq, the dissolution of Syria, and the opportunistic rise to prominence of Iran in the region, are all the step-children of that catastrophic invasion.

The coloring of the pieces that follow is also a product of those actions in the new century. From an attitude of relative buoyancy and optimism, the relatively anodyne portrayal of a part of the world that remains largely unknown to the American public, they have darkened and suffuse the reportage with suspicions of the deep state, more anti-Arab than the unthinking reflex that preceded them. The anti-Arab bias has now replaced an often-asserted, but nowhere believed, American commitment to even-handedness. Finally, the last three pieces reflect a weary resignation, and a sense that after all the tumult nothing has fundamentally changed in some parts of the region and they gradually resume their normal cast and cadence. Such is the capacity of the Middle East to shape, and impose its own interpretation of events on history.

The manuscript has been fortunate in its reader, a colleague and former intelligence officer in the region whom I persuaded to review the pieces. He brought his extensive knowledge of the Middle East to bear and he made suggestions of great merit, primarily with changes that, I hope, bring greater clarity to readers who may not be familiar with the history of the region. Any remaining gaps or uncertainties are, of course, my responsibility.

I

Arthur D. Little

IT WAS LATE DECEMBER, 1979 and I was on the phone with "G", a senior consultant at Arthur D. Little. We were discussing a job in Egypt and the subject turned to Arabic. It was one of the world's most difficult languages and would take years to master, especially if the study began as an adult. So, I said something about no one really being fluent in a language until he had lived in a country and spoken it on an everyday basis. But I had been exposed to the basics of the language, to modern standard Arabic, and that would enable me, in time, to acquire fluency. It sounded like something out of a course description, and was probably not the way to get a job. It was certainly not the way with *this* man who had a straightforward, not to say bumptious, approach to business. He was interested in results, not in a carefully qualified statement of why something may or may not be so. But it was my way and, on this occasion, it seemed to work.

It was my second time around with ADL, the first approach through the front door having met with the usual rebuff. But someone knew someone in ADL and he knew someone who was bid as a task leader on a project with the Egyptian telephone company. That was how you got a job. I was in my last semester at the American Graduate School of International Management, or Thunderbird, founded after the Second World War as the American Institute of Foreign Trade and located on an old air force base near Glendale, Arizona. With its offerings of area studies and languages, in addition to a faculty largely composed of ex-businessmen, it had since grown into the premier—some would say the only—American business school with an international focus.

But it was not a good time to be looking for work in the Middle East. The year began inauspiciously with the Shah fleeing Iran in January, and the downward spiral seemed to continue through the rest of the year. In February, the Ayatollah Khomeini returned to Iran, his followers seized power, and the US Ambassador to Afghanistan was kidnapped and killed. In April, Zulfikar Ali Bhutto was hanged in Pakistan, and Iran proclaimed the Islamic Republic in the same month. The Muslim Brotherhood murdered 62 sheikhs in Aleppo in June, and Saddam Hussein came to power in Iraq in the following month. The United States admitted the Shah for medical treatment in October and an already fraught situation turned toxic. In November, the American embassy in Tehran was attacked and 63 diplomats were taken hostage. Later in the month, fundamentalists seized the Grand Mosque in Mecca, with a mob trashing the American Embassy in Islamabad and killing two Americans over suspicion that we were behind the mosque events. In early December, another mob ransacked the American Embassy in Tripoli. This was followed later in the month by the Soviet invasion and seizure of power in Afghanistan. To put the capstone on a tumultuous twelve months the Dow closed the year at 838.74 and the prime rate came in at just over 15 percent.

However, there were occasional glimmers of hope. The Camp David accords signed by representatives of Egypt and Israel in September of 1978 opened the way to the peace treaty between the two countries a year later. The agreement also opened the coffers of aid agencies, primarily American and European, and they were soon lined up to extend credits to Egyptian public-sector entities. ADL, with a subcontractor, Continental Telephone, would eventually be awarded a contract to oversee American telecommunications projects implemented by AT&T and Ford Aerospace. A European consortium of equipment manufacturers, consisting of Siemens of Austria, Siemens of Germany, and Thomson CSF of France, headed the European effort. They would all win contracts to provide Egypt with equipment upgrades, the latest digital switches and the networks to connect them to each other and other networks, that would ultimately amount to several hundred million dollars.

But these latest developments lay in the future as I considered my options. Consulting firms bid on many jobs, only a handful of which materialized. By the time the bids were reviewed, the terms negotiated, and the contract awarded, half the people whose resumes appeared in the best-and-final document had probably moved on to something else. So, at a follow-up meeting with "G" in the lobby of the Biltmore Hotel in Los Angeles two days later we talked generalities and he gave me the sound advice to keep my options open and not count on anything, particularly on this job. And, by the way, had I approached any of the big-eight accounting firms?

However the job sounded interesting and I stayed with it. By the time the contract was awarded and the first people were on the ground in Egypt it would be mid-May 1980. By then I had been called to Cambridge for a second round of interviews. This was with senior consultants in the section and other members of the team. ADL in Cambridge was a large complex in Acorn Park, notorious for its Spartan concrete-block offices and Yankee work ethic. My first meeting was "G" himself who then ushered me into the office of a colleague, a kind of consulting type with a reputation for brilliance. For all I know he *was* brilliant, although I don't think he had worked anywhere except as a consultant. We talked in a desultory way about business until, very suddenly, he observed that Arabs must be capable of a kind of mental gymnastic, reading as they did from right to left while their numbers ran from left to right, just like ours did. It was an interesting observation. Then he took me over to a wall and showed me the framed cartoon of a camel with a handwritten caption in Arabic. It probably had something to do with their reputation for holding a grudge. Camels never forgot a slight. I was supposed to read the caption. But the handwriting was illegible and, anyway, most of those words had not been in our syllabus. I think I failed the test.

The next meeting was with "G"'s immediate boss. The discussion was anything but desultory. This man *had* worked and seemed to have come up through the school of hard knocks. We had both been officers in the Navy and that should have given me some caste. But he soon made it clear that he didn't like me, he didn't like the University of California at Berkeley, he didn't like the west coast, he didn't like government jobs, and he especially didn't like *this* government job. There was a sense of unreality about the man but I parried noncommittally and moved on. These first two interviews had been anything but promising.

This was followed by meetings with prospective members of the team. The first of them, "G" said admiringly, was well connected in Boston banking circles. He grilled me on what I knew about Cairo and seemed especially interested in tennis. Since I would go out as part of the advance team, I would be looking for an apartment for the visiting consultants. It had to be near a tennis court. But he left ADL shortly afterwards, probably gone back to some Boston-based investment bank, and never made it to Cairo. Next on the list was a boyish-looking guy whose expertise seemed to consist of a kind of extreme chutzpah. He had first interviewed with ADL in London and brought his girlfriend along on the trip. He billed the company for the cost of the two tickets and they had paid the claim. But at least he was friendly and had a framed print of "Mohammad" in good Arabic calligraphy on the wall.

The next two interviews were with African Americans and the interviews required a different kind of skill. I was supposed to be the one on trial but in a sense, they would always be. One man had developed a risk-assessment methodology for companies considering investment in the developing world and was interested in selling it. ADL was only a step along the way. The second man was a certified public accountant and, he was careful to tell me, the first licensed black CPA in the state of Georgia. But a later incident in front of the Nile Hilton in Cairo demonstrated why this chemistry was not going to work. We were turning into the hotel drive, "G" and I and the other two men, when a 1950s-vintage Cadillac pulled in, probably carrying some member of the old *Wafd*, the Egyptian political party founded after the First World War. With his unerring ability to strike the wrong note, "G" asked what model it was, as if blacks knew Cadillacs the way New Zealanders knew sheep. The two slumped, disgusted, in their seats. For a number of reasons, they weren't destined to last.

The final interview was with "L," the Greek-American whose dogged persistence had really won the contract. He worked like a beaver, with an intensity that often got in the way of his good sense. But he alone, among the people I met at Acorn Park, talked about Egypt and the client. He began as the project manager, since it was the practice in ADL that whoever sold the project managed it. He was not a very good manager and in the early days would make cash advances out of his hip pocket with IOU's written on the back of the hotel coffee-shop menu. So, shortly after the project began they replaced him with a more conventional figure who worked for Stanford Research Institute in Sa'udi Arabia and was known to an ADL vice president. But "L" took it like a man when they demoted him and kept on beavering. When he left Cairo five years later his section in Cambridge had forgotten about him. Actually, they ignored him when he came back and he spent several unprofitable months in Acorn Park looking for work, or just someone to talk to. Then he left ADL. It was kind of sad.

Somehow, I got the job. It would be as the finance and accounting resident in Cairo on a project with ARENTO, the Arab Republic of Egypt National Telecommunications Organization. At the time, the teledensity—the percentage of the population with a telephone—in Egypt was about one per hundred as opposed to something like seventy per hundred in more advanced countries. And the existing systems were old and inefficient. It was hard to believe but representatives of international companies had to fly to Cyprus on the weekends to place telephone calls. Since there was a direct correlation between the efficiency of a telephone system and the level of foreign direct investment in a country, this project was designed to shake ARENTO out of its statist somnolence and drag it into the late twentieth-century. Given the foreign policy thrust of the Reagan years this project would be only one of many that were intended to transform the primary infrastructure of Egypt and, incidentally, turn its economy from a socialist to a quasi-capitalist one. But the old socialist habits died hard, if they died at all, which we will see as our tale unfolds.

I say I got the job, but it wasn't easy keeping it. My first assignment was to examine ARENTO's existing accounting systems and to describe them in detail. Only then would the process of new system design begin. The skills required were not always those we had learned in business school. After a meeting with a manager in the fixed asset department I hoped that his knowledge of asset accounting was as developed as his knowledge of Islam. He looked slightly hyperthyroid anyway and his already prominent eyes widened as he rattled off all ninety-nine names of God—*al-Rahman, al-Rahim, al-Malik, al-Quddus, al-Salam . . . al-Sabur*—in order, in less than a minute. Just like that. It couldn't compare with memorization of the entire Qur'an, which some children had done, but it was still impressive. Very few of the Egyptian accountants spoke English and my classical Arabic wasn't much help. But I began to pick up the colloquial Egyptian that has served me well over the years. Spoken Egyptian Arabic, while it is widely understood throughout the Arab World, is regarded as hopelessly corrupt and my classical Arabic has never recovered from that early exposure to Egypt.

I also began to develop relationships with the Egyptians that would bear fruit later on. But these things weren't enough. I remembered the interview with the manager of the ARENTO Data Center, a man who knew very little about data processing but was concerned with, as he put it in Franglais, "my vacances." He hadn't had a vacation in years and saw our arrival as a way of putting pressure on his boss. I was translating and trying to convey the question as to whether there was an ARENTO way of computing, but the manager kept talking about his "vacances" and the interview ended inconclusively. I think "G" decided at that point that I just wouldn't do and that he needed an Egyptian in my place. He told me that he would write me a terrific recommendation, although I didn't know for what since this was my first experience in business and I had clearly failed the test. He later changed his mind and I stayed, but on the condition that I become fluent in colloquial Egyptian Arabic in a matter of months.

The condition, and especially the implication that I had misled him about Arabic from the beginning, particularly rankled. It would take several *years* to become fluent in the colloquial language and jumping through hoops wouldn't change that. So, I just hunkered down and tried to outlast him. It may not have been the most straightforward thing to do and it left a bad taste in my mouth. But, as I later learned, it was the Egyptian way. He had boisterous, backslapping manner that may have worked in the United States. But among the considerable gravities of the ARENTO finance committee it was, to put it charitably, unfortunate. He discovered early in the project that the extravagant promises of the proposal couldn't be delivered. So, he redefined them and ARENTO signed off on the changes. Then he sat back and hoped. In the end, everything worked out. But his boss hated government work so he must have spent many sleepless nights over the five years of the project. "G" was the kind of man you couldn't dislike but rather despised. There was something you couldn't put your finger on until he confessed that what most concerned him about Egypt was the fear of being taken hostage, like the embassy employees in Iran. He was simply the kind of man who didn't belong overseas. He told me that I had a bright future but it was always, it seemed, with someone other than Arthur D. Little.

The project soon developed the estrangement between the home office and the staff in the field that was common to overseas undertakings. The senior consultant in Cambridge in charge of each task—finance and accounting, inventory control, organization, training, billing, and planning—realized that reforming ARENTO was impossible, even in his own limited area. The scopes-of-work had been written in the United States and most of the task leaders had never seen Egypt before they promised to remake it in their own image. So, like "G", each one redefined his task, concentrating on visible deliverables. Those of us in the field were not very senior and we were clearly expendable, but we were *there* and could see needs developing that didn't fit in with the original scopes.

The task leaders from Cambridge would periodically fly in, expecting the kind of attention due a senior consultant in what was, after all, the world's first consulting firm. That was even allowing for the ADL culture, which was determinedly democratic. They would be breathless with overwork, having fit Cairo into a busy international schedule. They arrived from Bangkok or London or Rio de Janeiro, having read snatches from *Exodus* or *The Sphinx* or *The Key to Rebecca* on the plane to prepare them for work in the Arab World. It was obvious that some of them used the project as an excuse to see the pyramids. We talked long afterwards about the pair who arrived in Cairo one morning, having lost their luggage for which they roundly criticized the local administrative staff. They worked for the day, caught an evening flight to Luxor, saw the sights and were gone the next day. They later wrote a highly critical evaluation of the project.

The nice thing about the job was that I could write my own ticket, provided the deliverables were there, and I chose the project accounting area because it seemed the most interesting part of the work. There were loan covenants to read, many in Arabic, and I made my own translations and compared them with the original documents that may have been in English or French. It was the beginning of a habit of translation that has lasted for over three decades. Every year I translated the financial statements of ARENTO into English and provided copies to organizations like the World Bank and the International Development Agency or IDA. In time, I became the international finance department's own consultant. The discipline of making accounting entries in Arabic and adding large columns of Arabic numbers has never left me, an invaluable aid in sifting through the often-incomprehensible systems in this part of the world.

The discipline of double-entry bookkeeping was ingrained in ARENTO, and the debits always equaled the credits. But how they arrived at the result didn't seem very important. Information was not critical to management, so accounting became a hypothetical exercise. The current account, that governed relations between the accounting units, was always a problem. At the end of the year, the accounting managers gathered in Cairo where there was a feverish—and very uncharacteristic—burst of activity to make the numbers add up and close the books. Then, after awarding themselves a bonus, they returned to Alexandria, Tanta, Assiut, and Qena and relapsed into their old ways.

Under the circumstances, we could focus our attention only on a few limited areas where we could have some impact. The odds against success were illustrated by an incident early in our stay. We had scheduled a meeting with the finance committee to discuss the new accounts—in technical terms, the "chart of accounts"—that we had designed. At the last minute, the meeting was cancelled because, we later learned, the finance committee was meeting to discuss changes in the *existing* accounts. So, there were parallel activities in the finance area, one with the foreigners and the other where the real business of the company was conducted. And there was no question as to which was more important. We could do what we wanted but they would simply outlast us. So, we managed to do a few useful things like computerizing their payroll system where the savings in preparation time, were not, of course, realized in staff reductions. And we were able to introduce a telephone company chart of accounts into the projects area, only because they didn't have one before we arrived.

One of the Accountants

They were using the old accounts provided to all public-sector entities from the time of the revolution in 1952. The system was comprehensive but financially meaningless in a telecommunications environment and included accounts for every kind of commercial activity imaginable, from selling fabric to bee-keeping. There actually was an account in their books for "Bees, domestic." ARENTO could have assigned their own asset sub-accounts but they had not, and kept everything in an undifferentiated account called "equipment." That gave us the opening we needed. We brought in the retired controller of New York Telephone, a real old pro, and he spent several months under contract to ADL, drafting a comprehensive chart of accounts suitable to a telephone company in the late twentieth-century.

We designed new vouchers in Arabic with features to capture the above details in a format that could easily be computerized. And we trained a group of accountants, all of them young women, to deal with the capital expansion program. After Camp David manufacturers were lined up to sell ARENTO equipment and present invoices in their national variants of English. None of the women spoke English, so we trained them in the rudimentary written language. After a while they became experts in British-English, American-English, Austrian-English, French-English, German-English, Swedish-English and several other variants of the international language of business.

They were young, the oldest and leader among them, Madam Su'ad, being about thirty.

Madam Su'ad

The rest were much younger and a few were still in their teens. They worked in a separate room, away from the other accountants. They were ignored by the others but that was just as well because it prevented contamination and they did the only real accounting work in the company. They produced a monthly summary of "Projects under Construction," the detail by asset category with charges to accounts such as "French Protocols," or "Grants, American," accumulated by loan or grant number. The project accounts grew rapidly with the infusion of foreign money and the assets under construction soon became larger than the assets in service. That was another ARENTO problem. No engineer would accept responsibility for project completion, so the assets were typically not transferred to the "in service" accounts. That was less serious than it sounded because they still generated dial-tone—and revenue—and provided service to new customers.

As a group, these young women were the best accountants in ARENTO. In general, we found women better than men at the kind of detailed work required of accounting. Maybe that was because, for a man, work in the company was often a sinecure, and they had jobs somewhere else. It might be a repair shop for small appliances or a hole in the wall in the *suq* where he sold copper trinkets. A married woman also went home to a second job, but most of these accountants were single. But it wasn't just these women who stood out in ARENTO. Women in the company had risen to high positions and most of the implementation engineers we dealt with were women with authority over large numbers of men. I had seen computer classes in Egypt where the only male present was the teaboy.

On a visit to the company several years later I found the women still there, still hard at work, but removed even farther from the main accounting area. They were still seen as an extension of the foreigners long after the foreigners had gone. Most were now married with children and most were wearing the *hijab*, the simple wimple that was increasingly adopted by the urban poor in Egypt. But they were still doing their painstaking work and their monthly activity reports, the cumulative records of hundreds of millions of dollars' worth of sophisticated equipment, with accurate charges to foreign debt, were now being entered into a computer database. So maybe it was *we* who outlasted *them* after all.

The Hijab

The finance officers of the lenders came in a steady stream to the eleventh-floor office of the International Department in the Opera exchange building. I took it as a compliment the first time I was asked to be there for a meeting with one of them. It was interesting to see their different national characteristics. The Germans and the Americans were the easiest to deal with. The Germans seemed to be cut out of rough cloth and simply got on with the job. They seemed to like the Egyptians and were liked by them in return. The Americans were their usual cooperative and slightly deferential selves abroad. There may once have been the phenomenon of the "ugly American" but I never saw it in thirty years as an expatriate. Americans were always ready to see the other man's point of view, as long as it didn't interfere with their own interests. But I began to see my countrymen through the eyes of the undersecretary.

It was after a visit from the representative of Ford Aerospace, the network contractor. He was an old Iran-hand and had that fondness of some middle-aged American men for jewelry. He spoke expansively with his hands, displaying a pair of rings with a large diamond set in each. It was almost as if he talked just to show off the rings. On his left wrist, he featured a heavy gold ID bracelet. And on his chest, nestled among the white hairs, was a nicely-worked gold chain. After he left the under-secretary asked me, rather diffidently, why he wore all that jewelry. In the Arab World, they could understand a *woman* wearing that kind of thing, but not a man. Later, there was the story in the local newspaper about the American expatriate who had a cartouche made for his dog. Now, a 24-carat cartouche, depending on the weight, would have cost several hundred dollars, at the time about the per-capita GDP in Egypt. The reaction to the story in the faces of the Egyptians had to be seen to be believed.

In fact, the cast of characters on the project was as colorful as it was varied, although most were British. "C," the original office manager, was a retired colonel in the colonial police. He was a graduate of Sandhurst, the British equivalent of West Point, and during his career had been posted over most of what little remained of the British Empire. He first arrived in Egypt in 1956 in a parachute during the Suez War. Then it had been Betuanaland, Cyprus during "the troubles," and Nigeria. He ended his military career as chief of security in the Seychelles. After retirement, he attended a training course to prepare himself for administrative work. He would probably spend the rest of his life in out-of-the way places, working, drinking, and playing golf.

He had a ready fund of stories, from shooting lions in South Africa to undercover operations in Cyprus. His club became the bar at the Indiana Hotel in Dokki, the neighborhood of Cairo where we were headquartered. He would retire to the Indiana at the end of the day and drink until well into the night. His pretty young wife and two daughters seemed to accept it as the wages of expatriate family life. He drank only beer, tall Stellas brewed in Egypt under license from Amstel Corporation. It didn't seem to affect his weight, because he was small and wiry and never looked like he gained a pound. Maybe that was because he also gained a parasite after his arrival and was sick for most of his short stay in Egypt. He left after a few months, hired away by the subcontractor. That seemed an unfriendly thing to do, and it caused a brief estrangement between the two companies. Actually, the estrangement was there from the beginning, between Continental Telephone, a rough-and-ready operating company from Atlanta, and Arthur D. Little, among the greatest repositories of gray cells in the history of Cambridge Massachusetts. But it may have been as much his fault as Continental's, because he went back to Lagos, where his heart really lay, to work, drink, and play golf.

He was replaced by another character nearly as colorful in his own way as the original "C." His father had been in trade in India but in spite of that he bordered on the upper class. He dressed with a disregard of color and pattern that could only have been studied. With thick glasses and an unimpressive physique, he didn't look like an athlete, but put a racket or a club in his hand and he was unbeatable. He had been the expatriate squash champion of Iran and regularly shot golf in the low 70s. I remembered seeing him on the tennis court playing an American who came equipped with the latest racket and spotless white togs, down to the headband and wristbands. "C" was probably hung over and he was in his usual attire, dirty shorts and socks that had lost their elastic. He stayed on the baseline, a cigarette in one hand and racket in the other, and hit winner after winner.

He and his wife had two children, who were to be brought up just the way they had been. That meant that the boy was sent to boarding school in the UK at the age of eight. It may not have been the right thing to do, but that was the way it was done. His in-laws came to visit them in Cairo. The father was a medical doctor who had been in Egypt during the Second World War and, in a friendly sort of way, I asked him how the city had changed since he was last there. "I don't know," he said, "I was pissed the whole time." In Alexandria, they had to remove him from the stage when he went after one of the belly dancers.

The computer specialist was an old data-processing pro, also a Brit and with a hyphenated name at that, but relocated to the United States. While he took himself a little too seriously, at least he took the Egyptians seriously as well and they reciprocated the regard. He was a large man, about six feet tall, and weighed well over 200 pounds. But the weight was poorly distributed and there didn't seem to be an identifiable muscle anywhere in his body. He was shaped like a bull sea lion. He also had a fondness for jewelry and on a man of over fifty it looked a little ridiculous, especially when he lounged by the pool, the great expanse of white flesh covered only by the chains and the smallest of bikinis.

He had a large head, and we marveled at the IT knowledge that those prominent frontal lobes must have contained. He was also bald. That gave that part of his anatomy the look of a large melon, in which were set two tiny eyes and a small, thin-lipped mouth that worked uncontrollably when he was excited. He was also a bit of a raconteur with a ready store of photographs to illustrate his tales. The story of the truck that carried away a part of his house was a classic in the study of miscommunication between cultures. We were sitting in the office of the vice chairman of finance of ARENTO, an agreeable man but with only a rudimentary understanding of English. His response to almost every statement was "Excellent. Excellent, we must put everything in a good condition."

But this was different. There apparently had been a ten-wheeler parked on a hill above his house in the suburb of Cambridge where "S-P" lived. The emergency brake failed and the truck had come down the hill, crashing through the house and carrying away most of the family room. He was telling the story, complete with before and after photos, and he was on a roll. His excitement mounted as he described the carnage, and he was positively shouting as he told how his wife had escaped through the back door. The vice chairman sat phlegmatically though it all, muttering "Excellent. Excellent, we must put everything in a good condition." "S-P" and his wife didn't have children, but they had a Peekapoo on which they lavished their attention. He later bought jewelry for the dog. It would have completed the stupefaction of the Egyptians had they known.

ADL had apparently invested a great deal in the project management task and at a cocktail party the responsible consultant from Cambridge was talking about himself and his team. It was a *tour de force*. We had started the evening just chatting, but he spent the entire time talking about himself. It was now a couple of hours later, but he was still going strong. He had finished his own story, moved past that of his children and was now talking about his grandchildren. I had never encountered a self-centeredness so remorseless. He had been a test pilot in the Navy, and when I later saw a public television special on the X-aircraft, I was sure he was the man I saw climbing out of the cockpit. He had come to ADL after retirement and established a project management methodology and team. To read one description of the ARENTO project, you would have thought that it was nothing more than a showcase for himself and his team. But I don't think they were any more successful than the rest of us.

The French were the most difficult to deal with. The finance man from Thomson was always immaculately dressed, his shoes were always shined, and the fragrance of his cologne lingered long after he had left the building.

Street Scene, Cairo

He may have been in Cairo, and in the Opera exchange building at that, but he still dressed as if he were in Paris. My own experience with a pair of calfskin Ballys convinced me that sturdy footwear was preferable on the sidewalks of Cairo. But it wasn't so much his appearance, it was his manner: Cairo was an exile and, after Paris, that was understandable. He was particularly impatient with ARENTO's caution.

There was good reason for their caution. The undersecretary made the equivalent of about $100 a month and was asked, every day, to sign documents in a foreign language that committed the company to the repayment of millions of dollars in loans. There was no question that if anything went wrong they would come after the signatories. It led to a devolving of responsibility downhill, and we used to joke that the first signature you had to have was the teaboy's. I reviewed documents with the finance department on many occasions and it was always a painful process. We would review the language, word-by-word, sentence-by-sentence, page-by-page. When I thought that we had finished the first page and had moved on to the second, I realized that the undersecretary's eyes had returned to the top of the *first* page, and we went over it again. Under the circumstances, it was remarkable that they signed anything at all.

Trust was everything and small investments paid large dividends afterwards. When we had just arrived and I was describing ARENTO's chaotic fixed-asset system, the manager in charge was concerned about his son's application to a medical school in Boston. I helped him with the application, smoothing out the rough parts and bringing to bear what little I knew about the process of applying to American universities. The son got in, I'm sure on his own merits, but his father never forgot my help. When he later became undersecretary for Stores and Purchasing, a key position, he made life easy instead of difficult for ADL since he was responsible for approving our invoices.

The school application was a key to understanding the people in ARENTO. It was probably a cliché that Americans put their job at the top of a hierarchy, beneath which the others ranged in descending order of importance. The Egyptians emphatically did not. The chief accountant at ARENTO was as fine a man as I have ever known, the best example of a good Muslim, hardworking by his lights and unshakably ethical. I don't think he prayed five times a day although he put the precepts of Islam into practice on a daily basis. But he was a bureaucrat and the most important thing in life was seeing his two daughters through medical school. He clearly had his priorities right, and our brief was to get rid of people like him.

An average workday began in Ma'adi, the suburb south of Cairo where most Americans lived. It was described as "posh," but I always thought of it as a dusty little place. Dust was the bane of our lives. It was everywhere, so finely distributed that a dark coat in a locked closet in a closed room would be covered with dust the next time you took it out. There was even dust between the pages of books in the bookshelf. The street sweepers in Ma'adi spent most of their time cleaning up dust, although there was plenty of other rubbish as well. The first thing we noticed in the apartment after an extended absence was the characteristic odor of dust.

It rained in Cairo only a few times a year and the lack of rain meant that the trees in Cairo were generally dirty, although dusty may have been more descriptive. Then, when the occasional rains came, the combination of the water and the dust turned the city into a sea of mud. Women arrived in the office with the backs of their legs, fashionably encased in colored hose, spattered or caked in mud. The sewers would overflow and whole neighborhoods would be ankle deep in gray water. The incidence of water-borne diseases—what the government euphemistically called "summer diseases"—always rose at this time of the year.

Ma'adi had been fashionable under the British and had once been full of nice old villas. But with the new prosperity that came after Camp David landlords were pulling down the villas as fast as they could and putting up apartment buildings in their place. A landlord could recoup the cost of a building in a few years and, after that, it was all gravy. Tax evasion was not only a habit among landlords but, it seemed, a downright duty. Everyone got in on the action, including the foreign real estate agents who placed us in the apartments. A permit might be for five stories, but the building often climbed far beyond that. One consultant living in a ground floor apartment endured several years of construction activity, with illegal floors added above and the basement below excavated for a shop. He finally objected when alarming cracks appeared in a living room wall. Early in our stay, the Minister of Tourism was killed in his villa in another one of Cairo's neighborhoods. He and his family were buried under an illegal, ten-story apartment building next door when it collapsed.

Real estate was a problem, but for another reason. Under the laws that followed the revolution in 1952, rent control had gone into effect and it was not uncommon to see the ground floor of a large building rented to, say, a pharmacy for four Egyptian pounds per month. That amounted to about six dollars when we first came to Cairo. Later it was worth a third of that. A clever tenant would sublease the flat or apartment to a foreigner at the going rate, something like $1,000, and pocket the difference. But if an original tenant occupied the building the rent could not be raised and remained at the old, pre-revolutionary level. Much of Cairo real estate was deteriorating because landlords couldn't afford to maintain properties at those rents.

Public works had also been neglected during the Nasser years, while the country embarked on a program of military expenditures and expensive and wasteful projects like the Egyptian space program. The primary infrastructure—sewers, water, roads, and telephones—had deteriorated and repairing them was much of the reason why we, and others, were there. The Egyptians fixed what they could, but the maintenance work was poor. Roads were repaved, but the surfaces were poorly prepared and blacktop was laid down over piles of dust. It took only a few weeks for the potholes to reappear. Often, proper maintenance required tools they didn't have. I once transported in my own car a team from the Ministry of Electricity to fix the power cable to our building after it had been cut by a backhoe. They had the shrinkable splice closures, but I had to shuttle back and forth between the building and the *suq* to buy them pliers and fuel for their torch.

Road 9, the main shopping area in Ma'adi, was a scruffy little street where the merchants neglected even the sidewalks. That was probably because they were afraid of the tax man. They did very well in their little establishments, catering to the foreigners with slogans like "In God We Trust" emblazoned over the entrances. But they themselves always looked poor. It was like the cars. Upper Egypt was full of old cars, buried under the haystacks when Nasser came to power. Anybody with money had gone to ground after the revolution and it took a while for the habit of conspicuous consumption to return.

The grocery stores in Ma'adi were small and always smelled of a combination of cat droppings and rancid cheese. In the early days, there were shortages of everything, including staples like flour and rice, not to mention condiments like mayonnaise and catsup. We became very good at making tarragon mayonnaise. All you needed was a blender with a drip feed, an egg, oil, and a little tarragon. The stores were laid out vertically rather than horizontally, and that meant an army of clerks to mount the ladders and retrieve the items you wanted. The help was a characteristic of Cairo, and you never shopped unattended. The clerks were paid nothing and depended on tips. The owners were occasionally pleasant but for the most part they were too busy ringing up sales to waste time on small talk. The use of money was odd to an American. Checks were almost unheard of and Egyptians always carried cash.

My first experience in Ma'adi was buying appliances for the three flats in the building, and the girl in the store put the cash, the equivalent of about $6,000, in the unlocked drawer of a desk. There was no cash register, no security, and no record of the transaction. When we traveled with the landlord, selecting cabinets and tile for the kitchen and the bathrooms, he carried thousands of pounds in an attaché case. At each stop he would open the case to reveal bricks of brand-new 100-pound notes, still in the wrappers from the bank. The money got a workout and, with time, the bills—particularly the smaller denominations—became so frayed and dirty that the Japanese would handle them only with gloves. But there was very little theft in Cairo. There were plenty of stories of violence in the newspapers, but they tended to be crimes of passion or domestic violence. A man would kill his wife or a woman would stab her sleeping husband, generally over a suspected infidelity. The *bawwab*, or doorkeeper, for our building killed his daughter the year before we came. She was sixteen and had become pregnant. He threw her off the roof of the unfinished building. Everyone knew he did it, but the practice of honor killing was too deeply ingrained in the culture for anyone to bother much about it. He was never charged with the crime. But your money was safe in Ma'adi.

The Americans lived in Ma'adi primarily because of the school, Cairo American College or CAC. It was a large sprawling campus that included everything from kindergarten to the twelfth grade. The campus was a community center for everyone and, on the weekends British, Dutchmen, Germans, and Frenchmen as well as Americans could be seen walking, jogging on the track, or watching their kids play on the jungle gyms. It was also the gathering place for Americans in the event of an emergency, and always seemed too obvious to be safe. Old hands spoke of seeing Israeli planes coming in low over the school buildings during the war of attrition in the 1967–73 period. They were headed for targets on the Nile. Once they hit a nearby army barracks and afterwards the children watched the bloodied bodies being carried out of the building.

We always drove ourselves the twelve miles to the office, up the corniche that bordered the Nile. Others did not and I particularly remembered the sight of the manager of a large American project in the back seat of his chauffeur-driven car. They must have sharpened their pencils very fine when they bid the project because the vehicles were tiny Chevrolets, assembled in Korea. He was a tall man and looked comical, sitting in the back seat of this ridiculous car, reading the newspaper with his knees up under his chin. Our cars were Peugeot 504s, leased from Avis. They were the village taxis of Egypt, and the best of a bad lot. We eventually graduated to 505s.

Our offices were in the Dokki exchange building and they were barely adequate. The retired AT&T vice president who was later brought in as head of the project took one look at the place when he arrived and said that, God damn it, changes would be made. They were, but in a few months the toilets were overflowing again, the windows still didn't close, and everything else had returned to its original state. And this was in an exchange building where dust was death on digital switches. Egypt had a way of defeating the best of intentions. Our original quarters, almost our office, had been the Indiana hotel in Dokki. It wasn't fancy, but at least we were guaranteed rooms and the staff treated us like the old hands that we had become. There was a time when aircrews had to make reservations months in advance to be assured of a decent hotel room in Cairo. But when we left there was a surplus of five-star rooms in Cairo and more hotels were going up every year.

Dokki was actually pretty in the spring when the flame trees were in bloom. We were in the old flood plain of the Nile and the frequent excavations for new buildings revealed the value of the land we were occupying. Down they went, deeper and deeper, first men and then donkeys carrying away baskets full of rich black earth. It was the stuff of millions of years of deposits, topsoil carried down from the highlands of Ethiopia and deposited by the flood of the Nile. As recently as the mid-1960s, before the High Dam was competed, the river regularly flooded downtown Cairo.

Flame Trees, Dokki

The Egyptians dug everything by hand. We knew an American contractor who was erecting electrical power pylons and needed to excavate for the foundations. Each area was maybe 400 feet square by ten feet deep. When the excavation subcontractor arrived, it was a man and his three daughters with baskets. But very dramatically, as you mounted the Giza Plateau, the black earth ended and the desert began. The contrast was even greater since the green of the *birseem*, or clover, was *so* green. Only 3 percent of Egypt was arable, and that percentage was shrinking every year. The government was trying to encourage settlement in the desert, in places like Sadat City or 6th October City to the west of Cairo. But

Egyptians were notorious homebodies and people were reluctant to move. So, urban sprawl continued and arable land near the river was built on or excavated. The problem was that a farmer could get more for the topsoil by selling it to a brick factory than by sowing it. The government had mandated the use of concrete block in building instead of red brick, but it was another old habit that would die hard and the farmers were still scraping the soil.

Egyptian Desert

The Egyptian desert was not pretty, nothing like the magnificent golden dunes of the Sahara or the pink *Nefud* in Sa'udi Arabia. There were interesting areas like the Black Desert or the White Desert to the west, but most of Egypt was a dirty yellow-brown. Even as sand it wasn't worth much. At the ceremonial opening of a joint venture with Owens Corning to manufacture glass bottles someone mentioned that the sand had to be imported, the local product not being suitable for glassmaking. The gathering was interesting for its display of the old-boy network in Egypt. Many of the men present had attended Victoria College in Alexandria, once *the* school in the Arab World, graduating such luminaries as King Hussein, Adnan Khashoggi, Edward Sa'id, and Michel Shalhoub or Omar

Sharif. It was a pillar of the old colonial system where the boys went to "public" schools and were taught in English. The girls typically went to convent schools and learned French. After the Revolution Victoria College became Victory College, but it wasn't the same. There was a new branch of the school near us, in Digla near Ma'adi. But according to our Egyptian friends it suffered from the same overcrowding and lack of resources as the other schools in Egypt.

Founded in 1886, Arthur D. Little was the world's primordial consulting firm. Consultants now dot the business landscape. It was originally technology-based and had demonstrated that you *could* make a silk purse out of a sow's ear, that a lead balloon *would* fly, and that an old dog *could* learn new tricks. But, in spite of having spawned countless competitors and imitators, ADL eventually failed. Some said it never really adjusted to being a consulting firm as opposed to a technology firm. Others said that it was poorly managed and should have shed the financial burden of the Acorn Park property long before. One of the new breed in the 1980s even advised that the company enter into a sale and leaseback arrangement. There were probably other reasons, but in the end ADL succumbed to its inefficiencies. In early 2002, it filed for bankruptcy and protection from its creditors. The name was bought by a French company that retained the rights to its use. But ADL as we knew it was dead.

I worked for the company only in Egypt and Sa'udi Arabia and so knew the Cambridge culture from a distance. I was 100 percent billable, every day for nine years, and billability was gold in the consulting business. But on the first day I was *not*, it was down the road. In that respect, ADL was no different from Booz Allen, GTE, General Dynamics, Ronco, or Chemonics. To be fair, there was an understanding between the parties on the terms of the relationship: I received a salary and benefits and the company got the billability. I was not interested in occupying an office in Acorn Park, or McLean Virginia, or Washington DC. But there was something about ADL that left me with a bit of regret at its passing. Maybe it was the colorful personalities, or the fact that I knew it at a time when political correctness was not the rule. ADL was the last bastion of what seemed to be a kind of male-dominated, eastern-establishment culture.

A glance at the 1981 Arthur D. Little staff album showed that there were plenty of women and minorities working for the company, as might be expected of a firm with offices in Athens, Brussels, London, Madrid, Paris, Rio de Janeiro, San Francisco, Sao Paolo, Tokyo, Toronto, Washington, and Wiesbaden. But the company didn't make a thing of equal opportunity. With its private-sector focus, the project in Sa'udi Arabia was probably more typical than the ARENTO project, although in the kingdom there was always a question as to which was private and which was public sector. The vice president who periodically visited Jidda from the home office was also typical. He didn't really arrive but just seemed to glide into town. He had that silver hair and silver smile, and was an old Sa'udi hand in an odd sort of way. It was odd in the sense that he had been around for a while, but seemed curiously disengaged. He knew all the other old Sa'udi hands, but they seemed just as disengaged. They didn't speak Arabic and seemed to be the western equivalent of the Levantines—the Lebanese, Syrians, and Palestinians—who together with the Egyptians ran Sa'udi Arabia in the early days. We would sit around the office in Jidda and listen to him talk about what ADL was up to these days. We were all "ADLers," although some were more ADLer than others. He always emphasized how ADL circulated at the highest levels, and didn't bother with the small fry. There was some truth in that, and we were one of the few companies in Sa'udi Arabia whose employees didn't surrender their passports.

But at the highest levels we cultivated we often ignored the people necessary to make these consulting contracts work. There was always something a little childish about the behavior of the senior consultants, as if the enterprise they were engaged in was a game, and not just the game-playing paradigm fashionable in consulting circles. They seemed like children, too pleased with themselves and too careless with the careers of the people they moved around like pieces on a board. I don't know if they were playing chess or just checkers. I'm not even sure they played the game very well. There were stories of inefficiency and locals walking off with wads of cash. But those responsible were always rewarded with yet another promotion, yet more responsibility. In ADL, the saying was "fuck up and move up." There was an element of truth in the allegation. At the higher levels, they scratched each other's backs.

I later met a young guy who worked in Tunisia and wanted to be a consultant, preferably with Arthur D. Little. He had the combination of ambition and connections that would make him a natural. If he played his cards right he could look forward to years of plans and paradigms and games and algorithms. He was an incipient man with the silver hair.

2

The Arabists

OVER THE YEARS I have done a series of portraits of people I have called "Arabists," mostly in soft drawing pencil on plain white paper. Most were drawn from photographs and all are long-since dead, although Thesiger was still alive when I drew his portrait in 1991. They have been successively lithographed and digitized in Egypt, Sa'udi Arabia, Pakistan, and the United States. Although the first portrait dates from Egypt, Sa'udi Arabia was really where it all began.

The word Arabist is an odd one. In my experience it is little more than the subject of polite cocktail conversation in Cairo, whether so and so was an Arabist, the word itself uttered in hushed and reverential tones. Or maybe it was just what some pundits saw under every bed in the State Department. Actually, I met a few State Department Arab specialists in nearly thirty years in the Muslim world, but none was in a position to influence American foreign policy. They had all fought the good fight at one point but seemed resigned to a life of quiet ineffectuality, at least with regard to the core Middle East issue. The charge that the State Department was crawling with Arabists was an outgrowth of the same charge once leveled at the British Foreign Service with more plausibility.

In reality the people whose portraits I drew were more outsiders than anything else. Philby and Thesiger had all the establishment connections, the first at Westminster and Cambridge, the second at Eton and then Oxford. But they flew from official Britain as soon as they were able and never really went back. Gertrude Bell had the connections in spades and made good use of them in her travels through the East, but she died a suicide in Baghdad, far from comforts of her priveleged upbringing. Wilfrid Scawen Blunt's compulsive agitation on behalf of the downtrodden made him an outcast in his own country and his wife suffered by association. Lawrence and Burton were suspect as sometime cosmopolitans, both having been raised partly on the continent.

Palgrave was half-Jewish, and a Catholic and a Jesuit into the bargain. Doughty was a poet and a geologist who flatly refused to allow publishers to touch his often impenetrable prose. We can be thankful they weren't allowed to change *Travels in Arabia Deserta*. Niebuhr was a Saxon who tried to interest the academics in his painstaking work. But they wouldn't have him. Burckhardt left his native Switzerland as a young man, changed his name and to this day remains a bit of an enigma. Hogarth is the exception that proves the rule, although his obvious relish for out-of-the-way peoples and places makes him an honorary member of the caste. Outsiders all. But they all had connections, some lesser and some greater, with the Arab World and I have kept the title of "Arabists." But there will be no flowing robes or Arab gear among them, no Orientalist poses. They were all Europeans and that is how I chose to see them. Incidentally, they constitute a window on the Middle East opened by learned travelers to the region over the past 200-plus years.

Throughout I have struggled with the competing claims of fidelity and authenticity. The drawings are faithful to the originals, as they should be. The verbal portraits, on the other hand, are more authentic than faithful, if by that is meant a view of the subjects that is highly idiosyncratic and based on a lifetime's reading of nearly everything they wrote. They represent aspects of their characters that struck me as pertinent. In that respect they may be closer to caricature than portraiture, although they are based on the best possible evidence, the subjects' own words. Like most works of criticism the pieces may occasionally be provocative, but for that I make no apology. Finally, in this Internet age I have adhered to what might be called the "one click" rule. Rather than interrupt the flow of the text with footnotes I have chosen to leave any uncertainties to the initiative of a reader who may be unfamiliar with the subject of Arabian travel. Nearly every reference, whether to Trenchard, Liddell-Hart, Wooley, or Abduh, can quickly be clarified with the aid of Google and Wikipedia.

T. E. LAWRENCE (1888–1935)

The first portrait, of Thomas Edward Lawrence, is an example of a man who in many respects was *not* an Arabist. "Lawrence of Arabia" is a misnomer if only because no one in Arabia knows who Lawrence is. If he had to be "of" somewhere it probably should be "Lawrence of the Levant." That is where he got his start with a thesis on the Crusader castles of the area, and where the focus of the Arab part of his career lay. Other than a personal motive, movingly expressed in the dedicatory poem to the *Seven Pillars of Wisdom*, his one obsession in the entire Arab adventure was to "biff" the French out of Syria. And in that he failed. He spent a total of nine months in western Arabia and hated it the whole time. But expatriates today will point out Lawrence's house in Jidda, or in Yanbu' where he spent a total of nine days. Living with the Bedouin was, as he described it, "a death in life."

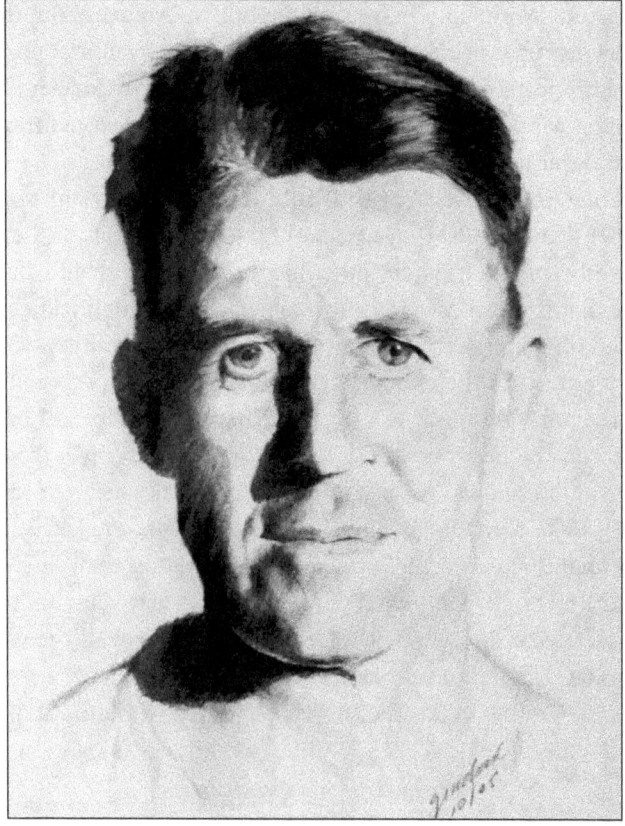

T. E. Lawrence

Part of the problem with Lawrence is that people do not take him at his word. "My proper share," he wrote, "was a minor one, but because of a fluent pen and a certain adroitness of brain, I took upon myself, as I describe it, a mock primacy." But his early publicist, Lowell Thomas (and ultimately Lawrence himself), was not given to understatement and no one believes the disclaimers. At its best, because of Lawrence's sometimes felicitous command of the language, the *Seven Pillars* can be brilliant. But the metaphysics are odd and home-grown and his writing is often too pat, evidence of a specious command of every situation because he seems able to describe it so well. E. M. Forster described the book as "nicely woven of Oxfordisms and Doughty." Oxfordisms there may be, but there is little Doughty other than an interest in geology and the watershed of western Arabia. Both Lawrence and Doughty *are* difficult to read, but each in his own way. Charlotte Shaw was closer to the truth when she said that the book was beyond style.

In the introductory chapter to the *Seven Pillars* Lawrence says that it would be "impertinent" to praise other Englishmen involved in the Arab Revolt. But his strong—and impertinent—criticism of the professional soldiers in the campaign must account for many of the bitter enemies he made. He was admittedly a neophyte at war, and his blithe invoking of Napoleon, Clausewitz, Moltke, and Foch seems gratuitous and amateurish in the worst sense of the word. He pulled some impressive legs with his theorizing, the most impressive being that of Basil Liddell-Hart, the preeminent military historian of the twentieth century.

He really wasn't a soldier, but a budding archaeologist and author, like his mentor David Hogarth. Had the war not intervened, we can imagine him as another Hogarth, or perhaps another Leonard Woolley with whom he shared a pre-war archaeological dig at Carchemish on the upper Euphrates. Neither man was schooled in his craft (there being no school of archaeology as such) but trained on the job. The absence of a professional syllabus meant that odd notions crept into their writings and both men were outspoken, not to say truculent, in their opinions. The son of a clergyman, Woolley eventually excavated Ur of the Chaldees and spent a great deal of time looking for evidence of the *person* of the historical Abraham, based on his reading of the Bible. Absent the war we can only imagine where Lawrence's predilections might have taken him.

He was inordinately fond of the northern Syrians and equally inordinately (the word almost defines him) averse to the Egyptians whom he knew from a short stint with Petrie at Abydos. Whether it was the British versus the Germans, the Syrians versus the Egyptians, the Ashmolean versus the British Museum, or Hogarth versus Gertrude Bell, Lawrence was a fierce partisan of his friends and his causes. It was a singlemindedness that would lead to Damascus and ultimately to that infelicitous compromise, the Hashemite solution in the Middle East. But if there was one thing he was *not*, it was inconsequential, and Lawrence as much as Churchill is responsible for the mixed legacy of the post-war king-making. Based on the traits manifest in those early years later participants and historians should have been warned.

As a writer Lawrence sedulously cultivated the society of literati like the Shaws and Thomas Hardy, and the *Seven Pillars* that eventually emerged was a more polished product than the earlier Oxford version. But his *real* book, his *magnum opus*, was to be an account of man's conquering the air, written from the inside. He spent the last fifteen years of his life in the Air Force as aircraftman Shaw. When he wasn't hobnobbing with Churchill or Lady Astor he *was* writing, but it was things like instruction manuals for boats used in air-sea rescue operations. Or treating other rankers to phonograph renditions of Brahms or Beethoven, having brought them to his cottage, Clouds Hill, on his Brough Superior motorcycle. A new Brough was provided by the Shaws every couple of years. The motorcycle eventually killed him.

His closest confidant became Charlotte Shaw and, reading their correspondence after her death, George Bernard Shaw realized that he really hadn't known either his wife or Lawrence. It was Charlotte who hounded Shaw into reading the manuscript of the *Seven Pillars*, and Lawrence afterwards allowed that Shaw was responsible for all the semicolons. Shaw, whose playwright's eye saw through the aircraftman pose, included a figure patterned on Lawrence in his play *Too True to be Good*, private Napoleon Alexander Trotsky Meek.

Lawrence's account of his years in the ranks, called *The Mint*, was published posthumously. It has the grace and readability of the London half of George Orwell's *Down and Out in Paris and London*, all English working-class, cuppers of tea and two slices. It is thoroughly depressing. As Lawrence aged he grew increasingly working-class in appearance. Photographs of him after retirement from the Air Force show, to Edward Sa'id's acute eye, a middle-aged Stan Laurel. He lived an ascetic life in his cottage, sleeping in a sleeping-bag and eating out of a tin. When the super-cerebral little man ran his latest Brough off the road in Dorset in 1935, the manuscript of *The Mint* was still in the custody of Viscount

Tranchard, head of the air force. No one remembers it today, but the *Seven Pillars of Wisdom* has lasted.

CHARLES M. DOUGHTY (1843-1926)

Charles M. Doughty

The same sort of thing happened with the second Arabist, Charles Montagu Doughty. He was also a writer—a poet—and his vision was to write a verse history of the primitive Anglo-Saxon race. The work was eventually published as *The Dawn in Britain*. He went down to Arabia in 1876 to see how other primitives lived and spent two years wandering over the deserts and lava fields of western Arabia, from Damascus to Meda'in Saleh, inland to Qasim, then back to the coast at Jidda. It is amazing that he lived through the experience, and he very nearly didn't, because he traveled as an "upright Christian man," a *Nasrany*, a term of opprobrium in the peninsula. He took the Arabic name *Khalil* not because it meant "friend" but because it was closest to the English of his Christian name, Charles. Such was his scrupulous, occasionally reckless, honesty. Doughty's Christianity was decidedly of the turn-the-other-cheek variety, and Richard Burton, a rough contemporary, found fault with him for his mildness and passivity—it was outrageous that an Englishman would allow himself to be so abused—as much as for his dislike of the Prophet and his religion. Throughout, Doughty calls the local sectaries "Mohammedans" (suggesting that they were followers of a particular man, not a religion) and one suspects the usage was not inadvertent. He financed his wanderings with a little quackery, an honorable tradition, and somehow emerged from the experience more or less intact at the British consulate in Jidda.

His account, *Travels in Arabia Deserta*, is a classic. Written in an odd, Spenserian English style, it was pronounced unreadable by publishers. It *is* difficult to read but, as Lawrence remarked, once you get into it, the book is a gold mine. Doughty was trained as a geologist and a generation of writers on the Arab World, including Lawrence, owe to him their habit of meticulous description of minerals and rock formations. The book made a minor contribution to an understanding of the watershed of western Arabia. But its real value lay in Doughty's description of the blighted lives of the aborigines among whom he traveled. No writer in English has described them better. However, it was not only the Bedouins but also his portrait of the Arab townsmen that gives the book its particular cachet. Where else would we learn that peninsular Arabs, in particular the *Ageyl*, those agents of the carrying trade in Nejd, would once have been expatriate workers in the region, hiring themselves out to Greek contractors during the digging of the Suez Canal?

In spite of its quaint style and the fact that the book was soon out of print, a whole generation of acolytes—the word is not too strong—virtually worshipped at the altar of Doughty. When early in the First World War the Arab Bureau in Cairo looked for a copy of *Arabia Deserta* they found only a dog-eared and poorly-bound copy in Bahrain. It served throughout the conflict as a kind of Bible of the tribes and personages in the Hejaz. In spite of Doughty's deep and abiding Islamophobia—he hated its influence in the peninsula—more sympathetic figures like Gertrude Bell and Philby didn't hold it against him, and their accounts of 'Aneyza, Bureyda, and Ha'il are full of references to Doughty's earlier work.

The Lawrence connection was interesting. As a young man, T. E. was obsessed with the medieval period in general and the Crusades in particular. He read Doughty's book as a preparation for his first journey to the Levant. Since the great man was still alive at the time, Lawrence wrote to him prior to leaving. When asked what his advice to travelers in that part of the world would be, Doughty replied, in effect, "don't go." Neither Lawrence nor Doughty was much of a linguist, and when Lawrence speaks of manipulating the Arabs with "delicately poisoned Arabic," I doubt that he was capable of it. Lawrence was responsible for a modest recrudescence of interest in Doughty after the war, writing the introduction to a new edition of *Arabia Deserta* published by Jonathan Cape.

Like Lawrence after him Doughty quickly closed the door on his Arabian adventure after he left the Arab World. He saw his primitives and didn't much like what he had seen. He seems to have financed his later poetry with proceeds from family investments in Malay rubber. Incidentally, he is known for the *Travels in Arabia Deserta*. No one remembers *The Dawn in Britain*.

RICHARD BURTON (1821–1890)

The third subject, Richard Francis Burton, *was* a linguist and one of the greatest who ever lived. He was also a poet who translated all the verse himself in his monumental, sixteen-volume *Arabian Nights*, intending to leave the prose to lesser mortals like his friend Steinhaeuser. Steinhaeuser's untimely death put an end to that hope. Burton said that what appears to be doggerel in the poetry of the *Nights* is because the original was doggerel. That may be so, but it seemed a cover for his often mechanical efforts as a poet.

At his worst, in books like *A Mission to Gelele, King of Dahome*, Burton can be a tedious cataloguer of useless facts, animated only by a spirit of animus. Even when he was sympathetic to his subject the endless etymologies, obsessive need to correct the errors of others, opaque asides (often in a foreign language), and prodigious displays of learning will tax the staying power of the reader who doesn't come armed with his Arabic, French, German, Persian (and Greek and Portuguese and Latin . . .) dictionaries, not to mention a glossary of geological terms and a Qur'an and a Bible. He often seemed to lack a good editor. But, in spite of it all, and if he wasn't much of a rhymester, he could be a hugely entertaining prose writer. An official penned the remark "flippant ass" in the margin of one of his early army reports. It may have been true, but Burton at his best is the most enjoyable of the Arabists to read.

Richard Burton

He has undergone something of a revival with the movie *Mountains of the Moon*, and several new biographies. The movie was silly and included a premarital liaison between Burton and his equally remarkable wife Isabel, complete with nude scene. It was not clear that he and Isabel ever got together in a marital sense, at least without Burton's hypnotizing her. For all of his scientific interest in the subject, there was something odd about Burton's attitude towards sexuality, and there was a little of Hemingway's braggadocio about him. One is reminded of the latter's displaying his riddled breeches at a meeting of the Oak Park, Illinois ladies club, to a collective gasp. Both men had a compulsion to shock and amaze, and it may be because both were raised in female-dominated households.

Burton's politically correct treatment of the Africans in the movie is misleading at best. He didn't like blacks, at least those who weren't Islamized, and considered them an ignoble race. This was in spite of his seminal anthropological studies and the fact that, next to Livingstone, he probably knew more about Africa than any Englishman of his time. Burton's deep and abiding Islamophilia led him to attacks on the other "religions of the book," some of them scurrilous. In *Wanderings in West Africa* he found the worst exemplar of the African in the returned slave from America, a clubhouse lawyer who was superficially Christianized and full of notions of the rights of man. In *The Jew, the Gypsy and El Islam*, Burton's vitriol against the Jews for their hostility to gentiles as codified in the Talmud, not to mention a millennium-long list of alleged acts of Blood Libel, was so incendiary that Isabel persuaded him to suppress it during his lifetime. After all, he had a career to consider and it made no sense to alienate a people of "unprecedented power and position" in England. The book appeared posthumously in 1898.

As far as the biographies are concerned, *Captain Sir Richard Francis Burton* has the merit that it covers Burton's early period in India, neglected in other accounts. But the author's gratuitous swipe at an earlier biography by Fawn Brodie, with the statement that a woman from California couldn't possibly understand a man like Burton, detracts from the book at the outset. The scoop about Burton's involvement as an active agent in the Great Game is credulous nonsense. The author uses Burton's sometimes picaresque adventures to tell us that he also travelled and was almost disemboweled in the Sudan, as if anyone cared.

Probably the best of Burton's many works is his *Personal Narrative of a Pilgrimage to el-Medinah and Mecca*. That is probably because it *was* so personal, although reviewers must have raised their eyebrows at some of the flippancies. He clearly was enjoying himself among a people whom he knew and understood. The element of danger in the pilgrimage has been overplayed. In the mélange of peoples and languages in Mecca his appearance and accent, that of an Afghan raised in India, would have been unremarkable and he appears to have easily passed as a Muslim. He was in far greater danger during his African explorations because of the climate and disease. Even during his trip to Harar in Somaliland, where he traveled openly as an Englishman, he was at greater risk because of the utter capriciousness of the Emir.

For an explorer to be first is everything and to be second nothing. But in a perverse sort of way Burton's life was a whole series of seconds. His refusal to accompany Speake on the first reconnaissance of Lake Victoria deprived him forever of credit for the Nile. He was a professional soldier who spent his military career in Sind, Afghanistan, and the Crimea, but always seemed to arrive too late to see action. In the foreign service he never got Syria or Morocco which he considered almost his birthright. Even his *Thousand Nights and a Night* was published just after John Payne's often-better version. The fact that Burton borrowed freely—and admittedly—from rivals and that his version was really only a forum for his poetry, footnotes, and terminal essay, exposed him to the charge of plagiarism. He was even accused of being ignorant of Arabic. "Yes, I don't know Arabic," he replied, "and I don't know the man who does."

The disappointments meant that Burton was often an unhappy man. In the foreward to the *Nights* he makes it clear that the great Arabian panorama was often his only solace during periods in "the luxurient and deadly deserts" of West Africa and the "dreary half-clearings" of South America. Instead, "the Jinn bore me to the land of my predilections, Arabia . . . in air glorious as ether, whose every breath raises men's spirits like sparkling wine." His "uncastrated" version of the *Nights* was published in 1885, to the delight of a few and the eternal scandal of many more.

Wilfred Scawen Blunt recalled seeing him in Buenos Aires in one of the black periods when Burton was drinking heavily. Blunt says he was the most sinister-looking figure he ever laid eyes on. Eventually posted as British consul in Damascus, Burton embroiled himself in an ill-advised venture, stemming from Isabel's staunch Catholicism. He was sacked and afterwards condemned to a series of minor postings. He and Isabel finally came to rest in Trieste where they spent his final days, he calling her "Puss" and she calling him "Jemmy." He died there in 1890 as the British legate and was buried in the Holy Roman Catholic and Apostolic Church, to the infinite disgust of his friends.

GERTRUDE BELL (1868–1926)

Gertrude Bell

Gertrude Margaret Lowthian Bell is an anomaly among the Arabists, a successful woman in a man's world. In fact, it was said, probably patronizingly, that she had the mind of a man. Like some early ground-breaking women, she had little sympathy for her sisters and was emphatically *not* a feminist. Having clambered aboard the vessel of intellectual and literary success and widespread popular recognition, it could be argued that she pulled up the ladder after her. But her focus was on individual achievement and the notion that she was speaking for anyone else, female or otherwise, was as foreign to her as the suggestion that she should be denied the fruits of her efforts simply because she was a woman.

In some respects, she was the consummate insider. More than any of the other Arabists she was born and bred to success. Her grandfather, the ironmaster and metallurgist Isaac Lowthian Bell, was one of the giants of the nineteenth-century industrial revolution, and the fortune he accumulated funded Gertrude's early exploits. Money was never an object—until much later in her life—and she was used at an early age to world travel and adventure. The Bells were also prominent in non-conformist circles and scientific and artistic giants of the mid-nineteenth century such as Darwin, Huxley, and William Morris were regulars in gatherings at the family home. But Gertrude counted not only non-conformists but also pillars of the establishment in the circles in which she traveled. She dedicated her *Amurath and Amurath* to Evelyn Baring, Lord Cromer, that epitome of late nineteenth-century British imperialism, and she could always count on the assistance of officialdom in her forays into the East.

But there was more to her success than privilege and exposure to the intellectual lights of the age. Surely, most of it has to do with the brilliance, high-spiritedness, and willfulness with which she was born. She excelled at most subjects in school—with the notable exception of religion—and attended Oxford in the only college then open to women, Lady Margaret Hall, where in two years she took an unprecedented first in history. She was an accomplished alpinist and attestations to her fearlessness and skill came from professionals in the business. Her languages, while not on a par with Burton's, were still exceptional and her early translation from the Persian of Hafez's *Divan* is still recognized for its quality today. Miss Bell so impressed Sir William Ramsay (incidentally, Hogarth's early mentor and *the* accepted voice on the archaeology of southwestern Anatolia), that he consented to the joint publication of *A Thousand and one Churches*: she would be responsible for the architecture while he would deal with the archaeology.

She was an inveterate traveler—on first exposure to the East she had been smitten—and, while none of her journeys was particularly dangerous or broke new ground, they were collectively a solid record of achievement. They also allowed her to acquire the knowledge that would be put to good use during and after the First World War. It would be silly to call her a spy, but she traveled in influential circles and kept her eyes and ears open. Her reports were always shrewd and insightful. Although Miss Bell was generally well received, she was still a woman and acceptance was not universal. There are stories of Ibn Sa'ud's mimicking her fluttering, bird-like chatter: "Ya Abdel Aziz, ya Abdel Aziz." It was inevitable that she would make enemies as she rose swiftly and assuredly in this male-dominated world, and an early detractor was Mark Sykes. He came from a background of equal privilege and seemingly effortless success, but he lacked her brilliance and his artless criticism reads like sour grapes.

It was probably inevitable that she would be compared with another prominent British figure in the immediate post-war Middle East, T. E. Lawrence. Recent biographers have examined the accomplishments of the two and there has even been the suggestion that *she* was the real "Lawrence of Arabia." The comparisons are as misguided as they were surely inevitable. There was really only *one* Lawrence for which, many believe, we can be thankful. Long before Lawrence, Gertrude Bell was associated in the mind of the British public with eastern travel and expertise. The East was her life, and she ended it in post-war Baghdad, in self-imposed exile, far from the wealth and comforts of her upbringing. She was not another Lawrence but an original Bell, and that should be more than enough for her most fervent admirers.

She decided early in her schooling that she was an atheist: she did *not* believe and, whatever else can be said of her, the decision by a child to dismiss out-of-hand a question that has occupied some of the greatest minds of mankind was a key to her make-up. Self-assuredness always seemed to be her greatest strength and the obvious lack of it at her end lends a poignant note to the trajectory of her life. For all of her advantages, she was prey to the absence of the one gift that would have brought her fulfillment, that of love. Her early attachment to a member of the British legation in Persia was dismissed by the family as infatuation for an impecunious diplomat, and she was given to understand that any serious relationship was out of the question. The later love of her life was Major Charles Hotham Montagu Doughty-Wylie, the married nephew of Charles Montagu Doughty. He was a legitimate war hero, killed in the early days of the Gallipoli campaign. In spite of several years of passionate correspondence and periodic trysts the relationship appears never to have been consummated.

She spent her final years working for the Iraq she had come to love. Earlier, she had written "I have drawn too deeply upon the good-will of the inhabitants of Asiatic Turkey to regard their fortunes with an impartial detachment . . ." After her machinations against Arnold Wilson, the British proconsul, succeeded in securing a quasi-independence for the Iraqis, she settled into the role of a kind of cultural impresario and the Baghdad Archaeological Museum was her baby. When she died in 1926 at the age of fifty-seven, probably by her own hand, this supremely gifted and accomplished woman seemed to have thrown it all away and joined the ranks of the outsiders. It was a tragedy of tragedies, not for Iraq, or the Arab World or the Middle East—she was, after all, a foreigner—but for herself. The lavish gifts, solid accomplishments, and public recognition couldn't insulate her against the emptiness within, although they did elevate her life beyond that of mere pathos. Hers is the saddest of stories.

WILFRID SCAWEN BLUNT (1840–1922), LADY ANNE BLUNT (1837–1917)

If Gertrude Bell suffered from a lack of love, it could be said that Wilfred Scawen Blunt enjoyed a surfeit of the passion. Born to a family of wealthy Sussex landowners, he apprenticed in the diplomatic service before settling down to married life as a country squire. As a youth, he was said to be too beautiful to live, and in an age when consumption was a great scourge—a brother and sister both died young of the disease—he was dogged throughout life by a weakness of the lungs. He seemed determined to make the most of what promised to be a short passage through this vale of tears by means of multiple affairs and compulsive infidelities. In expiation, he claimed the standing of a poet, no more accountable for his propensities than a lion for its teeth or a tiger for its claws. In the event he lived to the ripe old age of eighty-two, siring children by paramours, cousins, the wives of family friends, and occasionally by his own wife, Lady Anne King (Noel), the Baroness Wentworth.

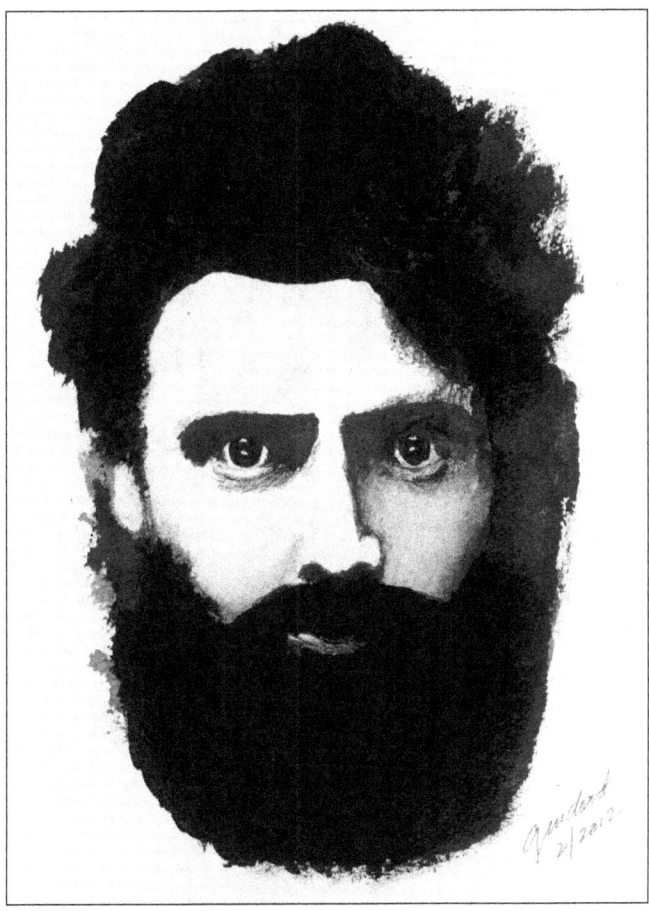

Wilfrid Scawen Blunt

She was the granddaughter of Lord Byron and Annabella Milbanke, Byron's "amiable mathematician . . . my princess of parallelograms." The grandmother was gifted mathematically but rather plain and the couple were together only long enough to conceive Ada, Lady Anne's mother, before the poet decamped for more exotic climes. The Byron connection would be important later when Blunt interested himself in the aspirations to freedom of downtrodden peoples. But if Byron's brief foray into revolutionary politics in Greece had a comic-opera quality about it, Blunt's decidedly did not and he was an outspoken and much heard (if most-often ignored) voice during the birth pangs of a free Egypt, India, and Ireland.

Lady Anne Blunt

Lady Anne was a tiny, in later life bespectacled figure who seemed to take after her practical grandmother, in whose company she spent her happiest days after the early death of her mother and subjection to a severe regime by her dour and humorless father. She was a tomboy, pretty if not stunning, and more at home in the outdoors than inside with others of her sex. She had an instinctive understanding of animals and her passion was for horses, which would later grow into the Crabbet Arabian stud. But the name Byron still meant something and if she always denigrated her facility with words, she was a gifted watercolorist, having studied with none other than Ruskin, and her paintings and drawings would grace their later books of travel. She played the violin and one of her instruments, the 1721 Lady Blunt Stradivarius, recently sold at auction for $15.9 million. She also absorbed languages like a sponge and acted as interpreter in their travels in Arabia, later becoming a creditable Arabic scholar. She was intrepid—the two of them together being fearless to the point of foolishness—and more than carried her own in the loading and unloading, riding, and occasional skirmishing that were a part of Arabian travel in the mid-to-late-nineteenth century.

It is for their travels that the Blunts merit inclusion among the Arabists, although with characteristic modesty they claimed to be just tourists. There is some truth to that as, after brief visits to Algeria and Egypt and knowing almost nothing of the language, they embarked in December of 1877 on their first journey in search of the *Kehilan*, the Arabian horse *par excellence*. They picked up the Euphrates a few days out of Aleppo and followed the river along its roughly 400-mile course to Baghdad, where they inspected the Pasha's stud. They were not impressed. Leaving the city surreptitiously (they found official attention tiresome) they struck out north through Sammara' and Tikrit to the vicinity of Mosul, where they turned west and then south-west across the desert to Tadmor, before reaching the coast at Beirut. An account of the journey appeared in 1879 as *Bedouin Tribes of the Euphrates*, by Lady Anne Blunt, "Edited with a preface and some account of the Arabs and their horses by W. S. B." They found the Bedouins and horses they sought and described many fantastic sights, including tamarisk thickets along the river, the haunt of lions that took domestic stock and an occasional child, immense flocks of sand-grouse, and herds of thousands of gazelles. You would have thought they were on the Serengeti. They viewed the natural aristocracy of the Bedouins with the practiced eye of those accustomed to sizing up horseflesh and clearly relished their time among these denizens of the Arabian steppe who enjoyed a degree of freedom unknown in the material and complicated West.

This was followed in the winter of 1878–79 by a second journey, across the Nefud to Jebel Shammar where they examined the stud of the then-greatest man in northern Arabia, Mohammed Ibn Rashid (they were not impressed) before departing with the Persian *hajj* caravan for points north. The crossing of the Nefud was especially notable. Palgrave had done it in the height of summer and gave it short shrift. Their description of the great red desert with its strange horseshoe formations, limestone floor, and exotic fauna filled in a blank in Western knowledge of northern Nejd. With their mares, greyhounds, and falcon the Blunts traveled as persons of quality and were treated as such by the Bedouins and Rashidis. A hellish "Persian campaign" surveying a possible railroad right-of-way then took them from Baghdad, skirting the no-man's land between Persia and Turkish Iraq to the Gulf at Bushire. Blunt was frequently prostrated by fever and diarrhea and Lady Anne played the role of nursemaid in addition to that of *caravanbashi,* ushering men and animals across a landscape peopled by hostile tribes and rivers swollen with snow melt. An account of the journey appeared in 1881 as *A Pilgrimage to Nejd, The Cradle of the Arab Race* "by Lady Anne Blunt, author of 'The Bedouin Tribes of the Euphrates.'"

In *The Penetration of Arabia* Hogarth opines that "their actual narrative will bear comparison with any other, concerned with the same ground, for sobriety and accuracy, as well as for observation and sympathy." Would that all tourists were half as observant. But here the plot thickens. Comparison of Lady Anne's journals with the text of the books shows that her brief notes were significantly embellished by Blunt when they were not ignored altogether. In fact, he not she appears to be the real author of the books, although she was complicit, copying Blunt's drafts for submission to the publisher. But this we needn't deduce, having it in her own words: "It is tiresome that everyone fancies that I am a writer," she wrote. "I can't do it, and nobody believes one's explanations because of W. having fatally insisted on sticking my name on the book of *his* travels." Blunt himself offers no explanation for the subterfuge. Lady Anne is characteristically self-deprecating, an attitude that seemed to dominate her married life.

Much of the reason may lie in a sense of inadequacy in what she viewed as her most important duty, that of providing Blunt with an heir. A son, baptized Wilfrid Scawen, was born in 1870 but died four days later. Twin girls were born prematurely in 1872 and both died within hours. There were several miscarriages, and she always had to weigh her reproductive health against the rigors of travel with her husband, often in inhospitable places. In the end, travel most often won out. A daughter Judith, born in 1873, was to be their only living child.

The Arabian travels were a brief episode in the Blunts' long and troubled life together, although in some respects they represented a watershed. When the second book was published in 1881 Blunt was forty-one, Lady Anne three years older and at the end of her child-bearing years. Blunt's instinctive sympathy for the underdog had been whetted by exposure to the Bedouins. His championing of the cause of Egyptian freedom in 1882 (he knew Muhammad Abduh, Jamal al-Din al-Afghani, and Ahmad Arabi Pasha personally) earned him no friends in official England. In the *Secret History of the English Occupation of Egypt* he would tell the shameful story of the bombardment of the forts at Alexandria and then the decimation of the poorly-armed *fellah* army by the British at Tel al-Kebir.

His early years as a diplomat meant that he knew many of the players and the often-devious uses of diplomacy, and he used the knowledge in the service of his Egyptian friends. It may be too much to say that Blunt's urging of Arabi to hold firm against British threats was responsible for the ultimate disaster. But it is undeniable that his agitation against Gladstone in *The Times* saved Arabi from the gallows. To the jingoes Blunt became anathema, and his increasing unpopularity in his own country led Lady Anne to lament that it cost her the only friends she ever knew.

He would later take equally unpopular positions on other imperial conundrums in Ireland, India, and the Sudan, the books equal parts diary and invective, at one point positively gloating over the defeat of British arms by the Dervishes. In *The Future of Islam*, drawing on the opinions of his friends Abduh and al-Afghani, he posited a special place for Britain in the "Mohammedan World" if they played their cards right. Needless to say, they didn't. He spent his declining years inveighing against the hypocrisies of the age, what with the scramble for Africa, the Boxer Rebellion, and the entry of America onto the stage in Cuba and the Philippines, not to mention Sarajevo and, finally in August of 1914, Armageddon.

Blunt became a teetotaler, toyed with vegetarianism, and advocated sensible wildlife management and animal rights. His poetry, increasingly put to political purposes, attracted as much vituperation for its content as admiration for its craft. At one point a delegation of young poets, led by Yeats and Pound, came to offer him homage but he found little to like in their efforts, composed especially for the occasion. In fact, he was a man who was as prescient as he was impetuous, correctly seeing the future of a post-colonial world but utterly incapable of bringing it about. In spite of the endless agitation, the succession of books and his undoubted fearlessness, there is something quixotic about Wilfrid Scawen Blunt. He combined his radical politics with casual acquaintance of half the royals and aristocrats, not to mention poets, politicians, and artists, of Europe. He was a social and aesthetic omnivore and might be accused of name-dropping if the diaries were not so natural and unaffected.

He once said that if he brought the Arabs some measure of freedom and established a stud devoted to maintaining the purity of the Arabian horse he would consider his life a success. He was more successful with the latter than the former. But it was Lady Anne's money and, equally importantly, her unrivalled knowledge of horseflesh that were responsible for the success. She labored on, increasingly distraught at his inattention and increasingly spiritual in outlook. She claimed to have had a vision during the "Persian campaign" and became a convert to Roman Catholicism. Welcomed into the Church by Cardinal Newman, she was confirmed by Cardinal Manning. The couple spent their autumn years sometimes together, more often apart, splitting time between their English stud in the summer and their Egyptian stud at Sheykh Obeyd in the winter. Blunt devoted himself to his affairs, poetry, and plays, inveighing against the destruction of all that was beautiful in the world by European civilization. His voluminous diaries contain almost no mention of his wife. A breach seemed inevitable and a formal separation (divorce was out of the question) in the summer of 1906 was the result. Blunt never visited Egypt again.

Lady Anne died in Cairo in 1917, having spent most of the war years in Egypt, with periodic visits to Sheykh Obeyd by the likes of D. G. Hogarth and Gertrude Bell. Having heard that Miss Bell could be overbearing she was prepared to dislike her, but found her well-informed and engaging. They shared reminiscences of Nejd. She never lost her longing for reconciliation with Blunt: "Through him," she wrote, "came all that made life worth living for me." Her constancy in the face of slights and infidelities reads like a tale from the *Thousand Nights and a Night*. Her journals during the years of Blunt's political activism deal almost exclusively with matters equine. Just before she died she completed the draft—at last—of *her* book, an account of the origins of the Arabian horse, much of it translated from the Arabic.

Blunt outlived her by five years, although his published diaries end in 1914. Their daughter Judith, as Lady Wentworth, carried on the family tradition managing the stud—after an acrimonious court battle with her father—that eventually would be worth millions. Her book *The Authentic Arabian Horse*, went through three printings, in 1945, 1962, and 1979, some of it unedited from the pen of her mother. Outspoken, irascible, and opinionated, but with an unrivaled knowledge of the Arabian horse, she was a perfect combination of her parents.

CARSTEN NIEBUHR (1733-1815)

Carsten Niebuhr

Among the least known of the group, at least in the English-speaking world, is Carsten Niebuhr. He was the mathematician and cartographer on the Royal Danish Expedition to Happy Arabia, or the Yemen, of 1761–67. He was the only survivor of a party of five professional, specially-trained travelers. The rest died of malaria, either in the Yemen or in India, within a year of their arrival in the East. Niebuhr himself was a German and a Saxon, and was almost an afterthought when the expedition was put together. Academically the least accomplished and the least presumptuous, he was the most observant and his contribution is the only one that is really remembered. Serious students of the European exploration of Arabia have always valued Niebuhr and in the *Lives of Eminent Persons,* published in 1833, this simple engineer from Friesland appears in the august company of, among others, Mohammed, Leonardo da Vinci, Michaelangelo, Newton, Galileo, Kepler, and Sir Christopher Wren.

Several members of the expedition were musicians and they carried their instruments with them. They gave periodic concerts, to the likes of an Egyptian bey or dignitaries in the Yemen. The Arabs, used to lighter and more lyrical pieces, found little to like in the formal European offerings. The expedition also traveled with plentiful supplies of wine and brandy, believing them safer than water. But the combination of the alcohol, hepatitis, yellow fever, and malaria may have been more than their livers could tolerate.

Niebuhr learned more than the others because he alone permitted familiar contact with the Arabs. Most of the others combined their academic pretensions with an unassailable belief in the superiority of Europeans. When Forsskal and von Haven died, Niebuhr patiently carried on their botanical and philological researches by himself. With characteristic modesty, he says that he wasn't really trained in either discipline but simply did his best. His best was good enough to set the standard for the next hundred years in Arab studies. Among his many contributions were the discovery of Serabit al-Khadem in the Sinai, the opening of Europe's eyes to the Himyaritic inscriptions in the Yemen, and the first complete copies of the Cuneiform inscriptions at Persepolis, leading directly to the decipherment of that script.

The original itinerary of the expedition was to have been via Tranquebar, a Danish colony on the Coromandel coast of India, before reaching Happy Arabia from the Indian Ocean and the east. However, the Mediterranean offered a more direct route and after stops in Marseilles, Malta, Istanbul, and Cyprus the party arrived in Alexandria in September of 1761. A number of factors, including a dispiute between the Bedouins in the Hejaz and the Mamluks kept them in Egypt for nearly a year. It would be their longest time together in any one place. Niebuhr put the time to good use, filling over 200 pages of his *Reisebeschreibung nach Arabien* or *Travels in Arabia* with material on Egypt, including the first detailed maps of Cairo and the Delta, a description of the commerce and ethnic and religious mix in the country, and a listing of the Mamluk beys who lorded it over the *fellaheen*. Egypt was followed by Sinai, the Red Sea. and the western seaboard of Arabia before finally reaching the Yemen, the ultimate object of their journey. There, they spent the first several months in the lowlands, Forsskal botanizing while Niebuhr gathered material for his map of the country. After much obstruction from the authorities, they eventually made their way to the highlands and San'a, arriving in the capital two and a-half years after their departure from Copenhagen, the original length of the expedition as originally planned.

However, they were a sadly reduced party that reached San'a. The two professors, von Haven and Forsskal, were dead from malaria, von Haven in Mocha and Forsskal on their incident-plagued journey up the escarpment from Ta'iz. Much of the purpose of the expedition seemed to have died with them. The surviving members of the party were intermittantly ill from what appears to have been the same disease. In spite of a cordial reception by the Imam and invitation to stay as long as they wished, their only thought was to get away as quickly as possible with what little remained of their health intact. They were in San'a for just ten days before the return journey down the escarpmant to Mocha where they took ship for Bombay. Baurenfeind and Berggren, the expedition's artist and European servant, died at sea and were committed to the deep. Kramer, the physician, died five montths after his and Niebuhr's arrival in India.

Now alone, Niebuhr returned to Denmark via Bombay, the Persian Gulf, western Persia to Shiraz and Persepolis, then Turkish Iraq where he spent nine months producing his by-now customary maps and decriptions of Basra, Bagdad, and Mosul. He departed Mosul in a caravan destined for Mardin and then Diarbakr in Armenia, before arriving in Aleppo to a welcome from a European community had long since given him up for dead. He spent the next six months traveling in the region, leaving a careful description of the ethnic and confessional kaleidoscope of an area that today constitutes Syria, Lebanon, Palestine, and Israel. Then it was across Anatolia by camel caravan, before Rumelia, Wallachia, Moldova, and Germany. By now he had abandoned all pretense of traveling as a European and, where possible, avoided the officialdom that had plagued the expedition in the Yemen. Instead, he just hunkered down and kept his eyes and ears open. His perspicacity from this lowered perspective remained intact.

Niebuhr turned up in Copenhagen in 1767, seven years after the expedition left, to an astonished but remarkably indifferent scholarly reception. His three-volume *Travels in Arabia, Description of Arabia*, and edited versions of the work of Forsskal, the botanist, are early, and mighty, contributions to Enlightenment science and Oriental studies. In *The Penetration of Arabia* Hogarth remarks that "It would be tedious to quote a hundredth part of Niebuhr's judicious observations." The books were originally written in his native low-German and have been partially translated into French, Dutch, English, and Farsi. Niebuhr wrote as he had traveled, alone, without the help of the professor who had dispatched the expedition, probably because the latter felt that, with the death of the other scholars, its purpose had been vitiated.

He eventually returned to his first calling as a surveyor and became a civil servant and tax collector in his native Dittmarches in Saxony. He suffered for the remainder of his life from recurrent bouts of fever, a result of the malaria that killed the other members of the expedition. He eventually went blind, having damaged his eyesight copying the inscriptions on the brilliant off-white limestone of Persepolis. He died nearly alone and forgotten, able to picture only in his mind's eye the fantastic shapes and sights and colors of his more than Sindbad's odyssey.

But he left an even greater lagacy in his son, the historian and diplomat Barthold Georg Niebuhr. The son was what we would today call "home-schooled" and in spite of his delicate constitution (or perhaps because of it), he absorbed his father's lessons like a sponge. His list of languages rivals Burton's and he is considered *the* seminal figure of nineteenth-century historiography. No less a figure than Goethe was among his many admirers. But more than the histories it is his letters that reveal him to be an intellectual of the first water with a knowledge as wide as it was deep. The father would undoubtedly have been proud if he knew that in the *Algemeine Deutsch Biographie* his own entry would occupy a single page, while that of his son would require fifteen dense pages. Today in Berlin, just off the Kurferstandamm, Niebuhrstrasse is parallel to Kantstrasse, just before the two intersect Leibnizstrasse. The son keeps the same eminent company that his father did.

J. L. BURCKHARDT (1784-1817)

If there is a name as esteemed as Niebuhr's among European travelers in the Arab World it is surely that of J. L. Burckhardt, although the question of his identity constantly recurs.

J. L. Burckhardt

Was he the Johann Ludwig Burckhardt of his christening, or the Jean Louis Burckhardt preferred by his biographer, or the John Lewis Burckhardt of his travels, published posthumously in English? Or, for that matter, was he Ibrahim al-Mahdi Abdullah Burckhardt as he was widely known in Cairo? What we do know is that he was a Swiss, born in 1784 in Lausanne to the second wife of a prosperous Basle merchant. The father knew Gibbon, then living in the city and in the throes of composition of the *Decline and Fall,* and was an outspoken Anglophile. This had serious repercussions with the outbreak of the French Revolution. Witnessing the prosecution of his father, who was tried for his life by the republican party, Burckhardt "imbibed at a very early age" a detestation of all things French and an admiration for all things English. After study at the universities of first, Leipzig and then Göttingen he left for England, arriving in the summer of 1806 with letters of introduction to prominent English men of science, among them Joseph Banks. Through Banks he came to the attention of the London-based Association for Promoting the Discovery of the Interior Parts of Africa.

The association was just then seeking a traveler who would fill a gap in European knowledge of the continent by joining the yearly caravan from Cairo west to Timbuktu and the Niger via the Fezzan, the area of oases in the Sahara south of Tripolitania. Burckhardt offered his services and was accepted, having in the meantime applied himself to the study of Arabic, chemistry, mineralogy, and medicine and steeling himself for the rigors of travel in remote and inhospitable lands. In January of 1809 he was sent to Aleppo where he was to acquire "the language and manners of an Arabian Musulman," thereby improving his chances of passing undetected in Africa. He was then to make his way to Cairo where he would join the next caravan bound for Timbuktu.

How these instructions were to play out over the next eight years is the story of Burckhardt's enduring contribution to a European understanding of the Arab and Muslim worlds. In Aleppo, he quickly discovered that his appearance and Cambridge-learned Arabic identified him as an obvious Frank, and that further schooling was necessary before he could pass himself off as an Oriental. The Association authorized an extension of his apprenticeship and he immersed himself in the study of Arabic prose and poetry, Islam, and the Qur'an. As evidence of his seriousness he translated *Robinson Crusoe* into Arabic and sent copies, in a fine *naskhi* hand, to his sponsors in Cambridge and London. He also began the peregrinations that would eventually result in the publication of *Travels in Syria and the Holy Land*, in the process becoming the first European since the Crusades to see Petra.

He arrived in Cairo in August of 1812, the goal of the Sahara and Africa now finally within reach. But the times were not propitious. The Wahhabi eruption into the Hejaz had led to a suspension of the western *hajj* and of caravans between Cairo and Timbuktu. Chafing at the delay, and with apologies to the Association, Burckhardt instead turned south to Nubia where he became the first European since Roman times to see the great temple at Abu Simbel. He almost missed it, covered as it was in drifted sand with only a single head visible. After penetrating the "Negro lands" as far south as Shendi, he turned to the coast at Suakin and crossed the Red Sea to Jidda. His *Travels in Nubia*, published in 1819, would be his only work on Africa, the ostensible goal of his journeys.

He remained in the Hejaz long enough to perform the pilgrimage rites, believing that the title of *hajji* would facilitate his travels in Africa. While there he was summoned to Ta'if where Mohammed Ali then was, prosecuting his war on the Wahhabis. Burckhardt was the object of amused regard by the Pasha, who had met him earlier in Cairo and found curious his passion for travel. Being himself an atheist the Pasha cared not a whit for Burckhardt's assumed identity as a Muslim, although he summoned doctors to test his *bona fides*. Burckhardt passed muster. Of more interest were the opinions of this "Englishman," since the Pasha knew that England had just defeated Napoleon and might now turn its attention to Egypt. Escaping the grasp of the tyrant Burckhardt made his way to Medina where he suffered an attack of dysentery that prostrated him for most of his three months in the city. His notes to the Association included "the most accurate and complete account of the Hedjaz, including the cities of Mekka and Medina, which has ever been received in Europe." It would eventually appear in *Travels in Arabia*, published in 1829.

Back in Cairo Burckhardt took a small house in the Turkish quarter and applied himself to his studies. These resulted in *Notes on the Bedouins and Wahabys* and *Arabic Proverbs and the Manners and Customs of the Modern Egyptians*, the latter demonstrating his mastery of the vulgar idiom. More importantly, the Pasha's ultimate victory over the Wahhabis resulted in a resumption of the African pilgrimage and an outward-bound caravan passed through Cairo in early 1817. Burckhardt made plans to join it on its return in December. But he was felled by a recurrence of dysentery and died, much lamented by Muslims and Christians alike, in October of that year.

In the end, he never made it Timbuktu. But the material he sent to his sponsors in London was evidence that his time was very profitably spent in the East. The volumes of travel and commentary, all published posthumously from 1819 to 1831, exhibit a learning that rivals Burton's, although they raise another question as to his identity. English was not his native tongue and the editors, while preserving the force and vigor of Burckhardt's observations, still had to reconcile the language of the notes with English phraseology and grammatical construction and purge it of foreign idioms. Behind the English mask the real Burckhardt remains elusive.

Today, a ten-minute walk from the Bab al-Nasr in the northern wall of the Fatimid City leads to the area identified in the 1811 French expedition map of Cairo as the *Tourab bab el nasr*, or the Bab al-Nasr burial ground. There, amid little lop-sided shanties and tumbled-down grave markers, appears a very Turkish-looking tomb, inside of which lies a marble coffin surmounted by a turban, also of marble. A plaque in Arabic marks the site of Burckhardt's final resting place after his too-short span of 33 lunar years:

> God alone is eternal.
> This is the tomb of the late Sheikh al-Haj Ibrahim al-Mahdi Abdullah
> Burckhardt of Lausanne
> (may God in His infinite mercy receive his soul).
> He was born in Muharram, 1199 A.H. He passed away in Egypt
> in the month of Dhu al-Higgah, 1232 A.H
> In the name of God, the Merciful, the Compassionate.

The memorial is fitting. From the time of his arrival in Syria in 1809 until his death in 1817 Burckhardt lived as a Muslim and was widely known as such. But the elusive prospect of Timbuktu may have been the deciding factor in his choice of creeds. He may have passed as a "learned Musulman," but a careful reading of his works suggests that he always viewed Islam as an outsider and remained a skeptical northern European to the end of his days. The corporal remains of J. L. Burckhardt may be found in Cairo, but we suspect that his spirit remains in Lausanne. Or, better yet, in London.

GIFFORD PALGRAVE (1826-1888)

Perhaps the oddest of this odd group is William Gifford Palgrave, the half-Jewish English Jesuit who traveled to central and eastern Arabia under the sponsorship of the emperor of France. Although he had been baptized in the Church of England, his father was a Jew and the official archivist of the House of Commons. One brother was a prominent poet and anthologist and another brother became governor of the Bank of England. Palgrave and Richard Burton were rough contemporaries and they took potshots at one another in the forwards to their books. They had a great deal in common, including an early promise amounting to precocity. Both joined the Indian Army before finishing Oxford, Burton in 1842 and Palgrave in 1847, and both were posted to the west coast of India. However, where Burton spent seven years in Sind, working on his languages and sharpening his powers of observation, Palgrave fell sick almost at once and was forced to convalesce in Goa.

Gifford Palgrave

There, he came under the influence of the Jesuits and converted to Roman Catholicism. After recovering, Gifford, as he was known, left the army and joined the Jesuit order. On ordination, he was posted to Syria where he spent many years as a missionary. He was present during the massacres of the Maronites and afterwards was sent to the British Isles to give a series of lectures on "the Syrian problem." The texts of some of the speeches in Ireland sound very Catholic, as only an Irish Catholic can sound.

He eventually left the Society of Jesus but, remaining in the Church, he tried to interest the Society for the Propagation of the Faith in a scheme to convert the Arabs of the peninsula to Catholicism. The Pope, understandably, was not interested in a venture with such a remote possibility of success. Palgrave then gained the ear of Napoleon III and secured his help in a journey to Nejd, the settled center of Arabia. Posing as leeches, Palgrave and a Syrian Christian traveled from Damascus via the Wadi Sirhan, Jebel Shammar, and Qasim to Riyadh, where they spent a month in the lair of the Wahhabi Emir before making their way to the coast at Muscat. *Central and Eastern Arabia*, the account of the journey, is dedicated to Carsten Niebuhr, ". . . in honor of that intelligence and courage which first opened Arabia to Europe."

Palgrave has always been controversial. In spite of an accurate portrayal of everyday life in central Arabia, conceded even by those who question other aspects of his account, the geographical details are often sketchy and his garrulousness is not redeemed by the claim that he is speaking not as a historian but as a reporter, repeating only what he heard at second-hand. Based on an examination of the itinerary Philby concluded that *Central and Eastern Arabia* was a fabrication and that Palgrave never traveled to Nejd at all.

Palgrave says that he "leveled" with his guides about his persona and purpose in the journey to Nejd. Unfortunately, he does not level with the reader and at the end we are still uncertain about who he purported to be and what brought him to Arabia. With his chestnut hair and blue eyes, his appearance immediately identified him as a non-Arab, although there were enough in the way of Turks, Georgians, Albanians, and Circassians in and around Arabia that he could pass for a Levantine Christian or even a Moslem. But it was not without alerting the finely-calibrated antennae of the *Nejdis* who, after their experience of the Egyptian invasion earlier in the century, had good reason to be suspicious of outsiders. The notion that a European, however thorough his knowledge of Islam and Arab practices, could pass himself off as a native is the stuff of *Kim* or *Greenmantle* and boys' adventure stories.

There is also something about Palgrave's attitude that grates. Where Burton asserts his knowledge of Islam and the Arab world, Palgrave assumes the same from the point of view of lofty superiority, and his orotund and oracular writing style is off-putting. His contempt for the Bedouins is perhaps a corrective to the more romantic picture subscribed to by some, but we wonder why he wastes much space on a people—faithless, witless, fickle, and scatter-brained—so unworthy of his attention. Finally, he seems conscious that he is writing a tale of adventure and we eventually become suspicious of too many fortuitous turns of events, complications of plot, and hairbreadth escapes. These devices may enliven *Robinson Crusoe* or *Gulliver's Travels,* but they do not inspire confidence in a work purporting to be a serious record of exploration. The Royal Geographical Society listened politely to Palgrave's account of Nejd but withheld the medal that should have gone to the first Englishman who crossed Central Arabia from north to south.

After the Arabian journey Gifford left the Church, although there is some question as to whether he returned to the Church of England. He seems to have become interested in his Jewish roots. He joined the British Foreign Service and was posted to Trebizond, from which base he traveled widely between 1867 and 1873 in the Caucasus. His account of that period, *Eastern Questions,* makes interesting reading today as the Soviet Caucasus falls apart. He married and was later sent to South America. He died as the British legate in Montevideo.

In *The Penetration of Arabia* Hogarth speaks guardedly and rather waspishly about Palgrave, alluding to his Jewish blood as the reason why he seemed to get along so well with the settled Semites of central Arabia. There was also the veiled suggestion that Palgrave could not be trusted. There may have been some truth in that, and he suffered from the disapprobation that often attaches to a renegade. But lest we leap to latter-day conclusions about the prevalence of anti-Semitism in official Britain, the similarity, again, of Palgrave's experience with Burton's should sound a cautionary note. Neither man was ever given a post commensurate with his ability. But both were in the civil service and what exotic flowers such as they ever blossomed in such barren soil? For all of his brilliance, Palgrave was no more successful as a diplomat than "ruffian Dick Burton," the "white nigger."

ST. JOHN PHILBY (1885–1960)

St. John Bridger Philby

Harold St. John Bridger Philby was perhaps the greatest Arabist of them all, if greatness were measured by the number of miles traveled. He had the advantages of the automobile and the ear of Ibn Sau'd and that made him, certainly, the greatest explorer of Sau'di Arabia. He was nearly as prolific a writer as an explorer. His early training at Westminster and Cambridge hardly fitted him for his later exploits, although to the end he retained a weakness for cricket at Lords. His almost obsessive need to tweak official noses didn't prevent him from prescribing precisely the same conventional upbringing for his stuttering son.

The son, christened Harold Adrian Russell but called Kim after the Kipling figure, tweaked official noses much better than the father. Eventually rising to be head of the anti-Soviet section of the British secret service, he was all the while a Soviet mole, having been recruited at Cambridge in the thirties along with Burgess and McLean. It was an astonishing indictment of the old boy network. Kim Philby was "the third man" but they could not, or would not, arrest him. He slipped across the border from Turkey when the heat became too great and died in 1988 in Moscow, a hero of the Soviet Union. But where his father was a legitimate, albeit insufferable, eccentric, it is difficult to see Kim as anything but the unfortunate product of his father's brutishness and neglect. His treason may have been responsible for several scores of deaths, although his importance in the broader East-West conflict is debatable. But there is something pathetic about the younger Philby, the bad teeth, ill-fitting clothes, chronic inebriation, and vacuous urbanity. He would cuttingly refer to American colleagues as "one generation removed from the plow," but spent his decling years in Moscow listening to, of all things, phonograph recordings of the Red Army band.

The father was a contemporary of Lawrence and the paths of the two men crossed on more than one occasion. In *The Heart of Arabia* Philby tells the story of meeting Sharif Hussein in Jidda in early 1918 where Hussein referred to him jocularly as "the Lawrence of Nejd." As Shakespear's successor he had come to coordinate the Sharif's efforts with those of Ibn Sa'ud. In the event, the Sharif was not interested in cooperation with Ibn Sa'ud and, to underscore the point, forbade Philby to return through his dominions. He made his way back via the Red Sea and the Persian Gulf.

Philby was also unsuccessful in convincing Ibn Sa'ud to take the fight to the Rashidis and the Turks. Only then would he merit the same attention and subsidy as the Sharif, although much of the lavish aid to Hussein bled into Nejd after all, in the form of golden guineas and arms as British largesse passed from the tribes in the Hejaz to their compeers to the east. Some of the arms eventually found their way to southern Persia. Ibn Sa'ud ignored the rifles but siezed all the ammunition he could lay his hands on. After the war Philby played a more conventional role in Mesopotamia administering recently-liberated territory. Later, he was Lawrence's successor in Amman when Churchill persuaded Lawrence to come to Cairo to help "settle" the Middle East once and for all. He complained that Lawrence's filing system was a disaster.

Philby had no truck with the Hashemites and after the consolidation by the Al-Sa'uds, he settled in Jidda as the franchisee for Ford and Marconi. He wasn't very successful as a businessman, although a type of tent in Sa'udi Arabia is still known as a "filbee" since he imported them. But he soon began his exploratory trips into the recesses of the peninsula and over the next forty years a torrent of books appeared, beginning with *The Heart of Arabia* in 1922, *Arabia of the Wahhabis* in 1928, and *Arabia* in 1930. They were followed by *The Empty Quarter* in 1933. Having finally persuaded Ibn Sa'ud to allow him to be the first European to cross the *Rub al-Khali*, he hoped to contribute to a solution of the riddle of the great unknown desert. But after completing the crossing, complicated by a case of badly inflamed hemorrhoids, he discovered to his chagrin that Bertram Thomas had narrowly preceded him, although by a different route. The book is among the hardest reading of his works, but in many respects it is the most typical. Only Philby could fill 364 pages with the "peerless monotony" of the desert. He was an indefatigable observer and the British Museum would be the recipient of the fossils, rocks, and minerals, shells, insects, reptiles, birds, and mammals collected during the crossing. Freshwater shells were evidence that, like the Sahara, the peninsula had once passed through a less arid phase.

Philby was a tyrant, and the account is spiced by disagreements with other members of the the party, followed by fits of peevishness where he would refuse to ride his camel or drink his share of milk. When asked why he was so disagreeable Philby conceded that God had made him so, but the Arabs inflamed him with their contrariness. *The Empty Quarter* was followed over the next several decades by *Sheba's Daughters, A Pilgrim in Arabia, Arabian Days, Arabian Highlands, Arabian Jubilee, Sa'udi Arabia, The Land of Midian* and *Forty Years in the Wilderness*. It was a first-rate record of exploration of the peninsula and no one before or since has matched its range and detail.

He converted to Islam, the cynics suggesting that the conversion was entirely opportunistic. It certainly allowed him access to Mecca and Medina. It also allowed him access to Ibn Sa'ud. His increasing influence with the king and his readiness to speak his mind—Philby always spoke his mind—became alarming to the sons and sycophants who surrounded the old man. One of the family's first acts after the death of the king was to banish Philby from the kingdom. He settled in Beirut, where he crossed paths with Kim, then in his own limbo between MI6 and defection to the Soviet Union. He was later permitted to return, but age and physical ailments had slowed him and his days as an explorer were over. He died in 1960, leaving behind an Arab wife and two sons who must still be alive somewhere in the peninsula. Sa'udis today think of Philby as a foreigner, an unbeliever, and a spy. He was certainly the first, probably the second and, equally probably, *not* the third.

But such is the ill-repute that attaches to the name Philby.

D. G. HOGARTH (1862-1927

D. G. Hogarth

David George Hogarth was an adult and *eminence grise* among the amateurs who constitute most of the Arabists. He was an archaeologist who dug with Evans in Crete after apprenticeships with Ramsay in western Anatolia and Petrie in Egypt and a stint as director of the British School of Archaeology in Athens. He was an expert not in the Arab World but in the eastern Mediterranean and Asia Minor. In *Accidents of an Antiquary's Life* Hogarth tells how, as a boy, his imagination had been fired by "the spacious world over which Alexander moved" and he was an admirer of all things Hellenic, although the race had lately entered a stage of decrepitude. His interests ranged over antiquity writ large. His canvas was typically broad, the sweep of his generalizations wide. In *The Ancient East* and *The Nearer East* we read of Greeks and Semites and pure Aryans from the "back of beyond," how the monotheism of the Semites would push back against the pure intellect of the Greeks and eventually result in the amalgam that we call the modern West. He also described the population pressures that, from time immemorial, had pushed the tribes out of the Arabian Peninsula, that "eternal motherland of vigorous migrants," and into contact with the settled peoples of Syria and Mesopotamia. It was a canvas and theme that would find resonance in some of the more purple passages of the *Seven Pillars of Wisdom*.

Like many Englishmen of his time, Hogarth was also a bit of a Turkophil with an instinctive sympathy for the Anatolian peasant, the unspeakable Turk, "unspeakable only in that he does not say much," whose strengths were courage, simplicity, and loyalty, and conscription his greatest fear. This old Turk was far preferable to the Levantine riff-raff who came to prominence with the revolution in 1908. Ensuring the integrity of the Ottoman Empire had been a pillar of British policy in the East for a century, out of concern for the potential impact of dissolution on the European balance of power. The First World War would put an end to the policy of temporization and afterwards the contest for choice bits of the Ottoman carcass began in earnest.

In 1908 Hogarth was named to succeed Evans as curator of the Ashmolean Museum in Oxford where he first noticed the exceptional promise of a student at Oxford City High School for Boys, T. E. Lawrence. It was the beginning of a remarkably close relationship, with Hogarth acting part father figure and part mentor to the young Lawrence. It was through Hogarth that Lawrence found work at the dig in Carchemish in 1911. But it is probably only by accident that they found themselves in Egypt during the First World War.

On the outbreak of hostilities in 1914 Hogarth joined the geographical section of the Naval Intelligence Division, having decided that he could not spend his time piecing out Hittite inscriptions while the country was at war. In 1915, at the age of fifty-three and with the temporary rank of lieutenant commander in the Royal Navy (shades of James Bond), he was sent to head the Arab Bureau in Cairo, responsible, among other things, for raising the tribes against the Turks in the Hejaz. In this incarnation, he was an "intelligence professional" (if the term is not an oxymoron) in an age when connections still meant more than expertise. Lawrence and the others in Cairo were too unorthodox to fit comfortably in an official harness. Hogarth was the man who managed them all. He was old enough, and had seen enough, that he was not prey to febrile impulses. In *A Wandering Scholar in the Levant*, published in 1896 he had warned of the danger of a kind "bohemianism" in the traveler who was a law unto himself, and he was always alive to the tendency by those of too great an individuality to wander off the reservation.

Although Hogarth's time in Arabia was confined to a short visit to Jidda in 1917 and there is no evidence that he spoke much Arabic, he became a specialist in the literature of Arabian travel and was sometimes known as "Hogarth of Arabia." In fact, there is probably no figure that better gathers together the various strains represented by the Arabists than D. G. Hogarth. In *The Penetration of Arabia*, published in 1904, he surveyed the contributions of, among others, Niebuhr, Burckhardt, Burton, Palgrave, the Blunts, and Doughty in opening the peninsula to the outside world. He later worked with Lawrence, Bell, and Philby. Only Thesiger escaped his reach.

Hogarth was also the principal author of a handbook, *Hejaz before World War I*, issued by the Arab Bureau in 1917. It was an attempt to compile everything known about this new theater of war, based largely on sources that appeared in *The Penetration of Arabia*. In the introduction to a 1978 reprint much is made of the "enigmatic figure" of Hogarth, suggesting that his archaeological work was really only cover for the raising of intelligence networks in anticipation of war with Turkey. However, none of his digs in Egypt, Crete, or Asia Minor was in an area that played much of a role during the war. But the suggestion that Hogarth was all the while a secret agent raises the question of the role of intelligence during the campaign in the Hejaz. In fact, if by "intelligence" is meant the foreknowledge of enemy plans, the best source, surprisingly, was what today we would call "sigint," the interception and decoding of enemy signals, largely due to the Turks' carelessness in use of the telegraph. Human intelligence or "humint"—Hogarth and other "spies" to the contrary notwithstanding—played a relatively unimportant part.

But it was "intelligence," if by the word is meant discernment, that led to the Arab Bureau's greatest success, effectively ending the war in the Hejaz. On a visit to Jidda Lawrence found the Arab Revolt in disarray, riven by amateurism in the worst sense of the word. But in Feisal, he discovered if not a prophet, at least a son of the Sherif malleable enough to follow him north where the real action lay. The blue-eyed Lawrence was a most improbable Arab, but with his immense drive and single-mindedness he set out to put things right. Auda abu Tayi may have been the mainspring of the descent on Aqaba as the Arabs maintain. But surely it was Lawrence who saw that Aqaba gave them the opportunity to link up with Allenby and their only chance to share in the spoils at the end of the war. As it turned out, they were there with the British, the French, and the Zionists in the "scramble for Arabia" and if the Hejaz and quasi-independence in Iraq and Transjordan were not the sum of Sharifian dreams, they were better than nothing. Without Lawrence, the Arab Revolt would probably have remained confined to the Hejaz in a permanent stalemate, investing the stubborn and unimaginative Turks in Medina. As director of the Arab Bureau Hogarth must take some credit—or blame—for this.

After the war Hogarth returned to the Ashmolean where he remained until his death in 1927. He resumed his geographical surveys with *A History of Arabia*, the first part of an intended series to include Syria, Mesopotamia, and Persia. A biography, *The Life of Charles M. Doughty*, appeared posthumously. In *An Oxford Portrait Gallery* his sister Janet, a childhood chum of Gertrude Bell, left a sketch of her brother's life. But there is still no definitive biography of D. G. Hogarth.

WILFRED THESIGER (1910-2003)

The last of these figures is Wilfred Thesiger who died a nonagenarian in northern Kenya. He was raised in Addis Ababa, the son of the British ambassador to Ethiopia and the nephew of the Viceroy of India. All the establishment connections were there. But England was only the locale of his school years and they were, incidentally, the unhappiest years of his life. There was a recent BBC special on the attempt of an old army veteran and white hunter to adjust to life in England. He had been evicted from his sprawling house and grounds in Kenya and a niece had videotaped his attempts at life in the UK. She showed him in a supermarket, filling a shopping cart with gin and later, drunkenly, trying to open a can of beans. I don't think he had ever opened a can in his life. It was comical and pathetic.

Wilfred Thesiger

Thesiger's account of his time in the UK in his latest book, *The Life of my Choice*, was a little like that, minus the gin. His first act in 1933, after an exile at Eton and then Oxford, was to return to Ethiopia and make a journey down the Awash from Addis Ababa to the Red Sea at Tajura. To call the Danakil, among whom he traveled, "wild" would be to put it mildly. They were intensely hostile to outsiders. They castrated their enemies and wore the testicles as trophies. The Italians discovered this to their regret and many Italian prisoners-of-war returned, if they returned at all, emasculated. Thesiger survived the passage intact, a remarkable journey for a twenty-three year-old.

Later assignments took him to Darfur in northwestern Sudan where he lived a kind of Jim Corbett life as a white hunter, shooting the lions that preyed on the tribesmen's stock. He shot them out of necessity, not sport. The courage of the tribesmen was extraordinary. Before his arrival they hunted the lions on their own, without firearms. There were always terrible mutilations and deaths when they eventually brought the animals to bay. Thesiger says he shot over seventy lions, but later became the classic poacher turned gamekeeper and a spokesman for the preservation of African wildlife.

The book was also a bit of a primer on the life of the tribesmen. He tells the story of the boy who was imprisoned after killing his new wife. The wife was circumcised in the Sudanese fashion, the inner labia and clitoris removed and the orifice sewn up, awaiting the exertions of the husband. On the wedding night the husband was to demonstrate his manhood by achieving penetration. But Husaini had used a tent peg to widen the opening. The wife laughed at him and told all her friends the next day. So he cut her throat. The sentence was commuted from death to life imprisonment and when Thesiger knew him he was out on good behavior.

From 1936 to 1938 Thesiger was in the southern Sudan amid the swamps with the Nuer. There the males also underwent mutilation, with tribal scars cut so deeply on both cheeks that they scored the bone. The agony of this passage to manhood was considerable, with the knife drawn repeatedly through the wound to ensure that the cuts were deep enough. They bled profusely and and the pain must have been excruciating, but the boys sat impassive throughout the ceremony. Any sign of flinching would bring shame on the family. Afterwards, ashes and cow dung were rubbed into the wounds to enure that the scars achieved the desired prominence. These swamp people were the most savage Thesiger had ever seen, and they went about utterly naked. They would stand and eat and urinate at the same time. It was an extraordinary book.

Thesiger returned to Abyssinia during the Second World War and served with the British forces that put Haile Selassie back on the throne. He then saw service in the Western Desert. After the war he was a member of the locust eradication team in Arabia, where he wandered with tribesmen over the fringes of the Empty Quarter. The title of the book about these experiences, *Arabian Sands*, says it all. This was followed by a period in Iraq among the Marsh Arabs. He eventually made his way to Kenya where he lived among the Turkana. He died in 2003.

He said in an interview near the end that he never set out with the intention to write a book, but instead to experience life. The books still came. I wonder that there will be another man whose life spans the kinds of change that have taken place in this part of the world. If nothing else, his refusal to accommodate himself to modernity makes him an attractive, if quixotic, figure. But the anachronism carries with it some anachronistic sentiments. He was a royalist and a partisan of Haile Selassie. Surely, there must be some middle ground between the old emperor and the murderous likes of Mengitsu. I was about to say that he is the last of a breed. But Thesiger was so unusual that he may have been one-of-a-kind. If so, he was the first and last of his type.

So there they are, outsiders all. They were all professionals in the sense that they knew what they were doing. But they were also amateurs in the best sense of the word in that they didn't take money for what they did. Oh, all other than Doughty and the Blunts had official duties that brought them to the Arab World and most accepted the King's guinea at some point in their careers. But it didn't influence what they said, and their outspokenness often got them into trouble.

The portraits I have drawn are perhaps not art at all, being something closer to illustration. All, with the exception of Thesiger, were dead when I drew them and all, with the exception of Niebuhr, Burckhardt, Burton, and Palgrave, were drawn from photographs. I am a competent draftsman but I also believe that drawing, like writing, is a voyage of discovery. There is enough of the unexpected or imaginative about them that I keep them on the wall for the pleasure they bring as well as reminders of a lifelong attachment to the subjects they represent.

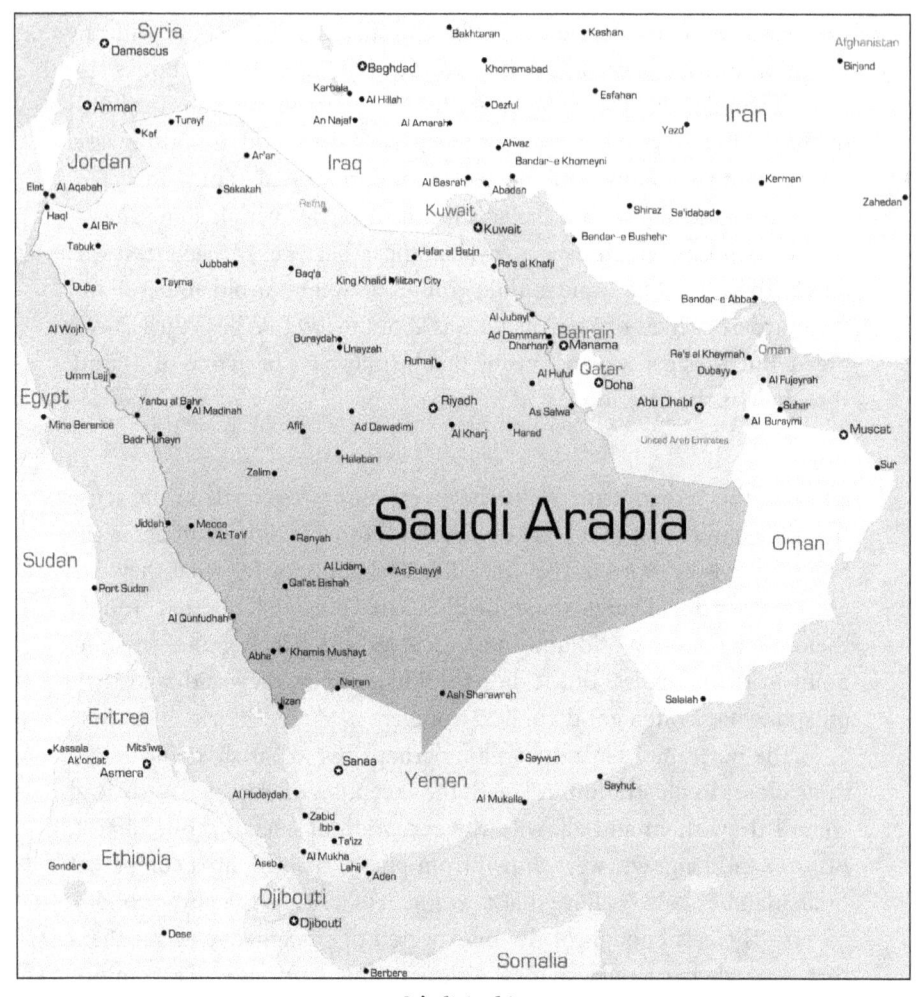

Sa'udi Arabia

3

The Magic Kingdom

It was still early on a May morning in 1986 when I reached Badr Hunayn, 150 miles north of Jidda and inland of Yanbu'. So, it was not yet the insufferable combination of heat and humidity that characterized the Tehama at the height of summer. The Tehama was the coastal plain of Arabia, extending from the Gulf of Aqaba in the north to the Bab al-Mandab in the south. Badr was famous as the site of a battle between the Muslims and the Meccans in the second year of the *Hijra*, or 624 AD. The Muslims were outnumbered by three to one, but the Prophet rallied them and they scored the victory that laid the foundation for all of their later successes. Badr also lay at the intersection of the road from Medina to the coast and the *hajj* route from Syria, and in 1986 it was still an intersection. This was my first long business trip in Sa'udi Arabia. Arthur D. Little was the consultant to Petroserve, the services arm of Petromin, the state-owned oil company. In the early 1980s, when the Sa'udis were flush, ADL had drafted a master plan to computerize all of Petromin's operations, from financial systems, through refinery operations, to marketing and long-range planning. Petroserve was responsible for implementation and ADL was the implementation consultant.

My part was the accounting, budgeting and personnel systems. The solutions were typically Sa'udi and lavish, with top-of-the-line American software, but Arabized and so available in either English or Arabic at the flip of a switch. For the Arabization, a stable of regional experts had been hired, although they sometimes struggled with the language of commercial usage which varied across the Middle East. But the real innovation was in the display on the monitors. Most computer Arabic at the time consisted of variants of the *handassa*, or engineering, script, made up of small horizontal and vertical lines, and visually crude. Here, the letters had been carefully drawn by expert calligraphers—laid out in large grids before being reduced to screen size—and the monitors were manufactured by a Canadian company especially for Petromin. The display was beautiful, easily the best computer Arabic in the market. The only problem was with the connection routines since certain letters required the use of more than one key, complicating the keyboard design. It was hoped that both the software and the display could be marketed by Petroserve elsewhere in the region. But the potential was too tempting. The big players—Microsoft and IBM—soon entered the market and Petroserve Arabic and the Canadian monitors were history. Microsoft Arabic became the standard and offered a menu with any script you wanted. The Petromin systems were based on IBM mainframes, although PCs, or personal computers, were beginning to cut into the mainframe market. IBM, of course, manufactured PCs as well.

There were projects across the kingdom, from Jidda, Rabigh, and Yanbu' on the west coast to Riyadh in the center and Dhahran in the eastern province. Each of the projects, including headquarters—Ahmad Zaki Yamani was still the chairman of the board—several refineries, an exploration company, a marketing organization, shipping companies, and a geophysical arm had a matrix of applications and the total of the project/applications numbered in the scores. So, we were in perpetual motion across the kingdom as the implementations unfolded. We were based in Jidda and generally flew on the longer business trips, either on *Sa'udia* or occasionally on the Petromin corporate jet. First class on *Sa'udia* in a Lockheed L1011 was always a pleasant experience, with swivel seats, plenty of legroom, a steady supply of Bedouin coffee and designer dates with almonds in the center. The corporate jet was even more luxurious. Once, for a trip to Riyadh to pick up visas for a family visit to Kenya, I had called the dispatcher and made the usual arrangements with the agreeable Brit who scheduled the departures. Aboard, I realized that I was the only one on the flight and that the air crew—the Lebanese stewardesses and expatriate pilots—flying this extravagance with gold-plated fixtures in the toilets, had been placed at my entire disposal for a purpose that could only be described as personal. The corporate jets were among the first things to go after a shake-up of Petromin management early in our tenure.

But this time I had persuaded the ADL project manager to let me drive. At the waist, from Jidda in the west to Dhahran in the east, Sa'udi Arabia was just over 800 miles across, about the distance from New York to St. Louis. From north to south it was 1,200 miles, about the same as the United States from El Paso to the Canadian border. The trip would take just over a week from coast to coast. There wouldn't be much time for exploration. This was, after all, a business trip and I would be seeing only a relatively narrow strip across the center of the peninsula, and that at seventy miles an-hour. But still it would a chance to put places to names that had figured in a reading of Sa'udi history. Most of the project cars were Chevrolet Caprices, still the vehicle of choice in the kingdom. They were big and powerful and had the added advantage of size in the event of an accident. Later, we would drive SUVs, and the four wheels allowed us to go off the road when we wanted. But the highway system in Sa'udi Arabia was very modern and 4x4s weren't needed for most routine travel.

However, this time I was in a little Honda Accord left over from the early days of the project, and I set out on a Thursday morning, the fifteenth of May. It was also Ramadan, the fasting month. This first leg would be repeated many times over the next three years. Rabigh and Yanbu', about 100 and 200 miles respectively up the coast from Jidda, were too close to fly, although there had been air service to Yanbu' in the early days. Both cities had refineries, although only the one in Yanbu' was operational. Yanbu' was the western equivalent of Jubail on the east coast and a considerable industrial city. So, there was a question as to whether Rabigh needed a refinery at all. But the Greek investor seemed to have friends in high places, because the project went ahead anyway. We often visited the site and always had lunch in the cruise ship the Greek tied up at the pier as a kind of floating hotel and restaurant. The little town was also an example of the inability of some Westerners to pronounce Arabic names. One of our subcontractors called it "Rabeeb." I tried to correct him:

> Ray, it's like two English words: raw, as in 'raw egg,' and big as in 'big fella.' Just put the two together: *Raw'-big*, with the stress on the first syllable.

But he never got it right, although I think he had graduated to "Rebeeg" by the time he left.

Yanbu' was the port of Medina, in the same way that Jidda was the port of Mecca. John Lewis Burckhardt had been there in 1811 when it was suffering from the ravages of the plague. The holy precincts were supposedly immune to disease, and the belief probably contributed to its spread. The most virulent strain was transmitted pneumatically, from person to person by aerosol droplets, and the frequent funerals and exchanges of sympathy between the mourners only worsened the epidemic. More recently, in 1917, Yanbu' had been the site of a critical battle in the early stages of the Arab Revolt. The Turks had driven Feisal and his Bedouins out of Yanbu' al-Nakhl, the palm groves several miles to the east of the town, and they had fallen back on Yanbu' al-Bahr, the town itself and port on the Red Sea coast. But the British had moved ships into the harbor in support and the Turks were halted. Lawrence tells the story in the *Seven Pillars of Wisdom,* how the Turks had lost heart when they saw the blaze of the ships' lights from end to end of the harbor and the points of the searchlights crisscrossing the plain. It was the turning point of the war in the Hejaz.

Hejaz Mountains

Here, I had driven up the featureless coast, past Rabigh and Masturah, before turning inland to Badr. The road led through the coastal range and Burckhardt, for one, had left a detailed account of its stages, although by a slightly different route. His caravan of Malay *hajjis* had headed directly north from Rabigh and picked up the road from the coast at Safra. But nearly two centuries later there weren't many places recognizable from his itinerary. The little booklet *Hejaz before World War I*, authored by David Hogarth and issued in 1917 by Arab Bureau in Cairo, included a description of routes between towns in the province, and this was one of them. The distance from Badr to Medina was about 75 miles as the crow flies, but the road was anything but straight, and it wound through little villages built of the flinty material that made up the mountains. The word "Hejaz" came from the Arabic root that meant, among other things, "to block... to bar... to isolate." All etymologies were suspect but this probably made sense: the mountains blocked access to the interior from the coast and vice-versa. Along with Mecca, Medina was one of the *Haramayn*, or the two Holy Cities, and unbelievers were forbidden to enter its environs. But there wasn't a "Muslims Only" sign on the highway, like there was outside Mecca, and on this occasion one unbeliever entered just far enough to buy gas.

Meda'in Saleh

On a later occasion a busload of us actually stayed at the Medina Sheraton in the outskirts of the city. We were on our way to al-Ula and nearby Meda'in Saleh, or the "Cities of Saleh, the striking group of Nabataean tombs that were the southern equivalent of Petra. Charles Montague Doughty had reported them in 1888 in his *Travels in Arabia Deserta*. They were carved in the sandstone monoliths that stood up starkly out of the desert, unlike the concentrated city of Petra in Jordan to the north. Some were spectacular, with multilayered cornices and elaborate entrance portals.

Roundhouse, Al-Ula

Al-Ula itself, just over 300 miles northwest of Medina, was interesting from a distance, an ancient ruin amid the palms. But our *tasriih*—the authorization that was needed for travel in the kingdom—didn't include al-Ula itself, although we did see Doughty's blockhouse and several old locomotives in the roundhouse at the al-Ula station. This station on the

Hejaz Railway looked like it had been left untouched after the war although the rails had been pulled up for use elsewhere. The railroad no longer ran south of the Jordanian city of Ma'an.

We had also stopped for coffee on the outskirts of Khaybar, halfway between Medina and Meda'in Saleh, where Doughty had looked for Jews, early occupants of the oasis. He didn't find any, the place being low-lying and feverish and occupied then by the descendants of black slaves. According to the Qur'an (or was it a *hadith* or saying?) one of the signs of presaging the end of the world would be the return of Jews to Khaybar. The drive back to Jidda from Medina could also be made by the inland, or Darb al-Sharqi or eastern route. The 277 miles was through a region of *harras*, or lava flows, memorialized by Doughty with cinder cones, little black pimples, standing up cleanly out of the plain.

Medina came at eleven fifteen after 395 kilometers, or 240 miles from Jidda. After buying gas I skirted the city and cleared the outskirts just before noon. From Medina, it was about 275 miles northeast to al-Rass, "the door to Qasim" and the heartland of Wahhabi Arabia. There were no projects in Qasim, and a more direct route would have taken me the 500 miles directly to Riyadh from Jidda. But it wouldn't have seen Qasim. I would be there on a Friday, the Moslem Sabbath, so there would be no loss of productivity. I would take the direct route back. After half a-day's drive from Medina, the early part through an outcropping of the *harrat Khaybar*, the field of black lava that covered thousands of square miles to the northwest, I was stopped by a policeman. He didn't understand the English of my passport and asked me where I had come from. I said "Jeddah," using the soft pronunciation we used among ourselves. But he didn't recognize the word, so I gave it the Najdi pronunciation "Jidda," a sharper sound, and then he understood.

After the *harra* the land was relatively featureless until I reached the Wadi al-Rimah, just short of al-Rass, although scuttling away by the side of the road I did see a *dabb*, the large lizard sometimes eaten by the Bedouin. They could be over a foot long and were a welcome source of protein, although other Arabs found the Bedouin appetite disgusting. An added attraction of Qasim was the al-Salman hotel, the Burayda Oberoi, run by the same chain that owned the Mena House Oberoi in Cairo, and I had made reservations for the night. Oberoi himself had been a busboy at a hotel in Simla, the summer retreat of the British in India, before he graduated to ownership of a chain of hotels across India and the Middle East. The Mena House was spectacular and I wanted to see what they had done in Qasim. But the al-Salman was a disappointment. It seems that Oberoi had sold out several years before, and I found myself in a standard second-rate Sa'udi hotel.

They broke the fast just after six thirty and dinner was a buffet in the hotel dining room. After the meal, I took a turn around the city but there was little to see in the gloom, with none of the Egyptian Ramadan nightlife. Burayda was not a friendly place, especially during the fasting month, the season *par excellence* for demonstration of the Wahhabi brand of the faith. This year it fell in May, not yet the hottest part of the year. But, still, it was nearly fifteen hours of fasting, from the moment before dawn when a black thread could be distinguished from a white to the *adhan* proclamation at sunset. In *Arabia of the Wahhabis* Philby, had noticed the churlish disposition of the citizens of Burayda. He thought it might have something to do with the water, which had a leaden taste. It was not apparent brushing my teeth in 1986.

Philby had come here with the Wahhabi army in the autumn of 1918, having finally persuaded Ibn Sa'ud that if he were to be taken seriously by the British he would have to do something useful against the Turks, like the Sharif was doing in the Hejaz. The Al-Rashids—the traditional enemies of the Al-Sa'uds—were friendly to the Turks and the smuggling of material and food into Medina was still taking place through Ha'il, the Rashidi capital 250 miles northwest of Bureyda. They were effectively breaking the blockade imposed by the Sharifian armies, although the "armies" by then consisted only of the tribal forces attached to Ali and Abdullah, Feisal by now having taken Aqaba and attached himself like a limpet to Allenby's British army in Palestine. Taking Ha'il would serve the interests of both the allies and Ibn Sa'ud. Or, so the British maintained. After months of urging by Philby, Ibn Sa'ud had finally consented to the campaign, although with ill grace.

Philby accompanied the army when it departed Riyadh in early August. But perhaps mindful of Shakespear's fate in an earlier action against Ibn Rashid—he had been killed, standing up very prominently in his British uniform and topee, or pith helmet, in one of the eddies as the tribal battle swirled around him—Ibn Sa'ud had left Philby behind in Burayda. In the event, the action was inconclusive and the reduction of Ha'il and unification of Najd would be left to another day, three years later and according to Ibn Sa'ud's own timetable. But this campaign against the Rashids and Ha'il had been ill-starred from the beginning. Ibn Sa'ud made it clear to Philby that he was moving against Ha'il only for the sake of the British since he had no immediate quarrel with Ibn Rashid. His real enemy was the Sharif in the Hejaz. But he had help from an unexpected quarter. The diplomatic bag in Burayda brought the news that His Majesty's Government were concerned that the campaign against Ibn Rashid would unnecessarily ruffle the temper of the Sharif. To underscore the point the British withdrew the offer of modern rifles previously made to Ibn Sa'ud. It was an unprecedented snub. Philby was furious. Ibn Sa'ud's pique probably concealed an element of relief.

I was gone early the next morning on the road to 'Aneyza, the sister city to Burayda and fifteen miles to the south. There, Philby had found an "open-handed hospitality" and a "complete freedom of any kind of religious or sectarian bigotry" that astonished him. Doughty had also spent several weeks there in 1878 after his escape from Khaybar. By comparison with his surly reception in Ha'il and Burayda, 'Aneyza had been an oasis of hospitality. Doughty's troubles were not over, however, and there would be a perilous journey to the coast before he found refuge at the British consulate in Jidda. In 'Aneyza, Philby found descendants of the Bassam who had befriended Doughty, and men who remembered the visit of *khalil*. I would later work in Petroserve with a Bassam from 'Aneyza whose openness and urbanity made him a worthy successor to the original. After a short tour of the environs, with groves of palms standing over kitchen gardens that were reminders of Doughty's time, I pressed on, the journey interrupted only by a flat tire near al-Thadiq, 175 miles south of the city.

If Qasim was a disappointment, the *Nafud* was not. The six-lane superhighway that connected Qasim with Riyadh crossed a portion of that belt of dunes whose praises Lady Anne and Wilfrid Scawen Blunt, among others, had sung. They were beautiful in the morning, a delicate pink in the rising sun, although I didn't see any of the *fuluj* that they constituted farther north. There, the pink sand was laid down over limestone basement material in great horseshoe arcs, at the bottom of which the white floor was visible, and they actually moved with the wind, marching imperceptibly across the limestone.

Dunes, Nefud

In the infrequent rains the dormant seeds would come to life and the dunes were briefly covered with a carpet of flowers. It was hard to imagine, but animals lived in the dunes, taking their moisture entirely from the plants. In 1971 a pair of Americans, anxious to experience travel the old way, had been allowed by the Sa'udis to follow the *Nafud* up the Wadi Sirhan to Amman by camel. But it was only on the condition that water and fodder be trucked in, or flown in by helicopter, every day. The wells were no longer maintained and no one traveled by camel any more. Why should they, when Toyotas were available? The impulse was in some respects romantic, although the peninsular Arabs were the most pragmatic, least sentimental people on the planet

After a transit of places with storied names—al-Sirr, Jabal Tuwaiq, Washm, al-Aridh—I arrived in Riyadh early in the afternoon, just over 250 miles from Burayda and 850 miles from Jidda. There was an Arabian Homes compound in Riyadh, but the Arthur D. Little corporate representative lived in his own detached villa. He was not an old Sa'udi hand, but the detached lifestyle made him seem older. If the odor of wine occasionally escaped from a room in a villa in Jidda, this house reeked of it, and of the beer fermenting in the bathtub. It was hard to tell where in the city he lived, since Riyadh seemed like several cities at once, all laid out helter-skelter. There was the old *suq*, and the area around the citadel that Ibn Sa'ud had stormed in 1902, the Petromin offices and the area around the Marriott. But there seemed to be no urban plan or zoning ordinances. The city was stitched together by a modern road system, and the civil works were impressive by comparison with those in Egypt. Actually, they rivaled the infrastructure in Europe or America.

Most of the Petromin entities served by the project were in Jidda or Dhahran, but the headquarters—including a computer center and a refinery—were here in Riyadh, as well as branches of Petroserve and Petrolube. The next three days would be taken up with coding issues as the old systems were adapted to the new software. There was a marked division of labor in Petromin. The vice presidents were Sa'udis but the systems programmers were Filipinos and the chief accountants were typically Pakistanis. The normal resistance to change was magnified by the divide. The Sa'udis were cooperative. It was, after all, their management that had hired ADL to oversee implementation of the new systems. And the Filipino systems programmers were prepared to do whatever was necessary to make it all happen. But the Pakistani chief accountants, the real powers behind the scene and seeing a threat to their traditional domains, resisted with every delaying device at their disposal.

The computer center at the refinery was memorable for an analyst by the name of Naqshbandi. It was the name of one of the most prominent Sufi orders, the Central Asian *Naqshbandiyya*, called after an early devotee. This man was very fair and looked Central Asian. In Farsi, the name meant "painter, one who adorns" but it was an anomaly in Arabia, the peninsular Arabs never having been sympathetic to painters or adorners. Sufism was largely a phenomenon of the outlying lands of Islam, of Central Asia, India, Anatolia, and North Africa. In the peninsula, prominent Sufis may have lived in the Hejaz or the 'Asir, but Najd had never been receptive to this more mystical branch of Islam. The zealots would say that Sufis weren't Muslims at all.

Ramparts, Diri'ya

There was something about the air of Riyadh that made it different, and somehow more authentic than the coastal cities. It was what made Sa'udi Arabia a different place. It wasn't a land just of Bedouins. The Al-Sa'uds, like the other family that tilted for primacy in the peninsula, the Al-Rashids of Ha'il, were merchants and traders, sturdy burghers occupying cities in Najd. They were citizens of al-Rass, 'Anayza and Burayda, and of Diri'ya before Ibrahim Pasha and the Egyptian army razed it to the ground in 1819. Ibrahim was the second son of Mohammed Ali Pasha and he was acting on behalf of his father who was acting on behalf of the Sultan in Istanbul, although father and son would later pose a much greater threat to Ottoman rule than the Al-Sa'uds ever did. It was in response to the first Sa'udi eruption that spread outward from Najd in the early part of the century. Wahhabi forces first sacked Karbala in Iraq in

1801, before turning to the west, reaching the Hejaz in 1806 and expelling the Turks from Mecca and Medina shortly thereafter. As was their practice they pulled down the domes over all the tombs they found, and had even attacked the green dome over the Prophet's tomb in Medina. In the attempt, several of the *Ikhwan* fell to their deaths from the heights and they took it as a sign. But it had been a near thing.

The Turks found this challenge to their nominal rule of the Holy Cities intolerable and the campaign of the Egyptians was the answer. But in Najd, Ibrahim was at the end of a 500-mile supply line, far from his base on the coast. Qasim was not a rich province and the Egyptians were at one point reduced to eating grass. So, after compelling the surrender of 'Abd Allah ibn Sa'ud, escorting him to Cairo and then Istanbul—where he was publicly paraded and then beheaded—they withdrew. Diri'ya had been the Al-Sa'ud capital and when the burghers rebuilt, they abandoned the site and the palms the Egyptians had cut down. They moved a few miles to the south and made Riyadh their new capital. *Al-Riyadh* meant "the gardens." Today the ramparts of Diri'ya were being restored in recognition of the city's importance in the history of the country. Now, stepped parapets and ochre walls again enclosed palm groves and leant the scene a look that had once characterized all of Qasim.

Although Riyadh had grown rapidly, not to say chaotically, and was full of gleaming new buildings, the look and feel of the old parts—the citadel, near where public executions still took place today—gave it an authenticity that Jidda somehow lacked. For the zealots of Najd, it was a place apart. The cities of Mecca and Medina may have been in the Hejaz, but there was always something foreign about the western seaboard and the real heart of Arabia lay here in Najd. In the early days, there had been only occasional European contacts with the center. In the east, the India Office was interested primarily in the Gulf trade and dealt with the pirate states only as impediments to the flow of goods. The agreements, or truces, hence "the Trucial States" of Abu Dhabi, Dubai, Ajman, Ras al-Khaima and Sharja were meant to ensure that the flow of trade was uninterrupted. With the exception of a few civil servants like Pelly and Sadlier—and, later, Shakespear and Philby—the authorities in Delhi or Bombay had never paid much attention to the central fastness of Arabia. There was nothing there to interest them. The same was true in the west, traditionally the responsibility of the Foreign Office exercised through Cairo. There, British governments were concerned primarily with ensuring that the rights of their subjects, mainly Indian, were observed during the *hajj*, or pilgrimage.

So long as trade flowed and British subjects were treated with the respect their passports deserved, the rest of the country was left to the Arabs. But by the early twentieth century the British had virtually surrounded the central portion of the peninsula. Starting in the northeast with Iran, whose southwest coast had been a British sphere of influence for decades, the string of British protégés continued almost uninterrupted. On the opposite coast of the Gulf were Kuwait, Bahrain, and the Trucial States. Then, in the southeast there was Oman and in the southwest the Aden Protectorate. In the west, the Hashemites were also British protégés, even after the old Sharif was replaced by his son Ali as king of the Hejaz. Across the Red Sea there was British Somaliland and then the Sudan and Egypt, joined together in their condominium. Finally, in the north there was mandatory Palestine, the Emirate of Transjordan and a quasi-independent Iraq, the last two ruled by Hashemites. Arabia was completely surrounded. When treaties were negotiated it would be between the Al-Sa'uds and the British: Gilbert Clayton would speak on behalf of the Imam of the Yemen, or Percy Cox, called "Cokkus" by the Arabs, would negotiate on behalf of the Amir of Kuwait, or some other civil servant would speak for the Sultan of Muscat. The Al-Sa'uds spoke for themselves.

In the final chapter of the story the Najdi *amir*, 'Abdal 'Aziz ibn Sa'ud, used the Bedouins to consolidate his hold over what would eventually become the Kingdom of Sa'udi Arabia. Gathering them together in settlements like Artawiyya and Ghat Ghat, he turned them from pastoralists into agriculturalists, weaned them of their predatory ways, reconciled their blood feuds, and infused them with the extreme Wahhabi vision of the faith. Then he turned them loose and as the *Ikhwan*, or brotherhood, they spread terror throughout the peninsula. They swept into the Hejaz in 1924, easily brushed aside the rickety edifice erected by the Hashemites and introduced to the coastal cosmopolites their version of puritan rule.

They also raided up the Wadi Sirhan into Transjordan and Syria, at one point reaching the outskirts of Aleppo. Along the way they laid waste to encampments and villages, massacring men, women and children alike. It was *not* the Bedouin way, where men were killed only when necessary and women and children never. The British responded with air power and occasionally strewed the bones of raiding parties over the waste. Eventually the *Ikhwan* grew arrogant and then unmanageable. Ibn

Sa'ud, always more a statesman than a religious zealot, called for restraint. When this was refused, he ruthlessly crushed them. It was a forgotten part of the country's history and young Sa'udis were always surprised at the story. Today, their utility as shock troops gone, the Bedouins were reduced to the status of policemen, providers of airport security, or members of the National Guard. They were little brown men, not the fat pink people we dealt with in Petromin.

The consolidation of the kingdom by Ibn Sa'ud—surely one of the great figures of the twentieth century—was almost the sole, legitimately Arab act of the postwar period. When Tai'f and then Mecca and Medina fell into the hands of the *Ikhwan* in 1924–25, the Hashemites—beneficiaries of British largesse while Ibn Sa'ud survived on a fraction of the sum—were ejected once and for all from the peninsula. For the British there seemed to be no imperial interests at stake. So, when Hussein refused to recognize the "arrangements" in Palestine and Iraq, he was abandoned to his fate. Indian Islam was aghast at the thought of the Holy Places falling into the hands of these wild men. But the die was cast. First Hussein and then 'Ali hired mercenaries, including Russian pilots, for defense against the *Ikhwan*. But they were no match for Najdi levies, with their hennaed beards, primitive tribal dances, and latter-day zealotry. These men were Arab in a way that the relatively urbane Hashemites were not.

Riyadh was, somehow, more Arab in that sense. It was in the highlands, at nearly 2,000 feet, and that made it seem even more remote. Where the coasts were low lying and feverish, unpleasantly humid ten months out of the year, Riyadh was hot and dry, or cold and dry. In the summer, the heat could be overwhelming. After a flight between air-conditioned airports and a drive to the Riyadh Refinery in an air-conditioned car, the 125 degrees Fahrenheit in the south of the city always came as a shock. The sun literally beat down and it was almost painful to look up. In the winter, the temperature could reach freezing, and there was sometimes snow on the ground. Then, Sa'udis would exchange their summer *thobes* for winter garments made of pinstriped wool. If Jidda and Dhahran were white cities, Riyadh was red or ocher and that seemed to speak of age and the desert and blood.

Teak Dhow, Qatif

From Riyadh, it was 250 miles to Dhahran and the Arabian Gulf. The Iranians called it the Persian Gulf. It was a straight shot, four hours on a good highway, parallel to the railroad that Ibn Sa'ud persuaded the British to build in the 1930s. The eastern province, or al-Ahsa, for some reason pronounced Hasa, had been another bone of contention between the Al-Sa'uds and the Turks, and Ibn Sa'ud descended undetected on the capital, Hofuf, at dusk one day in April of 1913. By the next morning Hofuf was his. The Turkish garrison, with its train of civilian officials and their families, surrendered and were given free passage to the coast. The garrisons of Qatif and Uqair followed shortly afterwards and Turkish Hasa was once more in the hands of the Wahhabis. It is interesting that this act of defiance of the Sultan-Caliph in Istanbul produced none of the hand-wringing and recriminations that accompanied the revolt of the Sharif in the west three years later. But then the Sharif, guardian of the holy cities of Mecca and Medina, would ally himself with a Christian power in a world war that had included a call for *jihad* from the Sultan. Then, the religious factor was more important, although the principle of defiance of legally constituted authority was no less at play.

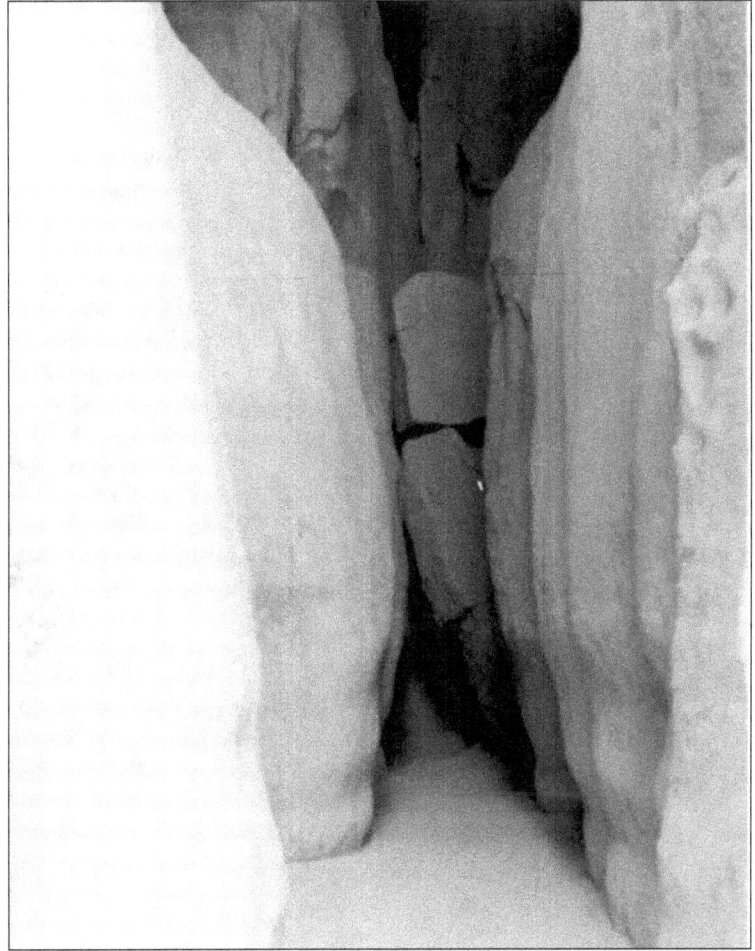

Caves, Hofuf

Dhahran was prettier than Jidda, and there were interesting things to see on the coast, in places like Qatif where old teak dhows still lay. Here, on the east coast, they still manufactured—if that was the word—teak dhows without the blueprints and tools of modern shipbuilding. In the shipyards—if that was the word—it was all tree branches, naturally shaped for the ribs, worked by adzes, hand drills, and the occasional mechanized band saw for the planks. The teak came, as it traditionally had, from India. The boats in the yards in Jidda were also handmade, painted in garish colors, but they were relics, no longer in use. Here, the unpainted teak made them look craftsmanlike and substantial, and they weren't relics. The old journey from Kuwait to Zanzibar and the mangrove swamps of East Africa, where a cargo of wool or dates might be exchanged for lumber, had gone out of fashion. So, had the pearling industry that occupied the sailors for the rest of the year. But these ships still plied the waters of the Gulf, literally coasting from Kuwait or Qatif or Dubai to their destinations along the southern coast of the peninsula, to Salalah, al-Mukalla or Aden. Now, they carried cargos of tires, refrigerators, and air-conditioners.

In Dhahran, there were several Petromin projects, including a marine construction outfit and a drilling firm, but we dealt mainly with Petmark, the marketing arm of the organization. Most of the Sa'udi staff were probably Shia, it being the Eastern Province. We always stayed in nearby Dammam, at another Oberoi that served the best Indian food this side of Bombay. This time, the hotel was not a disappointment. The huge Indian carpets and model of the dhow in the lobby said something about how cosmopolitan the east coast was, how it had always looked outward to Iran, Africa, and India. Then, after Dhahran, there was a detour to the south and inland to the chalky plains and hillocks of Hofuf. Even in early May it was hot, and the labyrinthine limestone caves in the hills among the palm groves were a welcome respite from the sun. From Hofuf, it was a couple of hundred miles back to Riyadh, and I was back in the city early the next afternoon.

Friday would be a travel day. Where the entry to Riyadh had been via a long loop to the north and Qasim, departure would be down the escarpment of *Jebel Tuwaiq*, the range that served as kind of spine in the center of the peninsula. After the escarpment, the 500 miles to Jidda was a straight shot, relatively featureless and boring, before reaching the northern extension of the 'Asir at Ta'if. In *The Heart of Arabia*, Philby had described the same journey in December of 1917 on an earlier mission to coordinate the activities of the Sharif and Ibn Sa'ud against the Turks.

It was part of the same effort that would result in the campaign against Ha'il in the autumn of 1918. And it held even less prospect of success. If anything, Ibn Sa'ud was less amenable to cooperation in 1917 than later. According to Philby his attitude was "one of consuming jealousy, rapidly developing into thinly disguised hatred" of the Sharif. But he reluctantly consented to have his case put before the British in Jidda by one of their own.

As for the Sharif, so hostile was he to any overture from Ibn Sa'ud that he forbade the British to approach Najd from his dominions. From the British side the solution to the problem was comical, if not pathetic. If the western approach was out, why not send Ronald Storrs, the Oriental Secretary in Cairo, to Baghdad, from which place he could travel to Riyadh and put the case directly to Ibn Sa'ud. Storrs may have been many things, a near-eastern scholar, an aesthete, a polymath, "the most brilliant Englishman in the Near East" according to Lawrence. But if there was one thing he was *not*, it was an Arabian traveler. The little caravan set out from Kuwait in early June 1917 when the temperature at nine o'clock in the morning was 123 degrees in the shade, and there was almost no shade. Storrs collapsed after two days, complaining of the heat, poor water, galling by the saddle, and having to "tear flesh with his fingers." The mission was aborted. It seems extraordinary that Gertrude Bell and Philby, both in Iraq at the time—Bell in Baghdad and Philby in Amara—and both experienced desert travelers, would have vetted so quixotic a journey.

Philby needed no encouragement to take matters into his own hands. The Sharif may have forbidden travel to Najd from the west, but he had no control over the east, and the approach from that direction would allow Philby to be the first Englishman since Sadlier to cross the Peninsula from east to west. The trip produced the usual dense Philby account, full of geographical and geological detail including descriptions of fossils he later sent for analysis to the British Museum. Philby was an explorer at heart and this early period was full of firsts, including a later journey south to the Wadi Dawasir and Sulayil. The center of Arabia in 1917 was still a virtual *terra incognita* for outsiders. In Ta'if the Sharif, after jocularly referring to Philby as "the Lawrence of Najd," had the last word after all. He rejected all talk of cooperation with Ibn Sa'ud and to underscore the point forbade Philby to return overland. The journey back to Riyadh was by ship and Kuwait.

In 1986 the descent from Riyadh was sharp and over the next several hours al-Ruwaydah, Halaban and Zalim came and went, breaking the monotony of the flat, before the climb to the nearly eight thousand feet of Ta'if. It had been just over eight hours from Riyadh. The green and relative cool of the highlands were a reminder that Ta'if was traditionally a refuge from the heat and humidity of the Tehama, a kind of Simla in the peninsula. The Ta'if Sheraton offered a respite from the heat and bustle of Jidda. In September of 1924 Ta'if had hardly been a respite. After their victory at Turaba, the *Ikhwan* lay just outside the town and they attacked one day, almost by accident, after Ali and his forces unexpectedly withdrew. Confusion reigned and by the time order was restored more than three hundred citizens were dead. The rest of the townspeople left their hiding places and streamed down to Mecca, preceded by rumors of terrible slaughter. It was the beginning of the end for Ali and the Hashemites, although Ibn Sa'ud saw to it that the *Ikhwan* were on their best behavior in Mecca and Medina. He was now on the world stage and knew how to play the part.

If the descent from Riyadh had been sharp the drop down the escarpment from Ta'if was sharper, and I had to stop several times when the odor from overheated brake linings became oppressive. In several places, the road had been washed away, requiring passage over an improvised detour. The detritus, made up of boulders and large trees, showed that the torrents here in the coastal mountains could be destructive. After skirting Mecca, I was back at home in Jidda at seven forty-five that evening. The odometer in the little Honda showed that it had gone 3,761 kilometers, or 2,279 miles, over the nine days. It had been a sprint by comparison with the measured pace of a camel. But at least I had put into context a few parts of the peninsula that had played a prominent role in the recent history of the country.

4

The Farm

Come and visit my farm. Bring your wife and daughter with you.

Jidda Skyline

MOHAMMED WAS A SA'UDI and the head of maintenance at the Jidda oil refinery. That meant that they wouldn't have to "Sa'udiize" the position later. Although he wasn't one of the young, American-educated systems engineers we worked with, he was still open and friendly and would have no problem meeting western women. Life for expatriate women in Sa'udi Arabia could be difficult, their movements limited by what seemed to be petty restrictions. In public, they weren't veiled but had to wear the *abaya*, a loose black gown that covered most of the body. They couldn't drive, or move around Jidda easily, although Jidda was not Riyadh. In three years in the city we never saw any of the *mutowwa'een*, the religious police who enforced, among other things, the dress code for women. The word came from the Arabic trilateral meaning "to obey" and their job was to enforce obedience. They were supposedly everywhere in Riyadh, but in Jidda we regularly saw Filipino girls in tight Levi's in the malls. That was why most expatriates preferred the city, although it didn't have the history—or the look and feel—of Nejd, the highland plateau in the center of the peninsula.

Jidda was on the west coast and, like other coastal cities, it had always been more open to outside influences. For that reason, it was suspect in the eyes of the religious purists, isolated in their highland fastness. Jidda was in the Hejaz and had always been full of Turks, Egyptians, Indians, black Africans, Javanese, Maghribis, and Hadhramis. They were all Muslims, but lacked the purity of faith as articulated in the middle of the eighteenth century by Mohammad bin 'Abd al-Wahhab, one of the zealots that Islam had periodically thrown up throughout its history. It was said that there hadn't been a reformation in Islam, but in fact there had been many reformations and 'Abd al-Wahhab was only the latest in a long line of reformers. He was supported in his spare unitarianism by Mohammed bin Sa'ud, a member of the Wuld Ali of the great 'Unayza tribal confederation in the heart of the peninsula. Their alliance ultimately bore fruit, and resulted in what would become the Kingdom of Sa'udi Arabia. Had it not, we might be dealing today with Rashidi Arabia or some other variant of the tribes and families that tilted for supremacy in Nejd.

When Mohammed first issued the invitation, I couldn't imagine what a farm in this part of the Hejaz would look like. And I was concerned that Martha and Laura might find it a trial. They were both troopers and veterans of the Arab world. Martha spoke Arabic and taught at the Sa'udia school in Jidda. Laura was only eleven, and her reaction to Sa'udi Arabia was that of a child, not a woman. We lived in Arabian Homes, the most upscale of the compounds in the city, and we might just as well have been in Andalusia or Southern California.

Arabian Homes

Laura would later look back on Sa'udi Arabia as a kind of idyllic time in her life. She had the run of the compound with her friends, and did what kids of her age did, making a clubhouse out of the detached utility room in our villa, playing with her friends and doing slightly wicked things like climbing over the compound wall when we weren't looking. The children were perfectly safe in Arabian Homes, probably safer than they would have been in Andalusia or Southern California.

The compound had the look of the Costa del Sol, all detached stucco villas with red tile roofs, swimming pools, and acres of vegetation. There were bamboos, banana trees, bougainvillea, and frangipanis that made the grounds colorful and fragrant in the spring. That was unusual in Jidda, because it had once been a miserable, salt-encrusted little place, built entirely of coral rock and desolate to a degree. In the old days, it was said, people would go down to the governor's house to look at *the tree*, there being only one in town. But in Arabian Homes, there was a riot of trees, and of bikini-clad women lounging by the pools. There was very little else for most women to do, unless it was taking exercise classes in the weight room, or practicing water aerobics, or bowling, or shopping at the little Safeway in the compound. There was a larger Safeway in the city, the biggest in terms of floor space I ever saw, and it sold everything from Australian beef and Indonesian fruit to oil portraits done to order by Korean artists.

It also sold five-kilo bags of sugar and cases of grape juice, the two combined together for convenience near the checkout stands. Most expatriates made their own wine, bringing the yeast back from visits to the United States or Europe, and most expat villas were also breweries, oenology centers, and stills. They weren't like the Aramco villas in Dhahran where, reportedly, the still was laid out in the blueprints. But the Sa'udis took a relaxed view of what expatriates did on their own turf. Television programs were taped abroad and brought back to be shown on the in-house station, much of the material originally appearing on channels in New York or Los Angeles. So, we occasionally saw things like the movie *1984*, featuring full frontal female nudity, in Sa'udi Arabia of all places. But there were other examples of the inconsistent Sa'udi approach to censorship. On arrival in the spring of 1986 my first media exposure was to an *International Herald Tribune* in the little Safeway with the photograph on the front page blacked out. It was the picture of a pilgrim carrying a cross on the Via Dolorosa during Easter celebrations. The same thing was said to happen, for different reasons, to *Vogue, Marie Claire, Cosmopolitan,* and *Seventeen.*

The most interesting event in three years in Jidda was the locust infestation. Locusts bred across Africa, from Mauritania in the west to Eritrea on the Red Sea, and the Horn of Africa, across the straits from the Arabian Peninsula, was often the epicenter of the outbreaks. If the summer rains were plentiful, the locusts would reproduce and hatch in the fall. After a short infancy and adolescence, the adults would begin their gregarious behavior, and they descended on Jidda one September afternoon in 1987. Some of the largest swarms ever reported had been seen in the vicinity of the Red Sea. This wasn't one of them, and they didn't block out the sun, but still they made for a rare sight. Seen on the ground they were about three inches long and sand-colored, their diaphanous wings covered with small brown dots. But airborne, the wings took on a silvery hue, and millions of them flashed brilliantly in the sun. I collected a few specimens and later cast them in plastic as paperweights. The Bedouins ate the locusts as they had traditionally constituted a protein supplement to their usual diet of dates and dried milk.

Mashrabiyya, Jidda

Actually, Jidda wasn't without interest. The city fathers were making an attempt to preserve the old parts, and the restoration was typically Sa'udi and lavish, with red granite pavements in some parts of the old *suq*. Even so it looked authentic, with the whitewashed coral rock setting off the weathered *mashrabiyya* woodwork. The streets were still narrow, and the enclosed balconies on opposite sides seemed to touch overhead. Signs identified the oldest buildings, including the *Beit abu Hama'il*, or the Abu Hama'il House, one of whose family worked with us in Petroserve. And then there was Eve's tomb, and the physiognomy of our common female ancestor was the same as when Richard Burton visited it in 1853. The tomb was maybe sixty feet long—people were bigger in those days, one of the young engineers in Petroserve soberly informed me. But the odd part was that it seemed to be forty feet from the head to the navel, and only twenty from the navel to the feet. It should have been the other way around.

I thought of these things as Mohammed and I made our way south from Jidda to his farm. I was driving. Martha and Laura had not come with us. The coastal area, or Tehama, was featureless, although the offshore coral reefs made diving a favorite pastime among expatriates. But there wasn't the wealth of fish found farther north in the reefs off Sinai. People said the Filipinos had eaten them all. After about ten miles we passed a junkyard, to which it seemed every derelict car in Jidda had been consigned. Highways in Sa'udi Arabia were lined with broken-down cars, or cars reduced to scrap by accidents, or cars that had been abandoned. Old timers said that in the early, flush days Sa'udis simply left cars by the side of the road rather than repair them. It sounded far-fetched, but this was a country where the far-fetched was often true. Even today after accidents the wreckage was left, supposedly as a cautionary tale to motorists, but it never seemed to have much of an effect. I remembered being passed on the shoulder of the Mecca road by a car that had approached so fast that I didn't see it in my rearview mirror. And I was already going about 150 kph, or 90 mph. The Mecca road was infamous, and a friend reported that he had become a little uneasy when the Sa'udi he was riding with reached 300 kph in his new Ferrari.

One of the engineers we worked with announced that he was interested in the business of recycling steel. It sounded like a good idea, and I imagined trucks like tank transporters collecting these scrap cars from the roads all across the kingdom. The landscape would be more scenic, the environment improved, and the country less dependent on the imported product. But he was a bit of a dreamer, and I doubted that anything would come of the idea. He was the one to whom I had turned over the preparation of the Petroserve Payroll Newsletter. It was supposed to be a guide to implementation of an Arabized version of American software, with tips, for example, on how to turn off the state income tax feature, or how to deal with overtime. But for him Petromin was either a tree with many branches or a trunk with many roots, and he spent most of his time working out the graphics of one or the other for the cover of the newsletter. The content went rapidly downhill.

We left the junkyard behind, but the impression of desolation remained. Everything was colorless, gray, or off-white. It was hard to imagine anyone actually farming this area. The plain was dotted with tufts of a blue-green bottlebrush and scruffy groundcover. But these were apparently enough nourishment for the camels, goats, and sheep that Mohammed raised on his farm. Because, as I would soon learn, it was a dairy farm and milk was the primary product. Twenty minutes after the junkyard we came around a low hill and approached an area with a large, fenced enclosure and a white fiberglass dome. We had arrived.

The dome was for 'Abdu, the Sudanese herdsman. He greeted us and began preparing the coffee and tea that were the staples of hospitality in the Arab world. Next to the dome was a rude lean-to, several poles supporting a piece of cloth to shade us from the sun. Under the lean-to was a machine-made carpet. It would be our home for the next several hours. The little scene had the look and smell of the desert, from the desolation around us to the fragrant bushes that fed the fire under the coffee pot. The first thimbleful of Bedouin coffee was refreshing after the drive, and it was followed soon after by thick, sweet tea. And so it went for the next several hours, coffee followed by tea, followed by coffee and more tea. 'Abdu was a perpetual motion machine, keeping the fire stoked and the hot beverages coming.

Occasionally he walked to the enclosure that contained maybe thirty goats and sheep, and the routine would be varied. The goats' baglike mammaries were full and the animals were uncomfortable. So 'Abdu relieved them and brought back cups of goats' milk. It was a welcome change from the coffee and tea, and the routine now became coffee, tea and goats' milk, before more tea and coffee. A gray Saluki, one of the whippet-like hounds the Arabs had used for generations to watch over their herds, lay near the enclosure. He was alternately bored and then alert, especially when 'Abdu approached his charges inside the enclosure. The sun reached its zenith, and then began its descent as the afternoon lengthened. It was early spring and the weather was pleasant, not the insufferable heat and humidity that characterized the Tehama most of the year.

Mohammed and I occasionally discussed news from the refinery, or a political issue, or maybe something about life in Jidda. But, for the most part, we just sat. It was enough to be taking our *kaif,* relaxing and enjoying our contemplative state, according to Hans Wehr's *A Dictionary of Modern Written Arabic,* our "pleasure, delight, well-being, good humor." It didn't get any better than this. It was just us and the elements, the fiberglass dome, the animals, the beverages, and the lean-to. There was a carpet under our haunches, God was in His heaven, and all was well with the world.

Then, the camels began to come in. They came singly or in groups of two or three, and introduced a new ingredient to our diet. We saw them approaching head-on, four slender legs and the great bulk of their bodies extending on either side. But the females were not pregnant, having already given birth that year. In fact, one female was wearing a large canvas diaper. 'Abdu was weaning her foal, and the diaper kept the foal from drinking whenever the mood struck him.

So, we took a shallow metal bowl, two feet in diameter, and approached the female. 'Abdu unpinned the diaper and began to milk, the liquid coming in a great foamy stream and quickly filling the bowl. Then he poured some of the milk into a liter container with a cloth filter on top. This removed any gross impurities. It was the climax of the visit, and I gradually finished the liter, and then another. The homogenized and pasteurized product was sold in the local supermarkets, and was supposedly healthier than cows' milk, having more calcium and less butterfat. But this was the unadulterated product. Afterwards, it was more coffee and tea, followed by milk, tea, and coffee.

At about 3 o'clock, by mutual consent, our *kaif* ended. We said goodbye to 'Abdu and left the farm behind. The drive to Jidda was brisk and I left Mohammed near the gate to the refinery where I had picked him up that morning.

Next time," he said, "you'll have to bring your wife and daughter."

But the plumbing at the farm would have to improve before they paid a visit.

5

The Yemen

WE HAD JUST LEFT San'a on the road to Ta'izz and I asked the driver the name of the first village we passed through. The difference between the leisured pace of a donkey or camel and hurtling down the escarpment by Toyota made it impossible to follow Carsten Niebuhr's itinerary very carefully. But at least I could ask Mohammed to identify the major geographical features along way. He did so unfailingly, long after I realized it was useless to try to write them all down. In the first place, his accent was unfamiliar and even the three Kuwaitis in the group had difficulty understanding him. Also he was chewing *qat*, the mild narcotic widely used in the Yemen, as he would over the next three days. It was like having a mouthful of cud. So it was almost impossible to distinguish the difference between close Arabic sounds. I would ask him to repeat a name several times before I thought I heard it right. Then I showed him the Arabic I had written to confirm what I thought I heard. That assumed he knew the correct spelling or that there *was* a correct spelling.

Niebuhr had made the same journey in 1763 that we were making in 1988. He had filled the text of his *Travels in Arabia* with details that appeared in the finished map. They were the reason for much of the tedium in the book. But he was responsible for maps, and you couldn't make a map without careful observations of distance and direction. He dealt in points of the compass and odd fractions of German miles, Danish miles, and various European leagues, along with latitudes and occasional longitudes. To be seen taking notes would have aroused suspicion among the guides, so he relied on his memory at night to write up what he had seen during the day. In spite of these shortcomings, his map of the Yemen would be unmatched in detail and accuracy for the next 150 years.

I knew the approximate equivalents of a Danish mile and a French league in English miles, but the odometer in the Land Cruiser was calibrated in kilometers. That added another bit of complexity to the calculations. In addition, Niebuhr's Arabic has come down to us through the filter of German orthography, and the German equivalents of Arabic sounds were different from those in English. So I was trying to do the same thing in the late twentieth century that Niebuhr had done in the middle of the eighteenth. His only tools were his ear, his pen, and his system of transliteration where Arabic names would be put into German equivalents for the book. It was theoretically possible to compare what he wrote with what was written today on a map. But, even here, there were problems. A few of the names were the same, but many had changed and many more had probably disappeared altogether.

In San'a I had seen a good topographical map of the country, with the text in Arabic, on the wall in the Tourism Authority where visas for travel inside the country were issued. It had been prepared by the Survey Authority of San'a under the direction of the Military Survey of the United Kingdom, and printed by a graphic arts firm in Zurich. It was beautiful, exactly what I wanted and I asked if I could buy a copy. For once, the answer seemed to be yes, followed by directions to the Survey Authority itself, near the Kuwaiti Hospital on al-Zubeiri Road. I found the building it shared with a group of banks and was directed to the office of the deputy director.

He listened politely but I could see that he was not sympathetic. Here was a request out of the ordinary and an opportunity to say no. And that was what he said, rather triumphantly, when I asked if a copy of the map was for sale. So, now in Arabic, I became more animated on the subject of my interest in the Danish expedition, why I had come all the way to the Yemen, and how the Yemenis had always been receptive to visitors with scientific interests. Some of it was true, and in the end, he agreed to let me have the map for 100 Yemeni Riyals, or about $8.50. But to show that he still held the upper hand, he said I could only have one of the 1:1,000,000 series, not the 1:1,500,000 series I wanted.

So I thought I had done a good bit of work that day, it then being just before the three p.m. closing time of the office on the eve of the holiday, the *Eid al-Fitr*. It wouldn't open again before I left San'a. I later saw a coffee-table book entitled *Yemen Rediscovered* in the hotel bookshop with maps of the Arabian peninsula and the Yemen, on facing pages. But they had been effectively censored in the English edition by gluing them together, although the French and German editions were intact. It was silly. The detail in the maps was of no use to anyone but readers of a coffee-table book and, anyway, I had just bought the the 1:1,000,000 topographical map at the Survey Authority. Or, so I thought. But since they didn't have a copy in stock, they would have to send it to me in Jidda. It never arrived. The deputy director had the last laugh after all.

SAN'A

My visit to the Yemen began in San'a. *Yemen Airways* had regular flights between Jidda and San'a. Sa'udi Arabia was full of Yemenis, particularly in the western provinces. Filipinos may have been the computer programmers, electricians, and other skilled workers and Pakistanis the accountants and financial managers, but Yemenis operated the gas stations and much else besides. It was almost impossible to buy a tank of gas, a battery, or a tire in Jidda, Rabigh, or Yanbu' unless it was from a Yemeni. Also, the countries shared a common, although partly undemarcated, border and there were several million Yemenis in the kingdom, many of them undocumented. All this would change two years later with the Gulf War. When Saddam Hussein invaded Kuwait in August of 1990 the Yemeni government publicly sided with the Iraqis and a mass forced exodus was the result. It would be the end of the Yemenis and their gas stations in Sa'udi Arabia.

On arrival in San'a I checked into the Taj Sheba hotel, part of an Indian chain that included the Taj Mahal in New Delhi, the Lake Palace in Udaipur, and the Lexington in New York city. "Taj" meant "crown" in Arabic and "Sheba" was the name of the famous queen. Of her, more below. I spent the next day looking around the old city. San'a lay in a dusty plateau at an elevation of about 7,000 feet. There was an historic section in the center of the city, whose peculiar highrise architecture had led UNESCO to declare old San'a a world heritage site. But although interesting in a gimcrack sort of way there was nothing in the city comparable to the monuments of Mamluk architecture that made Cairo the Arab metropolis *par excellence*. Outside the historic center San'a was nondescript, looking more like Tanta or Mansura.

Gingerbread House, San'a

Here, the walls were still standing on most sides of the old city. But they were of mud-brick and erosion had left gaping holes everywhere. Through the gaps these characteristic buildings appeared in sometimes startling contrast, looking like gingerbread houses with sugar trim. A *sayl*, or wadi, ran through the center of the city, and it clearly ran in spate during the rainy season. The bed was strewn with odd bits of debris, including the rusting hulks of several cars, the carcass of a large animal, ripe when the wind was right, as well as bones, paper, and plastic trash. In fact, plastic was the bane of the Yemen.

Bab Yemen, San'a

In some parts of the developing world the printing press was the greatest enemy of the environment. In Cairo paper debris was everywhere and mingled with chicken feathers and open sewers it made for a particularly offensive soup. But here, and everywhere else in the Yemen, plastic bags were the greatest offenders. An attempt was made to collect garbage, and there were actually dumpsters placed around the city walls. But they were full to overflowing and scrawny cats picked through the refuse. The people, too, looked scrawny. I don't think I saw a fat Yemeni in a week in the country. And everywhere, gazing benignly over the squalor, were posters of the president, Ali Abdullah al-Saleh. He was a military man, but even in uniform with the epaulets his head looked too big for his shoulders or maybe his body was too small for his head. If plastic was the bane of the Yemen, these military men were the bane of the Arab World. Here, the army had seized power in 1974, consigning the old Imam to the history books and bringing their own version of unbridled autocracy to the country.

The entrance to the *suq* was through the *Bab Yemen,* or Yemen Gate. It was a typical Middle-Eastern market and, unlike those in Cairo, Damascus, or Istanbul, it seemed to serve the everyday needs of the city. But it was just as colorful, largely because of the people. Most appeared to be slight and small-boned. Ears were especially prominent, the lobes often attached, but the points standing an inch-and-a-half away from the head. About half the women were veiled. There were also great white turbans, brightly colored skirts and shawls, and sashes with *jambeas.* The last were the curved dagger of the Yemen, still carried by every man in the country. But the steel was not particularly fine and they appeared to be mainly decorative.

The most prevalent commodity in the market seemed to be raisins. There were mounds of these little adjuncts to the grape industry, big and small, black, brown, red and yellow in color. It was said that a Yemeni could distinguish between forty different kinds of grapes and that they were available year-round. Most appeared to be grown to the east of the city on the Ma'rib road. There were also papayas, strawberries, blackberries, bananas, potatoes, green onions, tomatoes, squash, tobacco leaf, and coffee husks. I didn't see any coffee beans. Niebuhr reported that the Yemenis drank only *qisher*, a drink made from the husks, the beans traditionally being exported. The *suq* here was also full of beggars, many black and a few disfigured by what must have been smallpox. The disease was now eradicated worldwide, the last-known case having been isolated somewhere in the Horn of Africa in 1977. But it appeared to have been prevalent in the Yemen not many years before.

TO MA'RIB

The next day I made arrangements to go to Ma'rib. It was the site of the famous dam and the capital of the Sabaeans and lay about eighty miles northeast of San'a. The dam had been one of the wonders of the ancient world. We left in mid-morning and passed mile after mile of vineyards on both sides of the road. Then, fields covered with low scrub and grass appeared, with date palms in the distance. After a gradual ascent, we dropped steeply through two *'aqabat,* or passes, with weathered sandstone cliffs, into the plain where the dam and remains of the old city lay. Here, the grass gave way to a sea of golden dunes, finely rippled and sitting very stark against the black outline of the mountains to the north. They were a part of the *Ramlet Sabatain*, a southern extension of the Empty Quarter.

Ramlet Sabatain

After the coastal mountains this was a return to the high desert of Arabia. The sand gradually gave way to black volcanic debris, like the *harras* between Mecca and Medina. The remains of the city and dam appeared ahead in the dusty plain.

The dam, about 800 paces wide, had been built by the Sabaeans on a rocky foundation where the Wadi Dhenne cut through the hills. It was still recognizable by the sluice gates standing very prominently on opposite sides of the wadi. The gates with their attached walls remained but the body of the dam itself was long gone.

Sluice Gate, Ma'rib

Niebuhr and his party had not seen it in 1763, being in some haste to return to Mocha before the last English ship that year left for Bombay. Others would visit the site and leave careful descriptions, seeing evidence of related works and suggesting that the dam was part of a highly-developed system of irrigation of the surrounding plains. Its importance was attested by the reports of later historians and geographers, one of them maintaining that it would take a man on horseback over a month to cross the area of gardens watered by the dam.

The Sabaeans are mentioned in both the Old Tstament and the Qur'an and the region was once proverbial for its fertility.

Guard Ma'rib

There was some uncertainty as to the earliest date of the dam, with speculation ranging as far back as 1000 BC. It is known that the system was built piecemeal and underwent periodic renovation. The action of the wind, water, and accumulated silt periodically weakened the structure and there were occasional breaches, requiring extensive repairs. A break in 449 AD was recorded in an inscription near the northern sluice gate. It later failed catastrophically, sometime in the latter part of the sixth century, the event turning the fertile plain of Saba' back into the desert it had once been and has since remained. The failure was significant enough to merit mention in the Qur'an (34: 15–17). Afterward the inhabitants of Mar'ib migrated en masse to the Hejaz.

A wall running perpendicular to the barrage at the southern sluice gate was intact and contained stones bearing Himyaritic inscriptions. It appeared to have been built with material from a previous structure. There were other inscriptions as well, still very sharp, in the stones near the northern sluice gate. Oddly, the inscriptions, in the Sabaean-Himyar language, were known as Himyaritic although the people were generally known as Sabaeans. In fact, there had been both Sabaeans and Himyarites, but the terms "land of the Sabaeans" or "Saba'" had survived long after the Sabaeans themselves had been replaced by the Himyarites as the dominant people in South Arabia.

However the people were called, they had controlled an area that stretched inland from the Gulf of Aden to Ma'rib and south to the Hadramaut, as well as part of the Red Sea coast of Africa. The earliest references to Saba' occur in Mesopotamian historical documents dating from the second millennium BC. It is certain that there was a trading community in South Arabia from remote antiquity, supplying Egypt and Syria with gold, jewels, and spices. But the wealth of the country was based primarily on frankincense, an aromatic resin. There are references to Saba' in the Old Testament, in Genesis, Psalms, Ezekiel, Isaiah and Jeremiah. But the authenticity of the most famous of the Biblical accounts, that of the "Queen of Sheba," in I Kings 10, appears to be doubtful.

The earliest accurate description of South Arabia is probably that of Theophrastus, a Greek philosopher of the fourth-third centuries BC. Four South Arabian kingdoms—Saba, Kataban, Hadramaut, and Main—are listed as the sources of frankincense and myrrh. Theophrastus also mentions the mountainous nature of the country, the honesty of the "Sabaeans" in their commercial dealings, and the prevalence of sun worship among the people. Strabo, writing in the first century AD, described the first direct Western contact with the region, the military campaign of the Roman Aelius Gallus in 24 BC who was searching for the fabled spice lands. But plagued by a lack of preparation, ignorance of the country, and treachery of the guides, the campaign ended in disaster, although, it brought to the Roman world a better knowledge of South

Arabia and corrected errors in the earlier Greek accounts. Not much had been learned by 1763 when the Danish expedition, equally unprepared, also succumbed to disease and bad counsel in the Yemen.

An understanding of the script was eventually the key to untangling fact from fiction in the history of the area. Prior to decipherment notions of the fabulously wealthy Sabaeans in their remote Eldorado had constituted the stuff of legends in early works, including the Bible and the Qur'an. Niebuhr would make a modest contribution to the process. In his *Travels in Arabia,* published in 1778, he reported the existence of unknown inscriptions in the ruins of Zafar and this led to subsequent exploration. Copies were brought to Europe by Seetzen in 1810. Still later, the work of Halevy in 1869 and Glaser in 1882–84, 1885–86 and 1887–88 opened new chapters in an understanding of the area.

After the Muslim conquest the fortunes of Yemen had paralleled that of the larger Arab world. There had been first Omayyids, then Abbassids, and Fatimids, but the rule always tempered by Yemen's remoteness and the presence of local dynasties. The region's importance in trade, having declined with the advent of Christianity and the end of the Mediterranean's need for frankincense, saw a resurgence in the sixteenth century. The rise of the Ottoman Empire now barred the overland trade routes to the east and Europeans had discovered the direct route to India via the Cape of Good Hope. But Europe was still held hostage to middlemen on the route through the Red Sea and Egypt. The Portuguese set out to change that in 1507 by occupying the island of Socotra at the mouth of the Gulf of Aden. The effort was ultimately unsuccessful, but the major players were now engaged. The Egyptian Mamluks responded to the Portuguese threat with an invasion of the Tehama in 1516. But they were overthrown in the next year by the Ottomans, just as they were in Egypt. Turkish domination of Yemen lasted for a century, after which the first Imam was proclaimed and relative independence returned.

The history of Yemen since that time was a repeat of independence and isolation alternating with periods of foreign domination. The eighteenth century saw a resurgence of European interest in the country as a result of a new luxury commodity, coffee. Proceeds from the coffee trade financed a building spree in the country. The British occupied Aden in 1839, leading to the effective division of the north and south of the country. The nineteenth century also saw the opening of the Suez Canal and the return of the Turks, against whom sporadic risings took place in 1891, 1904 and 1911. But the country was unaffected by the revolt in the Hejaz during the First World War and Yemen remained loyal to the Turks. With the Turkish withdrawal in 1919 the Yemen lapsed into another one of its periodic periods of enforced isolation, the Imams attempting to insulate the country against corrupting foreign influences, especially after the revolutions in Egypt in 1952 and Iraq in 1958. The attempt was unsuccessful and revolution in the Yemen followed in 1962.

Earthfill Dam, Ma'rib

A new earth-fill dam, financed by the United Arab Emirates, lay about ten kilometers to the east and we drove to the top. The water was jade-green, almost a celadon color. But it was the only green we saw. Much of the terrain was mountainous, and even on the flat there were drifts of sand and areas of hard plutonic rock. The silt in the flat below the dam had once been cultivated. But we had just come eighty miles from San'a, two days ride on a horse and more on a camel, and had seen only a few areas that were sown. Al-Mas'udi's month of green by horseback looked like another part of the fable that surrounded much of South Arabia.

The old city of Ma'rib was a ruin, a dirt mound in the waste on which the new town had been built. A little boy showed me around and we wandered through empty shells in the dusty labyrinth.

Old City, Ma'rib

It didn't seem to be of remote antiquity, although there were stones with Himyaritic inscriptions in some of the walls. The construction was the typical mud-brick, covered with plaster. Beams in the ceilings were the tamarisk of wood-poor countries, irregularly shaped and covered with thinner sticks under a final covering of mud. Ma'rib was about equidistant from from the Gulf of Aden and the Red Sea, and that made it a likely place as the seat of the Sabaean kingdom. It was also on the imperial spice route that connected the incense lands of the south with Najran, Meda'in Saleh, Petra, and eventually Gaza on the Mediterranean.

Awwam Temple

On the way back to San'a we stopped at the Awwam Temple and the Temple of Bilqis, the Muslim name of the Queen of Sheba. It was another tale from an eclectic past, drawn out of the hoary mists of time and embellished according to the taste of the teller. The story was told in the

Bible, in I Kings, 10 and lists the gifts the Queen gave to Solomon and he to her: "And so she went to her own country, she and her servants." As told in the Qur'an (27: 20–40), the story reached Mohammed through Jewish sources, but appears to have Iranian influences as well with its anthropomorphism and talking birds. The difference in the two accounts is interesting. Kings I is primarily a glorification of the wisdom and prosperity of Solomon. The Queen returned a believer in these, and in the love of the Lord for Israel, but not a convert to Judaism. The Qur'an, for all of its supernatiural machinery, nonetheless has a clear moral message: the conversion of the Queen of Sheba to the worship of the one God.

The temple, dating from the fifth century BC, was devoted to sun-worship and a series of upright stelae, maybe eight feet high, gave it the look of a mini-Stonehenge. Walls made of the same stone completed the temple proper and the enclosure. Those inside were finely-dressed but the enclosure walls were crude with alternating, roughhewn black and dun-colored stones. The site had apparently been abandoned since the American Wendell Phillips and his Foundation for the Study of Man had been run off by the Imam in 1952 after several months of excavation. Many of the structures were covered, again, in sand and the pillars looked to be half the height shown in Phillips's *Qataban and Sheba*. Phillips and his team undoubtedly did important work, but a blurb on the dust jacket suggested that fantasies about South Arabia were not confined to the Bible and the Qur'an: "Wendell is a combination of Aladdin, Sindbad the sailor, and Ali Baba" gushed Lowell Thomas. It would hard to imagine a better listing of the ingredients of an "Orientalism" of the most superficial kind.

TO TA'IZZ

The next day was the beginning of the *Eid al-Fitr*. I met three Kuwaitis at the travel agency and we agreed to rent a car together. We would drive almost due south to Ta'izz, through Dhamar and Jibla, then northwest to Beit al-Fakih. From Beit al-Fakih we would go west to the coast at Hodeida, before returning up the escarpment to San'a. It would be a great loop and we would see the mountains, the sea, and the Tehama. We had only two days and the trip would be rushed. But it was the best we could manage under the circumstances.

The Kuwaitis were originally from the Yemen and they had come back to see their ancestral home. They looked more like Gulf Arabs than Yemenis, being relatively tall and sharply-featured, with none of the stunted look of the locals. They were also very westernized and we were soon purring over the plain west of San'a to the sound of Keith Jarrett and his jazz piano. The music was the final straw for my questions. That was just as well because Mohammed's answers were becoming increasingly perfunctory.

Mohammed

Over the next two days we would come to appreciate him as the most practical of men. Whether answering our questions, finding gas, locating a little roadside restaurant, or making copies of our visas he was a machine to answer our every need. The visas were a constant problem. They were on an 11"x14" form of the Tourism Authority, made out by hand in an original and carbon copies, listing our detailed itinerary. We had to surrender a copy at each police checkpoint. I left San'a with fifteen copies but soon ran out. Disgusted, Mohammed took the remaining one and made enough copies to last a week.

He never stood on ceremony, but would walk into a shop or to the head of a line and, after a booming *al-salaam aleykum*, would be instantly served. He kept a loaded .45 under the seat of the car and probably would not have hesitated to use it. He was dark and wiry, with the three requisites of every man in the Arab world: a wife, a mustache, and a cigarette habit. And like every Yemeni male who had reached puberty, he wore a *jambea* in his belt. I don't think he slept much during the trip, but that was all right as long as the *qat* lasted. We replenished it on the second day.

Escarpment

At the edge of the escarpment he made a concession to our astonishment by stopping so that we could have a look. A thousand feet below a stream meandered muddily through the fields and villages stood on little promontories, like old Mar'ib. The escarpment was terraced but was not green. It looked like the ground had been recently turned over in preparation for the seed. But if it was not green it still gave the impression of careful husbandry. Niebuhr had come this way in July of 1763, but in the opposite direction, laboring up the escarpment by camel.

It was about 160 miles from San'a to Ta'izz. We passed through the plain and Damar, and then Ibb, where we stopped for coffee. This time it was the real thing. The buildings were all of stone, with ragged awnings sheltering the little shops. As in San'a, the people were small and looked undernourished. In the little town of Jibla we stopped at a mosque outside of which a man was performing his ablutions at a green pool.

Ablution, Jibla

Inside, all was whitewashed and clean with Persian carpets covering the floor. A Sudanese *faqih*—or teacher and reciter of the Qur'an—presided and a combination of the quiet, the whitewash, the spotless white of the man's *gallabiya* and turban, and the chocolate-brown of his skin seemed to epitomize the serenity of the best traditions of Islam. Outside, horns honked, donkeys brayed, men bellowed, and women shrieked. But inside, all was peaceful and we lingered, not wanting to leave.

We pushed on to Ta'izz, Mohammed, as always, urging haste and insisting that we arrive before dark. On the way, we passed many fields of *qat*, festooned with discarded plastic bags. But even more of a scourge than the plastic was *qat* itself, the cultivation and consumption of which constituted half the energies of the people and, by some accounts, half the GDP of the country. We saw very little coffee, the trees having given way to this new staple. The country that once produced the best coffee in the world had been replaced by Brazil, Colombia, the Ivory Coast, Mexico, and Indonesia, to name only the largest producers. Yemen, where it all began, no longer even made the list.

In Ta'izz, the Mareb Hotel overlooked the city and *al-Qahira*, or Cairo, the hill that dominated it. After dinner I walked down the hill to buy film and in the store was asked if I was Russian. There appeared to be a clear division of labor in the country: the Russians were the military advisors, the Egyptians were the teachers and doctors, and the Sudanese staffed the mosques. The Yemenis themselves chewed *qat*. The Egyptians had been here since the civil war in the 1960's. It had been a time of rampant Nasserism in the Arab World and the Voice of Cairo fomented revolution against reactionary regimes. Revolt came to the Yemen in 1962 and the Egyptians had moved in quickly to support the rebels, reportedly using poison gas against the Sa'udi-backed royalists. The Egyptian military presence in Yemen—at one point there were tens of thousands of soldiers in the country—probably contributed to the disaster of the June War with Israel in 1967. The defeat by the Israelis had, among other things, put an end to large–scale military operations in Yemen. But Egyptian civilians remained in large numbers, mainly as teachers.

The next morning we wandered through the trim little city. In profile the cityscape was dominated by mosques, declared protected sites by UNESCO. The city sat in a swale, dominated by Mt. Sabir beyond the city walls. Unlike much of the rest of the Tehama there was no malaria in Ta'izz. Mosquitos didn't generally survive at the 4,500-foot elevation of the city, and the Aiyubids had chosen Ta'izz as their capital in the twelfth century, primarily because of its healthy climate.

The walls of Ta'izz were still intact in places and they marched resolutely up the promontory of *al-Qahira* and down the other side. Just as in Egypt, the word meant "the victorious." In the market I bought a *jambea* and ended the day with what I hoped would be a typical Yemeni meal. With his usual directness, Mohammed had pointed me to the nearest hole in the wall. There, the owner, looking slightly puzzled at the request, sent his son to a shop down the street where he bought a can of *ful medammes*, Egyptian broad beans, probably packed in California. I watched as he emptied the contents into a frying pan, added a chopped green pepper and served it piping hot. The beans were accompanied by flat bread and tea.

Mosque, Tehama

The next day would be busy: first Beit al-Fakih, then to the coast at Hodeida, and finally back up the escarpment to San'a. So we left early and that meant a stop for breakfast along the way. At the little roadside restaurant Mohammed was his usual model of efficiency. He elbowed his way to the front of the line, ordered the food with considerable brusqueness and served the tea, eggs, cheese, beans, and bread himself. It cost forty-five Yemeni Riyals, or about four dollars for the five of us. We were back on the road fifteen minutes later. In the eighteenth century Beit al-Fakih had been the emporium of the Yemen, the place where the coffee beans grown in the mountains were brought before being sorted, graded, and shipped to the wider world. Today it was a miserable little place marked only by a few domes, the resting places of local saints. We were now in the Tehama, a picture of desolation after the terraces in the mountains. Some of the structures looked African, round with plastered walls and thatch roofs. In fact, Eritrea was less than 100 miles away across the Bab al-Mandab. The two coasts were retreating from one-another at the rate of a centimeter per year.

The coast near Hodeida was low-lying and covered with beached *dhows* in various states of completion or disrepair. Like those in Jidda they were painted in broad stripes of red, blue and yellow. Lunch was fresh fish, split open and grilled, served with a hot red sauce. We were back on the road in the early afternoon, Mohammed, as always, being in some haste. There seemed to be no reason to stop in Hodeida itself. However, there was one bit of business we had not counted on and it would briefly detain us: we had exhausted our supply of *qat* and would need more for the trip up the escarpment. We stopped in an open-air market where *qat* was the principal commodity. Mohammed went from stall to stall, carefully sampling the tender shoots like some large primate as the banana-leaf wrappings were opened. He settled on a bunch and we took up a collection for the communal supply: it was 450 riyals, ten times the cost of our breakfast. Back on the road, we all chewed and I was reminded, again, of large-primate behavior. We carefully inspected each shoot with its attached leaves before inserting it into the growing wad in our cheeks.

The effect was not immediate, although we drank water which was supposed to accelerate the process of intoxication. The taste was not unpleasant, but the wad became considerable, distending the cheek by an inch or more. As we began the ascent through the foothills to the central highlands and San'a, I began to feel the effects of the *qat*. First, goosebumps appeared on my arms and my elbows began to itch. This was followed by not so much a high as a kind of pleasant euphoria.

Chewing Qat

Now, the hairpin turns and sheer drops seemed less alarming. Over the edge of one precipice we saw a tank, looking like an old Russian T-34. The successive escarpments were terraced and brown, having been recently tilled. In one, a man in a typical conical straw hat worked with a wooden plow and an ox. Political changes may have swirled about the Yemen for centuries but the man in the field represented a continuity that had outlasted them all. The fields were mostly planted in *qat* but we did see one of coffee trees and stopped for a photo. The trees were all leaves, no beans having yet appeared. The road followed the bed of a wadi and at one point the stream was fairly wide, fed by little waterfalls. A question that had occupied geographers for millennia was whether perennial streams existed in the Arabian peninsula. Early reports of these wadis in spate in the Yemen led some to conclude, erroneously, that there were. In fact, there were none.

Plowman

As we moved back up the escarpment, through ranges that would reach nearly 13,000 feet, the Yemeni weather system became clearer. The hot, moist air rose from the Red Sea until it came into contact with this mountain barrier. Unable to move farther, it broke against the mountains and released its burden of moisture. There were two heavy periods of rainfall during the southwest monsoons, in April and August. At these times rain fell in both the Tehama and the high Yemen above. The monsoons released about thirty inches of water a year and the wadis then ran in flood. Catchment systems had been developed to capture and store some of the water, which would otherwise disappear into the thirsty sands of the Tehama.

It was the presence of standing water that made the Tehama and the lower reaches of the mountains ideal breeding places for the mosquitoes that spread malaria. The disease killed five members of the

Danish expedition within ten months of their arrival in the country. Only Niebuhr survived, but he was subject for the remainder of his life to periodic fevers that would send him to his bed. I spent the last twenty-five miles to San'a ruminating on these details, feeling like a large ruminant myself with my load of macerated cud.

In San'a it was the Taj Sheba again. I had a final day before the flight back to Jidda. After the *qat* I was awake for the next several days and this allowed me to see more of the city. The gold in the market was the usual filagreed *baladi*, or "country," pieces that would constitute dowries. The silver was more interesting: fine old *jambeas* or daggers, elaborate necklaces, and pendants made from Maria Theresa dollars, traditionally called "French Riyals" even though they were minted in Vienna. The Arabs had always liked the look and heft of the silver Maria Theresas and the Austrians had continued to mint them into the twentieth century, still bearing the original 1780 date. They were the staples of Bedouin jewelry throughout the peninsula, the old ones worn nearly beyond recognition.

Today Yemenis said that fine workmanship in San'a was a thing of the past, having departed with the Jews who left in 1948. Numbering about 45,000, Yemeni Jews were transferred *en masse* to Israel in Operation Magic Carpet. They brought their skills with them and some sold jewelry in the big hotels in Jerusalem. But others faced the reality that they were unequipped to compete with the Europeans. It was in the early, heady days of the ingathering, before ethnic differences and the prejudices of the Ashkenazim diluted the dream. There were stories of Yemeni Jewish children being taken from their parents on arrival in Israel and placed in foster homes, the parents not judged by the authorities to be fit custodians. Along with the Moroccans and, later, the Falashas the Yemenis had become an underclass of Israel and they responded with their own Black Panther movement.

The presence of Jews in the Yemen was the reason for Niebuhr and the Danish expedition in the first place. It was thought by the most prominent Oriental philologist in Europe, Johann David Michaelis of the University of Göttingen, that a Jewish community still existed in the highlands of the Yemen where, he believed, an "eastern" dialect of Arabic was spoken that closest to Hebrew. What better way to explicate difficult passages of the Hebrew Bible than to ask native speakers of the language what the words meant. That lent the expedition a certain quixotic character. But Michaelis was not entirely mistaken in his notions. There had been Jewish immigration to Yemen from Palestine and Mesopotamia early in the Christian era. The original numbers were small but they made converts among the Bedouins and by the fifth century Judaism was widespread in the southwestern part of the peninsula. A period of Jewish ascendance ensued. However, with the arrival of Islam, conversion to the new creed quickly followed and the remaining Jews were tolerated against payment of the *jizya*, or head tax. Most Yemeni Jews were probably descendants of those early converts.

I bought a necklace stamped with the mark of one of the old Jewish craftsmen. The detailed work made it stand out from the rest of the pieces. There was also a *jambea* with a beautiful, silver filigree holder emblazoned with a Star of David. But at $1,000 it was more than I wanted to pay. I did buy a Spanish piece of eight, severely filed around the edges and now a rough hexagon, but with the cross still visible in the center. It had probably come from Peru in the eighteenth century, part of a payment for a cargo of coffee. It cost three dollars.

The flight to Jidda left the next day.

6

Monte Carlo

IT WAS HARD TO understand why the Finns were interested in Jordan at all. It was a little country with only five million people. Yes, it had recently liberalized the telecommunications sector and sold 40 percent of the state operator to France Telecom. And it had, with Morocco, the only functioning regulator in the Arab World. But the market was small and players like Nokia and Ericsson must have seen it for its symbolic not its real importance. Much of Jordan's attractiveness seemed to lie in the person of King Abdullah, successor to his impulsive, often maddeningly vacuous, occasionally disastrously mistaken, but always gallant father. King Hussein had been a decent man and he had somehow survived in a landscape peopled by dinosaurs: Nasser, Saddam Hussein, Hafez al-Assad, Ariel Sharon.

Abdullah was different, and a child of his time. Everyone who met him—Bill Gates, John Chambers of Cisco, Carly Fiorina of Hewlett Packard—came away impressed with his energy, openness to change, his grasp of technology and of its power to transform a people. They all wanted to do something for him and for his country, probably in that order. So they sent their minions in a steady stream through the Ministry of Post and Communications. We dealt on a daily basis with Microsoft, Sun, IBM, EDS, Cisco, HP, Compaq, Oracle, and countless smaller fry. In fact, they were the greatest drain on the slender resources of the ministry and the effort to manage their contributions was its greatest challenge.

Jordan had always been poor, even from the beginning when the neighboring Palestine mandatory administration had, by postwar standards, lavish budgets. Transjordan got what little was left. In an area awash in oil, Jordan had none and depended instead on a little potash, a little tourism, and a little charity. The lack of resources meant they had to be good at what they did and they were, in spite of a persistent inferiority complex. Jordanians always saw the glass half empty. Oddly, they shared that trait with Israel, their mighty neighbor to the west, although the two countries manifested it in different ways.

The other part of the equation was equally puzzling. DNA wasn't IBM or EDS or Nokia, but a little Finnish startup. Finland was like Jordan, another gallant little nation that had survived among regional behemoths. They held off the Russians in the Russo-Finnish war of 1939–40 until overwhelming numbers eventually wore them down. They were resource-poor except for wood and wood products, mainly paper. Unlike Norway and Russia they had no oil. But they were also good at what they did, which by 2001 had become mobile telephony. DNA wasn't an acronym like IBM or EDS but meant exactly what it said, deoxyribonucleic acid. It seemed an odd name for a telecom company but they weren't really a telecom, although they used mobile telephones to deliver their service. They were the new service provider in Finland, a saturated mobile market and the most competitive in the world. They aimed to differentiate their offerings by going after the power users and *personalizing* them. Hence the name DNA, the most personal thing that any of us possessed.

And then another piece of the puzzle fell into place. We would be joined by a couple of investment bankers from Bahrain, another little resource-poor country in a region of massive oil reserves. Bahrain had no oil, and had chosen financial services as its focus. There were now nearly 200 banks in the country, serving a population of a few hundred thousand. So, three little niche players would be gathered together in Monte Carlo, of all places, to talk business. The Monaco Grand Prix, one of the world's premier automobile races, would be thrown in for good measure. But that was no accident, because the Finns were also good at what the Europeans called motor sports, and Mika Hakkinen was the 1999 Formula 1 world champion. He and a rising young driver, Kimi Raikkonen, were both entered and we learned that the Finns had high hopes of a victory. The race actually set the tone for the meetings because DNA also had very high ambitions. They were not really a niche player at all. Jordan and Bahrain were just the opening gambit in the Middle East, a region of 400 million potential subscribers. After that, it was the world.

We left on May 24, 2001, flying Air France from Amman to Paris. Like most major carriers Air France had gone to a two-class seating arrangement and eliminated first class. But the business class space was small and cramped. They hadn't increased the size of the economy seats but simply put a console in the middle of a three-seat bank. That meant a little more elbow room but there wasn't much leg room. If this was business class, we could only imagine what it was like in the back of the bus. Actually, it was the only time in the next five days that we didn't go first class. DNA spared no expense and their attention to detail was meticulous, just like their service.

The first stop after passport control at Charles de Gaulle was a visit to a data center in a technology park in the outskirts of Paris. It was an extra, not part of the DNA program, but designed to fill the three-hour layover in France. Drivers with "Unisys" signs were waiting in the arrival hall. We bundled into two Mercedes taxis and hurtled at breakneck speed on a motorway through what looked like a series of light industrial parks. These Europeans *did* like motor sports. After ten minutes the driver pointed out the stadium where the French had won the football World Cup in 1998. He was a bit of a chauvinist and on the way back, a few hours later, he showed us where the Concorde had crashed. He said it had been caused by a piece of debris on the runway from a Delta flight and, so, was the Americans' fault.

At Unisys a pleasant Frenchman was waiting for us on the curb. It was a public holiday in France—the feast of the Ascension—and so a religious holiday in this most irreligious of countries. But Philippe was happy to be of service and, after we had been signed in and given badges, we took the elevator to a small conference room on the eighth floor. His program for us, hand-written on a flip chart, was tight but structured: twenty minutes for lunch, twenty minutes for lecture, and twenty minutes for a tour of the facilities. As usual, the French had their priorities right. The meal may have come under a plastic wrapping with the Dijon mustard in a little foil tube, but it was beautifully prepared and presented: smoked salmon, confit of duck, a main course of fish, vegetables and new potatoes, then cheese and a little creme caramel. All washed down with bottled water, gaseous or plain. It may have been France where wine seemed to come out of the tap. But this was, after all, a working lunch.

Over the meal we learned that Philippe was a veteran of the information technology wars and had worked in the United States. That accounted for his fluent but oddly-accented English. He really was one of us and it seemed that the IT business was seducing the best minds all over the world to American ways of thinking and doing. We asked how the French language was dealing with the assault of American IT terms and he just shrugged. It was an interestng problem. At a lecture in Amman earlier in the week, a Greek professor of economics at MIT had also spoken about the technology gap. Universities, he said, had traditionally been repositories of beauty and truth, and they had been reluctant to embrace this new IT truth. That accounted for the fact that highly-educated societies in Europe and America still had shortages of technology workers. So the seduction was not complete and some probably hoped it would stay that way.

The lecture was in IT-speak, all about "proof of concept" and "mix and match" of technologies. The tour was a look through a glass partition at a bank of servers, Cisco, Unisys, and others. It represented about a million dollars. Small potatoes. Then, after fifty-nine minutes, it was back into the two Mercedes and back at breakneck speed to Charles de Gaulle. The connecting flight to Nice was delayed but eventually we were airborne in an MD 80. It was more spacious than the Airbus. An hour later over Nice, far below in the crescent of the bay, an aircraft carrier appeared and I later learned it was the USS Enterprise. I had last seen the Enterprise in 1967 in Subic Bay in the Philippines during the Vietnam war. At the airport they were waiting with signs, this time saying "DNA." A courtly little Finn with mouse-brown hair greeted us, noticeable for the fact that he wore a pinkie ring, except that it was on his index finger.

As we collected the baggage we realized we were now on the Cote d'Azur, as glitzy and uninhibited a place as Los Angeles. A fantastic couple waited near the carousel, both looking to be in their sixties and both having seen better days. But they wouldn't give it up. He had unnaturally jet-black hair and his skin had lost much of its elasticity. A gold ID bracelet dangled from one wrist, and spotless white trousers covered what little remained of his shrunken buttocks. She was unnaturally blond, in stiletto heels, and age had not been kind to her face. She looked like Bardot, toothy, but what had once been voluptuous was now merely coarse. To his credit the man wrestled what must have been a dozen color-coordinated bags onto a pair of gurneys and they set off with a spring in their step. Later, before our bags came, we saw that they had missed one.

Then it was, again, into pair of Mercedes for the drive to the rendezvous with the yacht that would take us to Monaco. It think it was at Beaulieu Sur-Mer. On the strip, appropriately named *Californie,* there were already hookers in evidence, even though it was only about five thirty in the afternoon. The sailors on the Enterprise would be happier in Nice than in Bahrain, where they had probably just been. Our driver had lived in New Caledonia and with its proximity to Australia, he spoke good English laced with Australian slang. After half-an-hour along the coast we reached the harbor and crept in a series of hairpin turns down to the waterfront. There, we shifted to a small boat for the ride out to the *Fascination.* Our adventure was about to begin.

If the first Finn we met was small, the second was not. He was sitting in the fantail when we climbed aboard, dressed like one of the young Jordanians we worked with: clunky black shoes, black socks, black trousers, black shirt, and black coat. All that was missing was the black necktie. A piece in the New York Times a couple of months before had parodied the type, calling them yuppified and untypical. But they were not. Sitting next to him was a blonde with hair down to the middle of her back. But it was only when they stood up to shake hands that we realized how big they both were. His name was Hanno Muttola and the man with mouse-brown hair told us that he played for the Atlanta Hawks. I later looked him up on the Hawks roster and he was listed at 6'–11" and 247 pounds. He had played at Utah and had been on the team that lost the 1998 NCAA finals to Kentucky.

But he was open and unaffected and we chatted about basketball. Mention of the increasing numbers of Europeans in the league seemed to break the ice because he was very forthcoming about his NBA experience. The travel was grueling and he didn't have time to keep up his fitness regimen. He was not used to the run-and-gun style and had to learn to be more aggressive. But he was optimistic about the Hawks for next year. His English was almost unaccented. The blonde was his fiancee. They had both liked Utah.

We waited a few minutes over drinks for the Bahrainis to arrive and then weighed anchor. It was about an hour to Monaco, due east past Cap Roux and the Baie de St-Laurent to the Cap d'Ail before turning northeast to the breakwater outside the Port de Monaco. Inside, nestled among scores of sleek motorized yachts, lay the *Fair Lady.* We transferred again, this time to the *Fair Lady*'s boat to take us the rest of the way. She would be our home for the next five days. Built in 1927 she had recently undergone a multimillion dollar refitting, finished with the new paint that resisted salt water. At 135 feet long, she was about half the size of a World-War-Two destroyer. Her lines, with a nearly vertical prow, made her an anachronism amid the rakish giants on either side. But she had a few things the others did not, including lots of wood with its thirty-five coats of varnish, and enough brass fittings to keep the crew busy on a full-time basis. There was also a British crew that lent her a bit of tradition, and a couple of conference rooms suitable for IT presentations.

The *Fair Lady*

The *Fair Lady* was owned by the Sainsbury's of supermarket renown and the name brought back an odd memory. Sainsbury's had invested millions of pounds in Egypt in the late 1990s, buying up smaller markets and, incidentally, driving others out of business. With the beginning of the latest *intifada* word was circulated that the company was Jewish-owned and a boycott was organized. It was hard to say how much of it was politics and how much bureaucracy, because there also had been chronic problems with customs. But Sainsbury's had just pulled the plug. Poor old Egypt. They complained about the lack of foreign direct investment. But, just as in the Nasser years, they were experts not in attracting investment but in driving it away.

Below decks the stateroom was nicely appointed. There wasn't a piece of plastic in sight. The tiny shower had a head like one at the Dorchester and it discharged a torrent of hot water. On the bookshelf were titles that made the ship a little corner of England in Monaco: Peter Wright's *Spycatcher, Good Things in England, The Oxford Companion to Ships and the Sea,* and *English Eccentrics.* There was also everything you would expect in a good hotel room, little touches like cotton swabs, and Q-tips, and a few things you would not, including a silk DNA necktie (the logo tastefully woven into the fabric), a silk scarf, a polo shirt, and the ubiquitous American ball cap with Red Bull, Credit Suisse and Sauber Petronas logos. The last was Kimi Raikkonen's team. There was also a Nokia mobile phone with a picture of Raikkonen on the back. All the Finns wore it suspended by a tether around their necks. The welcome card was individualized:

> I would like to wish you a warm welcome as a DNA Finland Ltd's guest, to France and Monaco and I hope that you will enjoy your stay.
> I hope that our meetings are successful and that we can enjoy following the Monaco Formula 1 Grand Prix 2001.

It was signed by the managing director.

Back on deck after freshening up, we were treated to the the first of several days of cocktail parties and dinners. All the Jordanians, Bahrainis, and Finns were there, including the full DNA team with Hanno Muttola and his fiancée. Just before dinner it was rumored that Kimi Raikkonen was on his way and, sure enough, he arrived looking a little sheepish amid the glitter. He was dressed in faded blue jeans, a white tee-shirt, unbuttoned cotton-checked shirt, and a ball cap pulled tightly down around his ears. He looked like a kid, and I don't think he had begun to shave. We ate, drank and talked until well after midnight. Later, lying in my bunk, I reflected on this first day. It was as if they had mustered every famous

Finn and asked them to be there, because they were all gone the next day. But where were Mika Hakkinen and the guy who won the shot put at the Sydney Olympics? Maybe they would be there tomorrow.

The Big Screen

Breakfast the next morning was an antidote to the night before: fresh fruit, fiber, and plenty of black coffee. The schedule called for meetings all morning, general remarks by the managing director of DNA, followed by marketing and technical presentations by their respective directors. It was all laid out to the minute, like a battle plan. But the Finns weren't used to the Arab's sense of timing, or lack thereof. Jordanians weren't as bad as Egyptians, although they tended to drift late into everything. But, to be fair, it was as much the Finns' fault as the Jordanian's because we had an unobstructed view of the course and the seven-by-ten meter big screen showing close–ups of the races. The screen was topped by letters spelling out "GAULOISES," tobacco and motor sports still living together in Europe and still bucking the trend. The Formula 1 final wasn't until Sunday but there were qualifying heats and other races over the next two days. Discussions were impossible when the cars were on the track.

Monte Carlo

The course was laid out in the narrow, winding streets of the city. Barriers had been erected to protect shop fronts, high enough to obstruct from view of all but the tops of the passing cars. In our anchorage we were about 200 yards from the Avenue d'Estende and even closer to the Boulevard Albert 1er where the cars passed closest to the harbor. Monte Carlo was not a pretty city and scores of ugly high-rises crowded the waterfront. The effect was to reflect the sound of the unmuffled 800 hp engines back toward the harbor. When they all started together, they sounded like millions of angry bees:

BRRRRREEEEEEEIIIIIIIIIIIIIIIIIIIZZZZZZZZZZZZZZZZ

The Doppler effect was noticeable at first, but the course was so short that there seemed to be cars everywhere all the time, and the din became general. One of the Finns later called the noise infernal, and he was right. They passed out earplugs (provided by Red Bull Sauber Petronas) and while they helped, business discussions or even casual conversations were impossible when the cars were on the track.

The Finns may have had pull in Monaco, but there was nothing they could do about the noise. So the plan had to be altered and, like good generals, they made the best of the situation. The presentations began an hour late and we were just about finished with the first when, there it was, the sound of the bees again:

BRRRRREEEEEEEIIIIIIIIIIIIIIIIIIIZZZZZZZZZZZZZZZZ

We closed the doors but it was hopeless. There was nothing to do but to wait it out. The other presentations followed during breaks in the racing schedule. DNA had been founded in 1999 and was owned by thirty-seven local operating companies. They were heavily into mobile services and planning to offer third generation, or 3G, services in 2002. They saw 3G not as another means of Internet access, but as a different phenomenon altogether. Miniaturization of the appliances meant that you could never access large amounts of data with a handset—imagine trying to watch a big-screen movie on one of those little things. But there were other applications that serious users would want, like stock quotes or news bites. They were DNA's target market. Turnover to date in 2001 had been about 200 million Finnish Marks, or $29 million, and marketing expenses had been about thirty million marks, or about $4.5 million. We were probably part of the latter.

The Finnish regulator had helped by mandating the separation of network provision and service provision, and it was a model they were looking for elsewhere. That is, DNA didn't own any infrastructure but would only lease it to provide services. In an environment where European operators had paid fortunes for spectrum licenses and couldn't afford the infrastructure, it sounded like a sensible way to go. They were targeting power users of mobile services—students, entrepreneurs, consultants, trendsetters—and would provide services that were easy to use, personalized, intuitive and simply-priced.

The customer really would be king and that would allow DNA to compete in a market where all providers were thought to be the same. It sounded reasonable enough. In Jordan the *shebab*, or youth, in the ministry were already power users, addicted not only to mobile voice but also to data. One of them had even impressed John Scully, the former CEO of Apple, with his device at a conference in Cairo. I wasn't sure of the advantage of having some little snippet of news at work instead of at home that night, but there was clearly a market for it. In fact, mobile telephones were an unprecedented phenomenon and everyone wanted not only to talk on one but to be *seen* talking on one. Even the poor were prepared to sacrifice for service and the mobile system was often the only thing that worked in places where nothing else did.

The presentations were, of course, in English. And like all IT presentations, they were "interactive." That meant that we could ask questions. I later learned that there were two official languages in Finland, Finnish and Swedish. Everyone studied both in school and another language besides. Oddly, for this most Nordic of countries, Finnish was a Finno-Ugaric language and was distantly related to Hungarian and Turkish. I remembered meeting a Finn in Kuala Lumpur who said that when he worked in Istanbul he had little trouble picking up the local language.

Structurally it seemed incomprehensible and a short introduction to the language didn't help much:

> . . . Finnish is a synthetic language: it uses suffixes to express grammatical relations and also to derive new words . . . the simple word *talossanikin* corresponds to the English phrase *in my house, too*. The suffix -*ssa* is the ending of the so-called incessive case, corresponding to the English *in*. The suffix -*ni* is a possessive one, corresponding to *my* in English. And the suffix -*kin* is an enclitic particle corresponding to the English *too* . . .

Their English was heavily accented and the pronunciation of the "s" made the Finns sound a little like Greeks. But the most noticeable characteristics were a great deliberation—one of the Jordanians later complained about how slowly they spoke—and an odd stress on some consonants, particularly in names. Mikka was Mik-ka, Hanno was Han-no, Kimmi was Kim-mi, and so on.

Disruption in the schedule meant that the planned trip to Cannes had to be canceled and we had the first afternoon off. That meant relaxation in our staterooms and I started on *Spycatcher*. Peter Wright seemed a down-to-earth, practical English type, a little like Flinders Petrie. His father had been chief scientist at Marconi but when the father was laid off, Wright had to leave school. It was he, the pursuer of the enemies of capitalism, who had suffered from the baleful effects of capitalism during the depression. And it was the children of privilege—Burgess, McLean, Philby, and Anthony Blunt—who were the pursued. They were the ones who had turned to Marxism, although they hadn't really suffered at all. The book was written with the assistance of Paul Greengrass and it seemed to be Greengrass rather than Wright speaking in the Hemingwayesque opening line:

> It all began in 1949 on the kind of spring day that reminds you of winter.

Afterwards, it was very English and dated. It all seemed light-years from 2001, when scientists at Bell Labs had just passed 3.8 terabits of information, nearly four times the load on the Internet on an average day, over a single optical fiber cable in the course of a *second*.

Later in the afternoon we went ashore. Crowds were milling around the paddocks and gawking as teams in color-coordinated uniforms tended the cars. We mounted the steep green hill to the Place du Palais. There, a white-uniformed soldier was doing a march up-and-down in front of the palace. Actually, he looked like a hotel doorman and no one was paying him much attention. I bought a couple of rolls of film from a phlegmatic shopkeeper. The customer was *not* king in Monaco. It was a funny little place, a sovereign nation a kilometer long by 300 meters wide. On the way back to the boat we passed a large statue calling itself "Albert 1er 1297–1997." It was dressed in a religious habit although a scabbard extended in the back. This first of the Grimaldis, a band of Genoese adventurers, had entered the city in 1297 disguised as a monk. 1997 was their 700th anniversary in power. Monte Carlo was the capital.

That evening dinner was scheduled at the Hotel de la Voile d'Or. It was in Beaulieu sur-Mer, near where we had met the *Fascination* the day before. This time we went by van. At the restaurant the courses came in rapid succession, California cuisine in tiny artistically-arranged portions. I sat next to the finance director of DNA, a very fair blond whose husband was a motorcycle rally driver in his spare time. They had no children. She said that a typical Finnish meal was meatballs, although in the north they favored reindeer. In the short summers they suffered from a plague of mosquitoes, although there was no malaria. She had spoken to her husband that morning and in late May it was still only about five degrees centigrade in Helsinki.

Sandwiched between Sweden and Russia, Finland as a country was a relatively recent phenomenon. It had only separated from Sweden in the early nineteenth century, and the largely rural population and agrarian economy had kept it poor and insular. The language ordinance of 1850 forbade the publication of books in Finnish, except on matters dealing with "religious edification" or "economic benefit." Swedish was the only language allowed in administration of the country and Finnish speakers had to fight for their rights. Maybe that accounted for their drive. The northern part of the country consisted largely of Lappland and lay above the Arctic Circle. The Lapps seemed to have been the aboriginal people and were darker than the other Finns.

Not like me, said the finance director.

At the end of the dinner there were toasts to all three countries, and especially to Jordan whose national day it was. The managing director called it "Jordania." When he referred to Finland he said they were good at what sounded like "smorgasbord," but I later understood was "motor sports." That was all right, they were good at both. Back on the *Fair lady* we were greeted, as usual, at the accommodation ladder by one of the ship's company. Everyone was "sir," not in a deferential tone but one used by people who were comfortable with hierarchy, and the navy was about as hierarchical as it got.

The next day would be the Formula 1 trials. But they would be in the afternoon, and we thought we might spend the morning in Nice. With the Fins and the crew of the *Fair Lady* anything was possible. So we arranged to meet the *Fascination* just inside the breakwater and left at nine thirty. It was about an hour to Nice and we had to be back for a briefing on the race at twelve thirty, so that would give us just an hour in the city. There were the usual drinks and snacks along the way, and by ten twenty we were alongside the pier. The captain, a garrulous sort, seemed to know everyone, but an hour was the most he could negotiate with the Nice harbormaster. So we had to be back by eleven twenty. He told us to look for the *Place Garabaldi* and, from there, we would find the shopping area. We eventually found it and the Jordanians visited, of all places, a shop selling mobile telephone accessories.

Then we wandered back through the narrow streets of the old town. It looked a little like Switzerland except that the stores weren't as pristine and many of the people looked like—there was no way of avoiding it— like *Arabs*. But there was the usual European collection of antique shops, art stores, and butcheries featuring goats, kids, rabbits, and chickens in addition to the large ruminants. There were also cheese shops, bakeries, vegetable stands, and sellers of seafood. Mussels seemed to be in season. We were back on the pier at eleven twenty-five and underway shortly thereafter. Inside the breakwater at Monaco we waited for the boat from the *Fair lady*. The captain was in his element:

> Hey, bonjour! Hallo mon ami!

He was waving to the small boats that were plying between the bigger ones or zipping in and out of the breakwater. He used the argot that everyone seemed to think was understood by Americans everywhere, a kind of verbal pair of Levi's:

> I know everyone in zis fucking harbor. Hey, bonjour! Hallo mon ami!

The maritime police were there in their own small boat, monitoring the comings and goings, and warning some to cut their speed.

> What do these ships cost?
> See zat fucking one? We say about a million dollars per meter. So zat is fifty million at least.

It was one of hundreds in the harbor. Most were modern and sleek, with bows that cut sharply back from the vertical. If the bow of the *Fair Lady* stood almost straight up these new ones looked like knives. They were made of stainless steel and aluminum and were covered with that new paint. Most were brilliantly white. An exception was the grey monster that lay next to the jetty just inside the breakwater. It was about 350 feet long and higher out of the water than a modern frigate. It had small boats in the davits on either side and a helicopter on the fantail. They said it belonged to Bill Gates.

Motorized Yachts

In a discussion with the managing director I had mentioned the John Scully story and the phone in Cairo. He had worked for Apple during Scully's tenure and said that he may have been a visionary, but he had made perhaps the worst business decision of all time. It was before the rise of Microsoft and Scully had decided to keep the Apple operating system proprietary:

'We are in the hardware, not the software business,' he said.

That was the opening Microsoft needed. Without that decision it might have been Steve Jobs instead of Bill Gates on that monster in Monaco. The collective value of the ships anchored in the harbor probably exceeded the GDP of most developing countries.

Back on the *Fair Lady* we had been promised a preview of the qualifying heats by Mika Hakkinen's former manager. It would have to be quick because the heats began at one p.m. sharp. He had a large piece of flip-chart paper on which he had sketched the course, and he held it up against the bulkhead. They would start on the Boulevard Albert 1er and would have reached fifty-five mph at the first turn. After that they would rapidly accelerate to 160 mph up the Avenue d'Ostende, before slowing in a series of turns beginning at the Casino. The slowest part of the race would be at the Grand Hairpin where they would virtually creep at thirty mph in first gear. Out of that they would gradually accelerate and reach 160 mph again in the tunnel, emerging on Avenue John F. Kennedy. That's when the noise would be greatest. The whole course took a little over a minute. The qualifying record of 1 minute, 18.261 seconds had been set by Heinz-Harald Frentzen in 1997. It was certain to be broken this year.

The qualifying runs were important. There were very few places to pass and the pole position was critical. Only a few men were real contenders and we soon knew them on a first-name basis:

> I think Michael will be the favorite (he was referring to Michael Schumacher). Mik-ka may challenge and also David (he meant the Scot, David Coulthard). Kim-mi (he meant Kimi Raikkonen) is the hottest young property on the tour, but he will consider it a success if he finishes in the top ten..

We watched the drivers wedge themselves into their cars on the big screen, hunching their shoulders as they squeezed past the sides of the cockpits. The steering wheels were tiny. After a while the temperatures in the cockpits would approach sixty degrees Centigrade, or 140 degrees Fahrenheit. It was like being in a sauna. Maybe that's why the Fins were so good at it. Then, at one o'clock, it was the sound of the bees again:

> BRRRRREEEEEEEIIIIIIIIIIIIIIIIIIIZZZZZZZZZZZZZZZZ

For the next hour we could only gesture to one another, so great was the din. In the early going the times were in the 1:20 range, from drivers like Burti, Alesi, Panis, and Raikkonen. Then the big guns took to the course and the qualifying record was soon broken. Near the end of the hour Michael Schumacher seemed to have a lock on the pole position at 1:17.631. And then, on the last lap, seemingly out of nowhere, David Coulthard posted a time of 1:17.430. He would start first tomorrow. Schumacher was second and Hakkinen was third. His former manager was philosophical:

> David drove a very clever race. I think Michael was a little unlucky.

There had been a problem on Schumacher's last lap, just enough of a distraction to let Coulthard slip past. In what seemed to be the practice at Monaco, the first two drivers, Coulthard and Schumacher, were being interviewed together on the big screen. They looked surprisingly fresh after an hour in those cockpits. Tomorrow would be the real race and the manager promised to return to tell us the strategy of each team.

Lunch that afternoon was filet, huge pieces of beef with braised couscous pancakes, and tiny green beans. The chef on the boat was from California and had gone to culinary school in Berkeley. He wanted to open his own restaurant in San Francisco after he had made his stake. We had hardly digested lunch before it was time for dinner, baked tuna in pieces almost as big as the filets. The food came in an endless stream and I don't know how we got through it all. The featured attraction at dinner was a professor of economics at MIT, a Finn, who was also on the board of Nokia. The managing director said that he would advise us on telephony or economics or something. But he admitted that he really had only a layman's knowledge of the mobile telephone business. It sounded like Jordan was doing the right thing. Economics was another matter and he peppered his conversation with jargon from the dismal science. Like Hanno Muttola, he was gone the next day.

After dinner we took the motorboat ashore and walked up to the casino. The Jordanians had to plant their feet on firm ground every few hours, the gentle, hardly-perceptible rocking of the *Fair Lady* having already induced mild seasickness in one. The streets were packed as we walked past the paddocks where the cars and drivers were stabled. A few cars were visible under tarpaulins. We had seen one up close the day before and it was really only an engine, four wide tires, and some bits of sheet metal. No wonder they disintegrated when they hit a wall. It also illustrated how the race was as much a matter of luck as skill. The cars maneuvered dangerously close to one another and, at those speeds, someone else's mistake could mean disaster.

The crowd was festive but not misbehaved. The closest thing to football rowdies were a few Coulthard fans, including one huge Scot looking belligerent, and little incongruous, in a kilt. The *Nice-Matin* a couple of days later showed pictures of celebrities at the race, including the black footballer Edgar Davids *en promenade* and Naomi Campbell with the American rapper Puff Daddy. But for the most part this was a white, European gathering. Euro-Sport was a steady diet of motor sports, motorcycles, cars, trucks, and odd-looking things going up and down mountains.

We mounted the Avenue d'Ostende and then the Avenue de Monte Carlo to the Place du Casino. At midnight, the white pile of the building was brilliantly lit, looking like an elaborate confection. Inside were the green baize tables and the players intent on Punto Banco, Craps, Ruleta Americana, and Black Jack. We had a cappuccino at the Cafe de Paris while the power users indulged the new etiquette: hunched over, exchanging mobile telephone numbers by manipulating the tiny keypads. The really good ones used only one hand. Then we walked back to the Quai des Etats-Unis where the boat would meet us. At the accommodation ladder of the *Fair Lady* one of the staff was there to meet us, steadying the boat as we clambered aboard:

> Evening sir. Careful, careful, there we go sir.

Tomorrow would be the big day. Actually, it already *was* the big day.

The morning dawned clear and fresh. It had rained briefly on both Friday and Saturday but Sunday looked like a good day for a motor race. It would be busy. There would be Formula 1 warm-ups from nine thirty to ten, a Porsche-Pirelli Supercup at ten twenty, the Formula 1 drivers parade at eleven fifteen, the Renault Sport Clio Trophy race at noon, and the Formula 1 Final, the Monaco Grand Prix, at two o'clock. We would watch the race largely on the big board. The night before, on the walk to the casino, we had passed behind it and saw that it was made up of maybe seventy panels, each of millions of pixels. The resolution was excellent and the system broke down only a few times over the five days. The cars were so low that we only occasionally caught a glimpse of their tops, the cowls behind the cockpits, as they roared up the Avenue d'Ostende. But on the big board, we saw them all.

140 MIDDLE EAST TAPESTRY

Race Day

The city had been turned into a giant civil-works project, with moveable barriers lining the streets and temporary bleachers erected on the waterfront in the space not occupied by the high-rises. They were packed with humanity. The balconies of the hotels and apartment buildings were suddenly populous and pavilions had been set up on the roofs. A few were draped with banners featuring the red Ferrari stallion. In the harbor, the boats were flying the entire contents of their pennant lockers, their occupants in various states of undress in the bright sunlight. It was all very festive. At about one thirty Mika Hakkinen's former manager arrived, as promised, to brief us on the final:

> The race will be seventy-eight laps. Twenty-three cars will start. Since they start in a staggered line—one on the left and one on the right and so on—David and Mik-ka will be sandwiched around Michael. They will go out fast and Mik-ka will try to pass Michael. Then both McLarens would be in the lead. The Ferraris will have to go into the pits first, after about fifty-five laps. The McLarens will go into the pits after the Ferraris.

I think he said that the McLarens would be heavier since they carried more fuel. That was the reason for the difference in the pit timings. Both Coulthard and Hakkinen were in McLarens, with Schumacher and the Brazilian, Rubens Barrichello, in Ferraris. Barrichello would start in fourth position. So, of the twenty-three cars in the starting grid the McLarens and Ferraris would be evenly distributed in the first four positions: McLaren, Ferrari, McLaren, Ferrari. That was where the teams would come into play:

> If David and Mik-ka are in the lead, they can dictate the race and keep anyone from passing.

At least that was the plan. The race would be highly tactical, with very little passing. The start was critical and we would soon learn how quickly things could change. Kimi Raikkonen in a Red Bull Sauber Petronas was starting in fifteenth position. I think that out of loyalty to DNA we were pulling for him.

Shortly before two o'clock they passed out ear plugs (provided by Red Bull Sauber Petronas). At roughly eighty seconds per lap, the next hour and three-quarters would be nothing but infernal noise. We learned that the first would be a kind of practice lap and then it would be the real thing:

> Watch the five red lights on the big board. When they have all gone out the race will start.

We watched as they went out in series: five, four, three, two, one. Then, it was the bees again:

> BRRRRREEEEEEEIIIIIIIIIIIIIIIIIIIIZZZZZZZZZZZZZZZZZ

But something had gone badly wrong:

> What happened to David???!!! He's not moving!!!

The manager was shouting above the din.

> Oh, this changes everything!!! Now he has to start last!!! He'll be in the last position!!!

Apparently Coulthard's car had stalled, the computerized ignition system having failed. It had happened to four cars in the Austrian Grand Prix two weeks before, leaving them standing on the grid. By the time he started again Coulthard would be in the last, or twenty-third position. Those were the rules.

> It's not David's fault!!! It's the fault of the technology!!!

He was still shouting to those of us who strained to hear. Now, it was Michael Schumacher in the pole position with his teammate, Barrichello, in third. And now, the Ferraris had the McLaren and Hakkinen sandwiched between them. Barring a miracle, Coulthard was finished.

For the next couple of hours the race played itself out according to the cards dealt in those opening seconds. It was effectively over, almost before it began. Michael Schumacher, with a combination of position, a superb car, a good team, tactical skill, and a little luck prevailed while others fell by the wayside. The first to go was Nick Heidfeld, Kimi Raikkonen's Sauber Petronas teammate, in an accident on the first lap. Juan-Pablo Montoya went out on the third, also because of an accident. There were losses of steering, suspension, hydraulics, transmission, and engines that steadily reduced the field of twenty-three to the ten cars that finished the race. Men in color-coordinated jumpsuits were on the track removing the debris almost as soon as an accident occurred. The most crushing *abandon* was that of Mika Hakkinen on the sixteenth lap, because of a problem with his suspension. Since Raikkonen had already dropped off the board, it looked like there were no Finns left in the race. All the DNA staff were wearing their Sauber Petronas polo shirts and ball caps. So were we. But after the sixteenth lap one had said "It is a bad day for Finland."

As the race progressed the only question was whether the Ferraris could maintain their lead. After Hakkinen dropped out they were first and second and that's the way they finished. There was a brief moment of drama when Kimi Raikkonen appeared again on the leader-board. He had gone out, but not out of the race, and when he returned he was in last place. It was a small victory for Finland. As predicted, Schumacher went into the pits on the fifty-fifth lap and temporarily lost the lead to Barrichello. The big screen timed his progress—0.1 . . . 7.0—in seven seconds he was back on the track with a full tank and a change of tires. His brother Ralf in a Willams-BMW followed on the fifty-eighth lap, but the timer suggested something serious. When it reached twenty seconds it was clear that he was finished. Then Barrichello went into the pits, returning the lead to Michael Schumacher. He was back on the track in 6.9 seconds.

So it was Schumacher, followed by Barrichello, who finished almost where they had started. The difference in time—.431 seconds—suggested how close were the tolerances in the race. Michael Schumacher led from pole to pole, never seemed seriously challenged over nearly two hours and two hundred miles of grueling work, and still won by less than half a second. Coulthard worked his way from twenty-third back to fifth, largely because other cars dropped out. There had been almost no passing. Kimi Raikkonen finished tenth, five laps behind, but a success in his progress towards the big time. And if the din during the race was terrific, it wasn't much better at the end. Because all the horns on all the boats in the harbor of Monaco sounded before the noise of the engines had died away. On the big screen Schumacher and Barrichello were out of the cockpits at three fifty-five and at three fifty-six they were on the podium with Prince Rainier. Eddie Irvine was third. The Monaco Grand Prix was over.

The next morning we left for the airport at seven thirty. There was supposed to be a van waiting for us at seven o'clock but, in the only time the system broke down over the five days, it didn't appear. So the Finns called for taxis on their Nokias, and in a few minutes two black Mercedes were backing down the pier. Overnight, other boats had left and we had moved in one line. We were now tied up stern-to. After signing the guest book and posing for pictures, taken by the captain with a self-timer, we were given another of the ubiquitous American ball caps, this time with the name *Fair Lady* and the outline of a ship. It had been made in China. Then we said good-by to the crew and were gone. The Mercedes made their way past the barriers on what, the day before, had been the track and slowly accelerated to their customary speed. The signs—"Cannes, Toulon, Marseilles"—told us where we were. The landscape looked like California, and what was green would soon be brown and then golden.

At the airport we said good-by to the last of the Finns and checked in. But then our *Air Liberte* flight to Paris was canceled. So the United

States was not the only place where the traveler wasn't king. But it was handled by the ticketing agent with typical French nonchalance: the flight was canceled, these things happened, and if we didn't like it we could go somewhere else. Except that there was nowhere else to go. But there was another flight in a hour and from the air, as we circled away from Nice, we saw the Var river spilling its muddy contents into the bay below. The Enterprise was gone. Soon, the ground was a checkerboard of tiny farms. No wonder the French resisted any change in the EU regime of agricultural subsidies. Then, after half an-hour, we passed into the region of the French Alps and snow-covered peaks.

At two ten at Orly the French passed us to Royal Jordanian Airlines. Royal Jordanian actually was an improvement, with wider seats, more leg room, more amenities, more attentive crew. Even the food was better, and that was saying something. In the air we were able to reflect on what we had witnessed over the past five days: a very methodical, very thorough effort to woo us by a very determined suitor. These Finns were impressive. Not long after we returned the *International Herald Tribune* carried a piece reporting that Nokia had reached 34 percent market share in mobile handsets worldwide, and was working on 40 percent. Motorola and Ericsson were in the doldrums.

But in the exchanges the Jordanians and the Bahrainis had held their own. Both had won the confidence of the Finns. And beneath the glitz, the celebrities, and the endless supply of food, something of substance had taken place. A visit to the Finnish regulator was planned for September and after that, DNA would make a firsthand assessment of the Jordanian market. What could Jordan offer in return? Let's see, there were Petra and Jerash, diving at Aqaba, and some world-class IT firms. And they had a few rally drivers, but one of *them* was a king.

7

September Eleventh

IT WAS LIKE THE assassination of John F. Kennedy. We would all remember where we were and what we were doing when we heard the news that day. For some in the Ministry of Post and Communications in Jordan, it was the airport in Vienna. We had talked with DNA, the Finnish telecom, about a follow-up visit to Helsinki after our meeting in Monte Carlo. They were still interested in the Arab market and we were still interested in their expertise in data solutions for mobile providers. We had gone back and forth over a contract, or memorandum of understanding (MOU), that would make our relationship more concrete. They wanted a contract for consultancy services, with the invoicing and payment details to be worked out later. We wanted an MOU between the Government of Jordan, the Government of Finland, and DNA that would be a more informal arrangement. Ministries couldn't just award contracts without competition. In the end, we couldn't agree before we left Amman. So, we would leave the details to be worked out in Helsinki.

The Royal Jordanian flight left just after noon. But we were traveling with the minister and that meant the normal two-hour advance check-in would be waived. In fact, we boarded the plane just before takeoff. All the formalities had been taken care of, from stamping the passports to checking our luggage. It meant that we had the morning in the ministry to deal with last-minute business. About eleven fifteen we entered the big ministry Mercedes and, with the minister at the wheel, sped the twenty miles to Queen Alia International Airport. A slight delay meant that we spent ten minutes in the VIP lounge. Then at twelve ten on September 11, 2001, we boarded the Airbus for Vienna and then Helsinki.

The flight time was just under five hours. I sat next to a Jordanian who had an export business in Vienna and he gave me his card. You never knew when it might come in handy. After landing we made our way to the transit lounge when one of the Jordanians received a message on his mobile phone saying that something had happened in New York. Short messaging services were the rage in the Middle East, being convenient and relatively inexpensive. But it wasn't until we reached the main terminal building that we realized that it was something big. On a monitor in a video store was the sight that stunned the world. It must have been a delayed broadcast because both towers were still standing, but billowing black smoke. They looked like they might survive but an Austrian woman said simply "They're gone. Both gone." Then she walked away in tears.

There was nothing to do but watch in helpless, grim fascination. It was a kind of voyeurism, sharing the last, very public moments with the thousands who had died or were dying in the towers. But then reality snapped back and my first thought was for our daughter who worked at Rockefeller University in Manhattan. Laura had friends who worked in the World Trade Center and she occasionally visited them there. What if she had been in the building? But it wasn't just the building. What if all of Manhattan was threatened? The banner headline on CNN read "AMERICA UNDER ATTACK." There was already talk of broken gas mains and spreading fires from the vicinity of the towers. The number of hijacked planes was unknown, which only increased the uncertainty.

It was early morning in New York and the city would be full of commuters. There was no telling how many people had died. Some estimated that the number of staff and visitors in the Twin Towers on an average day ran into the scores of thousands. Imagine 50,000 dead. We sat in the lounge and reflected on what we had seen, but there was no comprehending the enormity of the event. Individual concerns filled the void. We tried the mobiles but they weren't much help. I couldn't get through to Martha in Cairo. All the lines were tied up. New York was impossible and we later learned that a key Verizon switching center had been in one of the towers. Five hours later in Helsinki we found the telephone system, one of the most advanced in the world, to be working perfectly and I talked with Laura on a clear line. She was fine and staying with her aunt on the upper east side. She had talked with Martha in Cairo and with my family in California. E-mails were bouncing back and forth between

San Francisco, New York, and Cairo. The Internet performed beautifully. An added bonus was that Laura's roommate had not gone to work in Tower 1 that morning. The Jordanians had other concerns: "God," said Mahmoud, "I hope it wasn't one of us."

In Helsinki, the hotel was the Strand Intercontinental in the center of the city. On television in the room, the only news was of the Twin Towers and the Pentagon. Bush looked like a deer caught in the headlights, and said something about an attack on "freedom loving people." But, to be fair, it was a reflex of the Cold War and he had not made the rhetorical adjustment to the new enemy. Someone deeply hated us, and it was not because of our love for freedom. There were other reasons and, to those of us who had lived in the Middle East for years, they were obvious. The BBC had already begun its coverage of Pakistan and Afghanistan whence, it was thought, the outrage emanated.

We hoped to awaken the next morning and find that it had only been a dream and the Twin Towers were still standing. But the events in New York and Washington were real, and they dominated the news in Finland. However, we had work to do and the program began with a visit to the Finnish Minister of Transport and Communications. He was young, in his thirties, and unlike the Jordanian minister he probably looked forward to a career in government. We discussed "issues of mutual interest"—how many times had I read the phrase '*ilaqaat thanayiyya* in Arabic—and we agreed that we needed a project to cement the relationship. The Finns had partners in IBM, Nokia, and Ericsson and they were looking to establish a presence in the Middle East. They would not require the separation of network provision from service provision. It had been done in Finland but was still too advanced for Jordan's developing competitive environment.

After lunch, we visited FICORA, the Finnish Communications Regulatory Authority. The director was a civil servant. So much for regulatory independence. But Finland had an interesting history of telecommunications. Under the Russians the Czarist authorities were interested only in the telegraph and left the telephone to the Finns. So, in a country with a population of just over five million there had once been over 500 telephone companies, many of them small cooperatives. Only about 100 remained today, but of the 100 more than fifty were classified as having significant market power. With so many companies, interconnection agreements, where providers agreed to connect to other providers' networks, had been highly developed. They generally consisted of simple commercial arrangements where the company completing the call added its charges to those of other providers and generated the bill. Oddly, with accession to the European Union and endorsement of the principle of "cost-based" interconnection, FICORA was in the process of hiring additional staff to administer the new, far more complex rules. It was the solution to a problem that didn't exist in Finland, but was the price of admission to the European Union.

Dinner was at the Palace restaurant on the waterfront. Both ministers were there and felicitations were freely exchanged between Finland and "Jordania." The managing director of DNA gave the welcoming address, and his voice had not changed since Monte Carlo. It was an instrument of astonishing force and timbre, especially when he laughed. The menu was lavish, the main course including fried reindeer fillet with cloudberry sauce. Desert was an assortment of Finnish cheeses. The wines were suited to each of the courses.

Back in the hotel room the news was a story of solidarity with America. NATO had invoked the mutual defense principle. Romano Prodi expressed what many Europeans—and all Americans—had felt for years: "In the darkest hours of European history America stood close with us," he said. "Today, we stand close by America." In New York, the first inflated casualty figures were coming down. It was amazing how many people had been evacuated from the buildings. But the smoking pile where the Twin Towers once stood would continue to emanate odd vapors for months afterwards, and Laura would write of crossing the Brooklyn Bridge and seeing the eerie parting in the skyline, a great maw that had consumed thousands, most of them without a trace.

More pieces of the puzzle were now falling into place. We learned that fifteen of the nineteen highjackers were Sa'udis from the 'Asir, the area south of the Hejaz on the western seaboard of Sa'udi Arabia. It was not well known, even in the Middle East. When I later told a Jordanian girl in the office that we regularly used to vacation there, she was surprised to hear that there were mountains in Arabia. So, she called a friend in Riyadh, but he couldn't place it either. That, we later learned, was because I had pronounced it 'Asir, not 'Asir. The difference between the two letters, the "*saad*" and the "*seen*," achieved by slightly thickening the sound, meant the difference in meaning between "juice" and "the mountainous district in southwest Arabia between Hejaz and Yemen."

So, she called him back and he said "Oh, yeah, 'Asir. I thought you said 'Asir." The distinction was almost impossible for us to hear or pronounce.

Highway, Asir

The region was beautiful, with mountains over 10,000 feet and wild almonds that scented the air in the spring. The highway south from Jidda was new and the journey was brisk. Along the way bees were fertilizing the white blossoms. Wild apes, their pink rumps bright as they scampered up the slopes, were a regular sight from the road. Typical *'Asiri* architecture was mud plaster, with horizontal slate ridges designed to shed the rain in the winter. The scene was similar to southern Sinai with jagged peaks through which the clouds dipped and clashed. We stayed at a hotel that was often in the clouds. It was wild and spectacular. The people of 'Asir—of Abha, Al-Baha, and Khamis Masheyt—seemed no different from people in Jidda, Rabigh, or Yanbuʾ or, for that matter, Riyadh, Qatif, or Hofuf. But we probably should have seen it coming.

Ape, Asir

In the 1980s Jidda hosted regular exhibitions on the Soviet war in Afghanistan. They were grisly and pathetic with pictures of amputees, not after the stumps had been surgically repaired, but jagged and torn flesh, men with limbs blown off, children holding up what remained of an arm or a leg. This was a holy war, and the other war in the region, between Iraq and Iran, showed that it was blessed to be maimed or killed for the faith. There were occasional views of the enemy, including one glass case with the bloodied uniform of a Russian soldier, the striped blue and white shirt of the *Spetznaz*, the Soviet special forces, and his identity papers. The photo in the passport was of a broad-faced Slavic boy and the picture with it could have been of a wife or girlfriend or maybe a sister. The purpose of the exhibits in Jidda—just as it was on Atlantic Avenue in Brooklyn—was to recruit Holy Warriors for resistance to the Soviets in Afghanistan. But they hadn't gone away when the Soviets pulled out, and we would probably have to live for years with the reality we had helped to create. There was more to it than Bush's "terrists" and "terrism." America was not an innocent in all of this.

The next morning there was only more dismal news in the *Financial Times*. We had just seen the extraordinary amateur video of the plane hitting the second tower. It been taken from almost directly beneath and showed the moment of impact, the 767 slipping into the building like a letter into a mail slot. One second it was there, and then it was not. There was something primal about the sight. It would be showed over and over again over the next several days.

Thursday, September thirteenth, would be spent primarily with the private sector. But presentations at Ericsson and Nokia would be sandwiched around a short session at the Ministry of Foreign Trade. Then it would be back to DNA for a look at their service offerings. Ericsson was a Swedish company, but it had a strong presence in Finland. The offices were in a large steel and glass building in the center of the city. When we arrived the Jordanian flag, with its little seven-sided star, was flying from the company flagpole. They had prepared a power-point presentation during which we learned that DNA had chosen Ericsson as its technical partner. The term "R & D" came up over and over again and we learned that research and development constituted 3 percent of Finnish GDP. After the presentation, there was a tour of a switching facility where a full-blown third generation, or 3G, system was demonstrated. It was a reminder of the combat information center on a destroyer, with the antiseptic walls and the low hum of the electronics. All that was missing was the dense cloud of cigarette smoke and the report of an occasional outgoing round.

The Ministry of Foreign Trade was on the waterfront with a view of the harbor and three large icebreakers in the foreground. They were being readied for the winter season. The minister sat behind a desk piled high with correspondence, files, books, and magazines, and peered at us over the jumble. We had a desultory chat about tourism before the conversation turned to politics. Finland had recently spoken out in favor of a Palestinian state and it caused the usual uproar in diplomatic circles. They had been forced to climb down.

Shimon Peres would later speak of "blood libel" after European criticism of Israeli military action in the West Bank. He was allowed to invoke the revulsion against historic anti-Semitism and the Holocaust to justify current Israeli brutality. And then there was the interview on CNN in which Peres discussed the refusal of Israeli reservists to serve in the occupation forces. This sexagenarian Jew, who had lived through the Nazi horrors, was allowed to assert without challenge that "soldiers must obey their orders." There was nothing sanctimonious about Sharon who, under cover of the attack on the Twin Towers, had moved into the West Bank the next day and killed seventeen Palestinians. He was clearly trying to piggyback on Bush's war on terror and it would be interesting to see if he would be allowed to do so. The last thing we could afford to do after September eleventh would be to get into bed with Ariel Sharon.

Lunch was at a club near the harbor. The main course was breast of pheasant and it continued the parade of spectacular meals in Finland. Seated at the next table was a group that included what looked like a classic European aristocrat: blond hair turning silver around the temples, receding hairline that revealed a fine forehead, and long, slender hands that gestured delicately or ate with an extreme economy of motion. But there was something about his look, with its bland gaze, that suggested he was *too* refined. We preferred the direct, not to say blunt, technocrats we were dealing with. With them it was all *ya ya* and no nonsense. Dessert would be at Nokia, half an hour away in the suburbs of Helsinki.

The journey by bus through the forest was a pleasant break from technology, and we saw why wood products had been the traditional Finnish strength. Nokia had started as a maker of rubbers—galoshes—and had evolved into a global technology giant. On arrival, we walked through a display of cellular telephones, from early ones the size of bricks to the fashionable little things of today, like the one with the picture of Kimi Raikkonen on the back that we had been given in Monte Carlo. Dessert was served during the presentation, which showed the company's worldwide reach. It was made by the chief technology officer, a man prominently featured in the book *The Nokia Revolution, The Story of an Extraordinary Company That Transformed an Industry*. Copies were provided after the presentation. On a slide with a map of the world, red dots showed the places where Nokia had a commercial presence. Blue dots showed development centers. There were already several red dots in the Middle East, but Jordan wanted to become a blue dot. We discussed how this might happen.

From a technology point of view, it was no longer a matter of language, since all known languages and scripts could be placed on the Web. Content was now the issue. For mobile data to be useful widely across the Arab World, it would have to be in Arabic. Jordan had good software developers, and a few world-class software development firms. If they could be paired with the Scandinavian technology giants, good Arabic-language content could be developed for export to the region. The level of Nokia's interest seemed to be indicated by the level of the presenter. So, there was a chance that it might become a reality.

We had coffee and a group photo in the glass-enclosed atrium. Then we returned to the city through stands of birch and evergreens for the meeting with DNA. The presentation showed that DNA was growing rapidly in the most competitive mobile market in the world. In fact, it was the fastest growing provider in Finland. Dinner that night was with the DNA finance director in another of Helsinki's finest restaurants. It was more fish.

Back in the room at the Strand, coverage of the attacks continued. The story of heroism on the plane that crashed in Pennsylvania was unfolding. It was a typical American story, just a bunch of guys getting together and doing something to make the world a better place. The hijackers included what was described as "muscle," but they were skinny kids and no match for the judo black-belts and rugby players. The police work was already impressive and revealed a pattern familiar to those who worked overseas. The hijackers had spent their last night at a strip club, attracted to the seediest manifestation of American culture. And they had learned how to steer an airplane, but not how to land one. It was the story of training the developing-world over.

The next day, Friday the fourteenth of September, would be the last working day of the visit. It began with another visit to the Ministry of Transport and Communications. They were a traditional combination, but increasingly an anachronism in a technological world. Egypt's telecommunications sector had been led for fifteen years by a former general in the transportation corps. But the Egyptians had recently created an ICT ministry, focused solely on telecommunications and information technology. Jordan was doing the same. However, old habits died hard and the little woman who made the presentation was from the old school. She knew it and we knew it and she knew that we knew it. So, there was a mischievous little twinkle in her eye throughout the poorly prepared slide show. She occasionally stood in front of the projector, so we couldn't see the slide. This was no super-smooth, technology-laden consultant presentation and, for some reason, that made it more believable.

Her commentary was laced with malapropisms: beauty contests were "beautiful contests," the regulatory environment became the "regulative environment," regulators must be flexible enough to "variate." There was a slide with a graph showing regulation on the vertical axis and time on the horizontal. The message was that the need for regulation decreased over time. That may have been true of Finland, but in Jordan it would first increase before competition, the best regulator, took hold. We asked a few questions but she was not very forthcoming; "we civil servants must have our own secrets." The session ended as playfully as it had begun, and we left having gained sustenance only from the fruit that was placed each of our places.

This was followed at midmorning by a visit to an ICT promotion agency like the one recently established in Jordan. The Finns used their mobile telephones for everything, from buying lottery tickets to paying for drinks in vending machines. More than 85 percent of banking transactions in Finland were done electronically. They had been using mobile phones for over twenty-five years with no noticeable health effects, reassuring to people who were concerned about the potential harmful effects of radiation on the brain. The real meat of the day, however, would be the joint strategy session that evening with DNA. But first there was to be "a special treat." We were escorted by the DNA attorney who had greeted us in Monaco. We knew he was a diver who regularly came to Aqaba for its coral reefs, so we thought it might have something to do with the water. It did.

We drove back into the country and to the vicinity of a lake, although there was nothing unusual about that in Finland, which had more than 12,000 square miles of inland water and thousands of lakes. As we entered the grounds of a resort it announced itself as "*Krapi Hotelli, Ravintolat, Savusauna.*" That meant a hotel, restaurant, and a smoke sauna. The last was the "special treat." We meandered down to a log building on the shore of the lake, where the sauna was located. Inside, Pekka produced swimming trunks for each of us, bought, he said, by his secretary. They fit. Then we entered the sauna itself, and it was infernal. The temperature was about eighty degrees centigrade said Pekka. That would make it about 175 degrees Fahrenheit. There were two levels of wooden benches, one above the other. It was too hot to sit on the bare wood, so we placed towels on the benches. But our feet still burned. Pekka said that most saunas these days were electric, but this was a real, old-fashioned one, and the wood was burning on a brazier just inside the door. A bucket of water with a large ladle sat nearby and he occasionally threw a ladleful on the brazier, producing a cloud of steam and heat that seemed to permeate every pore in our bodies.

After five minutes one of the faint-hearted left, although the phrase was more apt than I knew at the time. Saunas were not recommended for anyone with a heart condition. After a few minutes, we followed and Pekka led us down to another special treat: a dip in the lake. It was only September and this was not another Finnish favorite, ice-diving through a hole in the frozen surface. But still, the water temperature was probably about that of the air, five degrees centigrade, or about forty degrees Fahrenheit. The contrast—from 175 degrees to forty degrees—was supposed to be good for the health. So, we tiptoed down the wooden pier and jumped in, feeling the lake bottom oozing between our toes. And so it went, into the sauna followed by a dip in the lake, followed by a sauna and the lake again. After an hour of the treatment, I no longer felt the effects of the mild scoliosis in my back. Pekka said he had his own cabin on a lake and, like most Finns, did this all the time.

After a shower, we went to a conference room in the *hotelli* for the strategy session. Many of the issues discussed over the past several days were on the table and we agreed a joint plan of action. Then it was into the *ravintolat* for yet another Finnish meal. It was fish again, but this time the surroundings were more interesting than the food. The restaurant was a large wooden structure that looked like it might have once been a country house. There were wood stoves in every room and large old-fashioned sideboards lined the walls. It seemed old and very Scandinavian, maybe because of the wood and the light-yellow color of the walls, although it was a conflagration waiting to happen. But in a country where glass and steel were now the dominant building materials, there was something about the wood and the decor that seemed to transport us back to the nineteenth century and the world of Ibsen or Strindberg. But the Scandinavians we dealt with seemed very straightforward, not the tortured souls of that bygone era.

In the room at the Strand that evening coverage of the Twin Towers was moving into a more contemplative phase: why did they hate us, and why now? Individual Americans were liked the world over, so why this spasm of hatred for America? We would hear the questions repeated, over and over again in the next several weeks. When the answers finally emerged, they would absolve us of any responsibility for the events of September eleventh. Colin Powell said that Muslim nations had nothing to fear from the war on terror. I wasn't so sure about that. Israel and its friends in America would try to quarantine the atrocity, to fit it into a narrow conceptual box called "terrorism." Pundits would give us a little pop-sociology or pop-economics and tell us that the lack of jobs and democracy were the real villains. But it didn't wash. In fact, all of us—Europe, America, Israel, and the Arabs—bore some measure of responsibility for September eleventh, and it began with events in Palestine, that hard-scrabble little piece of real estate that, as someone remarked, had always manufactured more history than it could consume locally.

The dispossession of Palestinian Arabs by European Jews was an historic injustice. By the measure of the twentieth century, during which we had learned to harness technology to our blood lust, it didn't come close as a crime. Stalin said that one death was a tragedy but a million deaths was a statistic. Mao was probably the greatest criminal of the century. But if Palestine wasn't a crime, it was an injustice. Britain and then America had wrung their hands in attempts at evenhandedness, but that didn't lessen their guilt.

The Zionists had originally approached the Ottomans with a scheme for Jewish settlement in Palestine and the offer, in return, to deal with the unruly Arabs in the region. But the last thing the Sultan needed was another minority in the Empire, especially a stiff-necked one. So, the Zionists turned to the British government with the same scheme, and the same offer, and this time it fell on fertile ground. They first turned down Uganda before settling on what they really wanted, Arab Palestine. The Balfour Declaration in 1917 may have been issued by His Majesty's government, but the rest of Europe—even the notoriously anti-Semitic Russians—signed on. The Germans issued their own version, but it was too little, too late.

Some have suggested that the Balfour Declaration was about competition for the allegiance of "international Jewry." There was a desire, they said, to keep Russian Jewry in the war after the Revolution, since so many of the Bolshevik leaders were Jews. Or, it was an attempt to wean the wealthy and influential German Jewish community from the German war effort. Others said it was intended as a reward to the Zionist leader and director of the British Admiralty Chemical Laboratories, Chaim

Weizmann. He had developed a synthetic alternative for potassium nitrate, thus freeing the Empire from dependence on distant Bengal for that crucial feedstock of gunpowder. In one of the zanier episodes in the relationship, Weizmann would later propose that Palestine become the laboratory in which the grains of East Africa would be turned into fuel, thus freeing the Empire from dependence on Persian Gulf oil.

But all of these reasons missed the simple fact that Balfour, typical of his class and time, was raised on, among other things, the King James Bible and he believed in what he was doing. "Zionism," he said, "is historically important. It is more important than the desires and prejudices of 700,000 occupants of that ancient land." Here was no nonsense about "a land without a people," only a call to historical inevitability. But the 700,000, by now grown to several million, thought otherwise. They would protest against what the great democracies had in store for them, but they were helpless against the juggernaut. Ronald Storrs, the military governor of Jerusalem after the war, probably put their dispossession most succinctly:

> Palestine, hitherto a Muslim country, has fallen into the hands of a Christian power that has announced, on the eve of its conquest, that it intends to turn over a large portion of the country for colonization purposes to a nowhere very popular people.

The Balfour declaration was hedged about with qualifiers, designed to assuage the consciences of the drafters and ensure the irreconcilable rights of the parties, and it took an army of lawyers to understand what it meant. But to some, like Vladimir Jabotinsky, its meaning was clear. Armed with this clarity and a degree of ruthlessness, they moved to establish a Jewish state in all of Arab Palestine. Ariel Sharon, a latter-day Jabotinsky with the same clarity of vision and the same ruthlessness, is simply trying to finish the job.

Palestine today is a perpetual source of shame to Arabs, a reminder of their powerlessness in the face of the West. We in the West may see the injustice of Palestinian dispossession, the double-standard we apply to Israel and the Arabs, and an American foreign policy governed by the dictates of a powerful pressure group. The Palestinians see only their helplessness, and the desire is not so much for justice as for power, the power to inflict the same hurt that has been visited on them. Every Israeli incursion only deepens the sense of powerlessness and feeds the desire for revenge. As long as the wound continues to fester, it will be fertile ground for extremism and violence. Moderation hasn't worked and the example of Afghanistan showed that extremism did.

America used Usama bin Laden and the Islamic holy warriors to settle an old score with the Soviets: they bled us in Vietnam and we would bleed them in Afghanistan. In the Afghan program in the early nineties, it seemed that most of the people we worked with were either retired special-forces officers or Vietnam veterans. When the war with the Soviets was over and the score was settled, we walked away. In Pakistan, we left behind a culture of drugs and Kalashnikovs that the feudal society was unable to resist. The mess in Afghanistan was even greater, and the story of the civil war, followed by rise of the Taliban needs no retelling. The solutions to the multiple problems—Palestine, Pakistan, terrorism, extremism—were many and would tax the best efforts of everyone to solve them.

Jobs wouldn't do it alone, nor would democracy. Talk about jobs and democracy suggested that Arabs and Muslims were aggrieved only because they didn't have better things on their minds. If those 'Asiris had good jobs in the Jidda oil refinery, the thinking seemed to be, the Palestinian problem would go away and the rage would abate. There *was* a demographic problem in Sa'udi Arabia and a combination of the highest birthrate in the world and declining oil revenues meant that the per capita GDP of the Kingdom had dropped from something like $20,000 in the 1980s to $7,000 in 2001. Young Sa'udis needed jobs, but the threat of their idleness was to the ruling family, not to the West. It was true that only a kind of tribal democracy or consensus, the *majlis*, acted to check the behavior of the Al-Sa'uds. It wasn't democracy as we knew it and probably never would be.

But these weren't the real reasons for the rage. They were religious, linked to the underlying sense of powerlessness and fed by a deepening sense among Arabs and Muslims that it was all part of a Western plot. And Afghanistan, again, was a model. Islam had been great in its pristine state and a return to the practices of those early days—the dress, the beards, sequestration of women, cutting off of hands—would make it great again. Afghanistan showed that pious Muslims could defeat a superpower, and that was heady stuff. Usama bin Laden drew on a deep fund of resentment in the Arab and Muslim World and had asserted his power to inflict pain. We were going after bin Laden, but we also had to do something about the fund. With Palestine, Kashmir, Chechnya,

Mindanao, the Moluccas, and Bosnia still festering, and the Taliban quietly regrouping, the problem remains with us today. It will probably get worse before it gets better.

Saturday morning would be, as they said in the tour business, "free time." I was looking forward to a harbor cruise, and made the brisk, ten-minute walk to Market Square where the boats were tied up. The harbor was lined by open-air stands selling everything from the pelts of Arctic foxes to freshly-caught salmon. Sun Lines was leaving shortly and the hour and a-half cruise would take us first east, past the Suomenlinna Fortress, then north to the "beautiful canalroute," before returning west to the square.

A light rain was falling as we pulled away from the pier. The commentary was in Finnish, German, and English and we learned that Finland had been dominated as recently as the early part of the twentieth-century by Sweden. That was what the fortress was all about. The Swedes had been followed by the Russians and up until the collapse of the Soviet Union, Finland trod a very careful path between East and West. Passing the island of Santahamina we were reminded that the Finns had once been Norsemen. It was a bit of a stretch, thinking of these pacific people as the fierce Varangian guards employed by the Byzantines. The Finns were also Scandinavians, and Scandinavia had been the socialist utopia in the 1960s, the wave of the future. But then there was the Bofors scandal: they sold arms and paid bribes just like everyone else. It was followed the assassination of Olaf Palme, considered a secular saint until it was learned that he had presided over a Swedish nuclear-weapons program. Now, the Scandinavian utopia was in serious financial straits.

The "beautiful canalroute" was less beautiful in the mist. After landing, there was still time before the afternoon program, so there was time to see the Orthodox Cathedral across the square. It was very Russian, with gilt pillars, gilt candelabra, and gilt icons, some inlaid with pearls. Shrines with slender candles lined the nave. The contrast with the Lutheran church over the hill couldn't have been greater. There, the vanilla-colored walls were entirely bare, a testament to the simplicity and sobriety of Protestantism. Except the Finns drank nearly as much as the Russians. It was puzzling.

In the afternoon, there would be another special treat, and another Finnish passion: a hockey game. DNA sponsored a team, HIFK in the premier league, and they would be playing at a local arena. We sat in the equivalent of a skybox, plied with the usual DNA buffet and drinks. The teams were warming up when we arrived, and the sound of pucks slamming into boards echoed through the half-filled hall. The program consisted of 300 pages of statistics and color photos, including a section on what seemed like scores of cheerleaders. They needed that many because they were posted every ten yards or so throughout the arena. When a goal was scored they would leap up and dance mechanically, shaking their pompons, before resuming their conversations.

By game time, the arena was nearly full. It seated about 15,000 and the air was electric with anticipation. The game soon settled into a tactical test. It was not North American hockey and, while it was rough, there weren't any muggings. HIFK scored first and the cheerleaders did a little dance. There was a television monitor on the wall behind us, but it was still the odd experience of a game without instant replay. I wondered how we had done without it before. Later there was another score, but I was distracted and missed it. The stands erupted and cheerleaders danced, but how or by whom the goal was scored was impossible to say. It was history, the chapter closed forever. It seemed a problem worthy of Stephen Hawking. At halftime, we saw the crowd up closer and they were just a happy, slightly belligerent group of males enjoying themselves. HIFK won the game 3–2. We left with souvenir American ball caps.

Dinner that night was at Sundmans, another one of the best restaurants in Helsinki. On this last night, the talk turned to politics and the Finns and Jordanians discussed a solution to the ongoing crisis in the Middle East. Oslo had been a Scandinavian initiative, although all Oslo got the Palestinians was a doubling of settlers in the West Bank. Pekka, the lawyer, wondered if another attempt couldn't be made. At least they were addressing the root cause of the problem.

The next day would be a noon departure for Amman. This time we would go through Amsterdam. In the departure lounge the discussion of the night before resumed and Pekka seemed to be serious about a new initiative. The Finns had high-level representation in the EU and maybe something could be done. The flight took us southwest over Stockholm and then Copenhagen to Amsterdam. After a two-hour layover, it was KLM to Amman. But midway in the flight a change was announced: the airline would not allow the crew to overnight in Amman, so we had a crew change in Cyprus. We landed at Larnaca and spent an hour on the ground before we were airborne again. We flew south before reaching Egyptian airspace and then, probably somewhere over Sinai, turned north towards Jordan. We arrived at three a.m.

A defining moment had perhaps been reached in the Middle East. For all of his brutality and cunning, Saddam Hussein had it right during the first Gulf War when he called for a comprehensive solution. He sent Tareq Aziz in a fur hat to Moscow to initiate the "negotiations." We rightly told him that there was nothing to negotiate until the Iraqis withdrew from Kuwait. After the war, we tried—halfheartedly and under Scandinavian pressure—to facilitate a comprehensive solution. But the settlements made that impossible, just as they were intended. They were an insurance policy against "land for peace." They grew under Democrats and Republicans, Labor and Likud, and we wrung our hands and called them "unhelpful."

But they were, in fact, illegal under international law, violated the fourth Geneva Convention, defied more than a score of UN Security Council resolutions since 1979 and were contrary to the stated policy of every American administration since Carter. Still they continued their inexorable growth. Now, if we dealt resolutely with the settlements—and didn't sell Israel out, but sold the Palestinians in—and demonstrated that we treated everyone in the region equally, America might win broad-based support in the Arab World for its war on terror. It seemed obvious. A solution to the Palestinian problem was only a necessary, not a sufficient, condition for dealing with the extremists. That would require a long-term strategy, and the first thing would be to show the *integristes*, the fundamentalists on both sides, that their solutions didn't work. After that, it would be a long, slow process. It was a problem for everyone with a significant Muslim population, and that meant everyone in the region, the Israelis included.

The difference between 'Asir and 'Asir again reminded me the remark of one of our staff in Cairo. When our Palestinian marketing specialist reported that she'd forgotten her camera at a fruit stand in the Fayoum, he had said "That's the trouble with the Palestinians. You blame everything on the juice." It was witty, but contained a deeper truth. The key would be to remove this reflex, and after all was said and done, it was that. It was true that the return of Gaza and the West Bank—22 percent of the historic Palestine Mandate—was not justice, but it might end the overwhelming sense of powerlessness. Then, they could move on to the serious business of nation building.

8

Morocco

AFTER MORE THAN TWENTY years in the Arab World, it would be my first real visit to North Africa. I did spend fourteen months in Niger in the Sahel, and from Niamey Casablanca had only been a few hours away by air. It was a natural stopover on a flight to New York if you could escape the long arm of Air France. With Air France, everything went through Paris. However, the stay Niger had been too brief to take advantage of Morocco or much of anything else. But in March of 2002 there was a workshop for telecommunications regulators in Rabat that would include representatives from much of the Muslim and Arab world. From Jordan, we would fly to Casablanca with a stopover in Tunis. The first leg, slightly north of west would be over Crete and then Malta before the Mediterranean—the White Middle Sea in Arabic—narrowed to the choke point north of Tunisia. Then it would be slightly south of west to Casablanca.

The total elapsed time, with the refueling in Tunis, would be about seven hours, the equivalent of a transatlantic flight. In the air, there was almost nothing to see until the approach to Casablanca when the countryside appeared below in a patchwork of green cultivated fields. From the air, it looked a little like Europe, perhaps Provence. This first impression of Morocco was of a place different from the rest of the Arab World. It would linger at immigration and customs, where the formalities were handled with alacrity and efficiency by officials in civilian clothes. But outside the airport the look of Europe quickly faded.

We were met by a driver who would transport us the 110 kilometers to Rabat. The trip took between an hour and-a-quarter and two hours, depending on traffic. The road was potholed and it was half-an-hour before we reached a motorway. But it gave us a chance to see this part of Morocco up close. On the ground, it looked like East Africa or Central Asia. The color of the soil ranged from reddish-brown to ocher, and the green of the ground cover was primarily wheat, although the fringe along the road was dotted with white and blue flowers, wild artichokes, yellow mustard, and blood red poppies. The flowers were a product of the recent rains. It was the same scene we had seen the week before, driving up the King's Highway in Jordan. As in Jordan, the heavy rains had been welcome here after several years of drought. And also, as in Jordan, the green would soon turn to brown.

The red soil resembled that of East Africa, but the poverty and paler faces gave Morocco the look of Central Asia. There appeared to be none of the big Mercedes and BMWs of West Amman or even Cairo, but instead odd little French things, Peugeots, Renaults, and Citroens. That was when there *were* cars, because most people were on bicycles or walking. The rain may have been welcome but it was a trial for those on foot because the wet soil caked their feet and many of the gowns were spattered with mud. There were a few fully-veiled women, but most wore the *hijab*, the simple wimple that was increasingly adopted by the urban poor in the Muslim world. The men were generally in western dress, although a few wore the *burnous*, the hooded gown that gave them the look of inquisitors or members of the Klan. Children tended cattle in the fields, the latter looking like Holsteins, not the buffalos of Egypt. There was rubbish everywhere and clusters of single-story, concrete-block houses, without the antennas or satellite dishes that sprouted from even the camps in Jordan. Everything seemed dank and wet, and exposed metal was rusty. The population of Morocco was thirty million and counting, and the per capita GDP was about $1,200, less than that of Egypt. This was not a wealthy country.

Mohammed drove aggressively and it was surprising how many did not. Most of the other drivers made their unhurried way along one of the two lanes that constituted the typical road. He approached them at speed, flashing his headlights and passing when possible. His cruising speed seemed to be 150 km or 90 mph, and without these laggards we would have been in Rabat in less than an hour. Arabic was his first language and French his second. He understood very little English. We communicated in Franco-Arabic, although the Arabic was a constant adventure. The accent was difficult even for the Jordanians. Moroccans dropped vowels and combined consonants together into the combinations that were the enemy in Egypt. Part of the problem was the mixing of the three languages, French, Arabic, and English. Since the "ch" was used in French to express what the "sh" did in English, it often led to confusion. American commentators at first called the Moroccan miler Hicham al-Gorrouj "Hickam," like the airfield in Hawaii.

After an hour, we reached the outskirts of Rabat and entered the city through what I later learned was the *Bab al-Hadd*, or Sunday Gate. I noticed it because the next morning *Le Matin* carried a picture of the same gate and the same road and the same day on which we had entered, covered by a sea of humanity. Two million people, ". . . toutes categories sociales, professionelles et obediences politiques confondues . . ." had gathered in Rabat in solidarity with the Palestinians and in protest against Israel and America. The Israeli army had just been loosed in the occupied territories and public rage from Morocco to Bahrain, and everywhere in between, was palpable. The demonstrations were sometimes violent. The police in Jordan and Egypt, our two allies in the region, kept a tight rein on the crowds and cracked heads where necessary. America gave both countries money, but very little in the way of the political cover the regimes needed to placate their people.

We were booked into the Tour Hassan, originally built in 1914 and renovated most recently in 1999. It was now part of the Meridien chain. Inside, it was a riot of friezes, frets, arches, squinches, carved stucco, and inlaid wood. The staff were dressed in the jackets, pantaloons, and fezzes of the French era. Reproductions of Orientalist art, much of it done in Morocco, papered the walls. It was how European artists captured what they saw in the mysterious and sensual "East," although Rabat was west of every European capital except Lisbon. But that was the least of the contradictions in our fraught relationship with the Muslim world. The colors and shapes and sights of that world—from Andalusia to Samarkand—had always fascinated Europeans, while they were sometimes puzzled and sometimes repelled by the habits of the people who lived there. Both the fascination and the repulsion persisted to this day. Dinner was a *couscous royale* in the hotel restaurant. In spite of the authentic Moroccan setting it was a disappointment, consisting of a great pile of semolina topped with overcooked vegetables—zucchini, carrots, sweet potatoes, and cabbage.

In the middle, hidden by the vegetables, lay a couple of pieces of gray, fibrous meat. I think it was mutton. A hot sauce made it palatable.

The next morning was the scheduled opening of the workshop. But the desk clerk knew nothing about it. He suggested we check at the Hilton, a ten-minute cab ride outside the walls of the old city. We did and learned that the American delegation, concerned about the demonstrations on Sunday, had spent the night in Paris and would arrive that afternoon. The entire workshop—the venue and the delegations—had been moved to the Hilton since it was thought to be safer. The opening would be at three o'clock. So, there was time to see a little of the city. Rabat was one of the imperial cities of Morocco, and had first served as the capital under the Almohads in the twelfth century. But its importance waned in favor of Fez, and it wasn't until the Alaouites in the seventeenth century that the city reemerged from obscurity. When the French established the protectorate in 1912, Rabat was again chosen as the capital. There was much to see, ranging from the walls and gates that dated from Almohad times down to the twentieth-century architectural and urban planning contributions of Hubert Lyautey, the first French resident-general.

The Tour Hassan was centrally located within the ramparts of the city, some of them Almohad and others of later provenance. The most concentrated area of interest seemed to be in the *medina*— the "city" in Arabic—to the north and so I hurried west, past the modern cathedral of Saint-Pierre (it was closed and locked) before turning north on Avenue Mohamed V. That led past the parliament building towards the *medina*. This relatively modern section of the city had the look of parts of Cairo, with uneven and poorly-maintained sidewalks, nondescript office buildings, and spreading banyans. The trees were cleaner than those in Cairo, probably because of the recent rains. On Avenue Mohamed V, cheap clothing shops lined the street up to the Andalous ramparts. In the evening, young men would be hawking individual garments on the street corners.

Beyond the ramparts we passed into the *medina* proper where the street narrowed and the number of pedestrians increased. It was a replica of Fatimid Cairo, a bustling, open-air museum where the old mingled with the new. There were barbershops, patisseries, fruit vendors, bookshops, stands selling dried fruits and nuts, and shops selling traditional Moroccan dress, one suspected to Moroccans. Some butcher shops displayed haunches of beef, dripping redly onto the pavement below. But most carried the staple fare of the poor: sheeps' heads, sheeps' feet, duodenums, stomachs, and ilea. Outside, hung pink lungs with the windpipes still attached, looking oddly plastic and high-tech. The street was thronged with people, from the very young to the old and feeble, the latter picking their careful way through the melee. As usual in the poorer parts of the Arab World, they were still shown what little deference could be spared in the competition for space and resources.

Beyond the *suq*, on the boulevard Af Alou, the scene suddenly changed, emptied of both crowds and shops. To the west was the Bab al-Alou, and several hundred yards in the distance to the east, sat the brown pile of the *Qasbah* of the Oudaya. The approach to the *Qasbah*—North African for a fortified area and citadel—was flanked by the walls of the *medina*, penetrated by narrow alleys that snaked away to the south. Entrance was once through the Bab al-Oudaya, a magnificent monument to Almohad architecture in ocher monochrome. The single massive horseshoe arch was surrounded by carved fretwork and floral patterns delicately let into the surface. It was everything the busy gimcrackery of the hotel was not. It had been turned into an art gallery and inside were a couple of indifferent guards and walls with covered with canvas panels, over which great swaths of color had been abstractly applied. There was no one else there.

Back outside, access to the *Qasbah* was now through a smaller archway perpendicular to the larger gate. It led via a narrow winding passageway to the main street of the fortress, which was lined on both sides with shops and houses. The scene was simplicity itself: a sea of whitewashed stucco with pale-blue wainscoting, the arches around the doors painted a dark yellow. In the distance was a minaret in what appeared to be typical North African style, a massive, rectangular brick structure, with incised friezes and fretwork like the Bab al-Oudaya. It was different from the simple Ottoman tube, or the classic Mamluk minaret of Egypt with its square, octagonal, and circular sections topped by an open gallery. I later learned that the mosque was the Jamaa al-Atiq, the oldest in Rabat, and dated from 1150. The minaret had been restored in the eighteenth century.

Fifty yards beyond the mosque the street led onto an open, unpaved square, perhaps seventy-five yards on a side, where boys were playing football. Lining the square was a low wall, and below the wall lay an entirely unexpected sight: the muddy flow of the *Oued* (or *Wadi*)

Bou Regreg, looking like the Guadalquivir at Cordoba. And beyond the mouth of the Bou Regreg lay another unexpected sight: the Atlantic Ocean. Now, it all made sense, the weathering of the ramparts of the city, looking like the effect of salts from within or without, and the pervasive rust on exposed metal surfaces. Rabat was on the Atlantic, and now there was a whiff of sea breeze. It was as if, like some figure in the *Thousand Nights and a Night*, I had been picked up in the desert and somehow set down by the ocean. In a sense, I was.

There wasn't time to see Sale, on the opposite shore of the Bou Regreg. It had been a den for the corsairs, originally Andalusian, who preyed on Christian shipping well into the seventeenth century. But the scene was already different from the Mediterranean with, first, the breakwater, and then the great ocean beyond. It suggested an outward, not insular, orientation. The Iberians were the first to venture into the open ocean in sailing ships, not the oared galleys that lasted in the Mediterranean into the eighteenth century. It looked like these transplanted Iberians had followed suit. Between the ramparts of the *Qasbah* and the ocean was a cemetery filled with salt-encrusted headstones. I walked down to the beach with a group of French teenagers in the same assortment of T-shirts, baggy shorts, and ball caps worn backward as their American counterparts. Surfers in wet suits met us coming from the direction of the *Medina*, but the waves didn't look very impressive.

By now it was time to return to the Tour Hassan and prepare for the workshop. Then, another taxi ride took us over what would become familiar ground over the next five days, via the Avenue Roosevelt or the Place Abraham Lincoln to one of the several gates of the city. Then it was southwest, past the massive Chellah necropolis, to the Hilton. The taxis were little blue things, locally manufactured, and the metered journey cost the equivalent of an American dollar. The spelling of "Taxi" in Arabic, using the velar *tah*, was a source of amusement to the eastern Arabs at the workshop. They would have pronounced it "Tahksi."

The American delegation had finally arrived and it was impressive, including the chief researcher and the former chief technologist at the Federal Communications Commission (FCC), a lawyer and former aide to the chairman, and heads of foundations dedicated to the spread of telephony and the Internet. We would learn over the next several days that these Americans, whatever their position or experience—and in spite of a tendency to meet all objections with recourse to economic orthodoxy—were unfailingly polite, modest about their achievements, and interested in the problems of others. They were an example of the best we could offer to the rest of the world.

The opening session, where each delegation gave a description of the state of its regulatory regime, revealed a wide disparity among the attendees. Jordan, Morocco and, to a lesser extent Egypt, were in the lead, with functioning regulators that awarded licenses, approved equipment and tariffs, monitored quality of service, and assigned spectrum. The others—Algeria, Tunisia, Yemen, Lebanon and Afghanistan—were in the early stages of liberalization and could only look forward to steps the others had, haltingly, taken. The proceedings were in either French or English, with simultaneous translation into the other language. That was a problem for some—the Yemenis and the Afghans in particular—who spoke neither language very well. But this was a positive gathering. American emphasis on the market and the private sector, without adequate attention to the necessary regulatory checks, often left emerging economies prey to their most unprincipled elements. Russia was an example of how *not* to do it. This was an opportunity to help the Middle East and North Africa—MENA—countries get it right.

We adjourned at six o'clock and returned to the Tour Hassan in time to catch the evening news. Colin Powell had arrived in Rabat, beginning his leisurely grand tour of the Mediterranean basin. The next day it would be Egypt—or was it Jordan?—before inexplicably returning to Spain to show solidarity with the UN and the European Union, organizations we didn't normally care much about. Attendees said this was designed to give Sharon time to finish his dirty business, and I think they were right. With Powell, the words were often compelling but the substance was just as often lacking. He was in danger of becoming the Shimon Peres of the administration, lending the color of reason to its deliberations. But when the hardheaded men made the decisions, he was nowhere to be found.

There was another reason why Powell was of interest to the workshop, and that was because his son, Michael, was chairman of the FCC. It was a sensitive issue, and I recalled the driver in Egypt who said that if George W. Bush won the election, "don't ever talk to me about sons again." The Middle East was the land of sons—Bashar al-Assad, Qusay Hussein, Seif al-Islam Qadaffi. Even in Egypt Mubarak, who had not named a vice president, was said to be grooming his son Gamal as his successor. As Jordan looked for candidates to staff its own more independent regulator, modeled on the FCC, wags suggested that someone ask the foreign minister if he didn't have any sons. In Jordan, it was called *wasta*—or influence—a practice the ministry was doing its best to root out.

The next morning the workshop began in earnest. The Afghans arrived late, and I met them at the break. At the ITU conference in Geneva in 1999, they had been Taliban wearing local dress, *shalwar khamees* and *Chitrali* caps. These men were Tajiks from the Panjshir, in western suits and ties. They had flown from Kabul to Islamabad, to Karachi, to Abu Dhabi and then on to Casablanca. The leg from Amman had taken us over seven hours, so they must have been in and out of airports for most of the last twenty-four. Afghanistan needed more than a regulator. It needed everything—infrastructure, operators, and subscribers. Other countries needed less but, in terms of regulation, the issues covered on the first day were important. They included problems faced by all liberalizers: the organization of a regulatory authority and the establishment of the rule-making process. Jordan was going through a critical stage, even though their regulator had been in place for five years. The mobile system was in its infancy and the players in the sector—the ministry, the regulator, the operators and the courts—were all feeling their way as the relationships solidified. Our hope was that everyone would recognize that the ministry made policy, the regulator enforced it, the operators fell into line, and the courts intervened only as a last resort. A recent court decision in Jordan had set an important precedent that this was, indeed, how it worked.

Part of the problem with new regulators was that they were dealing with powerful interests, often used to exercising monopoly power. Monopolies always played hardball, especially if they had even more powerful foreign operators as partners. So, a new regulator was often reluctant to act, and the reluctance was understandable. Not only were the issues difficult, often more political than technical, but mistakes could be made. In Jordan, we used the energy crisis and the California State Public Utility Commission as an example. Regulators didn't always make the right decisions, and sometimes they made disastrously wrong decisions, as they had in California. But they had to decide, and no decision was often worse than a bad one. The "public" part of public utility regulation was also important, and the consultation process used by the FCC was a model to be emulated. The Jordanian regulator had placed laws, license agreements, and other important information on its website, although the information was largely static. And the ministry had published a policy—consultation paper on *its* website. These were good first steps, but the tepid response from the public showed that much more remained to be done.

With regard to independence we were surprised to learn that the FCC was answerable to Congress and that the Congress could, theoretically, order the commission to reverse a decision. We were all aware of the need for regulatory independence, but the Americans made it clear that no regulator was ever entirely independent. It was with subjects like this, with nuance, that the gap between the presenters and the audience appeared. It was something that even simultaneous translation couldn't bridge. I wondered how the translators dealt with the statement from one of the Americans:

> Our authority comes from the statute and we are constrained by the statute . . . we must pay heed in the first instance to our statutory constraints.

Translation, really simultaneous interpretation, was provided only between French and English. That left those most comfortable in Arabic or Dari out of the discussion. Simultaneous interpretation was a special skill requiring knowledge of several languages and an ability to think on your feet, often anticipating what a speaker would say. At lunch, one of the two translators in the booth, a professor at a local university, was enthusiastic about his work and provided a rapid French version of the above statement. United Nations translators said that it took 25 percent more words to say the same thing in Arabic as in a Romance language. But it also seemed to be true of the French, or maybe that was because the French speakers tended not to ask questions, but instead deliver long existential dissertations.

That night on the BBC there was more bad news from Ramallah, Bethlehem, and Jenin. Since the press was banned from most areas, we saw only pictures of Israeli armor moving into place. Some of the tanks and armored personnel carriers displayed the inverted "V" used by the allies during the Gulf War. That was presumably to distinguish them from the Palestinian armor. Sharon said that Israel was at war, and it was. The great, ponderous machine was moving into place. Armored bulldozers—those preferred instruments of Israeli policy—were again preparing to smash though flimsy houses and shops, leaving in their wake a trail of twisted cars, broken water mains, and severed power-cables. Just as with the "Grapes of Wrath" and other examples of Israeli tough love, the message seemed to be: let the Palestinians rise up and throw off the leaders who had brought them to this pass. Just as before, it would fail. If anything, Arafat, washing out his underwear in his besieged headquarters in Ramallah, was stronger than ever. In fact, his old enemy Sharon had thrown him a lifeline.

The next morning, breakfast was a buffet in the Tour Hassan. Despite the impressive interior, the service left much to be desired. The coffee came in a small pot, enough for a cup and a-half, and when I asked for another pot, it seemed to pain the dour maitre d'. He later had a very public row with one of the waiters. Then, a little *tahksi* carried us through the center of the city and out through the southeastern gate before turning southwest towards the Hilton. This gave us a view of almost the entire, mile-long expanse of the southern ramparts of the city. They had been built by the Almohads in the thirteenth century and were being restored around the gates. They were maybe forty feet high and red or brown in color, depending on the height and angle of the sun. Where the restoration was complete, the surface was smooth. But elsewhere it had been eaten away by salt or wind and had the rotten look of the walls around old San'a. To our left, the Chellah necropolis lay over an area of many acres. It was the resting place of another ruling dynasty, the Merinids, and the guidebook said that behind its imposing walls lay an oasis of peace and tranquility.

The second day of the workshop covered rural access, competition, interconnection, licensing, and liberalization. The day was long and the material was dense. Rural connectivity was a key in most developing countries. Teledensity, or the percentage of fixed telephones in the population, was in the single digits or low teens in most of the countries in the room. But given family size and urban concentrations, the situation was actually better than it appeared, and most people in the cities probably had access to a telephone. Rural areas were harder, being more expensive to reach, but a new technology was helping. The mobile revolution—and it was truly a revolution—had made the traditional measure of teledensity meaningless. Mobile infrastructure was cheaper and easier to deploy, and mobile telephones were changing even rural peoples' lives. There had been a lot of hype about the "information revolution," but this was for real. Prepaid cards, accounting for 90 percent of subscriptions in poor countries, meant that people could ration their scarce dinars or pounds or dirhems. If anything, the hype was understated with the mobiles.

The remainder of the day was devoted to ways to make it all happen, to reach more people with affordable service. There was one subject, however, that got everyone's attention: voice over the Internet protocol, or VoIP. The technology, in which voice was packetized and treated as just another form of data, could also change poor peoples' lives. It was cheaper than traditional voice and, in spite of the fact that it had been banned in many developing countries, it was easy to deploy, hard to detect, and widely used. The question was why anyone would want to ban it. The short answer was that it threatened the business plans—some said the viability—of developing-world telephone companies. They were heavily dependent on the hard currency earned in the old, bilateral accounting system that governed traditional voice telephony. Not only that, but the Internet had reversed the financial flows. Instead of sharing the revenue with developed world operators, those in the developing world now had to pay for access to the backbone. It was a recipe for financial disaster, with the associated problems of lost public-sector jobs and dwindling hard-currency reserves. It was so controversial that the organizers put off discussion of VoIP to the roundtable on the last day.

Dinner was a Moroccan special at the Tour Hassan, sponsored by the organizers. It consisted of relays of flakey meat-filled pastries, fish, and chicken. After the couscous of the first night, it restored the reputation of Moroccan cuisine. The meal also gave the presenters and delegates a chance to exchange views on an informal basis. The Americans I spoke to were cautious, but some were as disturbed as the Arabs at what was happening on the West Bank, and at our incomprehensible reaction to it. Unspoken was the issue of the influence of AIPAC on the conduct of our policy in the Middle East. Americans hotly denied it and we, alone, refused to recognize what everyone else in the world had taken for granted for years. We still ritualistically referred to the "perceived" American bias towards Israel, but George W. Bush had taken off the gloves and everyone knew it was more than a perception.

The third day was devoted to spectrum management. It dealt with the competing needs for the radiofrequency spectrum, by definition a scarce resource everywhere. It was a sensitive issue in the Arab World, given the authoritarian regimes and the need of the security services to monitor transmissions. The military and security people generally took whatever spectrum they needed, and what was left was allocated to civilian use. But, again, the difference with the United States was less clear-cut than we thought. After September eleventh, national security needs for spectrum had become more urgent in the United States, and the competition for what little was left was more intense. The problem in the Arab World was that the line between military and civilian use of spectrum was not clear. That was a concern for potential investors, who would not risk their investments without the assurance that the resource was managed on a rational and predictable basis. The general remarks on spectrum were followed by discussion of the third generation, or 3G spectrum.

The developing world had the advantage that it could watch and learn from the developed world before it took the leap. The experience with 3G to date, with ruinous amounts paid for spectrum in Europe, financial crises in operators, questions about the usefulness of the service, and suggestions that it would be years before 3G generated positive cash flows, made the decision an easy one. The day ended with a visit to ANRT, the Moroccan regulator, in its modern and spacious facilities. In spite of lingering institutional conflicts in the relationships between the government, the regulator, and the operator, Morocco was well on its' way to establishing a sound regulatory framework. Unfortunately, much of the authority of the Moroccan regulator existed in the person of the sitting director-general. And because of what was said to be a lack of political support, he was leaving, on his way to a position with the World Bank. When I called a week later for advice on a numbering issue, he was already gone.

The fourth day of the workshop would deal with a few remaining telecom issues, such as cost-based pricing, before taking up the Internet. Costing was a complicated issue, compounded by the fact that the developing world generally lacked the accounting systems that would make the cost basis work. The Internet was the real threat to the old order and, although it hadn't yet had the revolutionary impact of mobile phones, it was well on its way. The presenter cheerfully told us that it was a "disruptive, invasive, and insidious technology," this to an audience in the most thoroughly-controlled region in the world. But he was right, and to the credit of the Jordanians, the Internet was not filtered there. They had looked into filtering and come to the conclusion that it was expensive, invasive, subjective and, ultimately, ineffective. Instead, individual or institutional responsibility would be encouraged. That was not to say that chat rooms were not monitored for political content, and sites were occasionally shut down.

Jordan had taken the right decision and was even looking to the Internet as a partner in its e-Government efforts, although that required Arabic content. The population of the country was young, with over 70 percent under the age of thirty. At nearly 90 percent, literacy in Jordan was probably the highest in the Arab World. Jordan was an exporter of IT talent to the region, particularly to the Emirates. But more than 60 percent of Jordanians were Palestinians, and the "troubles" across the river represented a constant threat to the stability of the country. The combination of Islamist sympathy, political disenfranchisement, simmering resentment, and unemployment made for a potentially explosive mix. The young king had identified IT as the engine that would transform the country. It was a gamble, but he really had no other choice. Everyone was trying to ensure that it worked.

The final session, a round table discussion, dealt with VoIP. It was not a theoretical issue for telecom authorities, as it threatened their traditional cash flows. Everyone agreed that cheaper international calls were good, but that the transition would have to be carefully managed. It was here that the Americans seemed to miss the point. The Internet had reversed traditional financial flows, and was now sucking resources out of the developing world and *into* the developed world, particularly to the United States. Economic orthodoxy taught that consumers were better off with lower prices, but the consumers weren't the only ones involved. Developing-world telephone companies were sources of vital hard currency. They also employed thousands—too many thousands—but simply turning them into the street in an environment of high unemployment was not an option. Preaching orthodoxy was easy if you were the immediate beneficiary, and the Egyptians suggested that there was a bit of hypocrisy at play here. Fortunately, no one brought up steel, where the United States had just imposed an implicit tax on consumers in order to protect its own inefficient producers. The final act of the workshop was a clarion call for better communication and collaboration among regional regulators. The cynics tried to forget that Arab unity had been an elusive goal for at least a century.

The return to Amman was uneventful. After Tunis, the flight path seemed to be direct to Amman, over Israel and the occupied territories. In the first few days after September eleventh, KLM had forbidden its aircrews to overnight in the region and, on a flight from Amsterdam, we had stopped in Cyprus for a change of crew. Then, it was a long detour south to Egyptian airspace before turning north to Jordan. Now, with Jenin directly beneath us, we flew on. It was a measure of the indifference of the world to the events taking place below. That would have to change before a solution was forthcoming.

Jordan

9

The Hejaz Railway

THE FLYER READ "THE famous Marriott train ride goes Hawaiian this year." It was a charity affair, sponsored by Prince Ra'ed bin Zeid, and a chance to ride on the Hejaz Railway, known largely in Jordan for its part in the "Great Arab Revolt" of 1916–18. In the West we called it simply the "Arab Revolt," its greatness having become controversial, like so much else in the Middle East in the postwar world. The railway connected the Turks with remnants of their peninsular empire and it was the only link with Medina when the Sharif of Mecca raised the tribes against them in June of 1916. After the war, it was the primary reason why Amir Abdullah chose Amman as his capital, rather than Salt, the larger and more cosmopolitan—if that was the word—city to the northwest. In 1921 Amman was a sleepy provincial town, home to many of the Chechens and Circassians who found their way to the Middle East after the Russians emptied the Caucasus of much of its Muslim population with their victory over Shamil in 1857. But the railway ran through Amman, not Salt, and the die was cast. By the early twenty-first century, the city had grown to a population of nearly two million and was home to two Jordanians in five.

Construction of the railway had been financed by the Ottomans through pious subscriptions of individual Muslims, including deductions from the salaries of Turkish civil servants and members of the Ottoman army. But it also attracted contributions from the likes of the Sultan, the Shah of Iran, and the Khedive of Egypt, as well as from the sale of honorifics such as *pasha* and *bey*. Intended to facilitate *hajj* traffic, it was designed to transport pilgrims from Damascus to Medina—and eventually to Mecca—in a fraction of the time previously required. The overland traffic from the west consisted largely of two streams. One flowed from North Africa and Egypt, passing through the Sinai to Aqaba, and then down the western seaboard of the Hejaz—Wejh, Yanbu, Rabegh, and Jidda—before turning inland to Mecca. The other started in Damascus, having previously concentrated the streams from Turkey and the Balkans, and flowed southwards to Ma'an, Batn al-Ghul, Mudawwara, Tebuk, and al-Ula before reaching Medina. From Medina, it was south over the old *Darb al-Sharqi* (or "Eastern Route") to Mecca. Pilgrimage had always been a trial, a test of strength and faith by Muslims able to muster the will and the finances required to make the journey.

The seaborne flow, largely from India and Java in the East Indies, was arguably less rigorous, although the dangers of the sea were not to be dismissed. But the overland journey had particular dangers and discomforts. A *hajj* caravan consisted of a polyglot horde of horses, camels, mules, donkeys, and human beings. Some pilgrims rode in elaborate litters slung to the sides of camels, or suspended between two animals, front to back. Others rode the animals themselves. But most pilgrims were on foot and the toll on shoe leather and, ultimately, on feet must have been fearful. They traveled at a camel's pace. A loaded animal made between two and three miles per-hour and, assuming a fourteen-hour day and 1,000 miles from Damascus to Mecca, that meant over forty days on the road.

Somehow, they all started and stopped at the same time, the halts announced by the report of the little brass cannon carried for that purpose. It was useless for much of anything else, certainly defense. There were the inevitable problems of sanitation, water, food, and fuel for tens of thousands of human beings and animals. Most pilgrims preferred to be in the middle of a mass that extended for miles from beginning to end, and meandered on either side for scores of yards. That was because outriders and laggards were tempting targets for the Bedouins through whose territories they passed, not to mention the danger of falling ill and being left behind. Burckhardt tells of a belief among the Bedouins that men who fell were carried off by female demons "in order to enjoy their embraces," city dwellers being choice morsels for those used to the "food of the desert." In reality those who died along the way were hastily buried in shallow graves, scratched out of the unyielding soil. The resting places were soon visited by carrion eaters, winged and otherwise.

Throughout the nineteenth century most caravans were escorted by a ragtag band of cutthroats armed with a motley collection of weapons and led by an *Amir al-Hajj*, for whom the assignment was a plum. That was because they carried valuable goods, including the *kiswa*, the covering of the *Ka'aba* embroidered by tradition in a workshop in the Citadel in Cairo, as well as the stipend to be paid to the custodians of the Holy Places. The latter was elaborately calculated and paid to extended families depending on the responsibility and degree of consanguinity.

The weapons were not needed if the agreements with the Bedouins were kept. That was because the *hajj* caravan also carried money and cheap cloth—much of it beginning in the eighteenth century from France— with which to buy them off. The system generally worked. When it didn't, a problem could bring traffic to a halt. Jabarti tells the story of Hussein Bey in 1760 who decided to put an end to the extortion by these wild men. He succeeded, but only briefly. Calling their chiefs to a parley where the usual bribes would be paid, he surrounded them with his *Maghrabis* and killed them all. Later, on his return to Cairo, he carried their heads triumphantly through the Bab Nasr. In the short term, it may have been gratifying, but it stopped western *hajj* traffic until a new agreement could be worked out with the wild men and their equally wild women. So, the overland route had its dangers, but the greatest problem was the simple fatigue associated with a difficult journey of a thousand miles through a harsh and unforgiving landscape. Because of variance in the lunar year, the *hajj* could take place in the winter when the influence of the sun was moderated. But at the height of summer it could be a torment.

So, pilgrimage truly was a trial of strength and faith. When the caravan returned to Cairo there would be the thrill of anticipation as the great stream flowed into the area around the Birket al-Hajj, the lake whence it had set out several months before. There were ululations and tears of joy as family members greeted the new *hajjis* who had completed the pilgrimage, one of the five pillars of Islam. But there were also lamentations and bitter tears shed over those who had not withstood the rigors of the journey. The railroad would significantly reduce the mortality, if not the extortion. A train could still be derailed and the loss of life could be considerable, particularly if the Bedouins were not compensated for the loss of their yearly stipend. But the greatest gain would be in the relative comfort that would allow more people to safely undertake a journey of four days instead of more a month. Purists might have argued that it would thereby become too easy, and the faith not sufficiently tested. But the gain in the lives and souls of the faithful outweighed such considerations.

The railroad was conceived during the nineteenth-century railroad boom, although construction didn't begin until 1901 and the early twentieth-century. In addition to the hostile terrain and the equally hostile Bedouins, there were engineering challenges, including varied topography, the ever-present risk of flash floods, and occasional steep gradients. From the vicinity of Mudawwara to Batn al-Ghul the rise was nearly one in five. The work was completed in 1908, largely by German engineers and Turkish soldiers, and the railroad was soon transporting 30,000 pilgrims a year to Medina. Still, it was a fraction of the hundreds of thousands who converged on Mecca every pilgrimage season. The line from Medina to Mecca was never built, the Sherif viewing the extension as a transparent Ottoman attempt to interest themselves to an even greater degree in his affairs. It probably was.

When the Turks joined the Central Powers in November of 1914, they were ensconced in Medina. There, despite the outbreak of the Arab Revolt in the Spring of 1916, they remained for the duration of the war, supplied primarily by the railroad. Lawrence says it was intentional on the Arabs' part, with the Turks invested in the city and reduced to eating the transport that would otherwise have made them mobile. Having lost Mecca in the first Arab rush, they could not, or would not for reasons of prestige, abandon Medina, the second city of Islam. If the Turks came out and fought, they would have been a formidable force in the field. It was estimated that 20,000 Ottoman troops were tied up during the war, defending Medina and garrisoning the railway. If loosed on the Gaza-Beersheba front, they might have tipped the balance in the Turks' favor. Even if defeated they would have been a burden and the allies would have to feed them in prisoner-of-war camps. So, the train-wrecking enterprise by a few intrepid British and French sappers and their Arab auxiliaries was designed to keep the Turks in place and the railroad functioning, but just barely. Like much of the *Seven Pillars of Wisdom*, it all sounds a little too pat.

But pat or not, the demolitions were real and the reputation of the experts among the Bedouins grew proportionately. When Newcombe ran out of explosives, the wild men said, he would gnaw the rails with his teeth. Hearing the report of the spectacular explosions on the railway, one tribe requested "Send us a Lurens and we will blow up trains with it." But Lurens, or Lawrence, was only one of several train-wreckers, and not even the principal one. "This isolated picture throwing the main light on myself," he said in the introduction to the *Seven Pillars*, "is unfair to my British colleagues . . . My proper share was a minor one, but because of fluent pen, a free speech, and a certain adroitness of brain, I took upon myself, as I describe it, a mock primacy." Garland, Newcombe, Peake, Davenport, and Hornby, some of them professional sappers, worried the rails on a full-time basis. Lawrence, a novice but a quick learner, set mines when it served immediate ends, such as testing a new kind of explosive device or isolating a station prior to attacking it.

He eventually became proudly economical in his use of gun cotton. The early experiments involved spectacular explosions that sent pieces of engines or tenders hurtling scores of yards into the desert. His later efforts were directed at bridges, and they weakened the spans just enough so that the Turks were forced to complete the job of demolition before they could begin to rebuild. But most of the seventy-nine bridges Lawrence claims to have destroyed were not like the large structure that crossed the Syrian Yarmuk gorge at Tel al-Shehab, the scene of a spectacular failure in July of 1917. Rather, they were small series of arches and spandrels that crossed *wadis* and allowed occasional floodwater to pass without carrying away the elevated rail bed. Their destruction required the labor of days, not weeks or months, to repair, carried out largely by Serbian work parties. They can still be seen today to the east of the Desert Highway, the older spans delicate structures of two, three or four arches, made of dressed limestone blocks. The newer ones are square, functional concrete.

After the war, the heavily damaged section of the railway between Ma'an, 130 miles south of Amman, and Medina was never repaired. North of Amman it continued in service. In the early twenty-first century, a train still ran to Damascus twice a week, at the equivalent of $3.50 a ticket and taking twelve hours to make the 150-mile trip. With modern highways, not to mention air travel, it was only the very poor or the occasional history buff who rode the rails. But at least one investor was eyeing the railroad right-of-way as part of a fiber-optic cable route linking the Mediterranean with the Red Sea.

The flyer, distributed by the Marriott in Amman, stated that the adventure would begin on a September afternoon in 2002. The price (JD forty or about fifty-six dollars) covered transportation, dinner, and drinks. That meant a bus ride to Um al-Hyram station, the train journey to Dab'a castle, the buffet dinner, and a bus ride back to the Marriott. I looked for the castle, but it was not among the eighteen castles listed on the map provided by the Jordan Tourism Board. And it wasn't listed among the palatial residences in the excellent *The Umayyads, the Rise of Islamic Art*. But someone on the train later said they thought it was near the Queen Alia International Airport, and that would have meant southeast of Amman. After nightfall, a waxing crescent moon appeared to the right of the train and remained low in the sky for the duration of the trip. That would have been to the west, so it looked like we were going south after all. The schedule said the train trip would take about two hours. I don't think we ever built up speed to much more than twenty miles an-hour. So, with the frequent stops, we were probably about twenty-five miles to the southeast of the city. That would have put the castle in the rough vicinity of the airport.

The bus ride took twenty minutes, through an area of east Amman that had once been a Palestinian camp and was now grown into a neighborhood. It was the usual hive of small shops that announced where the owners had come from: Haifa and al-Khalil, or Hebron, Nablus and al-Quds, or Jerusalem. It didn't look affluent and was characterized by that bane of modern Jordan, clusters of young idle males. When we arrived at the station the train was waiting, the locomotive already getting up steam and belching connected puffs of black smoke. A tender and seven little wooden cars were lined up behind it. The rolling stock was odd, the cars looking old from the outside, but covered with cheap particleboard panels in the interior. They were festooned with Heineken posters, inside and out. The locomotive was an impressive bit of railroad technology, great four-foot wheels and all the linked mechanical parts that made it work. But it burned fuel oil, not the coal or wood of the original engines. The Turks' appetite for wood to feed the locomotives had meant the denudation of much local forest during the war. Here, the second car was a tanker that carried fuel oil.

Kella, al-Ula

From the platform of the engine, seven feet above the ground, the fireman invited me aboard. He showed me a few gauges, and explained the function of each. The firebox was open, glowing redly. He said that the engine was "maybe fifty years old." That could mean anything, but it was clearly not one of the original machines. We had seen several of these in the roundhouse at al-Ula, just north of Medina in the late 1980s. Al-Ula had been a station on the Hajj route before it became a railroad station, and Doughty had spent several weeks there on the journey that was later memorialized in *Travels in Arabia Deserta*. The *kella*, or fort, where Doughty stayed was still there, and both it and the station were close to Meda'in Saleh, or the Cities of Saleh, the Nabataean tombs that were the southern equivalents of Petra. But where Petra was an enclosed city, these stood up starkly out of the desert. The locomotives then had been much smaller and more primitive than this monster, and one bore the information that it had been built in the Rhineland in 1906.

Meda'in Saleh

The history was interesting but it soon became clear that this was not going to be a journey into history, but a party. In the first car, there were now many passengers: a young Jordanian couple, a pair of Australians, a Brit, two Swedes, a South African, a German, and an Indonesian. Most of the foreigners worked at embassies and most had that slightly adventuresome streak and world-weariness that characterized expatriates in general. We talked briefly about September eleventh and most were uncomfortable with the demonization of the region. The Marriott staff were dressed in Hawaiian shirts and shorts and were clearly enjoying themselves. Music was turned up so that conversation became impossible, it being a firm belief of Middle Easterners that the sum of all Westerners' desire is disco music turned up at the highest possible level.

At six forty-five the whistle sounded and the train pulled out of the station, accompanied by Chuck Berry on the sound system. Traffic was stopped at the first crossing as this odd phenomenon, an old train plastered with Heineken posters, blaring 1960s rock music, and carrying obvious expatriates in the early stages of inebriation, crawled by at twenty miles an-hour. The people in the cars, most of whom probably had places to go and things to do, watched bemused. Some even waved. It was a touching characteristic of Jordanians, and of Arabs in general, that they indulged us with as much humor as they did. The staff passed out handfuls of hard candies, individually wrapped and we threw them to children watching the train pass. The music became more modern as we progressed south, from the Everly Brothers and Elvis, to Nat King and Natalie Cole, then to things I didn't recognize. By the time we arrived at the castle, they were playing something with a chorus of *al-salaam aleykum* over and over again, a kind of Islamic disco refrain. The car wasn't large, but the seats were arranged on the sides facing the center so that there was room in the middle and it soon filled with dancers. The Indonesian was indefatigable, making elaborate gestures with his hands that looked very Asian. A steady stream of waiters somehow made their way through the melee carrying trays of canapés.

The outskirts of southern Amman soon passed and for the next couple of hours we crawled over the hardscrabble landscape of central Jordan. The fields rose and fell in long swells, most of them covered with stones and little else. Occasionally there were signs of cultivation, stubble where there had been wheat earlier in the year, or walled enclosures containing neatly-tended olive trees. Families sat in clusters around the infrequent houses and watched this odd procession pass. We stopped for several minutes, for no apparent reason, at one crossing and it was soon lined on either side with honking cars and trucks. Then the sun went down and the only things visible were the new crescent moon and the lights of the highway several miles away to the west.

We arrived in the vicinity of the castle at about nine o'clock. The flyer said that there would be a walk of a kilometer from the train, and the winding path was marked by hundreds of candles in foot-high paper enclosures set a few feet apart. When we were near, someone threw a switch and Qasr Dab'a loomed up suddenly out of the blackness. Dab'a meant female hyena, the original denizens of the place. It looked a little like the Qasr al-Kharrana we had seen several weeks before, but without the circular towers. Here the familiar brown limestone was covered with signs of the sponsors: the Marriott, Royal Jordanian Airlines, National Car Rental, Pepsi, Heineken, and HSBC. Tables were arranged on one side of a central path with the buffet on the other side. In front of the castle was an elevated dance floor. We were going to rock the night away here in the middle of the desert, and the next several hours were filled with food, drink, and music. When I left at midnight, stumbling 100 yards over an unlit *wadi* to the bus, they were still hard at it, the Indonesian still in the lead. The last bus was due to leave at one o'clock in the morning.

So, the famous train ride had been a disco party with a little local color thrown in. As for history, the Marriott had transported us about as far back as the era of Johnny Mathis. One of the organizers said that there were roughly a hundred on the train, down from twice that many the year before. At forty JD a head, that was only 4,000 JD, or about $5,600. After the food, drinks, and transportation, not to mention the labor of lighting every one of those hundreds of candles, that can't have left much for the Al-Hussein Society for the Rehabilitation of the Physically Challenged.

10

The California Zephyr

AS THE PACE OF the march to war in Iraq quickened, Americans in frontline states the Middle East were thought to be at risk and were evacuated. Located strategically between Iraq and Israel, Jordan had always been in the thick of things, acting at different times as a dumping ground for refugees, a springboard for guerilla action, a buffer between the combatants, and occasionally as an actor in the little tempests that had wracked the Middle East over the last six decades. In 1948 the Jordanian Arab Legion had been the only Arab army to hold its own, taking East Jerusalem and the West Bank. In 1967, in spite of Israeli warnings to stay out, Jordan had come in, and in the process lost both. For King Hussein, the ultimate survivor, it had been a choice between the territories and his throne and he had chosen the latter. It was a matter of survival for the Hashemites, largely against the Palestinians who constituted 60 percent of the population of the country. Black September in 1971 was a further reminder that the King was prepared to deal forcefully, not to say ruthlessly, with opposition to his rule.

In 2003 the throne no longer seemed at risk but the new king, Abdullah, was widely felt to be too close to the West and too distant from his people. His first formal speech from the throne had caused general embarrassment, not to say derision, because of his poor command of Arabic. The informal and technologically-savvy style that made him a favorite of the likes of Bill Gates and John Chambers threatened to leave his impoverished and politically neutered people behind. The latest *intifada* in Israel and the West Bank was covered on a daily basis in Jordanian newspapers and grisly pictures of the aftermath of Israeli assassinations of activists, not to mention house demolitions and general acts of oppression, were a regular feature of Jordanian life. The people were seething with resentment of Sharon and the Americans who backed him, having now abandoned all pretense of neutrality in the conflict. The effect of F-16s, Abrams tanks, and Apache helicopters being used against Arabs by *Americans* instead of Israelis was something that no one could predict. The George W. Bush administration had reportedly canvassed the regimes in the region and was assured that they would not object if we went after Saddam. But that ignored the feelings of the people, for whose benefit, at least rhetorically, we were so solicitous.

There had been talk of waiting out the war in Cyprus, where we would have been closer to the client. But that was ruled out and in late February 2003, a month before the outbreak of the war, we flew to Washington, DC where we would gather and maintain contact with the client by e-mail. We left for the airport at night in a driving rain. After a career when international flights were always economy, for some reason we flew business class, although the first leg on KLM to Amsterdam was in a 737 and only marginally better than the back of the bus. An African-American across the aisle was wedged into a bank of three seats where his bulk spilled into the adjoining seat and his size-sixteen shoes spent most of the time in the aisle. When we got off in Amsterdam I saw why. He was about 6'-6" tall and must have weighed well over 300 pounds.

In the business class lounge at Schipol what appeared to be an Indonesian or Malay busied himself on the other side of the bank of seats where we were sitting and I thought that it was probably a good thing that he had the opportunity to work in the Netherlands, even if it was only as a cleaner in the airport. The remittances sent back by expatriate workers were important to countries like Indonesia, Malaysia, the Philippines, Sri Lanka, and Pakistan. Then I realized that he was a passenger. The cleaner was a uniformed Dutch lady.

Northwest restored the reputation of American carriers: the seats in the DC-10 were wide and spacious, there was plenty of room between them, and the middle-aged stewards and stewardesses were pleasant and attentive. The pork in mustard sauce sounded better than it tasted. The announcements from the cockpit were in that characteristic American idiom: "please return to your seats before we DO begin to make our descent," "please be sure that your seat belts ARE securely fastened," "please remain seated until we HAVE come to a complete stop." Most of us did.

The captain was his usual, slightly-deferential American self: "For those of you who have not returned to your seats, we would request that you to do so now. And please remain seated until we have pulled up to the terminal building and come to a complete stop." What he really meant was to say "God dammit sit, sit down NOW and stay in your seat until I tell you to get out of it."

It was a constant problem, that American reluctance to tell other people what to do. In spite of alleged American unilateralism, we struggled mightily to convince our American consultants that other people were looking for direction, not consultation. I remembered the retired American executive who was advising Telecom Egypt on marketing. He had years of experience with Bell South and began his presentation to Egyptian senior management by asking for their opinions on the subject. It was a struggle to move the process along and afterwards the Egyptians wondered: "Why is he asking us what *we* think?" they said, "*He* is the expert." But even in Jordan we were not very successful in spite of a direct order to our consultants to tell us what they would do if they were all-powerful. The advice that eventually came was sound, but so full of qualifiers—it was only an example of what *might* be done, they couldn't tell other people what to do, etc., etc.—that its effect was lost. The British were much more direct. The minister would eventually ask "Why do I feel so much more confident with British than American advice?" Nuance was fine, but with developing world clients it was better to be direct. It should be said that this worked with telecommunications marketing. How they lived their lives was another matter.

It is always slightly alarming coming back to the United States from the Middle East. For all of the opportunity it offers, America is a tough place and arrival at an American airport must be a shock to a foreigner. This time the driver of the cab into the city was a Pakistani, but not from Lahore for a change. There were about 300 licensed Pakistani cab drivers at Dulles, he said, and only three were not Punjabis. He was originally a Kashmiri and seemed offended when I asked if he was a *mohajir*, or refugee from India. He left Pakistan in 1988 and never looked back. Pakistan was unbelievably corrupt, even more so than we knew who saw only small corruption on a daily basis. We talked about the Himalayas and the Karakorams and he said he had done a tour of the mountains before he left since he knew he would never go back. America was a land of opportunity and he had no problems after September eleventh.

It was hard to figure Washington DC. Mason and Dixon had placed it among the slave states, although just barely. But there was something about the city that seemed to make it sleepy and southern. Maybe it was the taxis—Lincoln Continentals seemed to be the favorite vehicle—all driven by men of color. I later learned that most of them were from Ethiopia. The only movie I saw in ten weeks in the United States was *Gods and Generals*, heavily subsidized by Ted Turner and featuring himself, gap-toothed and grinning, in a cameo appearance as a Confederate officer. It was a view of the Civil War from a Virginia perspective, with Robert Duvall as a very believable Robert E. Lee. But the most memorable part of the movie was the beard of the man who played Stonewall Jackson. Burton said that the only people who *ought* to wear beards were the Persians, and it was that kind of beard, full and dark and rich. In spite of an investment of what was said to be $80 million of Turner's own money, the movie dropped like a stone off the charts.

We stayed at the Embassy Suites at 22nd and N, a prime location and within easy walking distance of our temporary offices on Connecticut Avenue between L and K. It was an odd combination of a family hotel and what appeared to be the destination for every Russian delegation that came to Washington. Americans ate huge quantities at the complimentary breakfast, but the Russians really tucked in, probably because it was free. Weekends allowed us to see the city, and its layout seemed more like a European than an American city. Georgetown was nearby, but was a little too cute. The walk to the Mall, then across the river to Arlington and the Iwo Jima Memorial took half a-day. At the memorial, bigger than I imagined it, an older American was lecturing a Danish family about the men who raised the flag. They hadn't all been marines. Iwo Jima seemed the epitome of American willingness to sacrifice in war, and cost over 26,000 dead and wounded in twenty-six days of fighting. The American public accepted casualties in those days. The searing experience was still written on the faces of the hard men when they gathered fifty years later on the island to remember, captured in a PBS special. They hadn't forgotten, and some were still consumed with hatred of the Japanese. Back across the river I felt strangely disembodied at the Vietnam memorial, maybe because my experience in war couldn't compare with Iwo Jima. There had been the same Pacific and the same brilliant blue of the water, the same naval gunfire and lingering smell of cordite after the guns had gone silent, the same Asia with its damp, humidity, and odor of stale urine, even the same tough marines in Danang. But it somehow wasn't the same and I was almost apologetic as I listened to the guy in the Legionnaire's cap who talked about the war. I didn't tell him I had been there too.

The walk to the office in the morning took me by Borders at 21st and L, where the window featured the latest books on our latest war. I remembered watching the long, drawn-out election of 2000 at the Marriott in Amman, vaguely pulling for Bush if only because it seemed to promise a return of Bush-Baker and a willingness to get tough with the Israelis. For all of his reported empathy with the Palestinians, Clinton had presided over a doubling in the number of settlers on the West Bank. Sure, George W. Bush was a marionette, a front man for his father's friends, and I remembered being surprised as the recounts went on that he actually seemed to *want* to take charge. He would have to do better as President than in the debates, where he did a kind of rope-a-dope, letting Gore take his best shots with a curious passivity. He was hard to take seriously with those small eyes set too close together in his head, the narrow, pursed lips not to mention the narrow mental bandwidth, the short fuse, the slightly pigeon-breasted strut, arms akimbo. He seemed puny. If the father, for all of *his* verbal gaffes, was slightly larger than life, this man seemed smaller than life.

But there in the window at Borders was *Bush at War* by Bob Woodward. Having responded to September eleventh by launching a few smart weapons at a medieval enemy he was now being treated like a reincarnation of Hannibal or Alexander the Great. Then, there was Bernard Lewis, working overtime in his self-appointed mission as interpreter of Islam to the West. The sins of the son probably shouldn't be visited on the father, but the fact that Lewis's son had been the head of policy analysis at AIPAC, concerned about not leaving "fingerprints," would forever detract from his father's credibility. When Bernard Lewis talked about the importance of guilds in medieval Islam, I listened. I wasn't so sure about the rest of it. The piece in the *New Yorker* after 9/11 had been simple-minded and tendentious. And *What went Wrong? Western Impact and Middle Eastern Response* was a series of pre-9/11 lectures to which a post-9/11 conclusion had been hurriedly appended, and it asked the wrong question.

The problem seemed to be that the great intellectual and technological accomplishments of the Arabs, achieved when the Arab and

Muslim World was most open to outside influence, had been replaced by a latter-day focus on a pristine simplicity and closing of the door to the outside world. But the Arabs and Muslims had always been early and enthusiastic adopters of technology, and the twenty-first century was no exception, with amplified muezzins and the computerized Qur'an. Some of the most popular screen savers were verses from the Holy Book. The real problem seemed to be that Islam had a monopoly on virtue, and so had not developed the kind of give and take that the modern political world required. It had withered not technologically but politically. Even that put it poorly: it really hadn't withered at all, nothing had gone wrong. It simply hadn't gone *right*. Islam didn't have a tradition of the separation of church and state and was struggling with a system of governance that was not up to the demands of a complex world.

Most of the models that had been tried in the region—royalty, socialism, parliamentary democracy, even military autocracy—were borrowed. Like most borrowed things they didn't fit very well. Personal virtue enjoined on the believer had always been more important than institutional virtue in Islam. As Olivier Roy had argued, there was no Muslim philosophy of government other than to be guided by an ethical man, although the Iranian model was an attempt to reduce it to some form of system. But if it was politically primitive, the emphasis on individual ethics had made a significant contribution to the world, and when the all-encompassing Muslim order had finally passed, for all of its shortcomings, we would be poorer for its passing.

Then, there was Dore Gold's *Hatred's Kingdom: How Sa'udi Arabia Supports the New Global Terrorism*. Gold seemed the embodiment of the unhealthy relationship between the United States and Israel. Was he an American or an Israeli, or was he both? Whatever he was, his book seemed the opening salvo in the next war, this one on Sa'udi Arabia. Described in reviews as the "former Israeli ambassador to the United Nations," a "Middle East expert" and an "internationally known Middle East strategy expert," Gold purported to open the eyes of the average American to the hatred of America being taught in the schools of Sa'udi Arabia, our supposed ally. What the average American probably didn't know was that Gold was born in 1954 in Connecticut. His religious Zionism led him to emigrate to Israel in 1980, where he became, of course, "a specialist in the relationship between Israel and the United States." He was an early and vociferous enemy of Oslo and became Netanyahu's advisor on foreign affairs. He remained close to Sharon. *Hatred's Kingdom* disappeared from

Borders after a couple of days, either because it sold out or because—like *Gods and Generals*—it didn't sell.

Daniel Pipes was there as well, and *The Rushdie Affair, The Novel, the Ayatollah, and the West* had been reissued. He made a show of objectivity, of trying to cover fairly all points of view, but there was something about Pipes that was shrill. He had an agenda. The one book that didn't seem to have an agenda was Samuel Huntington's *The Clash of Civilizations and the Remaking of the World Order*. That was odd, given the apocalyptic title. But Islam was seen honestly for what it was, a philosophical, ethical, and aesthetic phenomenon of historical importance. That was in the past, but it would be a major force in the future as well, its greatest opportunity—or threat, depending on your point of view—being demographic. Muslims were multiplying faster than the rest of us, and that gave them an energy, and their predilections an urgency, that we lacked. On reading the book the clash seemed less dramatic than advertised, and contained the perfectly reasonable notion that future strife would probably be on the margins of the world's great civilizations. Islam was surely one of them.

I didn't see anything by Edward Sa'id. In his long championing of Palestinian rights, Sa'id was for years the only voice that took up the cause in the United States. For this he paid the price, even in circles that supposedly valued academic freedom. But for all of his courage Sa'id was an intellectual bully, his offerings were often intemperate, and they tended to be too personal. Maybe that was because he *was* such a lonely voice. The latest piece I had read was an account of his life, growing up in neighborhoods like Zamalek and Ma'adi in Cairo. *Out of Place, a Memoir*, was fascinating, but it had redefined the genre of autobiography as revenge. Fu'ad Ajami, too, was on the back shelves, not up there in the front window with *Hatred's Kingdom*. It was odd that when writers in English wanted a reasonable "Arab" who spoke the truth about mainstream Sunni Islam, they would have chosen a Lebanese of obvious Iranian extraction, born a Shiite, and an intellectual émigré who had left Beirut and lived for the past several decades in the United States. That isn't to say that he wasn't often right, and he appeared to be the only Middle Easterner who had actually read Burton and Lawrence, Doughty, Palgrave, and Niebuhr. *The Arab Predicament* told some hard truths about the region. But Ajami paid the price for his honesty, and was regarded by many Muslims as fundamentally unsympathetic to his own kind.

More authentic, perhaps, was a collective effort that resulted in the *Arab Human Development Report* by UNDP. There, a group of Arabs from the region had attempted to redress what they believed were the shortcomings of the accepted assessment methodology, and had gerrymandered the model to dramatize the Arab deficit. Most conspicuously gone was "per-capita GDP," replaced by, among other things, "womens' access to power." The combined effect was a dramatic drop of the Arab World in the rankings, although the process produced some absurdities. Now ranked number fifty-seven, well ahead of any Arab country surveyed, was the Solomon Islands. I looked at the CIA website and learned that this island grouping in the South Pacific was characterized by deforestation and soil erosion and most of its coral reefs were dead or dying; that the lingua franca was Melanesian pidgin with English spoken by only 1–2 percent of the population; the government type was "parliamentary democracy tending toward anarchy;" and the legal system was English common law "which is widely disregarded." There were no elections, and severe ethnic violence and an empty treasury had led to "serious economic disarray, indeed near total collapse." Information technology was supposed to be the savior in the new, networked world, but the piece included the cheery note that in the Solomons "telecommunications are threatened by nonpayment of bills and the lack of technical staff, many of whom have left the country." Presumably men and women had equal access to the chaos that remained.

The United States itself would fare poorly if measures like "availability of affordable health care," "incidence of violent crime," or "mean difference between highest and lowest levels of compensation" were included. The point was that you could probably produce any result you wanted. But the UNDP report was an honest effort to address the problems of the Arab World, and it was immediately picked up by friends—and others—to show that "we" had been right all along. The Arabs themselves were finally getting it. After all the talk about weapons of mass destruction and defiance of UN resolutions, the invasion of Iraq was designed to impose the kind of change called for in the report, in the process making the country an ally of Israel and America. But no one paid much attention to the statement in the introduction that the occupation of Arab lands was the most serious impediment to development in the region.

I had always wanted to take the train across country. But it was expensive and time consuming by comparison with air travel. I had driven several times from the east coast to California and it was a good way to get to know the country, but it was even more expensive and time-consuming than the train. The last time, in 1969, it had taken a week of steady driving and with gas, motel stays, and food cost about $1,000. Here, the train fare was $733, one-way from Union Station in Washington DC via Chicago to Emeryville, just north of Oakland. One-way air-tickets, I later learned, were much less expensive. But it really wasn't a question of expense. No one took the train because it was more economical, although I did meet a traveling salesman who took Amtrak from Chicago to Omaha because it *was* cheaper. By the time he calculated the drive to the airport, the lost time with increased security, a rental car, and a motel stay, he was better off on the train. And with a laptop he could be productive along the way.

But the real reason to ride the rails was to see the country. Amtrak online offered several accommodation options, including First Class Superliner standard, deluxe, and family bedrooms. I chose the standard bedroom and it was adequate, with the same efficient—some might call it cramped—use of space as aboard a ship. For a couple much beyond middle age, the deluxe would have been necessary. If nothing else, the climb into the upper bunk was beyond the ability of anyone who qualified for membership in AARP. By the time I bought the ticket I was already a veteran of Amtrak online, having virtually commuted up and down the east coast between Washington DC and New York city. Reassuringly, the answer came back a few seconds later that the reservation was confirmed: the "Capitol Limited" would leave Union Station, Washington at 3:10 p.m. on March 17, 2003. We would arrive in Chicago at 8:30 the next morning. The "California Zephyr" for Emeryville would leave at 2:15 that afternoon. The transcontinental trip would take us through the three major mountain ranges in the country, the Appalachians, the Rockies, and the Sierra Nevadas. We would cross the major rivers, from the Potomac in the east, the Mississippi and the Platte in the midwest, to the Humboldt and the Sacramento in the west. With the exception of the Gulf of Mexico we would touch all the major bodies of water in the United States, including Chesapeake Bay, the Great Lakes, the Great Salt Lake, and San Francisco Bay. And we would transit the major geographic areas of the country—the east coast, the Midwest and the west. That left out the south, but Washington DC seemed to be in the south and that's where we started.

The metro from Dupont Circle was convenient to Union Station, but not with several bags, and I took a cab. If all Dulles cabbies were from Lahore, in the city they all seemed to be from Addis Ababa and this man was no exception. He had been an engineer in Addis, he said, and was reduced to driving a cab here. But there was something wrong on the afternoon of March 17 and as we headed from Washington Circle east towards Union Station we found the way blocked at every intersection. Police directed the flow northwards and the combined detours soon produced gridlock. So, after a half-hour ride that took us only a few blocks from where we started, the cabbie dropped me at the Farragut North Metro station. I descended into the bowels of Washington—the metro lies deep under the city—and emerged fifteen minutes later at Union Station.

It seems that Dwight Ware Watson, a tobacco farmer from Whitakers, North Carolina, had driven his tractor into a shallow pond at Constitution Gardens and refused to budge. He claimed that he and other farmers were being driven out of business by unfair government policies:

> 'I don't give a damn no more,' Watson said. 'If this is the way America will be run, the hell with it. I'm out of here. I will not surrender. They can blow my ass out of the water. I'm ready to go to heaven.'

Pictures showed him wearing an army helmet with American flags "bedecking" the tractor. The Washington Post carried the story and the standoff ended a day later. But while it lasted many streets were closed, creating a massive traffic jam. Watson also said he was against America's pending war with Iraq and March 17 was only two days from the unleashing of the first wave of shock and awe on Baghdad. So, officials were understandably nervous about a crazy man allegedly armed with explosives a few blocks from the White House. Everything seemed to have ended peacefully, but on the train, we didn't know. Aside from the *Toledo Blade* early the next morning and the *Chicago Tribune* and *The New York Times* later in the day, we wouldn't see another newspaper or a newscast before we reached California. That wasn't much of a loss because a month of exposure to media in America had left the impression that the quality of public discourse—except on public television—was abysmal. Everyone seemed to have about thirty seconds to get whatever it was off his or her chest, and they most spent their time shouting at one another.

On the train, the standard bedroom looked smaller than on the website. It was actually two seats facing one another along the long-axis of the car, separated by about four feet of legroom. The seats folded towards one another to make the lower bunk. The upper bunk was a single unit, folded up during the day. Both seats had an unobstructed view from the window. It was not the kind of thing you would think about beforehand, but depending on the direction and the time of the day, one side of the train was preferable to the other. The direct sunlight could be uncomfortable. The porter, a young African-American kid named Jamil wearing civilian clothes, directed me to my berth on the north side. On the Chicago-Emeryville leg I was on the south side and that meant the sun all-day long.

At 3:10 p.m. the Capitol Limited pulled out of the station, on schedule. That was a good sign, but it wouldn't always be so. There wasn't much daylight left as we headed northwest to, first Rockville, Maryland and then Harpers Ferry, West Virginia. Harpers Ferry arrived at 4:21 on schedule, and we sat on the siding for ten minutes above the Potomac—or was it the Shenandoah?—while passengers boarded the train. John Brown had seized the arsenal here on October 16, 1859 before being captured by Colonel Robert E. Lee. The raid led indirectly to the Civil War. It wasn't until the Vietnam War a hundred years later that the country went through a similar experience of discord and dissension. Ronald Reagan led us out of *that* national funk but, in the process, we had become uncritical cheerleaders of whatever military adventure the executive branch drummed up. There had been Tripoli, then Grenada, Panama, the Gulf War, Kosovo, Afghanistan, and now Iraq. They were all sold as patriotic acts. The enemy this time seemed to be France. The scenery after Washington had been anything but uplifting, a bleak landscape of leafless trees, pools of stagnant water, mobile homes, and rusting cars. There was almost no snow on the ground. Dinner was in the dining car with an elderly couple from Miami on their way to Cleveland. Cleveland came at 2:28 the next morning, passengers awakened out of a sound sleep by the jolt of mail cars being added at the end of the train.

At 4:30 we reached Toledo and Jamil wrestled a heavy bundle of newspapers on board. Bush had given Saddam his forty-eight-hour ultimatum the night before and *The Blade*, published by Block Communications Inc., was unsparing in its view of the justifications for this particular war. Commenting on the furor caused by the remarks of James Moran the week before, the editor opined:

> Whose National Interest?
>
> Mr. Moran isn't alone in linking White House policy to Israeli interests . . . Stanley Heller, American and Jewish, has tried to keep his co-religionists honest for 20 odd years. In a Feb. 20 article at *www.antiwar.com*, he cited 'rabid neo-cons'—some of whom, 'like Richard Perle, Douglas Feith, and David Wurmser, actually worked for Israeli think tanks writing grand papers for (Likud) Prime Minister Netanyahu on how the U.S. and Israel should take apart and reconstruct the Middle East,' and who now hold key roles in shaping U.S. foreign policy . . . We owe it to Americans to tell them the whole truth, that part of the war drive is being fueled by a wacko militarist clique from Israel and its interlocking bands of American Jewish and Christian supporters' . . . He is not alone. In the Feb. 23 (London) Observer Ed Vulliamy, and in the March 3 San Diego Union-Tribune, James O. Goldsborough speak in the same vein—of America's first religious war and proponents' visions of empire . . . Is this what Americans want? Does Israel have too strong a hand in our foreign policy, or do its interests merely coincide with ours? Americans won't know without open discussions free of political repercussions and stifling accusations.

Breakfast came somewhere between South Bend and Chicago with a traveling salesman who represented a software company. But he was middle-aged, not a techie, and could just as well have been peddling petroleum products or magazines. He spent most of his time on the road and loved his work, about which he talked without interruption. The upcoming war was a distraction:

> They don't understand us and we'll never understand them.

At eight thirty-five we passed a sign announcing a measured mile and we covered it in fifty seconds. Fog off the Lake Michigan shrouded the early morning view until, with a shock, we met another train. The relative speed of 140 mph meant that the two joined and then parted very suddenly, and so close that we could have reached out and touched the other cars. Then as we approached Chicago there were extensive rail yards and names on the cars that would become familiar over the next four days: Conrail, Norfolk Southern, Procor, Seaboard System, The Nationwide Boxcar Pool, Winchester & Western Railroad, Central Soya, Union

Pacific Fruit Express, Golden West Service, Cyro-Trans, Union Pacific Chilled Express, Western Fruit Express, and Santa Fe.

The numbers I had seen were not current, dating from the 1980s. But railroad usage was probably not the kind of thing—like mobile tele-density—that changed on a daily basis, and so they were still broadly representative. Among the top-ten railroading countries in the world, in terms of the length of track the United States was the leader. In fact, at 322,000 miles we had more track than the other nine—Russia, Canada, India, China, Australia, Argentina, France, Germany, and Brazil—*combined*. In terms of freight service, measured by ton-miles, we were second to Russia, although that had probably changed with the collapse of the Soviet Union. There were still pullmans, open-top hoppers, covered hoppers, gondolas, tank cars, vert-a-pac cars, two-level rack cars, boxcars, refrigerator cars, stock cars, and cabooses sprinkled among the above, but most were either containers themselves or carried containers, and rail transport was a major economic factor in America. But in terms of passenger service, we weren't even close. In first place was Russia, with over 206 million passenger miles. The figure for the United States, 6.5 million, was miniscule, less than half of that of Romania in tenth place. If anything, the development of low-cost and regional airlines over the last two decades had probably reduced the number even farther. Amtrak ran a chronic deficit and depended on Congress for a lifeline to stay afloat.

At nine twenty there was a switching problem and we were delayed, backing then inching ahead with a series of uncomfortable lurches. Finally, we were underway again and pulled into Union Station, Chicago at ten forty-five a.m., an hour and fifteen minutes late. Union Station was cavernous but welcoming and after a few minutes I found the metropolitan lounge for first class passengers. That meant those of us with sleeping car reservations. It was like a business class lounge at the airport with comfortable sofas, chairs, coffee, and juice. Outside, it had been the usual train station bustle, with an unending stream of announcements for connections to Madison, East Lansing, Detroit, Columbus, Cincinnati, and Milwaukee. Rapid transit service to O'Hare left from the subway station at the corner of Clinton and Congress streets, two blocks south of Union Station. In the last month, we had taken every kind of public transportation in America, from cabs to buses to the New York subway, from Amtrak to airport shuttles to the Washington metro. For a country that supposedly didn't have much of a public transportation network, it was surprisingly convenient and efficient.

Chicago was its usual muscular self. We were on the verge of war and for the *Tribune* of March 18, 2003 this was no time for second thoughts:

> Exile or War
>
> More than six months after he took his case to the United Nations . . . President Bush declared Monday night that time had run out . . . He affirmed his oft-stated resolve that the risk of inaction eclipses the risk of action. He said that if conflict is to occur, it should not be at some future time—and deadly scope of Hussein's choosing . . . how the Iraqi dictator threatens the future of peaceable nations . . . by sharing his deadly playthings with terror brokers . . . Yet Americans have waited a year for those who flatly opposed the war . . . to offer their own credible plans for disarming Hussein . . . to let fear of his revenge immobilize us is to admit that his weaponry is too lethal to tolerate . . . Resolution 1441, which offered one last chance to a nation that had 16 prior resolutions, is 131 days old. That is too long—and thus long enough.

But were weapons really the reason for the war? Colin Powell's performance before the Security Council had been vintage Powell—smooth and avuncular, but very short on substance. Aamr Sa'adi, Saddam's technical advisor, whose performance in the run-up to hostilities had been equally smooth, probably put it best: "A superpower ought to be able to do better than this." As for the resolutions, over the last twenty-five years there had been at least sixty-five Security Council resolutions dealing with the Middle East. We had vetoed thirty-four of them—where we were the only dissenting vote—probably because they were not "balanced." Of the thirty-one that passed, most dealt with Israel's behavior as an occupying power and sixteen of them, dating to 1978, invoked the fourth Geneva Convention and called for the immediate cessation of settlement activity and the dismantling of existing settlements. Yet unlike Saddam, who allegedly pretended to cooperate with the resolutions but did not, the Israelis didn't even bother to acknowledge them. And we, who had effectively eviscerated the Security Council with our unwillingness to enforce its will, now invited it to act lest it become irrelevant. Our performance boggled the mind.

The *New York Times* editorialized on the same day with "War in the Ruins of Diplomacy" and was more nuanced, coming down somewhere between the *Blade* and the *Tribune*:

> America is on its way to war . . . Diplomacy has been dismissed . . . The country is at a decisive turning point, not just in regard to the Iraq crisis, but in how it means to define its role in the post-cold-war world . . . This page has never wavered in the belief that Mr. Hussein must be disarmed. Our problem is with the wrongheaded way this administration has gone about it . . . When this administration took office just over two years ago, expectations were different . . . the new president looked to have assembled an experienced national security team . . . But this did not turn out to be a team of steady veterans. The hubris and mistakes that contributed to America's isolation began long before the attacks of Sept. 11, 2001 . . . In the Middle East, Washington shortsightedly stepped back from the worsening spiral of violence between Israel and the Palestinians, ignoring the pleas of Arab, Muslim, and European countries. If other nations resist American leadership today, some of the reason lies in this unhappy history . . . The result is a war . . . fought almost alone. At a time when America most needs the world to see its actions in the best possible light, they will probably be seen in the worst. This result was neither foreordained nor inevitable.

It would be interesting to see how these three views of the war played out.

At five minutes after two we were called to board the California Zephyr for San Francisco, via Denver. It would take sixty-six hours, or just under three days. The real rail journey was about to begin. The come–on was enticing:

> WELCOME ABOARD! You are traveling on board the *California Zephyr*, an Amtrak Superliner train. While on board, you will be experiencing the utmost comfort and service in train travel and witnessing some of the West's most spectacular scenery . . . THE FUN STARTS HERE. There is a lot to see and do aboard the *California Zephyr*, from relaxing, socializing with family and friends, or enjoying a wonderful meal. Please listen for announcements of the specific times and locations of activities, and most of all, have fun.

This time the conductor was in uniform and he pointed me to a berth on the south side of the train. It was in the last car, although there would be others added over the next several days. We climbed past the luggage storage area to the second deck and the sleeping compartments. That meant a nice elevated view of the passing scenery and in the four days

I didn't use the Sightseer Lounge. This would be home for the duration: the same seating arrangement as on the Capitol Limited, so a passenger could sit facing either east or west. Bedding—a thin mattress, sheets, and pillows—was rolled up on the upper berth that was hinged and sat at an angle overhead. The lighting was dim, but there was also a small reading lamp above each seat like the little lights on an airplane. An electrical outlet and fold-down table allowed the use of a laptop. There was no Internet access. A sound system connected to the intercom and provided light entertainment. A curtain on the inside and shade on the window provided privacy at night.

At the head of the car was the bathroom—compact and stainless-steel like an aircraft bathroom—and a small galley. Coffee and tea were available as long as the attendant kept the water hot. Jamil had been very efficient and we would see if the new guy was as good. The dining car was two cars away, through another sleeping car with deluxe accommodations. They were individual little rooms with their own baths. Beyond the dining car was the Sightseer Lounge that served complimentary cocktails in the evening. The food was the highlight of the trip. My only previous experience of overnight on Amtrak had been a trip from Dallas to Wichita in the late 1970s where the meal service consisted of cold sandwiches served by an attendant wearing a broken pair of eyeglasses. The glasses seemed to say everything about the service. Here, there was almost too much food, it being America, and the quality and variety were surprisingly good. The dinner menu included filet mignon, regional seafood selection (generally salmon), home-style roast pork, and roast chicken. A selection of red and white wines was available for a little extra. A uniformed attendant usually came through the car taking reservations for the sittings, which were at 5:30, 6:30, and last call at 7:30.

The train pulled out of the station promptly at 2:15, heading just south of west towards Naperville, Illinois. By the time we cleared Chicago the sun was low in the sky and there was little to see of what was advertised as the most beautiful train trip in North America. The first sitting at dinner came soon afterwards and we were seated in the dining car in order of our arrival. At the table were a husband and wife on their way to Redding to see friends and a tough little retiree setting out on yet another lease on life somewhere in California. The husband was a CPA and spoke with a nasal tone that I later realized was due to a hare lip, masked by a thick mustache. He looked like he was in his mid-sixties but didn't have a gray hair in his head. The retiree seemed to be congenitally disadvantaged and talked endlessly, but cheerfully, about her physical ailments. She had raised two families, hers and her second husband's, but it hadn't been a happy marriage:

> The best thing he ever did for me was to die.

We were in the same car and regularly had meals together over the next several days.

I awoke early on March nineteenth. Fields of what looked like alfalfa lined the tracks on either side and just after dawn a feedlot appeared. Soon after, the first snow of the trip began to fall. It came at first softly and then in heavy, slanting drifts as we passed Fort Morgan, Colorado, an hour behind schedule. Phillips unleaded gas cost $1.69/gal. in Wiggins when it would already be over $2/gal. in California. Breakfast was a choice of fresh-squeezed juices, eggs-to-order, French toast, pancakes, bacon, pork-sausage patties, turkey-sausage links, and potatoes or grits, with toast or biscuits. There was also a Continental breakfast, but in the middle of America on the eve of a war, fruit and yoghurt didn't seem appropriate. The snow was falling more heavily as we approached Denver and we crawled slowly towards the city. What had before been slanting drifts were now nearly horizontal with the wind. We later learned it was the heaviest snowfall in a century in the area. At nine o'clock the switching yard was covered with snow and the switches had to be thrown by hand, something that would become familiar as the day progressed. We arrived at Union Station, Denver at ten a.m., two-and-a-half hours late, to what looked like a ghost town. The city was covered in drifts four feet deep, and the streets were deserted except for an occasional emergency vehicle or snowplow. We stretched our legs, as the Route Guide said we could, but there was no danger of wandering too far:

> Time is limited, so be sure not to leave the station waiting rooms or platform area.

On the platform, I chatted with a young couple and their two kids who were also expatriates of a sort, returning after a couple of years running a dive shop in the Caribbean. We agreed that things looked different from the outside. There were no newspapers available.

The few cars in the yard told us that we had left the Midwest behind: there was an occasional Chicago Northwestern System, but most were Union Pacific, Southern Pacific, Missouri Pacific Lines, Denver and Rio Grande, and Santa Fe. After an hour, we were underway again. The next stop would be Fraser-Winter Park, a ski resort. The timetable said it was 1,100 miles from Chicago and two and-a-half hours from Denver, but we were already well behind schedule and steadily lost time over the rest of the day. There were two engines ahead of us with crews to dig out the switches. The conductor kept us posted on our progress via the intercom. I didn't realize it, but there was a chain of command on a train. The route guide said that conductor "is in charge of all crew members aboard and is responsible for the collection of the tickets and the safe operation of the train." This one was a garrulous sort, and came on regularly to tell us the latest happenings.

As we climbed into the Rockies our progress became slower and then we came to a complete stop:

> Ladies and gentlemen, this is your conductor speaking. We are experiencing a little difficulty ahead. These switches are buried and it takes a while to dig them out. They are attached to a system of red and green lights and we have to wait for the green light before we go ahead. Now, we know there is no train coming the other way, but we still have to wait for the green light. Those are the rules. On behalf of Amtrak we apologize for the delay.

It was silent and beautiful in an eerie kind of way. There was nothing but a sea of white under a low cloud cover. In fact, it was like being at sea in the middle of the Pacific. Then evergreens began to appear in individual clumps, almost the first green we had seen since we left Washington DC, two days earlier. As we made our way to higher elevation they appeared with greater frequency until the mountainsides were carpeted with them. Individual branches were bowed down under the weight of the snow, frosted like gingerbread men. Actually, they looked more like embryos.

At twelve twenty we came to our first tunnel and we waited while they dug out the switch. On the other side, there was another problem: a group of deer were on the tracks and we couldn't get by them.

> Ladies and gentlemen this is your conductor speaking. We have a small problem ahead. There are deer on the tracks and we're going to have to move them off. It is understandable for the animals, since the snowdrifts are so deep that the track is the only place where they can move. I'm going to have to get down myself and see if I can't hurry them along. Otherwise, we are simply going to have to go through them. We don't like to do that, but in some cases, there is no other choice. There should

> be no problem for the train—we are heavy enough that we won't derail. Again, on behalf of Amtrak we apologize for the delay.

I could only imagine the snow turning pink as we plowed through the animals. But they moved, and as we passed we saw six does on a little hill by the side of the track, all panting heavily.

At two forty a bull elk cropped unconcernedly by a little stream, fifty yards to the south of the train. An hour later at 9,329 feet we came to Moffatt Tunnel and the Continental Divide. A light snow-shower fell while we waited for the tunnel to vent the exhaust from the engines ahead of us. Then, it was dark for fifteen minutes while we passed to the other side of the continent. At four fifteen we emerged to a blue sky and the sight of skiers on the slopes. A 124-car train, loaded with coal under a light dusting of snow, sat waiting on a siding on the other side of the tunnel. At four fifty-one we pulled into Fraser-Winter Park, five hours and forty minutes behind schedule. The Route Guide said that the park billed itself as "the ice box of America" because of winter temperatures of minus fifty degrees Fahrenheit. At five forty-five we moved briefly, but it was a false alarm and it wasn't until six fifteen that we were underway again:

> Ladies and gentlemen, this is your conductor speaking. Union Pacific supplies the two locomotives ahead of us and we pay them a lot of money to keep us on time. But this is their railroad and we can't go until they say so. Again, on behalf of Amtrak we apologize for the delay.

In the fading light, we watched tobogganers as they were lifted to the top of the hill, then careened down crazily, occasionally spinning before coming to a stop at the bottom. Then, it was back up the lift for another run.

At dinner, we were a different group: a Japanese girl who had been an exchange student in Arizona, a lawyer, and a bookkeeper. The girl was an adventuresome sort—no one in Japan did this kind of thing. Her English was very good and she was just seeing the country, but her parents were not happy. The lawyer was originally from Florida but had gone to law school in Denver and had stayed on in Colorado:

> I was accepted at Pepperdine law school but when my father learned that it was near Malibu, he said 'no way.' I grew up near the sun and the sand. Here, there is plenty of work. I live in Grand Junction and on the way to work in the morning I can tell the time just by where the elk herd is on the mountain. Yeah,

I heard there was heavy snow in Denver, but they don't know how to deal with it there. Denver is really only western Kansas.

No one at the table was in favor of the war.

So far, the trip had been beautiful and we couldn't disagree with the Route Guide:

> Certainly, it is the most comfortable way to travel between Chicago and the great cities of the West. But as you twist through the narrow canyons and towering peaks of the Rockies . . . you won't be thinking about where you're going. You'll be thinking about how glad you are that you took the California Zephyr to get there.

But it was dependent on the time and the season. We had already passed through Galesburg, Illinois, the home of Carl Sandburg, and the site of a debate between Abraham Lincoln and Stephen Douglas; Omaha, the birthplace of President Gerald Ford, Henry Fonda, Fred Astaire, Marlon Brando, and Malcolm X; and Glenwood Springs, Colorado where Doc Holiday was buried and Teddy Roosevelt stayed at the Colorado Hotel. But the last two places had been at night, and in the dead of winter there would be even less to see.

I awakened at five thirty the next morning. Outside, there was still a foot of snow on the ground, but we were through the Rockies. At six thirty-five leafless trees appeared again in a creek bed, bare limbs above the red earth and scrub. Then we went through a chain of rugged mountains that from the map must have been the West Tavaputs in eastern Utah. The feathery red-gray brush near a creek was beautiful in the early morning light. We had swung around and were now heading northwest by north towards Salt Lake City. We reached Provo, at seven fifteen, now eight hours and forty-five minutes behind schedule. A solitary tree showed a slight tinge of green, and then another, struggling against the brown. A few minutes later it was Orem, home of Word Perfect. It was odd that IT companies had located themselves in this Utah fastness, and in a couple of months SCO out of Lindon would take on IBM over alleged infringement of its Unix patent. Then, there were more mountains, the Uintas, in their starkness looking like the Tian Shen, the Heavily Mountains, in Kazakhstan. A pheasant—a ring-necked rooster—scurried away from the tracks before exploding into flight. At the Lehigh City Power

Department, every vehicle in the employee parking lot was a pickup. This was a country of rugged individualists, but the downside was the auto junkyards that were a regular feature of the little towns.

We reached Salt Lake City at 8:27 a.m. I was beyond counting how far behind schedule we were, but the delay in the Rockies meant that we would not see the other advertised highlight of the trip, the Sierra Nevadas. The spires of the Mormon Temple were visible above the station building. Utah was the New Zion, the Promised Land for the Mormons, the earthly paradise wrested out of the wilderness after the hostility of the Gentiles. The place seemed downright biblical with the little towns of South Jordan and West Jordan just outside Salt Lake City and the Great Salt Lake itself. In the spring of 1860 Richard Burton had made an overland journey from St. Joseph Missouri to Salt Lake City, before going on to the fleshpots of San Francisco. It was part of a plan to visit three celebrated holy cities, Mecca, Harrar in Somaliland, and Salt Lake City, and had been memorialized in *The City of the Saints*. The account of his picaresque adventures in the American west was vintage Burton. It was probably his best book after the *Pilgrimage to El-Medinah and Meccah*. There was the usual encyclopedic treatment of the natives, of the Latter-day Saints, and American Indians, but enlivened by a little booze, a little bravado, and a little braggadocio. Deseret was an English and Anglo-American thing, and you almost couldn't imagine an Italian Mormon or a Spanish Mormon. Brigham Young was a man you could look in the eye and trust, and the Mormon women were uncommonly attractive. All the newspapers in the station were sold out.

At nine ten we were underway again, past a 163-car train in the siding with four engines in front and two in the rear. But it wasn't going anywhere, the pass we had come through still being snowbound. There was a change of crew in Salt Lake City and the new conductor, Dave, was more garrulous than the one before, if that was possible. We learned that Denver was still closed down, with more than 4,000 passengers stranded at the airport. Later, Dave came through the car and said that we were at war. So, after six months it had finally happened, although it had been in the works far longer than that. It was later reported that the first of forty cruise missiles in the "decapitation attack" began to rain down on Baghdad at about 5:30 a.m., March 20, local time. That would have been about 8:30 p.m. Central Time on March 19 when we were in the vicinity of Parachute, Colorado.

We were now heading due west, along the southern shore of the Great Salt Lake. A derelict telegraph line, the poles crooked and the broken lines dangling forlornly, ran along the tracks for mile after monotonous mile. At nine thirty-five we passed a Kennecott copper smelter, but for the next couple of hours there was nothing to see in this abomination of desolation. If we had just left God's country, this seemed utterly Godforsaken. At about eleven o'clock we passed the Bonneville Salt Flats and then into Nevada. In the distance to the west there were snowcapped mountains, their peaks in the clouds. The headwaters of the Humboldt River rose to the north and the tracks followed the course of the river through the surrounding mountains. The little stream looped back and forth to the left, right, and beneath the train, with occasional mallards and Canada geese afloat among the reeds. But it hardly seemed like a real river, nothing like the Potomac at Washington or the mighty Susquehanna where it emptied into Chesapeake Bay.

It was now March 20 so the sun would have been just above the equator. We were at about forty-one degrees north latitude, heading west, so the sun lay to the left of the train all day long, halfway up the sky. After a while it became oppressive and I closed the curtain. Passengers on the other side of the aisle had north light, but the advantage was relative. There simply wasn't much to see. Just before one o'clock we came to a halt:

> Ladies and gentlemen, may I have your attention please. We have some folks working on the line ahead of us and just as soon as Union Pacific gives us permission to go through their work order, we'll be on our way.

After we were underway again he came on to tell us that there had been an avalanche in the Rockies and we were the only train that would get through that day.

For the next six hours, it was more of the same. There was an occasional deer, a jackrabbit, once a coyote skulking away from the line in the dying light. Ranches with herds of cattle and horses came and went with mind-numbing regularity. At three forty Dave came back on to tell us about "the famous Indian chief, Winnemucca" so we must have been near the town of the same name. The Little Humboldt joined us at Winnemucca but it didn't seem to make much difference in the volume of water. Around seven o'clock we passed by Humboldt Lake and then the Carson Sink. In Sparks gas was up to $1.97.9/gal. at an Exxon station, and at 7:25 p.m. we pulled into Reno, the casinos ablaze in the dark after the sun glare of the day. According to the timetable, it should have been 9:20 in the morning and we would be about to begin the climb through Donner Pass in the heart of the Sierra Nevadas. We soon began the climb, but there was nothing to see in the dark. They hadn't planned for an extra sit-down dinner so Dave passed out sandwiches after we left Reno. Then, it was fitful sleep until we arrived at the Emeryville station at 2:20 a.m. on March 21. But the day was not quite over.

A van took us to the Jack London Station in Oakland where I planned to catch the train to points east. The produce district was already alive with activity, Mexicans having replaced the Italians of forty years before, but there was no BART station. There were also no cabs and this was *not* a place you wanted to be at three o'clock in the morning, so the van dropped me at the Marriott at twelfth and Broadway. The nice Hispanic night manager let me sit in the lobby after I told him that I was a veteran of the Marriott chain. It was true that we had stayed at Marriotts in Cairo, Riyadh, Ta'if, Islamabad, and Amman for years. BART began service at four a.m. and I caught the first eastbound train. So, from Washington DC it had been about 3,600 miles and just over seventy-six hours, door to door. The price of the train ticket was odd, the fare itself only about $120 and the rest of the $733 for "accommodations." The return, direct flight to Washington, bought online for $112.50, cost about the same as the fare.

In Walnut Creek, the little cow town had long-since been transformed into a high-tech emporium. It was full of comfortable people, couturier outlets, and cavernous gourmet emporia featuring sushi bars, French wines, and two-inch-thick pork chops. America's good intentions were on permanent display. But the subject of the war was contentious and it *was* like the Civil War, separating brother from brother. After a few acerbic exchanges, we agreed not to discuss it at family gatherings. I discovered that it was a matter of personalities and that what George W. Bush *was*, was less important than what he was *not*: He was not Bill Clinton, and that seemed to be enough for his friends. There were some who simply couldn't abide the sight or the thought of one or the other. In that atmosphere of animus, the war seemed unimportant and simply slipped between the cracks.

11

Home

I ARRIVED BACK IN Amman two days after I left the United States. The flight from San Francisco was about as uncomfortable as any I can remember, with the seating so cramped that I couldn't read when the man seated ahead of me reclined the seat. I couldn't hold the book far enough away to see the type. It was claustrophobic. The officious woman at the Northwest counter said that, in spite of the fact that I checked in three hours before flight-time, they had no bulkhead seats available. They were all reserved for frequent fliers.

Amsterdam was cold and dark under a cloud cover and I had six hours to kill. So, I took a Spartan little day room at the airport and slept for a couple of hours. When I woke up I watched CNN and the latest news from Tora Bora. We were pounding the remnants of al-Qaʾeda and American special forces were engaged. It was light years from Vietnam and impossible to imagine these guys smoking joints and listening to Jimmi Hendrix on the headphones. Then the news cut to an American veto of a UN resolution calling for protection of the Palestinians. Sharon was completing the unfinished business of 1982, the destruction of Yassir Arafat and the PLO, and we were either unaware or indifferent. Probably the latter. The two clips in combination represented American triumphalism at its worst. It didn't seem possible that we could be simultaneously bombing Afghanistan and turning Ariel Sharon loose in the West Bank, but it seemed to be working.

The connecting flight to Damascus and Amman left at 5:50 p.m. and I checked in at about five o'clock. The 767 was full, all 200-plus seats, mainly with young, Middle Eastern–looking males and women with children. The men had to be relieved to be going where they no longer excited suspicion. A little boy named Khaled sat next to me. He looked to be about ten and his very polite mother was seated across the aisle. His manners were impeccable and his English was textbook-perfect until I spoke to him in Arabic and then he switched. Like most kids he manipulated an electronic game console effortlessly and then switched to the headphones and what sounded like hip-hop. He was from Homs, he said, a city north of Damascus. Just before landing his mother filled out the arrival cards for her brood. The passports were all American.

The announcements from the cockpit were in Dutch, followed by English. That was fair enough on a Royal Dutch Airlines (KLM) flight. But I don't think anyone apart from the stewardesses understood the Dutch. The language sounded silly and the pilot equally so. I thought of Srebrenica, probably unfairly. In the East Indies, the Dutch had been the authors of as brutal and self-interested a colonial policy as any on record. In the Balkans in the twenty-first century they had undertaken to protect minorities and had failed scandalously. The stewardess commiserated with me on the lack of space and she seemed to be saying: "If these people didn't breed like rabbits there would be more room for you."

In Damascus, the plane emptied with the exception of about thirty of us. Then the cleaners came aboard, hard-looking middle-aged men wearing headscarves. In America, they would probably have been Mexicans or Salvadorans. After a wait of about half-an-hour we took off for Amman, although we were detained by "incoming traffic." I couldn't imagine who that might have been. Damascus was not Amsterdam. In Amman my bag arrived, always surprising since I had last seen it in San Francisco it seemed like days before. The ride to the apartment was uneventful. Nali, the Sri Lankan maid, had been there the day before and everything seemed spic and span. On the plane, I had plowed through Judith Miller's *God has Ninety-Nine Names*, if only because Edward Sa'id had savaged it as being utterly without value. But I thought it was a workmanlike—or a workwomanlike—attempt to tell the story of twenty-five years covering the Arab World, allowing for obvious gaps in language, culture, and historical perspective.

12

Tel al–Shehab and Mudawwara

I HAD ALWAYS WANTED to see a couple of places in Jordan, one in the far north of the country and the other in the south, that had figured prominently in the Arab Revolt. The first was Tel al-Shehab, the village north of Amman where a major railroad bridge crossed the gorge of the Yarmuk River. As reported by Lawrence a raiding party attempted to destroy it in November of 1917 and had spectacularly failed. But as Martha and I were to discover, it was not in Jordan at all, but in Syria. Crisscrossing the area just south of the border between the two countries, we could only look wistfully at the gorge from the heights of Um Qais, the ancient Gadara, known for the Gadarene swine in the New Testament. Um Qais was worth a trip in itself, with its black basalt ruins, including a spectacular amphitheater, temple, and streets bordered by what may have been little shops that were remarkably still intact. A long avenue trailed away to the west, down to the celebrated hot springs. The springs were still there, prized for their medicinal properties. Partially excavated structures lined the avenue and we often wandered among the tumble-down walls and subterranean churches. The little cafe above the ruins served one of the better *mezzes*, or finger foods, in Jordan, although maybe it was the view that made it so.

In the immediate foreground to the north was the gorge of the Yarmuk river, maybe five miles away. Beyond, another five miles to the northwest, lay the Sea of Galilee with the Israeli towns of Hammat, Kinneret, and Poriyya on its southwestern shore. Beyond Galilee lay the Lebanon. To the east were the Golan Heights. Um Qais sat near the northernmost point of Jordan where the Yarmuk formed the border with Syria. In the *Seven Pillars* Lawrence says that the westernmost bridge over the gorge at Um Qais had been the primary target of the raid. But the defection from the raiding party of the transplanted Algerian, Abdel Qadir, had ruled the bridge out. A secondary target, the bridges at Wadi Khalid, also lay below villages occupied by Algerians and these, for the same reason, were also out. So, on the last day the Arabs had hurriedly chosen the easternmost bridge at Tel al-Shehab as the target. From our perch in the little cafe the gorge was plainly visible and what looked like a railroad bridge lay due north, maybe seven miles away. The modern map of the area didn't show a Wadi Khalid, but it looked like the area where bridges might have been. The road leading to the area was restricted, controlled by several checkpoints, as might be expected in the border area that separated Israel, Jordan, and Syria. So, Tel al-Shehab remained a mystery. Maybe the village was gone, and maybe the bridge hadn't been "major" at all, but that in itself would be interesting information.

Amphitheater, Um Qais

I later made second attempt to find the site, this time alone and farther east. From the description in *Seven Pillars* it appeared to lie between the Syrian town of Dera' and Jordanian Ramtha, but I wasn't sure where. Martha and I had been in the area south of the border earlier in the year, touring old Roman basalt towns set in rolling fields. Lawrence reported the going very slow in the rain, which turned the area into a sea of mud. The water table in this region lies close to the surface and creates a spongy layer of soil that would have accounted for the heavy going for the raiding force in the winter of 1917. It seemed to match the area where we had been.

So, I drove north to Ramtha and at a group of shops near the border I stopped to ask if they had heard of Tel al-Shehab. A couple of men at one shop selling cheap cooking utensils said yes, but it was in Syria. I had a Jordanian *iqama*, or identity card, and they said they thought I could cross with that. Tel Shehab—they didn't use the definite article—might have been the site of a railroad bridge, but when I mentioned the war one of the men said something about Salah al-Din, referring to events of the eleventh century. So, I told them about the raid in 1917 and they stroked their chins and allowed as how it might have been so. But to get there I would have to take a Syrian taxi. So, when a yellow Syrian tax passed by, going south towards Amman we waved and it went about fifty yards before doubling back. I told the driver I wanted to go to Tel Shehab, see the bridge and come back. The twenty-five dinars out and back seemed reasonable. I joined two young guys in the cab, the one next to me wearing an Oakland Raiders jacket. I told him in Arabic that it had been my team, but I don't think he knew anything about American football.

The trip that followed was anything but direct. The two passengers were fares the cabbie would deliver in Ramtha. After about a kilometer we left the main road and went up a little hill where we dropped them off, before heading back towards the center of town. I was now in the front seat. The cabbie parked on a hill and asked me to get out while he used a screwdriver to open the glove compartment. In it were several cartons of Marlboros and he disappeared for a few minutes before returning. He was probably doing a little side business with the cigarettes, although I couldn't imagine that they were cheaper in Syria than here in Jordan. His name was Mohammed and he was originally from Dera'. He had a kind of stunted look, with gaps between his teeth that showed when he grinned. Everything he did was at a frenetic pace.

He said the car was a *model thalatha wa saba'een*, a '73 Dodge with a manual transmission, the shift lever on the steering column. You forgot how big American cars once were until you got into one. This one seemed loose, but powerful. We hurtled up the street before doubling back again. "*Benzene*" said Mohammed. After the gas we turned around again, this time heading towards the border. He was going about sixty on the city street and I asked him to slow down. He said that he already had. The windshield was cracked in two places and it was a reminder of the little Fiat and the driving trip to Ferghana in Uzbekistan.

At the border, a couple of policemen looked at my *iqama*, or Jordanian identity papers and said "*wain al-jawaz?*" I said that my passport was in Amman and that I understood that it was possible to go into Syria—only to Tel Shehab and back—with just the *iqama*. They said "*no, no, problem, problem*." It turned out that I needed my passport after all. So, Mohammed backed through the gate and turned around before hurtling back to the shop where I had left the car. I gave him five dinars and we agreed I would return in a week with my passport. But I never made it back to Ramtha. I later found Tell al-Shehab on an Encarta map of the Sea of Galilee and it was north of the border, and the only road that reached it was the one through the border at Ramtha. So, the men in the shop had been right after all.

The second town, Mudawwara, was the southernmost in Jordan and the map showed it to be only a few kilometers north of the Sa'udi Border. For overland traffic, it was where the customs and passport formalities between the two countries took place. But, as I would discover, there were actually two towns of that name, al-Mudawwara and al-Mudawwara *al-jadida*, or *New* Mudawwara. New Mudawwara was the border town, and old Mudawwara was twenty kilometers to the north. I was looking for the old town, although it probably had not been a town at all but a station on the Hejaz Railway and a fortified Turkish post during the First World War. It was the only source of water on the railway between Ma'an and Medina and so was the key to Medina, 400 miles to the south. The Arabs had first tried to take the post in September of 1917, in spite of the fear of their British advisors that success might lead to a Turkish abandonment of Medina. That would not only turn 20,000 Ottoman troops loose on the northern front, but also transfer railhead to Ma'an. Neither development would have been welcome to the British or the Arabs. That first attempt had failed, as had several others, and it wasn't until August of 1918 that the Egyptian Camel Corps finally meted out the fate that Mudawwara had so long avoided. Lawrence tells the story of the failures and the ultimate success, first as a principal in a tribal raiding party and later as a guide with mixed forces consisting of British, Egyptians, and Arabs.

Bedouin, Wadi Rum

All of this was in an attempt to put context to the story told in *The Seven Pillars of Wisdom*. In addition to the accounts of contemporaries, part of the context was the lay of the land itself. It looked from the map like the most direct route to Mudawwara was through Ma'an, and then south to the Sa'udi border. But that would have missed Wadi Rum where the raiding parties had started. From the Desert Highway 200 miles south of Amman the signs pointed to Ma'an and al-Mudawwara, and at the interchange I turned off, heading first east and then south. Ma'an was drab and uninteresting, and at an unmarked fork in the road I mistakenly turned right instead of left and wound up back where I had started, at the interchange on the highway. Something was telling me that I should continue towards Aqaba and approach Mudawwara from the Wadi Rum side. The map didn't show a track between the two places. But I had a 4x4 and the route had been passable for armored cars in 1918, so surely there was a way.

A swirling fog shrouded the pass at Ras al-Naqb before the first breathtaking view of the flat, thousands of feet below. Then it was New Quwayra followed by Quwayra—an advanced logistics base during the war—before the turnoff to Wadi Rum. I had first been to Rum in 1975 and had spent a week with the Desert Patrol near the fort built by Glubb Pasha. It had been a working fort then. But the Desert Patrol seemed to be mostly ceremonial these days. The fort was still there, but abandoned and in a ruinous state, and the village of Rum had grown up around it in a kind of tumble-down disarray. Concrete block houses and electricity were undoubtedly improvements for the Huweitat, the Bedouin tribe inhabiting the area, although some preferred the old ways. Outlying areas among the sandstone monoliths were still dotted with black tents. At the police station in the tourist complex the officer on duty, repeating the orthodoxy, said the only way to Mudawwara was through Ma'an. He consulted an Arabic map of Petra with a tiny inset of Jordan and, sure enough, it showed the highway south from Ma'an. But it also showed what my map didn't, a dotted-line track from Rum east to the highway, and we discussed how it could be done. There were apparently two ways, one north and then east, the other more directly east. He thought the direct way would take about an hour and a-half to Mudawwara, with the other route taking a little longer.

A young Bedouin in western dress was listening to the conversation and said that he knew the way. So, we went outside to the map of Rum posted on a bulletin board in the tourist complex to look at the route. The complex was authentic in an odd sort of way, housed in original boxcars from the Hejaz railway and offering Bedouin handicrafts, painted ostrich eggs, and books, including copies of the *Seven Pillars* in English, French, German, and Italian. We traced the two routes on the map and agreed that, since it was already afternoon, we would start early the next morning. His name was Youssef and I wrote it in Arabic on the map the policeman had given me.

Do you have a mobile phone?' he said. "Take my mobile number.

So, it was settled. I would spend the night in Aqaba and return the next morning for the trip to Mudawwara. An hour and a-half each way and an hour at the site meant that we should be back at Rum around noon, although I wasn't sure about the estimate.

It was twenty-seven kilometers back to the highway from Rum Village. Part of the reason for waiting until the next day was to avoid the drive to Aqaba in the dark. Martha and I had done it once before and it was probably the most lethal stretch of road we had ever encountered. The thirty-mile portion between the port and the Quwayra plateau had been under repair and in places it was reduced to two lanes. The gradient was very steep and winding, and up and down the road from the port crawled a regular stream of truck-and-trailer rigs carrying everything of bulk—mainly fuel-oil and gasoline—that came into Jordan. During the Iran-Iraq War it had also carried everything of bulk that came into Iraq, the Persian Gulf being effectively closed to northbound traffic. A few Jordanians made millions out of the trade. In the dark on the unlit road that night it was not unusual to find yourself wedged between trucks, often without taillights, going ten mph, up as well as down. Passing was almost impossible, and even if it were, there was another rig ahead going just as slowly. They would loom up, unexpectedly, out of the gloom. The problem was compounded by the fogs that often crept up from the Gulf. It had been nerve-wracking, an experience I was not anxious to repeat.

But the repair work had been completed and a divided highway, separated by a wide median, now carried north and south traffic. In some places, highway work left scars in the landscape. Here it seemed orderly and regular, almost puny next to the great alluvial fans that poured down from the heights and the detritus left after flash floods that occasionally swept through the gorge. Everything that had been painstakingly built up over months or years could be carried away in a matter of minutes. We always thought of Jordan as small—little king, little country— sandwiched between regional behemoths. But there were parts of Jordan that didn't seem small, and this was one of them. The road wasn't on the scale of the Karakoram Highway that connected Pakistan and China. But the gorge was an extension of the East African rift valley system and the same geological forces that shaped the Olduvai Gorge in Kenya had been at play here. The earth displayed itself in all its nakedness, plutonic rocks occasionally exposed where succeeding layers of sandstone and then limestone had been worn away, before the whole was fractured and upthrust, permitting lava flows to spill out over the exposed surfaces. And, everywhere, faulting that moved whole blocks up or down or sideways, often tilting the layers in odd attitudes.

Like other settlements in Sinai the town of Aqaba seemed to spill out of the gorge and there was a permanent downward tilt to the water. Jordan had hopes of making it a high-tech center, and there was already an economic free zone and ASEZA, the Aqaba Special Economic Zone Authority, responsible for development. There were a few good hotels and decent diving in the reefs of the Gulf, although there wasn't the wealth of marine life further south. But, as a McKinsey consultant had recently advised, Aqaba needed more "golf" before it would attract investors and the yuppified work force to staff the enterprises they would bring. There would have to be more in the way of entertainment, amenities, schools, and connections to places in and beyond the region. There was only one flight per day into Aqaba, a prop plane from the old Marka airport in Amman, and that would have to change as well.

The Aqaba Movenpick hotel made an attempt—largely successful— to integrate itself into the surroundings. It had the same ocher, mud-brick look of the hotels at Petra and the Dead Sea, oriental carpets and mosaics in the lobby, and an enclosed bridge that carried pedestrian traffic over the street to the beach and the water's edge. At 51 dinars (about $75) for a single room with a sea view, the price was right. Americans had recently seen a drop in the dollar, and European vacations cost half-again what they did a couple of years before. But here, safely in the dollar zone we were insulated against the fall. The Middle East was largely a dollar zone, and oil was still priced in dollars, to the dismay of the Gulf producers. It was another example of how deeply Americans and Arabs were linked, and the ties were not just commercial. For all of the talk about terror, we had a whole litany of shared values with the Arabs: belief in a monotheistic God, the importance of religion in daily life, devotion to family values, hostility to socialism, and a deep commitment to private enterprise. By those measures there were probably no people on the planet with whom we had more in common.

In the early afternoon, the town was asleep and many of the shops were closed. But it came alive in the evening and the streets were thronged with single men and strolling families. The prices in this free-zone were a fraction of those in Amman. There were considerable savings, particularly on liquor and nuts. A fifth of Haig scotch cost 3.5 dinars, or about $5, the same price as a kilo package of mixed pistachios, hazelnuts, cashews, and almonds. There were probably similar bargains in everything from small appliances to bedding. Most of the staff working in the shops seemed to be Egyptians, Christians from Cairo or Alexandria or Malawi, and they were, as usual, happy to speak in their own inimitable dialect. Even Jordanians loved to hear Egyptian Arabic, probably because it was a reminder of years of exposure to Egyptian movies and soaps, to the antics of actors like 'Adel Imam and Mohammed Hineidi.

But the Egyptian connection was more than a linguistic one, and there was something about Aqaba that seemed very Egyptian and dated. The owner of one shop called, appropriately, the "Khan al-Khalili," said that they were trying to attract foreign tourists, but that with the war in Iraq Americans and western Europeans were now staying away. Instead, they were now looking to the east, to Hungary, Poland, Bulgaria, and the Czech Republic. A sign on his shop window was in Hungarian. It was a reminder of the old flirtation between Egypt and the Eastern Bloc. But this time it was out of necessity.

> I have lived in the United States, and I have an American passport. But I am ashamed to call myself an American. They said there were weapons of mass destruction in Iraq, but they were lying.

It was a sentiment deeply felt throughout Jordan, probably understandable in a country whose business—and livelihood—had always suffered from insecurity in the region.

But even more than the shops, the streets had the feel of the Middle East, and it was not the Middle East envisioned by the high-tech dreamers. Even in early March it was warm and humid, and we could just as well have been in Jidda or Dhahran. As usual in the Arab world, families predominated, the women generally wearing the *hijab* and pushing baby strollers, the bearded men often carrying small children. The restaurants, featuring large tables with the plates inverted, waited for family traffic.

The food was plentiful but bland. There was no concern about crime, violent or otherwise. You were as safe walking in an Arab city—with the notable exception of Baghdad, Basra, or Mosul—as in the smallest of American small towns. It wasn't exciting. There wasn't the anticipatory air of wickedness of an Asian city, or the vibrancy of a big American city. Instead, it was just a collection of normal people going about their everyday lives. I often thought of Arabs as the most pedestrian people on the planet. But there was something to be said for normalcy and security.

On the BBC later in the day Tony Blair was giving an earnest defense of the invasion of Iraq. He spoke about a "mortal danger" to the West, and how this was not "a time for cynicism of the worldly wise who favor playing it long," whatever that meant. But I was having trouble connecting the danger with the scene I had just seen in the town. Because the people I saw were just like the people of Baghdad, only much safer. Thirty years of dictatorship, war, and sanctions had reduced Iraqis to an impoverished, brutalized, and deeply-religious mass. But at least they had been safe. Bush and Blair had resorted to the most shameful scare-mongering—with visions of chemical weapons, sophisticated delivery systems, and mushroom clouds—to justify a war on a pathetic, broken-down dictatorship. The man in the shop was right and the Iraqis had probably destroyed most of their weapons long before the war began. Not everyone had gotten it wrong. Hans Blix, Rolf Ekeus, and Scott Ritter had gotten it right, but their advice was inconvenient.

So far from pursuing weapons of mass destruction, Saddam apparently spent most of his time in the run-up to the war writing novels. The tyrant's favorite movie was said to be *The Godfather*, and he probably believed that in the end we would make a deal, just like the Corleones. Bush said that Saddam Hussein "hated America." Now, Osama Bin Laden may hate America, but Saddam and his unspeakable sons did not, monopolizing the technology, pornography, and violent crime that are such characteristics of our culture. Those same things are now being democratized, and Iraqis must wonder if they are better off for it.

Dinner that evening was in the Italian restaurant in the hotel. I was the only one there, although the clerk at the front desk said the hotel was half full. The waiters were a Filipino girl from Manila and an Egyptian Christian from Assiut. I had been to both places and they were anxious to talk about their homelands. But Manila today was different from the Manila of 1967, although the girl couldn't have known it then:

> Was Marcos still in power? Let's see, he left in 1979? But that was before I was born, sir.

Now, she said, the Philippines was very corrupt. Jordan was safe. The Egyptian spoke about the Holy Family, how they had spent six months and five days in Assiut during their sojourn in Upper Egypt. Egyptian Christians always wanted to talk about religion. The darker side for the two of them was that Filipino women were harassed even in Jordan, abused by employers who demanded sexual favors in return for sponsorship. And for all of their country's being the intellectual leader of the Arab World, Egyptians were rather despised by Jordanians as common laborers.

The next morning it would be Wadi Rum and Mudawwara. But it took me fifteen minutes, tacking back and forth over the tilted plain before I found the road to the north. That was odd since there was only one real road out of town, but it was poorly marked. I had nothing to declare at the customs checkpoint and a sleepy guard waved me through without stopping. At Rum Village Youssef was waiting, having exchanged his western dress for a clean white *thobe* and red-checked *kufiiya*. We stopped by his house and several brothers and sisters, and then his father came out to see us off. I asked the father how long it would take to Mudawwara and he said about an hour and a quarter, maybe longer.

We made our way through the cinderblock houses and pitted roads of the village and soon were in the pink sand of Rum. It wasn't long before we stalled for the first time. It took skill to drive in the desert and, as I was to learn, infinite patience. It was a repeat of a similar experience in Sinai, where the Bedouins said they had learned sand driving from the Israelis. When they stalled, westerners tended to gun the engine, but that only dug the hole deeper. So, we exchanged places and Youssef took the wheel. It was clear that he should drive. He sized up the situation and simply eased—you might have said "willed"—the car forward before we resumed our customary fifteen mph over the sand. He was heavy and dark and I would soon become used to his large hand hovering over the shift lever, expertly moving it to 4 wheels when needed, but using 2 wheels when it was not.

Wadi Rum

I had bought a "Wadi Rum Tourist Plan" at a bookshop in Aqaba the night before. It had a good layout of the *jebels* or mountains, and showed a few oddities, like a photo of "The Seven Pillars of Wisdom," a formation of seven spiral peaks near the entrance to the complex, as well as a chart showing the fixed constellations that were visible from Rum all year round. It also contained timetables for camel and horse trips to Aqaba and Petra. Both took five days. Youssef said a man named David had done the Mudawwara trip by camel a few weeks before. But we were soon lost in the immensity of the place and after we turned left at *Jebel Khaz Ali*, the map wasn't much use.

Abdullah

The valley floor was covered with tracks the Bedouins made in their Toyotas, and we generally stayed in the tracks. But Youssef spotted a Bedouin tending a flock of sheep in the distance and we bounced over the sand and scrub to consult with him. He was looking for Abdullah who, he said, knew the area well.

> His father is Sheikh Tleyhan. He will be sheikh one day.

Abdullah was at his tents. So, with this bit of intelligence we bumped back to the track before making a wide circle to the left towards what looked like an impassable barrier of hills. But there was a pass over a drift of soft sand and ten minutes later we arrived at a black tent, outside of which sat a cluster of men. Sheikh Tleyhan was maybe fifty years old, very dark and blear-eyed, looking like he had cataracts. Abdullah was young—he said nineteen—and sharply featured. A third man poured tea while his children, bright-eyed little creatures with their father's prominent ears and dressed in dirty western hand-me-downs, dashed up and posed for pictures. After tea, our complement now complete, we bounced back through the pass and set out for Mudawwara.

We would be together for the next six hours. Abdullah was nearly as quiet as Youssef was voluble. But together they kept up a steady stream of one-sided chatter, talking of everything under the sun, from girls to the weather. Did Abdullah have a *khalawi*, or mobile telephone?

La'a.

The "no" was firm. Youssef explained why Abdullah probably never would carry a *khalawi*:

> The Bedouins don't like to depend on other people. When they want to do something they just do it.

Youssef had been given *his* phone by the man from MobileCom in exchange for help in siting towers in the area. They even discussed the utility of GPS, or the geographic positioning system, and it was clear that Youssef saw its promise, where Abdullah did not. The two boys had been in school together, although they were separated by a year.

> It was a military school in the village. We studied Arabic and English and history and religion. They gave us everything, even lunch.

It was Youssef, not the future sheikh, who was the natural leader.

Our heading was generally east and after half an-hour we bounced into a little village and an oasis of green—tamarisks and olive trees—with concrete-block houses and a paved road. Youssef said it was called Om Misheer, and it was obvious that there was artesian water nearby. It was a reminder of a dinner at an Italian camp in 1975. They were involved in a water project, and it may have been at the same place. The Desert Patrol sergeant had driven me in the Land Rover from the fort at Rum and left me with stern, parental instructions not to be late coming home. The Italians had been good-natured and there was a great deal of banter during the evening, most of it at the Bedouins' expense. The meal had been Aqaba whitefish over mountains of rice. But the thing I particularly remembered was the full bottles of Scotch—Vat 69—set at every other place on the table. We went through several bottles during the meal, and that was probably the reason why I didn't remember much about the evening.

The first attempt by the Arabs on the station at Mudawwara had been in September of 1917 and it would be Lawrence's introduction to Rum. Even the "unsentimental" Huweitat had told him that it was beautiful. The place left a lasting impression. The only problem with Lawrence's description was one of spaciousness, not of scale. It was just as red and massive as Lawrence described it. But the overwhelming feeling of Rum was one of openness, not confinement and even in Lawrence's "avenue," the thousand feet of height was nothing compared with the ten-thousand feet of distance that separated the two ramparts.

There had been troubles with the clans, all Huweitat but jealous of one another and jealous of Auda Abu Tayi. Lawrence reports that he spent much of the time trying to soothe tempers in the much-reduced raiding party. The Auda figure was played by Anthony Quinn in the movie *Lawrence of Arabia*, and he actually looked like the Auda of photographs. The only contemporary who both left an account of the campaign and saw the movie, was the formidable Richard Meinertzhagen. He was Allenby's chief of intelligence during the war, and he and Lawrence had occupied rooms in the same Paris hotel during the peace conference. The portrait of Lawrence in Meinertzhagen's *Middle East Diary* was not flattering and was later used by Lawrence's enemies in accounts that amounted to little more than character assassination. But Meinertzhagen had enjoyed the movie as it "brought to life some precious memories," although he thought that Jack Hawkins was miscast as Allenby and Peter O'Toole as Lawrence was "too tall and sad."

The raiding party set out on a September dawn, the weather "mild, perfect as an August in England." They estimated they would reach the wells near the Mudawwara station about sunset on the second night. That would have meant a distance of about fifty miles, given the normal pace of a camel and ten-hour days. The track on the map in the *Seven Pillars* showed the direction to be first south of east and then southeast. As it turned out, they had watered at the wells in the late afternoon and then crept forward to a hill overlooking the station in the blackness of the new moon. The station was very long and stoutly built and the garrison seemed to consist of about 200 men, too many for the party to which the troubles in Rum had reduced them. So, the next morning they had gone on several miles to the south where a high embankment and a little two-arched bridge provided ideal cover for an electronic mine. After a long wait through the heat of the day a train appeared and activated the mine. It had been an outstanding success, with the Stokes mortars and Lewis guns taking a heavy toll of the Turkish troops who survived the thunderous explosion that destroyed the engine and tender. Lawrence's long, eight-page description of the detonation and the aftermath, the Turkish civilians, household goods, and the looting, made the incident obvious as the model of the train scene in the movie. The Arabs had three men lightly wounded.

Lawrence says that he had been too busy to notice the surroundings and provides little description of their progress out and back from Rum. But he had noticed "twenty miles of hard mud" that might have enabled armored cars to reach the station. Our track in 2003 was more east than southeast, and so we emerged on the line well north of the station itself. There was considerable topographical diversity in the fifty miles, and the red ramparts of Rum soon gave way to lesser rock outcroppings, standing up starkly out of the dun-colored sand. The day was overcast and that may have contributed to the effect. Youssef said that there had been an unusual amount of rain that year, but the "green" that he pointed out was really more gray-green, or blue-green scrub.

After about half-an-hour from Om Misheer we descended to a broad surface that stretched away for miles and looked utterly flat, reflecting the faint light like a mirror. It was the Batn al-Ghul, or "belly of the desert demon," and after the heavy going of the sand Youssef opened the car up to about ninety km/hour. This was obviously Lawrence's "hard mud." It was alluvial and the car kicked up such a choking cloud of dust that we had to close the windows. I wondered whether this was the "Devil's Anvil" of the movie, the stretch in the raid on Aqaba that had been dramatically—and portentously—described as the last barrier before the descent on the port. But it was more likely that David Lean had conflated it with the Nefud, which the raiding party did not cross, into a kind of cinematic Death Valley. Omar Sharif, as the Ali Ibn al-Hussein figure, had pronounced it impassable to humankind.

However it was called, cross it they, of course, did. In reality, the Batn al-Ghul was fertile after the artesian water in the area had been brought to the surface. Now, large center-pivot irrigation devices appeared, feeding acre after acre of *birseem*, or clover. Youssef said that in season they turned the animals—goats, sheep, and camels—loose in the fields. After several miles, the flat narrowed to a kind of choke point and here the hand of man had intervened once more. A large, triangular-shaped fenced compound appeared, bordered by a paved road for a mile or so. The fence was new and about ten feet high, over the top of which appeared reeds, the yellow heads prominent among the green. Youssef said it had been built by Sheikh Makhtoum bin Rashid al-Makhtoum, and that its purpose was for "ducks." I later looked up Makhtoum on the Internet and learned that he was the Vice President of the United Arab Emirates and the ruler of Dubai. In the Forbes Billionaires List of 1998 he was listed at number eighteen, with over $10 billion of holdings largely in oil and oil services.

The "ducks" seemed to be what Youssef now called *hubara*, or bustard. Because several now appeared between the fence and the road, looking like a cross between turkeys and small ostriches. Now, it all made sense. The Emiratis were inveterate hunters of the bird and the bustard population of Baluchistan was being systematically reduced by Gulf Arabs. In the mid-1990s the Pakistani authorities had been under pressure to stop issuing hunting permits. But here Sheikh Makhtoum seemed to be raising them, like salmon farming. Between cracks in the fence we saw a large, artificial lake with levees and dams and many reeds. On the other side of the road, at the top of a steep mountain, up which a dirt track crawled precipitously, appeared several large glassed greenhouses. Who knew what else the Sheikh had up his sleeve in the area.

After the flat and the artificial marsh, the desert reappeared. But this time it was brown, not pink or white, and drifts of golden sand had blown up against the east side of the carved and incised, chestnut-colored hillocks. The brown was from flints that lay everywhere on the surface. They were not sharp like obsidian, but blunt with little air pockets where they had cooled after having been thrown up out of the earth. It was more evidence of the lava flows that had occurred millions of years ago and covered earlier deposits of limestone and sandstone. The lava seemed to be everywhere, but Youssef said that we would reach Mudawwara "just after the *wadi*." Fifteen minutes later the *wadi* appeared, a barely perceptible depression in the lava with a little green scrub that indicated subsurface water. But there was nothing that looked like a railroad, much less a station in view. We were now over two hours into our hour-and-a-quarter trip, although Youssef said that was because we had stopped for Abdullah.

Then, in the distance we saw a truck and then another. It was the highway from Ma'an to the south. We bumped over to the road and I took the wheel, Youssef having earned his keep in the sand. He said he had a "Bedouin driver's license," but I didn't know what, if anything, that meant. The smooth going was a relief, but it was obvious we were still well north of the station. After fifteen minutes a road sign announced Mudawwara, and then another one saying that it was another twenty kilometers distant. So, we had probably gone due east before picking up the highway. The railroad right-of-way lay twenty yards to the east of the road. Most of the little bridges were no longer intact. After another ten minutes, we came to a police station announced by several eucalyptus trees and an unmanned, striped barrier. It was raised and open. And beyond the barrier were two brown buildings by the side of the railway, separated by about 150 yards. At a little store by the side of the road several men said this was Mudawwara station. We had arrived.

South Mudawwara Station

Allowing for the difference of eighty-five years, the scene was just as Lawrence described it. According to the account in the *Seven Pillars* the station was very long and made up of several stone buildings, and this complex stretched perhaps a quarter of a mile from the police post in the north to the last building in the south. The water tower was gone, but Lawrence reported that it had been dynamited, spattered in "single stones across the plain" after the fall of the station in 1918. The police post was white, but clearly had been painted and looked just like the southernmost building, across from which we were now parked. It was brown, of dressed limestone blocks, with a verandah behind four stone arches. A eucalyptus stood in front. It was single story and flat roofed, fifteen feet high and maybe fifty feet long by twenty feet wide. A black tent lay behind it, on the other side of the railroad right-of-way that was covered with pebbles. The tracks were long gone. On the western side from which we had come, there was a hill or knoll, maybe 500 feet high and about half a mile from the tracks. This had obviously been the height from which the raiding party had looked down on the station on that moonless night in 1917.

We drove across the road, up a little incline and parked next to the building. A teen-aged girl came out and said, yes, of course, I could look around. Inside, there was no furniture except in the rooms that served as sleeping quarters. On one wall a mural with Kalashnikovs and raised fists announced solidarity with the Palestinians. Out the back door the children of the family raced around, frantic in their excitement, all wanting their picture taken. Even the girl, after putting on her *hijab* and adjusting it demurely, consented to a photograph. But back at the car Youssef and Abdullah were nervous about something, and they wouldn't tell me what the problem was.

So, we agreed that they would stay well away from the house, on the railroad right-of-way, and follow me up to the next building, 150 yards to the north. It was a repeat of the one I had just seen, except that there was a windmill and a little pump house nearby. The northernmost building in the complex was the police station but we all agreed that we wanted no part of that. And later it seemed that this was the problem all along. I could go into the house, but the police would think that the two young Bedouins were going after the girls. Youssef and Abdullah were well-spoken and cleanly dressed in white thobes, but that wouldn't matter. My experience with the police was that they were not ill-intentioned, but capricious, and it was always best to give them a wide berth.

But we had seen what we came to see. New Mudawwara and the border held no interest and we headed back the way we came. It had taken us nearly three hours and the odometer showed that it had been 118 km, or about 75 miles. That confirmed my suspicion that we had not taken the direct route, but more like the two sides of the triangle. At a roadside kiosk, a mile past the police station Youssef asked me if I had any "small money." I gave him a couple of dinar notes and he came back with Hostess Twinkies and Pepsis for himself and Abdullah.

The trip back to Rum was the reverse of the trip out. There were first the brown flints, then Sheikh Makhtoum's waterworks, followed by the Batn al-Ghul, the white sand and then Rum itself. We bumped through the sand with its fringe of gray-green brushwood, over the little rise and then across the flat to Abdullah's tent. He would go back with us to the village, and went inside to collect his things. Other than two Italian tourists on camels that morning, we hadn't seen a woman since we arrived in Rum. But from the women's side of the tent came the sound of a shrill female voice, Abdullah's mother I imagined, telling him not to forget something like his toothbrush. But given the general state of Bedouin dentition, it probably wasn't a toothbrush. In the Sinai, the children all seemed to have a brown stain halfway up the incisors, and the teeth here didn't seem much better. The addition of Hostess Twinkies and Pepsis to their diets wasn't helping matters.

Back in the village we dropped off Abdullah and bought gas. I had started that morning from Aqaba with a full tank, but the longer route and the heavy going meant that now there was only a quarter left. We went down one of the little potholed streets to a concrete block hut where a Bedouin sold gas in twenty-liter jerry cans. After the gas, it was back to Youssef's house. His father asked how we had fared, words to the effect of "How did my boy do?" I said that he had done a fine job. And he had, with the direct and commonsense attitude of most Bedouins. But there was more to Youssef than that. He wasn't so tied to the old ways that he couldn't adapt to the new. He told me that he had finished school and that his profession would be tourism. I wished him the best and paid him the thirty dinars we had agreed for his services.

On the way to the highway I gave an Egyptian from Malawi a ride to the project where he worked. Shortly after the junction it began to rain, at first in large, single drops then more steadily. The rain soon washed most of the sand from the outside of the car, although the inside was covered with a fine pink film. The road was good, with stretches where the posted speed limit was 110 km/hour. But you had to be careful since there were radar traps along the way and we had been stopped several times in the past. At a checkpoint near the Ma'an interchange a man in black uniform waved me over, a little disconcerting since the *mukhabarrat*, or secret police, generally dressed in black. But he was only looking for a ride to Amman for another policeman who was waiting by the side of the road. I could hardly say no, and for the next several hours the tall, pleasant but very quiet man sat at my side. He *nazala*, or descended, with profuse thanks just south of the airport. I was back in the apartment as night fell, having covered nearly a thousand kilometers in the two days. It turned out that the expense was a little more than the gas and the 30 dinars I had given Youssef. The going over the sand and flints was so rough that the thick rubber padding under one of the motor mounts had sheared off and it cost another 30 dinars to have it replaced.

And what of the station at Mudawwara? On the 31st of December 1918, three months after the first raid, another party set off from Quwayra for the railroad, this time in eight Rolls Royce armored cars and tenders. Colonel Joyce, nominally the senior British officer with Feisal's army, was in command. By sundown they reached the bluff overlooking Mudawwara where the Arabs had made the first reconnaissance that September night. Lawrence says that it was the first time that he was in a fight as a spectator. The description was vintage Lawrence, a kind of combination schoolboy prank and parody of real soldering. They didn't have the numbers to take fortified buildings and so contented themselves with shelling the little station north of Mudawwara. Four months later, in April 1918, another regular force under the command of Alan Dawnay, with Lawrence having "delicately" offered himself as interpreter, methodically reduced several stations to the north of Mudawwara. But the inevitable looting after the fall of the stations at Shahm and Ramleh north of the fort meant that most of the Arab force had melted away by the time they reached Mudawwara. It was another reprieve.

Finally, in August 1918 the Egyptian Camel Corps took the station convincingly. Lawrence accompanied the force only as far as Rum. But the action was yet another source of friction with the long–suffering British at Aqaba and Quwayra. It seemed to Hubert Young, quartermaster to the Sherifian forces, to be just another one of Lawrence's "stunts." He tells the story in *The Independent Arab*, how they finally took the station convincingly and inflicting over 150 casualties.

The actions around Mudawwara occupied many pages in the *Seven Pillars* and included some of its most stirring accounts, with the first description of Rum, reflections on geology, Semitic religions, and tribal politics, the mining of a heavily-laden train, and thoughts on the difference between guerrilla and regular warfare. It was typical Lawrence, humorous, philosophical, and slightly self-deprecating. So far from the self-aggrandizement of which he is often accused, by his own admission Lawrence was a real participant only in the first raid, and wasn't even there when the station fell at the end. He freely admitted the superior knowledge of the regular soldiers attached to the Arab cause, only disagreeing on what could or could not be done. Much of the friction with the regular soldiers may have come from Lawrence's blithe presumption of intimacy with General Allenby, all the more galling since it was probably true.

It is appropriate that the last word should be Young's. For all of his clashes with Lawrence over logistics, he recognized the little man's genius. When asked if Lawrence could have accomplished what he did without the almost limitless supply of golden guineas, he replied that he certainly could not. But no one else could have done it with ten times the amount. The question eventually became whether Lawrence really *did* anything at all. Critics in the West said that he and the Arabs did very little in the war to earn their freedom. His Arab critics said that *he* didn't do anything, but *they* did. The dispute will probably never be resolved to everyone's satisfaction. But at least with the drive to Mudawwara a part of the context had become clearer.

13

The Jordanians

THEY WERE A PALESTINIAN, a Circassian, and an Armenian but they were all emphatically Jordanian. It was what seemed to set the Hashemite kingdom apart from other countries in the region. Elsewhere, ethnic and religious tensions simmered beneath the surface, although they were often denied and the official line consisted of paeans to the unity of the country. That was not to say that there wasn't ethnic or religious friction in Jordan. The political system favored the native east-bankers over the more-numerous Palestinians, and tribal forces in the government and military were the greatest supporters of the throne. But tensions seemed to take a less lethal form than in other countries in the region. Maybe that was because the Hashemites were not really native to the area and from the beginning had to trim their sails to the prevailing winds.

They were the descendants of cosmopolites who had divided their time between comfortable captivity in Istanbul and a brief period of rule in Mecca during and immediately after the First World War. They were part of what came to be known as the "Hashemite solution" in the Middle East. In Damascus Feisal, third son of the Sharif of Mecca, ruled briefly after the war despite local grumblings about his Bedouin leanings and entourage. Syria had serious centers of power, from the great merchant families in Damascus to the Turkified elite of Aleppo, to the Druse isolated and relatively independent in the remote Huaran, not to mention the Alawites in the northwest and the always refractory Bedouins and Kurds in the east. None of them, with the possible exception of the Druse, played much of a role in the Arab Revolt, a tribal uprising largely confined to the Hejaz before it became an appendage of Allenby's army in Palestine. And none of them figured in the calculations of British king-makers, T. E. Lawrence chief among them. The elites of Syria chafed at the imposition of a Hashemite sovereign on the country, although they conceded that Feisal was preferable to the French. In the end, they got both. The brief flirtation with independence was terminated by a French army and ended with Feisal, ejected and forlorn, sitting on his baggage in the train station in Dera'a. He was later the beneficiary of British skullduggery and made king of Iraq.

In Transjordan, the Hashemites had to carefully navigate their way among the shoals of not only the sectarian and ethnic divide, but also of great power rivalries. Abdullah, the second and most politic son of the Sharif, having announced that he would eject the French from Syria after they deposed his brother, marched north from the Hejaz with his ragtag army and set up camp across the Jordan, constituting a thorn in the side of both the British and the French. The British had by this time acceded to French control of Syria, having traded a free hand for the French in that country in return for Mosul and a free hand in Iraq, in effect selling out their Hashemite allies. Abdullah's fulminations and periodic cross-border incursions threatened to upset the new arrangements, bringing with them the possibility of French retaliation. The British responded by separating Transjordan from the mandated territory in Palestine, although some argued that Lord Balfour, in his munificence, intended to deed everything between the Mediterranean and Iraqi border to the Jews. They bought off Abdullah at a cost to the exchequer far less than that of Palestine and recognized him as Emir of the new entity.

With the possible exception of Salt in the north there were no large urban centers in the country. Amman at the time was a small town inhabited largely by tribes and the Circassians and Chechens who had been introduced by the Turks as a stabilizing element in the region. There were also Armenians who had survived the massacres and found refuge in the country. But there were few merchant elites and so Abdullah cultivated the tribes and the Circassians to maintain himself in power, a bit of triangulation that became necessary as increasing numbers of Palestinians—west-bankers—streamed across the border from mandated Palestine as Arab-Jewish tensions increased. The stream became a flood after 1948 as Arabs were largely cleansed from what would eventually become Israel.

By the end of the twentieth century the Palestinians had come to constitute a majority in Jordan and a series of kings would continue to use constitutional means to dilute their influence. The constitution gave disproportionate weight to the tribes and east bankers. It was perhaps the habit of careful maintenance of the balance between competing interests—tribal, ethnic, and political—added to Abdullah's native shrewdness, that contributed to the Jordanian Hashemites' moderation. That was not to say that they could not be ruthless when there were threats to the throne, and Black September in 1971 showed that they were capable of answering force with force. They were autocrats, similar in some respects to other autocrats in the region, but different also in their fundamental decency.

Which brings us back to the three men mentioned at the beginning of our tale. They were all senior executives of Jordan Telecom and members of the board of the company. If Jordan stood out in the region for its moderation, Jordan Telecom stood for the competence of its senior executives. They told stories of regional conferences where chairman of another—unnamed—telecom company stayed in his hotel room rather than exhibit his ignorance in meetings with his peers. Not the Jordanians. They were in the forefront in the Arab World, not only in the company but also in the formation of a regulator, a necessary first step in liberalizing the sector. The board had taken the decision in the mid-1990s that they would liberalize both the fixed-line and the mobile sub-sectors and they asked for American help to make it happen. It was a reversal of the normal practice, where the Americans would decide that liberalization was necessary and attach covenants to loan and grant agreements to bring it about. It goes without saying that the Jordanian model was the more successful.

I knew the three only after their retirement. Two were consultants to the Ministry of Post and Communications (MoPC) and the third was chairman of the Telecommunications Regulatory Commission (TRC). I found the first two in the back room in the ministry to which they had been consigned, barely visible through a thick haze of smoke. One had a cigarette habit and the other smoked small cigars. Both had an inveterate mistrust of foreign consultants and my reception was hardly enthusiastic. Abu Jamil appeared to have been a redhead with a fair complexion that sixty-plus years of exposure to the Middle Eastern sun had burnished to a deep scarlet. He was a large man, weighing close to 250 pounds and an Armenian Catholic originally from Cilicia, or Little Armenia, an area that straddled the border between Syria and Turkey. He was a graduate in engineering from the University of Baghdad and had risen to become head of network planning in Jordan Telecom.

He and I eventually became friends and we later made it a practice to stop by his house on Christmas Eve where the conversation flowed freely. His wife looked to be about twenty years younger and was very pretty. Their children, a son and a daughter, had, like their father, done well in school and looked forward to careers in the telecom business. In that respect, liberalization had been a boon and there were several alternatives to the old fixed-line monopoly company, now majority-owned by France Telecom.

The family were all-Armenian and they appeared committed to holding up the side. When I looked for a tailor in Amman Abu Jamil recommended an Armenian downtown. When I looked for a tinsmith to have my copper pots re-tinned, Abu Jamil recommended another Armenian downtown. In one of the unintended consequences of the genocide the Turks afterward couldn't find anyone to tin their pots. Like many crafts in northeastern Anatolia it had been an Armenian specialty. Abu Jamil smoked like a chimney and combined with his weight and type-A personality, he looked like a cardiac waiting to happen. But on this first meeting he wouldn't speak to me.

That was left to his more diplomatic cohort, Abu Omar, a Sunni Muslim and, I believe, a west banker. He had taken a second wife later in life and had small children by her. If Abu Jamil was voluble and wore his opinions on his sleeve, Abu Omar chose his words with a great deal of deliberation, a good trait in the regulator he would later become. He had led the Jordanian effort in the brief spring after Madrid when Jordanians and Israelis were negotiating, among other things, telecommunications agreements, and he could always be counted on to take the long view. Abu Jamil was a tough negotiator who argued shrewdly and persistently, but Abu Omar was a conciliator. That made him the natural leader. But the fact that he was a Sunni Muslim, the dominant sect and overwhelming majority in the country, may have contributed to the dynamic between the two. Abu Omar spoke with the confidence of one born to rule. No pyrotechnics were necessary. They were in many respects the stereotypical Christian and the stereotypical Muslim, embodying the confessional divide in the country. But they came as a package and were inseparable except for their opinions, which were often diametrically opposed. They were like Mutt and Jeff except that they disagreed good-naturedly on almost every subject imaginable.

The third member of the group was another Abu Omar, a Circassian whose forebears came from the Balkariyya autonomous region in the Causcasus and he was, in fact, very Caucasian in looks. Where the Circassians in Egypt had been brought in as chattels and enjoyed the kind of perverse prestige that came with their servile origin—they effectively ruled the country for 500 years—the Circassians in Jordan came at a different time and under different circumstances. When the Russians completed the conquest of the Caucasus with their victory over Shamil, they cleansed the area of much of its Muslim population, although some Muslims left voluntarily rather than suffer alien rule. Those who left passed through Bulgaria before making their way to Turkey where they found refuge among their coreligionists. Many were subsequently sent south by the Ottoman Turks to settle the land across the Jordan, where they were concentrated in the Wadi Seer area around Amman. In time, they came to constitute a wealthy, landowning elite.

With the coming of the Hashemites after the war, Circassians were drafted into the bodyguard of the king. The army was Bedouin and the bodyguard Circassian and together with the scattered east-bankers, they represented a counterweight to the Palestinians in the country and constituted another piece in the mosaic that made up modern Jordan. The Circassians maintained a strong sense of community and some of the staff we worked with still spoke the old language at home. Abu Omar didn't wear his Circassian identity on his sleeve, maybe because of a reputation that represented a holdover from less settled times. Someone later said he was the only Circassian he knew who didn't pack a pistol. He didn't wear his religion on his sleeve either, maybe because the Circassians were relatively recent converts to Islam, many of them having been Orthodox Christians well into the eighteenth century.

He was known as Abu Omar junior and where Abu Jamil and Abu Omar senior had, in effect, been put on the shelf in retirement, he was made head of the Jordanian regulatory authority, or TRC. It was he who suggested that the other two constituted a resource that could be tapped as liberalization unfolded. Like his namesake, Abu Omar junior was thorough and methodical, an approach that inevitably earned criticism from the firebrands in the sector. As competition was introduced the old monopoly provider reacted like monopolies everywhere with behavior that, while it may have been prejudicial to new entrants, still fell on the right side of the law. The firebrands wanted Jordan Telecom taken down. Abu Omar junior's ingrained caution, combined with the untested powers of the regulator, made him choose his battles, like his words, very shrewdly. I never knew a man who read a memorandum—in either Arabic or English—more carefully. As we helped to shape the regulatory framework we hoped that government would make policy, the TRC would ensure compliance, the operators would conform, and the courts would intervene only as a last resort to adjudicate disputes. Abu Omar junior was not about to provoke unnecessary conflict as the parties in the sector maneuvered to find their way in the liberalized landscape.

Eventually, each of the three found a permanent place in the new environment. Abu Jamil remained as a senior advisor to the ministry where his knowledge of the old monopolist was put to good use as he held France Telecom ownership to account for promises made in the license agreement. Abu Omar senior was named to the new five–member, full-time TRC and he brought his characteristic measured approach to its deliberations. Abu Omar junior remained at the TRC where his talents were put to good use as, in effect, the second in command. Let others grandstand. He would continue to read and speak carefully. All three were forces for good in the successful Jordanian effort to open the sector to competition. There was justice in that, as they were representatives of the board that had conceived the idea in the first place. In that respect, they were Jordanian through and through.

14

The Bach Festival

IT WOULD BE A week of unadulterated Bach and a respite from the persistent bad news that plagued the Middle East in 2004. The year was really no different from any year in the past sixty years in the region. Only now it was more so, with the United States engaged in suppressing a civilian insurgency in Iraq through the application of massive military force. Abu Ghraib came as a shock to the sensibilities of everyone in the Middle East who had looked to America as a paragon of respect for human rights. There had been no reports of Israeli sexual abuse of Palestinian detainees over the years, perhaps because it was too inflammatory. The Israelis, as they were tireless in reminding us, still had to live in the neighborhood. So where did the Americans learn this tactic? Because sexual debasement was a particular humiliation in the Arab World. Young Arab males, frustrated by their repressive societies and no different from young males anywhere else, were enthusiastic consumers of western pornography if the figures for Internet usage in the Middle East were to be believed. But it was the product of the debauched and depraved West, indulged in private. Public nudity was nonexistent and years of exposure to dressing rooms in health clubs in the region had been a schooling in the prudishness of the average Arab male. Clothes were changed in little cubicles with curtains, and signs on the walls cautioned against appearing in public without "bathing costume."

Maybe it really was, as Seymour Hersh would later suggest, that advisors to the administration had recommended a classic "Orientalist" canon, Rafael Patai's *The Arab Mind*, as their textbook on the humiliation of Arab males in an effort to extract actionable intelligence. If so, it would reinforce the notion that "Orientalism" was nothing more than a means of asserting Western control over the East. It would also call into question the efforts of the "Orientalists" who had arrogated to themselves the role of interpreters of Arabs and Muslims to the West.

The immediate backdrop in early May was the prison abuse scandal, with the ominous warning that worse was yet to come. The *Bachfest Leipzig 2004* seemed an escape from the drumbeat of bad news, particularly in Jordan, according to several Pew Reports the most anti-American country among those surveyed. An earlier poll showed that 99 percent of Jordanians had a negative view of the United States. Jordanians trusted Osama bin Laden over George W. Bush by a figure of 57 percent to 3 percent. But the hostility was an undercurrent, not expressed openly. That was because the authorities kept a tight lid on popular outpourings of emotion. After all, Jordan was a friend in the region with a long history of CIA involvement at the highest levels. Americans with buzzed haircuts had been everywhere in Amman in the run-up to the war, and the country served as a venue for the detention and interrogation of notorious bad actors. After a period in the doghouse in the early 1990s with their rhetorical support for Saddam in the first Gulf War, Jordan was back on the gravy train, with $450 million in annual aid. On a per-capita basis that was nearly double our contribution to Egypt, although only a tenth of the aid to Israel. So, in spite of deep popular hostility to America, Jordan remained an ally, although the events in Iraq were putting a strain on the relationship. The delay of a meeting with Bush in late April was King Abdullah's recognition, albeit a feeble one, of the strain.

I left Amman on Thursday May 13, the day marking my twenty-fourth anniversary living and working in the Muslim World. The experience had been primarily in Arab countries, but included stints in Baluchistan and the Northwest Frontier province of Pakistan, and Niger in old French West Africa. I had cut my teeth in the region reading *Al-Ahram* in Egypt in the early 1980s with its dismal, day-by-day account of the Israeli siege of Beirut. The reportage on events in Iraq was like that earlier experience, except that this time it was Americans who were the perpetrators. Civilian deaths in Iraq were probably approaching the 20,000 killed in Beirut, although nobody bothered to keep count. If the Americans wanted to maximize their influence in the Arab World they should put their considerable resources into dealing with the intractable Palestinian problem, imposing a solution if all else failed. If we really wanted to see American troops greeted as liberators, we should put them in the West Bank, unthinkable as that seemed.

There was another reason why Bach seemed a good antidote. Several years before I had bought Christoph Wolff's *Johann Sebastian Bach, The Learned Musician* and the book was a constant companion during the week in Leipzig. Wolff listed nine areas of "compositional art" in which Bach excelled, from fugues and canons to church cantatas. Among the last, particular favorites were recordings by Kurt Thomas and the Gewandhaus Orchestra, Leipzig. On a closer reading it appeared that Thomas, like Bach, had been cantor in Leipzig, from 1957 to 1960. All the above names and genres would become familiar over the course of the week.

Leipzig was in the old East Germany or GDR, and the city and its Lutheran churches, some of them venues for the festival, had played an important part in the collapse of the Soviet system and the fall of the Berlin Wall. It had been a moral force for good. But all this lay in the future as I laid plans for the week. It would be Air France from Amman to Berlin through Paris. Then, the train southeast to Leipzig. I had called the Bach Archive beforehand and was assured that tickets to the events would be available in Leipzig. In fact, only once was a concert sold out and, even then I found a seat. But I did make hotel reservations for the week at the Hotel Deutscher Hof, and confirmation of an "Einzelzimmer—Du + WC—Frühst." from the Leipzig Tourist Service arrived within a few minutes by e-mail. That meant a single room with a shower and water closet, plus breakfast.

Air France was the usual pleasant traveling experience. At midmorning, Charles de Gaulle was the familiar series of ellipses through which it seemed only too easy to gain access to Europe. There was a three-hour layover and then a bus ride to another Airbus for the 2:55 flight to Berlin. Low clouds lay over most of northeastern Europe, and it was only after we descended that the green of Berlin appeared. It didn't have the look of a major city, if only because of the canopy of forest that seemed to surround it. At an airport information desk an attendant helped me make hotel reservations. I said that I had come from Jordan for the Bach Festival and would take the train to Leipzig the next day. So, I wanted a hotel near the train station. The Bleibtreu on Bleibtreustrasse (or Bleibtreu street) was within walking distance of the Zoologischer Garten station.

The strangeness of Berlin increased on the ride to the hotel. About ten minutes from the airport we turned onto Kaiser Friedrichstrasse and passed through an area of tattooing and piercing establishments, massage parlors, tanning salons, and block-long "erotik" emporia. A pipe, a foot in diameter and painted a lurid pink, ran the length of the street before it elevated over an intersection. The city looked down at the heels. But the area around the hotel was decidedly upscale with outlets of the major couturiers. I later learned that it was considered the Champs Elyseés of Berlin. The hotel was set well back from the street, so inconspicuous that I passed the entrance several times before finding it. The first-floor room was small and the furnishings were unlike anything I had seen before. Nearly half the floor space was taken up by the bathroom, whose door was a single hinged glass-and-plywood partition, four feet wide. It looked Japanese. The fixtures were crude, of functional brass with cruciform handles. The bed was hard and the pillows were small and thin, a reminder of the Hotel Uzbekistan in Tashkent. There were remotes to control the lights and the television, and the phone was a mobile device. Those who grew up expecting a fixed-line telephone in every house, not to mention every hotel room, forgot that in the developing world a fixed telephone was a luxury. Mobiles were now cheaper and easier to deploy.

The evening and most of the next morning would be spent in Berlin before the afternoon train to Leipzig. The first order of business was dinner, and I asked the girl at the front desk if the hotel restaurant served German food.

> Oh no, the food here is international. She seemed slightly offended.
> Where would I get a good German meal?
> Try the Leibniz-Klause on Leibnizstrasse. Go down the Kurfürstendamm three blocks and then three blocks to the right.

Leibniz-Klause, or Leibniz's Retreat, was a pleasant, airy place served by friendly ladies in peasant dress. If it was a German meal I wanted then I must surely have the Reisen Eisbein, and how about a little Kartoffelsuppe to start with? That was potato soup Kaiser Wilhelm style, with Troutkaviar. When the Eisbein, or pickled knuckle of pork, arrived it was more like a shoulder than a knuckle, covering most of the plate. Somehow, there was room for a thick puree of peas with bacon bits, sauerkraut and boiled potatoes. Even after I had removed the quarter inch of fatty skin surrounding the meat and eaten down to the bone, it was still too much. The meat came with horseradish and a pot of sharp mustard.

If I wanted a week of unadulterated Bach, the other attraction of Germany was pork and I indulged it to the full. Pork was available from Christian butchers in Cairo and Amman, and we had eaten wild boar in Islamabad and even "white beef" in Jidda. But it was an occasional treat, and this was a chance to have it prepared by experts. My resolve broke down only once in the seven days. On the return to hotel I passed Niebuhrstrasse just before crossing Kantstrasse. The streets in Berlin all seemed to be named after famous Germans, although I didn't know if this was Niebuhr the traveler in Arabia or Niebuhr the historian.

The next morning, I made reservations for an afternoon train to Leipzig. The station was on the edge of the Tiergarten, which seemed to be to Berlin what Central Park was to New York. The guidebook provided by the hotel described the area as hunting grounds for local rulers in the sixteenth and seventeenth centuries, before being developed as a park in the eighteenth century. Somehow it had survived the immediate postwar need for firewood. On this spring day, it was lush and green, intersected by little streams and carpeted with wildflowers. I walked along the western fringe for fifteen minutes before reaching Strasse des 17. Juni—or, June 17th Street, so-called after the revolt of East Berliners in 1953—and turning east towards the Brandenburg Gate, which looked from the map to be a couple of miles away. Closer, in a roundabout, was a column surmounted by a winged figure, the Goldelse, and only up close did its proportions become apparent. This was no slender classical structure, but a massive segmented column, now blackened with soot, topped by the violently gold and very Teutonic figure of victory. It stood about 200 feet high. Was it the Franco-Prussian War she was celebrating?

The Tiergarten

Bicyclers and joggers filled the footpaths that dipped in and out of the green on either side of the avenue. After fifteen minutes, I reached the monument to the Soviet conquest of the city, bracketed by a pair of vintage tanks and topped by the usual massive Soviet statuary.

Soviet Tank

The Russian march across eastern Europe had been an orgy of rape, and it was said that two million German women were violated. From the back, the Brandenburg Gate was obscured by scaffolding and it was only on the other side and the Unter den Linden that its familiar contours appeared. The park with its bucolic setting was suddenly transformed into a wide boulevard with shops and hotels. A map of the city before reunification showed that almost the entire Tiergarten, with the exception of a little hernia that protruded through the wall on the southeast side, lay in the western zone. Even so, its 1,300 acres of almost tropical cover seemed a perfect setting for the kind of Cold War activity chronicled by authors like John le Carre. But that could have been only in the spring and summer, because most of the trees would lose their leaves in the autumn, and in the winter it would be a sea of naked limbs.

I walked up the Unter den Linden a few blocks before turning back towards the Brandenburg Gate and the Tiergarten. Then, it was a reverse of the walk back to the hotel. I had clearly not seen much of Berlin, and only a few of the pre-World-War-II monuments. The Nazi period, the Cold War, and the post-Cold-War period—with the exception of the Soviet monument and the Kurfürstendamm—were utter blanks. But there seemed to be little architectural homogeneity in the city. The guidebook mentioned work by "famous" architects, "most renowned" architects, "star" architects and "French star" architects, and the city had obviously been a fertile ground for international designers in the reconstruction after the war. This gave Berlin an energy, a kind of main-street boosterism that seemed out of character for what had been the stern capital of Prussian militarism.

Just after noon I checked out of the hotel, whose odd little rooms looked like they had been designed by a star architect, and made my way back to the Zoologischer Garten station. At noon, the place—bordered by fast food joints—was thronged with people. Most of them seemed to be wearing Levi's. Jeans represented a kind of American casualness and freedom, not to mention a German fascination with the American west. The train to Leipzig was direct, with only a couple of stops and would take just under two hours. Ten minutes later, through an area dominated by an odd combination of high-rises—what looked like the space needle followed by a massive domed, Baroque cathedral—we arrived at the Berlin East station. Then it was into the outskirts of the city before reaching the suburbs and then the countryside. Acres of what looked like industrial-use, brick structures were abandoned and covered with another western import, graffiti. It was wild and colorful and psychedelic and accompanied us all the way to Leipzig. In the little villages, a few new roofs—the bright orange of their tiles contrasting with the washed–out dun color of their neighbors—suggested a recent infusion of wealth. But the dominant feature in all the towns was the church, its spire towering over the secular space and I reflected that I was in a Christian country again. I would later discover how mistaken I had been.

The countryside looked to be very fertile, with wide undulating fields bordered by dense stands of forest. The fields were planted in what looked like mustard, the color suddenly brilliant after the pervasive green. It was almost painful to look directly at the yellow. In the forest, some of the oaks were not fully in leaf, but there were occasional stands of pine of a uniform height, most of the trunks bare to within a few feet of the tops. After an hour, we reached Wittenberg and windmills, all turning slowly, began to appear on both sides of the train. They were very modern, looking like those that dotted the Altamont Pass in California, but so slender that it was hard to see how the wind could find a purchase on their three-sided sails. The outskirts of Leipzig soon announced themselves, nondescript except for the graffiti, and at 3:16, on schedule, we arrived in the city station. It had to be the mother of all Bahnhoffen with an enclosed area under a massive, domed and reticulated glass-covered roof that was the equivalent of about twenty football fields, set side-by-side. Escalator access to several layers of shops multiplied the commercial space many times over.

I took a taxi to the Deutscher Hof. After five minutes, we pulled up outside another nondescript brick building with several broken windows, the glass covered with graffiti. We had arrived. Inside, dressed in stone-washed Levi's, the proprietor—and desk clerk, telephone operator, bellman, concierge, waiter, and general factotum—greeted me with a burst of incomprehensible German. He had been waiting for me. There was nothing to sign, no credit card impression to take, and no guide to the hotel amenities, such as they were. The room was on the third floor and the elevator was conveniently located next to the front desk. Room 301 was neat and clean, very simple with a small single bed and European style coverlet inside the sheet. The bathroom was also new, clean and functional, equipped with two thin towels. There was no mini bar, no television, no telephone, no room-service menu, and no guide to the city. I later learned there were a Westin and a Marriott in town, but that they were fully booked with the Bach Festival. But the Deutscher Hof advertised "gunstige Zentrumslage and komfortable Zimmer," a central location and comfortable room, and that was all I wanted.

I had time for a change of clothes and a brief discussion with Herr Friedrich about the location of the Thomaskirche, where the opening of the Festival would take place at six o'clock that evening. We traced the way on a dog-eared city map to the church. It would take about twenty minutes. I would wear a groove in the cobblestones of that route over the next week.

Thomaskirche

At the church, the ticket office was open and there were still good seats available. The concert began with the Sinfonia in D Major by Bach, followed by a series of lectures delivered by, among others, Prof. Dr. Dr. H. C. Christoph Wolff, Harvard professor, director of the Bach Archive in

Leipzig and, incidentally, author of *The Learned Musician*. I suppressed a thought of Basil Fawlty ("Oh, so you're *two* doctors . . .") and tried to catch a sense of the lecture. But my previous exposure to German consisted of translations of Carsten Niebuhr's eighteenth-century Saxon into English, using a dictionary of the literary language published in 1939. So, I was helpless with the spoken word. But I had come for the music not the words. The program resumed with a Bach Motet BWV (Bach-Werke-Verzeichnis, or List of Bach's Works) 225, the Cantata BWV 190, and ended with a piece by Mendelssohn. The musicians and singers were in the organ loft above and behind us and the magnificent sounds filled the church from on high.

Dinner in a little restaurant near the hotel was a breaded pork-cutlet with potatoes and cauliflower. When I asked for bread the lady appeared several minutes later with two slices of what looked like Wonder Bread, this in a country with more varieties of dark bread than Carter had little pills. She took only cash. Back in the hotel room, I reflected on this first day. I was in Leipzig, tickets to the concerts were available, I was familiar with the venue and had already experienced a taste of what was to come. The hotel was adequate and the Schweinefleisch was plentiful. But after the Tiergarten, the Brandenburg Gate, a couple of trips to the Zoologische Station and a round trip to Thomaskirche I had probably done a half-marathon on foot that day. A painful inflammation of one leg bothered me for the rest of the week. But it was a small price to pay for the music. There would be no newspapers, no television, no Internet, no e-mail, and no telephones for the next seven days. It would be just Bach and pork.

Leipzig Motif

Leipzig—or something between Leipzij and Leipzitsch in the Saxon pronunciation—was a moderate-sized city in Thuringia, the state in the geographic center of reunified Germany. It had always been an important crossroads for trade, from the Italian cities north to the Baltic, and from Russia and Poland through Germany to the west. Importantly for Bach, this included not only trade but also musical influences, particularly from

Italy. The city's wealth—judging by the provenance of the buildings that lined the walk to Thomaskirche—appeared to date from the nineteenth century. In Bach's time the church lay just inside the city walls, beyond which there were only fields. In time, the fields had been overlaid with the streets and buildings of the growing metropolis. There appeared to be a characteristic Leipzig architectural motif, all the buildings consisting of four stories with regular facades and classic windows and doors, surmounted by pediments and raking cornices. Dormer windows showed that there were rooms in the attics that made up a fifth floor. This gave a uniformity and human scale to the city. Half of the buildings today appeared to be boarded up and covered with graffiti. Of the other half, some were in use and others were enclosed in scaffolding as the facades were renovated and the interiors refurbished. Outside the medieval walls, the city in 2004 looked like it was getting back on its feet.

Bach Statue, Leipzig

Johann Sebastian Bach (1685–1750) had come to Leipzig in 1723 after stints as organist in Armstadt (1703–1707) and Mühlhausen (1707–1708), court organist in Weimar (1708–1717), and Capellmeister in Cöthen (1717–1723). These were all locales within seventy-five miles of one another in Saxony and Thuringia. He came from a family of professional musicians. His father, Johann Ambrosius Bach, was one of nine cousins and third-generation descendants of Johannes Bach, a town musician in Gotha. They included Johann Christian Bach, Johann Aegidius Bach, Johann Nicholas Bach, Johann Christoph Bach, Johann Michael Bach, and Johann Gunther Bach. All of them lived between 1640 and 1716, and all were town musicians, organists, composers, or cantors. The name Bach meant "rivulet" and was originally Hungarian, or at least came from somewhere in the Hapsburg domains.

But if he came from a long line of musicians, Sebastian carried the family tradition to new heights, creating perhaps the most extraordinary corpus in the history of music. The twenty years in Armstadt, Mülhausen, Weimar, and Cöthen had been mainly devoted to academic keyboard and orchestral works. But the Leipzig period was devoted to what had become a passion in Bach's middle life, "a well-regulated church music." Leipzig was an opportunity to integrate the latest trends in French and Italian opera with his own thorough grounding in counterpoint into the new genre, the sacred cantata. He envisaged five complete yearly cycles, only half of which have survived, although there is some question whether the last two ever existed as such. This required a regular artistic output—roughly a new cantata per week—that would have taxed the stamina of a lesser man. There was some "parody" involved, that is, the reuse of previous material in new settings. But, even so the sustained work and uniformly high quality of the Leipzig years was phenomenal.

One appeal of Bach was that he was a hardworking, no-nonsense, hands-on musician. Not only was he Germany's—and probably Europe's—premier keyboard and organ virtuoso, having developed a revolutionary fingering technique that allowed new departures in performance, but he was also an expert in the design, tuning, and operation of what Wolff calls the most sophisticated piece of machinery in eighteenth-century Europe. Bach never lost his technician's interest in the craft of organ building and made trips to other German cities to test newly built organs. His sense of the importance of acoustics in performance was legendary, and he could immediately identify which venues were suitable, and which were not, for musical performances. After testing Gottfried

Silbermann's new pianoforte, Bach's highly critical comments nearly scuppered development of the instrument until Silbermann swallowed his pride and adopted the recommendations. Added to his seminal use of the keyboard as a solo concerto instrument—the 5th Brandenburg being probably the first to do so—the nineteenth-century fashion of the piano concerto as the virtuoso performance *par excellence* probably owed more to Bach than to any other single figure.

He was also irascible, a tempestuous employee, a hard negotiator, and a hard drinker. A week's expense report for one of his early organ-testing trips, to Halle in November, 1713 shows a claim for, among other things, eighteen groschen for beer, which Wolfe calculates would have bought thirty-two quarts at the then-retail price. He liked to retire to his composing room in Leipzig with a bottle of brandy. He was nobody's fool and while he could be obsequious on paper to his courtly patrons, he was never groveling. With two wives he fathered twenty children, of whom ten lived to adulthood. We suspect that his sons would have found the old *perruque* (wig) a difficult and demanding father, if he did nothing more than require from them the same high standards he set for himself. Not all responded equally, and there were some ne'er-do-wells among the Bach sons. One, Carl Philipp Emanuel, probably achieved more in terms of musical acceptance in society than his father. But in spite of his sometimes-rough edges, Bach was deeply religious and his sacred cantatas and passions contain some of the most moving music ever written. When he finally succumbed in 1750 to a painful eye disease, probably brought on by untreated adult-onset diabetes, it was with a fine Christian acceptance of his fate.

The next day, Saturday May 15, was the beginning of the Bachfest in earnest. It would last until the twenty-third, and over that period there would be over seventy scheduled events in twenty-two venues throughout the city. Most of them were within a half-mile of Thomaskirche. I had to be back in Berlin for a flight early on the morning of the twenty-first, so that meant the Gottesdienst in der Liturgie der Bach-Zeit, or divine services in the liturgy of Bach's time, on Thursday morning the twentieth, would be my last event. It would be eventful, a lesson in the integration of the sacred cantata form into the eighteenth-century Lutheran liturgy. It would also be Christi Himmelfahrt, or the Feast of the Ascension, which accounted for the extensive service in midweek. So, after breakfast—a buffet of cold meats, cheeses, pumpernickel and fruit, with coffee served by Herr Friederich—I made my way back to the old city and the 9:30 Mass, this time at Nikolaikirche. The service included motets by Monteverdi and Palestrina, sandwiched around chorales and organ pieces by Bach, and ended with motets by the twentieth-century German, Max Reger. But more interesting than the music this time was the church itself. That evening, I learned from an architect who had come from Munich for the concert, that this was where the revolution of 1989 had begun. "It started in that very church," he said.

It seemed that after months of demonstrations and a physical blockade of the church, during which the police and *Stasi*, or State Security Service, had arrested hundreds of demonstrators, events had come to a head on October 9, 1989, 450 years after Luther preached another revolution, the Reformation, in Leipzig. On that night thousands assembled for "peace prayers," joined by 600 *Stasi* and communist party members in the church itself. But the effect of the Sermon on the Mount had been electric. Before the end of the service, messages of solidarity from civic figures, including Kurt Masur, conductor of the Gewandhaus Orchestra, were read out. Thousands left the church carrying candles in a nonviolent protest, to join the tens of thousands waiting outside. Faced with this massive outpouring of sentiment, the police and security forces withdrew. The party and its ideological state collapsed a few weeks later, brought down, it was said, by an alliance of art and religion, music and the gospel.

From the outside, Nikolaikirche looked massive and crude, of unadorned brown sandstone surmounted by a series of steep, slate-gray roofs. But inside it was elaborately decorated in eighteenth-century style, with fluted columns topped by elaborate capitals of green palm fronds that spread onto the vaulted ceiling. The ceiling itself, arched separately over the nave and transept, was covered with geometric designs, executed in tan and green. In the apse, there were two large paintings over the main altar, and the sides were papered with portraits of church dignitaries. Elevated galleries around the sides allowed overflow crowds and were occasionally used for small orchestras or choral groups. The church sat about 2,000 worshippers.

The floor was of geometric green and white marble. The back of the pews, painted in white enamel and numbered with brass plaques, struck the average worshipper about chest high. That allowed a little angled railing on the top to be used as a book rest. The only objections to the space from a musical point of view were that the columns, two feet in diameter, interfered with the view from some vantage points, and the acoustics were occasionally poor, with a voice drowned out by an accompanying trumpet. The church appeared to be immaculately kept. That wouldn't always be the case with churches in Leipzig. A week's attendance at Nikolaikirche, Thomaskirche, Lutherkirche, Evangelisch-reformierte Kirche and Michaeliskirche would reveal a wide range of styles and attention to maintenance. But there was one constant in these German Protestant churches: they all had little footrests, but no kneelers. In a week of divine services in Leipzig, I didn't kneel once.

Back at the Bach Archive I bought tickets for the week. Prices ranged from fifteen to fifty Euros for the major concerts, and ten to thirty Euros for the lesser ones. The most expensive tickets didn't always guarantee a good seat. The morning Gottesdienst, or divine services, were free and a bargain at twice the price. Otherwise, it would be a week of old favorites. I signed up for one tour, to Halle, with performances of pieces by Handel, Bach, and Dvorak. The morning services were a learning experience and pieces I was not familiar with, particularly preludes and fugues for organ. And in spite of the fact that I was looking for a week of unadulterated Bach, the festival was, after all, entitled "Bach und die Romantik," or Bach and the Age of Romanticism. That meant a heavy dose of Brahms, Dvorak, Schumann, and particularly, Mendelssohn. Felix Mendelssohn Bartholdy had played a major role in resurrecting Bach's music in the century after his death, and his music was co-featured throughout the week.

The days were long, and several times I returned to the Deutscher Hof near midnight, having left early that morning. The church services in Bach's time could last for three hours, with an hour for the sermon alone. In 2004, they weren't quite that long but still could take up most of a morning. Afterwards there might be a grilled bratwurst bought from a sidewalk vendor. It was a serious sausage, served in a round roll like a hamburger bun, so it had the odd look of a combination American hot dog and hamburger. A pint of beer complemented the sausage. Today, the fifteenth, there would be a concert of motets and cantatas by Bach and Moritz Hauptmann at three p.m. in Thomaskirche. They would be followed by the Goldberg Variations in Nikolaikirche at five o'clock. Finally, at eight o'clock that evening, would be the first major concert in the spacious Gewandhaus, the concerto "fur 3 Klaviere" by Bach and two orchestral pieces by Mendelssohn. The evening concert was a bit of a disappointment. The seat was not very good. I had the most expensive ticket, but was seated in the E section, well above those in sections A through D. I wondered what a ten Euro ticket would have bought. Then, the 3 "Klaviere" turned out to be pianos, not harpsichords, and lacked the brilliant sound of the strings being plucked rather than struck. The pianists—an American, a Chinese girl, and a German—were all very good and were called back for several bows. Four seemed to be the going rate for a really good performance.

At the intermission, I chatted with the architect from Munich. He was another enthusiastic amateur, and had come up five hours by train for the concert. He was almost apologetic:

> I am an architect, but my *mother* was a musician.

He was a westerner but if he resented paying the "Ossi," or Easterner, tax he didn't say so. That was when he mentioned Nikolaikirche and the revolution. The walk back to the Deutscher Hof near midnight was in a light drifting rain.

The next day, the sixteenth of May, would be nearly as busy. First there was the divine service in Thomaskirche. It was a Sunday, and so a full-blown service with the liturgy sung in a tenor plainsong by the Pfarrer, or parish priest, Christian Wolff. It sounded very medieval, even Catholic. A piece by Brahms accompanied the Introit, and then the congregation joined in singing "Ehre sei Gott in der Höhe," ("glory to God in the highest.") I was astonished to hear the Japanese man sitting next to me—bandoliered in camera equipment—following the notes in the little mass booklet and singing in a fine tenor voice. The Japanese, apparently great enthusiasts of Bach, were regulars throughout the festival. After the reading from the Old Testament there followed the epistle and gospel and the Bach Cantata "Du Hirte Israel höre," ("You Shepherd of Israel, Hear,") BWV 104. The sermon, delivered from the elaborate elevated pulpit by Pfarrer Wolff, apparently dealt with the present, and I caught the words "anti-communist," "Karl Marx," "democratic," "problem," "Internet," and "innovation." As he spoke he used his hands like Colin Powell, regularly aligning his speaker's notes with the tips of his fingers, the palms turned upward.

But this liturgical reverie was to be interrupted. It was now nearly eleven o'clock and time for departure for Halle. We boarded the bus in front of Thomaskirche and, as we wound our way through the city it was clear that the festival venues represented only a small part of Leipzig. Founded in the early twelfth century at a crossroads of trade routes, the city had suffered heavily during the Thirty Years War. But a period of rapid growth beginning in the eighteenth century had confirmed its reputation as not only a trading, but also an artistic center. The core of the city—and almost the geographic center on the map—was a rough square enclosed by the old medieval walls, now the Ring Road. The square was about 800 meters on a side, easily walkable in a few minutes. Inside lay the venues for most of the Bachfest: there was Thomaskirche, followed by the old Rathaus or city hall, then Nikolaikirche and the Opera House. To the north were the Gewandhaus, a modern concert facility built in the latter years of Communist rule, the new Rathaus and parts of the Universities of Leipzig and Wohnheim. The medieval center still appeared to be a focal point of the city, but the activities were decidedly modern: crowds of shoppers, tourists, and students filled the space and outdoor rock concerts competed with the Bachfest. Industrial cranes bearing the logo of Hochtief, our old acquaintance from Sa'udi Arabia where the company had built the Jidda airport, showed that the city fathers had plans to further modernize the area.

The core of this core—and almost in its geographic center—was the old city hall, a medieval three-story building that had been restored and now enclosed open space, shops, restaurants, and concert venues. Katherinestrasse was a north-south artery on which sat Gottfried Zimmermann's coffee house, where many of Bach's secular pieces would have been featured in weekly concerts. In the summer, they would have been in the garden, during winter in the house itself. The street was still there but the building was gone, destroyed during the Second World War. From this medieval center, the modern city appeared to radiate for miles in a series of circles. The whole was intersected by several rivers, the Pleisse, the Weisse Elster and the Parthe, which all seemed to come together to the west of the medieval city. An excellent watercolor by Felix Mendelssohn, painted in 1838 and featured in the Wolff book, showed the Thomaskirche, the western gate of the city, a mill and the Pleisse river, all within a few hundred feet of one another. In 2004 what appeared to be the Pleisse was little more than a storm-drain across the street from the church.

We soon passed into what looked like industrial suburbs with the familiar sight of abandoned brick buildings covered with graffiti. The area looked depressed and there were many black faces in the streets.

I recalled reading a scathing indictment of German colonial policy in West Africa before realizing that the book had been written during the reign of the GDR that had, of course, disavowed all responsibility for the nation's past. Then, it was into the countryside and a repeat of the train ride from Berlin, with alternating fields of wheat and mustard, stands of dense forest, and occasional windmills, all turning slowly. The guide for the tour was a girl from Halle, who lectured in German and halting English. It seemed that Halle had grown up around the salt industry and the name had something to do with halogen, a nonmetallic chemical element. The symbol of the city was a half crescent and stars, which stood for the saltpan and salt crystals and was *not* the Turkish crescent and star, as some suggested. That was probably understandable, given the Turkish presence in Germany. The most frequent fast food joints—next to the bratwurst vendors—seemed to be shops selling *doner kebab*s, that staple fast-food of the Middle East.

George Frederick Handel was born in Halle in 1685, the same year as Bach, and only about seventy-five miles from Bach's birthplace in Gotha. But the two men, arguably the giants of eighteenth-century music, never met. Their trajectories were very different, Handel having become Anglicized, a court favorite and social lion in London, and a very wealthy man. He probably came as close as anyone to being an eighteenth-century superstar. He never married and outlived Bach by nine years. The city would have its own Handel Festival in June. Bach plied his vocation quietly in the less cosmopolitan settings of Saxony and Thuringia, crafting his music as a means of supporting a growing family. He would be forced to deal with the early deaths of one wife and half his children. Infant mortality was the rule in eighteenth-century Europe, but it can't have lessened the loss. This regular reminder of the transitory nature of human existence probably contributed to the religious focus of Bach's later music.

The New and the Old, Halle

Hans Dietrich Genscher, the federal foreign minister who played an important role in reunification, had also come from Halle. In spite of the fact that the city was in East Germany, Genscher had never forgotten his roots. But if she was a bit of a Halle booster, the tour guide was unsparing in her description of what it had become in the early eighteenth century: "A sordid tinderbox of crime, alcoholism, and prostitution." That was perhaps because the venue for our concert would be the

Frankeschen Stiftungen, or the Franke Foundation. It was a "registered charity" founded as an orphanage by August Hermann Franke at the turn of the eighteenth century. Three hundred years later it was still in operation, ministering to the poor and disadvantaged, although its survival had been a near thing. After reunification, it took intervention by a circle of friends to save the foundation buildings from condemnation for a throughway. It was now back in business in its vocation of "social and pedagogical-reform projects." Halle was losing young people to the west, 70,000 or a quarter of its population having left since reunification. Only 10 percent of those who remained were practicing Christians, although I wasn't sure, here in the heart of Christian Europe, what they had since become. From the top of the foundation building there was a good view of the surrounding city, the medieval slate roofs and church spires competing with the occasional modern mid-rise.

I later chatted with the guide about the pietism to whose dour tenets Franke had subscribed and we discussed another eighteenth-century figure who had grown up in its shadow, Johann David Michaelis. He was the foremost Oriental philologist in Europe and the moving force behind the Royal Danish Expedition to Happy Arabia memorialized by Carsten Niebuhr. She had heard of Michaelis, was interested in the story and I promised her a copy of the book when it was published. The remaining hour before the concert was devoted to a tour of the "curiosities," a typical eighteenth-century collection featuring pickled fetuses in jars, Eskimo implements carved from whalebone, an entire ten-foot whale rib, Red Indian clothing, and, suspended from the ceiling, a stuffed crocodile much the worse for wear for its 300 years. The material dispatched by Niebuhr from Bombay would probably have found its way into a similar collection in Copenhagen.

Outside the curiosity room, in a little area devoted to astronomy, was another reminder of the Danish expedition: an exhibit of the transit of Venus. The passage of the planet across the face of the sun occurred twice within eight years on a regular cycle and was due again on June 8, 2004. Earlier, it had represented to the astronomers of Europe the chance of a lifetime to calculate "the astronomical unit," one of the fundamental building blocks of Newton's mechanical universe: the distance between the earth and the sun. In 1761 a measurement of the transit had been the first scientific task of Niebuhr on his journey to the Near East, just as it would be for James Cook in his expedition to Tahiti eight years later. And in a little exhibition room on the ground floor there was yet another link to the Danish expedition, a Bible translated into Tamil, prepared for use in Tranquebar. Tranquebar was the combination trading and missionary post established by Denmark on the Coromandel Coast of India and had been the original destination of the expedition on its way to the Yemen. It was later decided to go by way of Egypt and the Red Sea.

This was interesting stuff, but it was only a sidelight in a musical event. After coffee, we were invited to take our seats in the hall for the chamber concert. Oddly, we were permitted to take anything—cameras, backpacks, shopping bags—into the concert hall except our jackets. For some reason jackets were *verboten* and had to be checked. After a little welcoming speech by the management we got down to serious musical business. The concert consisted of a sonata by Handel, followed by an overture and sonata for piano and violin by Bach and, finally, a couple of pieces by Dvorak. The music was the highlight of the festival thus far. The violinist was brilliant and he was called out for the four ritual bows, and then for an encore. The Japanese were particularly enthusiastic.

The trip back to Leipzig was the forty-five minutes of the morning journey in reverse. Overhead, contrails suggested that Thuringia was still a crossroads of trade, this time of the aerial variety. The day was half over, but it still promised to be busy. At five o'clock that evening in Nikolaikirche there would be the Ascension Oratorio by J. S. Bach followed by an oratorio by his second son, C. P. E. Bach. That would be followed at eight o'clock in the Altes Rathaus by what looked to be another highlight of the festival, the 5th Brandenburg concerto and two orchestral suites by Bach. The five o'clock concert was a disappointment. The acoustics in the church were again a problem, and there was a long pause between the two pieces with a great deal of milling around while they rearranged the furniture and the performers. I left after the piece by the father and had a chicken stew with wild rice and fresh mushrooms at a nearby restaurant. They had no pork but were featuring *spargel*. It was sold by the kilo and the half-kilo, at prices that approached that of meat, and was apparently a German seasonal favorite. It turned out to be asparagus.

If the earlier performance was a disappointment, the concert at eight o'clock was not. The Old City Hall venue was small enough to be intimate, yet still accommodated a full orchestra, although the full orchestra for an eighteenth-century concert was surprisingly small. When the Armonico Tributo Austria assembled they were only eighteen in number, led by a first violinist who acted as the conductor. For the Brandenburg, they were reduced to eleven, minus the horns, trumpets, and the timpanist. The 5th

Brandenburg had been written in 1721 during Bach's Cöthen years for the Margrave Christian Ludwig as part of a group of pieces demonstrating instrumental virtuosity. Wolff argues that it was the first time that a solo keyboard instrument played so prominent a role in a concerto. Moreover, its virtuoso nature suggests that Bach probably wrote the solo part for himself, in preparation for a contest with a rival. So, it was a keyboard tour-de-force, and the harpsichordist did it full justice. I was able to base my judgment only on years of listening to recordings of the piece. But to my untutored ear, the execution that night was the equal of anything I had heard on Deutsche Grammophon or Archiv.

After the intermission came the orchestral Suites Nos. 2 in B Minor and 4 in D Major, the orchestra reduced still further to seven players. It was remarkable that those seven could generate the orchestral sound that the suites required. They were patterned on a French genre incorporating overtures and dances into orchestral pieces. Bach used the French overture many times in his cantatas, although these pieces were two of only four that have survived as such. The sounds filled every corner of the hall and as the last note died away it was followed by rapturous applause. To their credit, audiences in Leipzig generally avoided the standing ovations that seemed to be the rule everywhere else, and the enthusiastic individual who immediately leapt to his feet generally stood alone until he sat down again. Another characteristic of the festival seemed to be the youth of the performers and their obvious pleasure in the pleasure they had given, as measured by the applause. It had been a spectacular day by the time I walked back to the Deutscher Hof at nearly midnight. This time, the elements cooperated and there was no rain.

We had now moved into the weekday rhythm of the festival. That meant the morning divine services, but only workshops during the day until the major evening concerts. Since I didn't understand German, the workshops would have been a waste of time, so there was a chance during the day to explore the city. The *Mette* or Mass on Monday morning was in Lutherkirche, which appeared in the map on the edge of a large park midway between the hotel and the old city. From the outside the church looked dark and gloomy, with the usual steeple standing 350 feet above the ground, half of it soaring beyond the highest roof. It was of red-brick and had been built relatively recently, probably in the nineteenth century. Inside, it was even gloomier with the pews, railings and choir stall all of dark wood. The only touch of color was provided by a small copy of Leonardo's *Last Supper* and three crudely painted windows, executed in a kind of bluewash and orangewash, over the altar. On the other side, there were four similar windows, which the early morning sun had not yet illuminated. The altar itself was a simple table with a white altar cloth and a few candles. If Luther had railed against the excesses of Rome, this church was the perfect antidote.

The state of repair was poor. Paint was peeling everywhere and there was evidence of water damage in the ceiling. If Thomaskirche and Nikolaikirche had been carefully preserved, this church looked like it had suffered from decades of neglect. I arrived early and the soloist, a boy playing the harp, was already hard at work, going through his paces. As the church filled I recognized a few faces from the days before, most of them middle-aged men with variants of facial hair, several carrying backpacks. Their consorts were equally severe in the simplicity of their dress and the no-nonsense buns in their hair. The church looked like it seated maybe 400, a fraction of that in the other two.

The service began with pieces by Palestrina and Antonio Lotti, sung *a capella* by the Leipzig Vokalromantiker, nine men of very different sizes, shapes, vocal ranges, all dressed in black. The big men seemed relaxed, the little men assuming a kind of aggressive pose, chests puffed out and arms akimbo. For almost the first time in the week the words of a scared service—"*Agnus Dei, qui tollis peccata mundi*"—were familiar, and they sounded particularly sweet this morning. This was followed by a prelude and fugue for organ by Bach. The notes generated by the mighty machine—with its metal and wood pipes, wind chests, bellows, pedals, and keyboards—too often meant a kind of awful din. Here, the sounds made the rounds of the different acoustic surfaces in the nearly-empty church, often clashing and tumbling over one another, before they all came together in a final apotheosis. The fugue was followed by another Bach piece, this time for harp and choir. The boy took his place at his instrument and on a signal from the choir leader, launched into the introduction to a Chorale, BWV 484.

The performance was fine, his fingers brilliantly dexterous on the strings, although he later missed an opening and had to back up and start again. It was the only glitch I remember hearing in the Festival. The harp piece was followed by the Ansprache, or sermon, delivered by the priest, Dr. Peter Amberg. With the exception of the familiar Vater, Sohn und

Heiliger Geist it was back to impenetrable German, although Dr. Amberg seemed to enunciate his words with particular clarity.

After the speech, there were more harp and choral pieces by Bach and several by Mendelssohn. The morning's performance ended with two "traditional" pieces, "Swing Low Sweet Chariot" and "Joshua fit the battle of Jericho." The Negro spirituals, both sung in English, might have transported us from eighteenth-century Germany to the American South. But they were more variations on the traditional pieces than the pieces themselves, the simple original tunes replaced by harmonic elaborations. And if we couldn't do justice to the name of Bach, even less were the Leipzig Vokalromantiker able to replicate the rhythms of the old-time religion. The words were there — "Swing low, sweet chariot, coming for to carry me home"—but they sounded very different. The German translation provided in the program captured even less of the sense, and I tried to imagine a "susser Wagen" coming for to "mich heimzubringen." But it was a good effort and the morning ended on a jaunty note. The harpist received an especially warm round of applause.

By midmorning the overcast had cleared and it was shirtsleeve weather. At the Gewandhuas Shop I found several CDs, including a Kurt Thomas recording of three more cantatas. After a bratwurst and a beer, I returned to the hotel for a bit of reading and a rest, stopping along the way at a deli. It carried a good selection of Italian pastas, French cheese and wines. I asked the proprietress if she was from Leipzig.

> I am Thuringian.
>
> Are things better than they used to be?
>
> For me, yes. But not for the old people. Now, they are saying that things were better ten years ago.

In the old system, it was said that people pretended to work and the state pretended to pay them. But at least they had jobs, affordable food, health care, retirement benefits, and a future. Now, many had none of these things.

The concert that evening in Thomaskirche featured the Sanctus in C Major and the Mass in B Major by Bach and the Messe Solonelle by Charles Gounod. This time it was free seating and I arrived early to find a seat in the pews just behind the apse. They ran along the main axis of the church, rather than the normal seating arrangement, and allowed a view of the organ loft whence the sounds would come. The Bach Masse was a "Lutheran mass," minus the Credo, Sanctus, and Agnus dei, not a full-blown Catholic mass that might have taken close to two hours. Some of us drifted off during the Mass but we awoke during the pyrotechnics of the Gounod piece, dating from 1855. It went on and on, and just when you thought it had ended there would be another burst of codas, cadenzas, and flourishes until the whole thing came to a climax with the combined sound of the orchestra, organ, and choir that threatened to bring down the roof. Afterwards, we all sat back in our seats, exhausted. This was followed by a Schweinerückensteak and Pilgerpfad at Lotter & Wiemann in the Altes Rathaus. That meant a pork "back steak," and white wine. The steak was like a New York strip, braised on the outside with just a hint of pink inside, and served with dense potato pancakes and sauerkraut. After a coffee at the Bachstub'l behind the church, I was back in the hotel just after 11 o'clock, early for these evenings.

The Gottesdienst the next morning, Tuesday the eighteenth, was in the Evangelisch-reformierte Kirche, a gray stone structure just off Jahnallee and outside the walls of the old city. Inside, it was as light and airy as the Lutherkirche had been dark and gloomy. It dated from the eighteenth century. The pews, arranged in a semicircle around the altar, were all blond and provided with cushions. It was an exception during a week of hard benches. The organ faced the congregation and seemed to produce a sound that was more manageable. Or, maybe the acoustics were just better. The church sat about 200. The program began with the Prelude and Fugue for organ in G Major, BWV 541, by Bach. The piece had been selected by the father as the audition piece for his oldest son, Wilhelm Friedemann, in his application for the post as organist at St. Sofia's in Dresden. Wilhelm Friedemann got the job. This was followed by a Mendelssohn *Te Deum*. The proceedings ended after exactly an hour.

This left the bulk of the day for sightseeing before the concert that night. A first order of business was the train schedule back to Berlin. The Hauptbahnhof was only a few hundred yards down the ring road from the church. Direct trains ran several times in the afternoon, so the return journey did not appear to be a problem. The visit was a chance to explore a little of the commercial activity under that stupendous roof. It was like an American mall with space for everything from watchmakers to grocers. The entire southeast portion of the second floor was taken up by a grocery outlet, and food was not cheap in Leipzig. Most meat was priced at over a Euro for 100 grams, $12 per kilo or nearly $5.50 per pound. And that was just for the average cut. The cheapest was bratwurst at about $2.15 per pound. I wasn't sure what the outcome of the banana wars had been, pitting small Caribbean producers—and former European colonies—against the Central American giants. The Americans were far more efficient and it was felt that the little producers needed protection. Tariffs on the American product were the sticking point. Germans were the greatest consumers in Europe of bananas, and here the Caribbean product from Martinique were priced at 0.96 Euros per kilo while American Chiquitas cost 1.99. So, if Leipzig were the measure, it looked like the Europeans had won the war.

On the way back to the Altes Rathaus I stopped at a bookstore where I bought the latest Grosswörterbuch Deutsch-English to complement the Cassell's *New German Dictionary* I had been using for years. In addition to the latest terms it had the advantage of the modern script. I also found that the cost of postage to the United States was extortionate at over a Euro for a postcard. It was no wonder that *Deutsche Post* was thriving while post offices elsewhere were struggling to survive in the electronic age. Dinner was a Musikerschmaus mit Puffer, a musical special consisting of strips of smoked pork and vegetables served over a potato fritter, and a Riesling at the Bachstub'l.

The concert that evening was in a smaller venue of the Gewandhaus and included pieces by Johann Christian Bach and Mendelssohn, followed, after the break, by the concerto in A Minor for violin and orchestra by J. S. Bach. The soloist was a very pretty Canadian and she did not disappoint. The *News*, a broadsheet handout produced every day of the festival, agreed. The next day it opined that she had "filled the solo part in Bach's showpiece with refreshing vividness and a virtuosity full of energy." It was not so generous with her rendition of the earlier Mendelssohn piece, pronouncing it lacking in "lifeblood." But the audience was wildly enthusiastic at the end.

Wednesday the eighteenth completed the tour of Leipzig churches with Michaeliskirche, a massive, neo-Gothic stone structure located 500 meters north of the Reform Church. Stained glass windows depicted the Birth, Crucifixion, and Resurrection and the light-colored wood of the pews and pulpit was elaborately carved. Squat sandstone columns with Corinthian capitals framed the central space. The church had been built in 1901–04. The music was mostly organ and choral pieces by Brahms,

Schumann, and Mendelssohn and ended with a transcription for organ by Franz Liszt. The pastor, Michael Markert, actually made the sign of the cross at one point during the mass, the only occurrence I recalled during the week in Leipzig. Afterwards I asked him if the name "Michaelis" meant any one in particular, and he said no, it just referred to St. Michael.

Michaeliskirche

But I would find evidence of Johann David Michaelis later that afternoon. In the Leipzig University Library a few blocks from Thomaskirche, I found a copy of his 1762 "*Fragen an eine Gesellschaft . . .*," (or "Instructions to an Expedition . . .") It was small, maybe four by eight inches and an inch thick. But into it Michaelis had packed all the questions raised by his lifetime's study of the Hebrew Bible. The small type included Hebrew, Syriac, and Arabic characters in addition to the Latin. I had seen another original, although in poor condition, in the Bancroft Library at Berkeley. But this little treasure was beautifully preserved. The very helpful librarian looked online for the antiquarian bookstores in town but was not optimistic that I would find anything so rare. I had already been to one and the man just smiled when I mentioned Michaelis and Niebuhr.

Dinner was in the Auerbachs Keller, as the name indicated a cellar below the street level. Inside, it was doing a booming business and looked like it could seat nearly as many as Thomaskirche. I had a Bauernpfanne, Saxon plowman's fare and, in honor of the season, a carafe of Spargelwein. The main course was a dish of gratineed potatoes and sauerkraut, topped with a pork cutlet. The concert that evening in Nikolaikirche consisted of the Bach cantatas BWV 105 and 147, followed by a Mendelssohn Kyrie and cantata. The BWV 147 piece included the familiar tune "Jesu, Joy of Man's Desiring." If only a fraction of the cantatas had survived how many similar pieces, melodies that might also have become favorites over the years, were gone, lost forever. After the performance, a few homeless men assumed their familiar pose outside the church, on their knees with hands outstretched, cupped as if holding water.

Thursday would be the last event and time for a summing up of the week. It was, appropriately, back where it began in Thomaskirche. The Bachfest wasn't over, and there remained three days of performances that included sonatas, inventions, preludes and fugues, suites and cantatas by Bach, not to mention the Mass in B Minor and the mighty St. Matthew Passion. But it was over for me, and I made my way to Thomaskirche that morning early, to have a final look at the church. It was very different from Nikolaikirche, not tucked away in a narrow medieval lane, but sitting very prominently on the Martin Luther Ring Road, its white triangular facade and neo–Gothic portal acting like a beacon to the faithful. A little booklet, *Thomas Church in Leipzig*, provided the details. At sixty-three degrees, the roof was one of the steepest in Germany. From the back, the brown sandstone that surrounded the apse was a departure from the white, and the 200-foot steeple, with its square base followed by octagonal sections and little open gallery, was an interesting echo of the classic Mamluk minaret in Cairo. Back in the front of the church the musicians had begun to arrive, most on bicycles with their instruments in soft cases on their backs.

But it was inside that the difference with the other church was most striking. If Nikolaikirche had undergone a lavish eighteenth-century remodeling, Thomaskirche seemed to have been frozen in time. It was beautifully kept, but crude, and the lines from its fifteenth-century founding remained intact. Instead of being fluted the columns were plain white octagons, and the thin ribs supporting the vault were of porphyry. The word from the Greek meant "purple," but someone had decided to paint them rust-red. It looked like a coat of industrial primer, unevenly applied with hints of the underlying white showing through. Where the ribs came together at the peaks, little floral patterns had been painted around the intersections. But the most jarring feature was the Gothic arch that framed the nave. It had been painted in the Islamic *ablaq* style, with alternating bands of brick-red and white, the intervening space up to the vault looking like it had been bricked over. The altar itself was lavish, with the festive Pauline altarpiece displayed throughout the week. It was eight gilt panels depicting scenes from the life of Christ around a central figure of the same. It looked like a Coptic *heykal*, where icons would have portrayed similar scenes. Stained glass windows on one side—honoring the fallen in World War I, Gustav Adolf, Bach himself, Martin Luther, the Emperor, and Felix Mendelssohn Bartholdy—completed the gross lineaments of the interior.

There were other features to be seen that morning including the neo-Gothic pulpit, the tomb of Bach (moved here in 1950), and the memorial plaque on a column recalling the sermon delivered by Luther from that spot on Pfingsonntag, or Whit Sunday, 1539. But if the Reformation had won the day in Leipzig, there were enough Roman remnants to make one wonder how thorough the conversion had been. As the congregation gathered for the mass on this Feast of the Ascension the proceedings had a medieval, almost Catholic flavor. This time, there would be no interruption. The liturgy would be read by the Pfarrer, Christian Wolff, with the sermon by our old friend, Dr. Peter Amberg. An organ prelude by Bach opened the service, followed by the choral "*De Ascensione Christi*" in Latin. This was followed by another Bach prelude and then a Bach Kyrie in German. A series of exchanges between the pastor and the congregation then followed, sandwiched around the Gloria from the original Bach Magnificat. The epistle was chanted in plainsong by the deacon before the congregation sang the hymn *Nun freut euch lieben Christen gmein,* or

"Dear Christians, One and All, Rejoice." Everyone seemed to know the tune and it rose in a mighty chorus of 2,000 voices to the porphyry rafters. The Gospel was then chanted, again in plainsong, before the opening notes of Bach's Cantata no. 128 broke in on our medieval reverie.

It was only then that I realized how revolutionary Bach's music must have sounded to the congregations of his time. Here, we had been lost in our Latin plainsong and reflections on Mark 16, 14–20. But suddenly, the sounds of an opera from somewhere south of the Alps burst from the organ loft above us. The text might have celebrated this particular feast day, and the music made up of chorales, recitatives, arias, and duets. But, whatever else it was, it was unmistakably celebratory with its complex melodies and contrapuntal elements, full of the boundless self-confidence of the late Baroque. Celebration was appropriate on this day, the commemoration of the Savior's rise to heaven, and falling in that part of the liturgical year when music was permitted. Bach never wrote down to his audience and he used his knowledge of the composer's craft in these cantatas. But they were not dry, academic exercises. Instead, they incorporated the latest secular genres into the musical celebration of a living faith.

Energized by the cantata, the congregation launched into a three-verse choral celebration of the Trinity: "*Wir glauben all an einen Gott . . . Wir glauben auch an Jesus Christ . . . Wir glauben an den Heiligen Geist . . .*" This was followed by a short exchange between the priest and congregation before Dr. Amberg monopolized us for the twenty minutes of his sermon. Afterwards, about two-thirds of the 2,000 took communion, the evolution taking another twenty minutes as two long lines approached the apse, ranged themselves in groups and received both bread and wine. They drank from a common chalice. During the distribution of communion many elements of the liturgy in the little pamphlet passed and the service rapidly reached its conclusion. We were released after a final fugue for organ by Bach. The Mass had taken just over two hours.

The service had been a window into the religious practice in the age of Bach. The program notes suggested that the Sunday service had been as much a political, cultural, and civic as a religious event. But what, if anything, did it say about the state of religion in Germany today? Even allowing for attendance at the other churches in Leipzig, the collective faithful probably represented only a small fraction of the city's citizens. The booklet on Thomaskirche had ended on a pathetic note, reflecting that only some 60,000 out of 500,000 Leipzigers now belonged to the

Evangelical Lutheran Church. The challenge was not some new dispensation, but the gradual erosion of belief in the saving message of Christ. Christians now faced "the raw climate of pluralism." "Pluralism" probably meant the distractions that competed for peoples' attention in a modern, secular world. The old unity, with its belief in the message of the Gospel, had been sundered. In spite of a week's effort, I was no different from the rest. A month before I had seen *The Passion of the Christ* at Mecca Mall in Amman, while most Jordanians were avoiding public places out of fear of terrorist attacks. The violence of the movie had been out of all proportion to the theology. In fact, it was unsustainable without the theology and, in its absence, seemed gratuitous. It was too much. I didn't believe and therefore couldn't emote. But here, there was perhaps hope in a less fervent belief.

As long as St. Thomas Church remained "a place of lived faith," it would never be reduced to "a mere museum." Instead it would remain a place of lived faith reaching out to those seeking consolation and direction. It was probably the best that could be hoped for. And remnants of the old belief lingered amid the new pluralism. The ballpoint pen I bought in the bookstore behind Thomaskirche bore the little ditty *Jesus liebt Kinder*: "Jesus loves children." It was also useful to remember that this same faith had recently brought down a state. And as I hustled out to do a little last-minute shopping in Leipzig, I discovered that all the shops in this non-Christian city were closed for the day on this, the Feast of the Ascension.

Herr Friedrich had the bill ready on check out. In the sole concession to hotel practice in the twenty-first century, he accepted a credit card. It had been a week of nostalgia, and over a beer at a pub in the train station there sounded the familiar strains of another old favorite:

Sixteen vestal virgins . . . As the miller told his tale.

It was Procol Harum's "A Whiter Shade of Pale" and something about the medieval lyrics and the elaborate organ solo made it a fitting conclusion to the *Bachfest*. Bach would probably have noticed. The train ride to Berlin was comfortable and measured, unlike the cramped rush of air travel. The Holiday Inn on Bleibtreustrasse had become a part of the chain only in 1995, but it was a return to familiar ways, with a fixed-line telephone and washcloths in the bathroom. It was also an unwelcome return to hotel exchange-rate practice: the dollar was posted at 0.7 euros and when I asked the desk clerk what had happened over the week, he motioned downward with his thumb. But in the newspaper the next day the rate was virtually unchanged, so the hotel was taking nearly a 20 percent premium. Dinner was a disappointing Sauerbraten at Leibnizklause. The potato dumplings and braised red cabbage were good, but the meat was so soft that it had almost turned to mush.

At Charles de Gaulle the next day the transfer was swift and the flight to Amman left on time. In the air, an *International Herald Tribune* was a return to current events and the wars in Gaza and Iraq. In Rafa Israel was behaving with its customary ruthlessness. In Iraq, the United States was working out a deal with the Mahdi Army to avoid the same. They had just raided Ahmad Chalabi's headquarters in Baghdad. In Jordan he was known as "Jalabi," and the news was a reminder that his Amman house was a block from our apartment in Abdoun. At the airport in Amman we waited half-an-hour for the bags and I chatted with a Brit who was on his way to Baghdad to do file transfers. There were also a couple of Americans in hunting vests who were also going to Baghdad. What big game were they pursuing? Were they "private contractors," those rent-a-Rambos favored by the Pentagon? At least they were adults. Another article suggested that behind the concertina wire in Baghdad we had assembled relays of Young Republicans to run Iraq. You didn't want someone building a beacon of democracy with preconceived notions.

In Leipzig, the effect of "a well-regulated church music" had been effervescent: spirited, and of short duration. But the recent history of the city showed what good people could accomplish if they spoke out.

15

Feelers

TODAY I WAS APPROACHED by the CIA. The man on the phone was pleasant and probed noncommittally before revealing the name of the agency he represented. Was I an American citizen? My resume showed the kind of experience that might be of interest to his organization. The standing joke in the extended family that was that I really *was* a spy. The fact that I had lived and worked over most of the last thirty years in places like Egypt, Sa'udi Arabia, Oman, Pakistan, Niger, and Jordan could mean only one thing. But I had never seriously considered the CIA. Now, it seemed to make sense. Here I was, fluent in spoken Egyptian Arabic, an experienced translator from Arabic to English, with some knowledge of Farsi and wide contacts in the Arab and Muslim worlds from teaboys and drivers to businessmen and ministers. I had firsthand knowledge of how we were perceived in this important part of the world. But it had been gained as a byproduct of technical assignments—demining, policymaking, computerization, privatization, and regulation. Finally, someone would put the broader cultural knowledge to work. It wasn't really a matter of patriotism, although there was a sense that I could help my country understand the feelings of Muslims toward America. And the fact that the CIA was engaged in practices for which we prosecuted individual Japanese at the end of the Second World War didn't even cross my mind. It was just business. I had a skill to offer and they had a need for that skill.

But as we talked that morning I had a growing sense that this wasn't going to work. There was something odd about the conversation, and the man I was talking to. I couldn't quite put my finger on it until I remembered the Navy, forty years before. Did I live near Frisco? He was from the east and really didn't know the west coast. Yes, my hometown was near San Francisco. The firm he represented was interested in individuals working overseas. Would I be willing to travel extensively, be gone maybe half the year? Yes, I was prepared to travel. How was my Arabic? On a scale of one to five—where five represented native fluency—how would I rate my ability in the language? I said that it was about three and a-half, since there were subjects—religion and the arts, for example—where my vocabulary was limited. I recalled the conversation in Arabic I had with an Egyptian lab technician in California a couple of weeks before. He was from Mansura in the Delta and he wanted to know where I was from. "I was born here," I said. "No," he insisted, "nobody can speak Arabic like that unless he was born in Egypt." It was flattering, but the signals that you are not a native speaker can be minute, the kind of thing that allows an American to immediately spot a Canadian. Or, it was like the Russian girl we met on the train from Tashkent to Bokhara. Her English was flawless and she said that she was from Seattle, but something immediately said she was not. In Egypt, I was sometimes mistaken for a Syrian or a maybe a Palestinian. But if they expected me to pass myself off as an Egyptian we were probably not going to do business.

The conversation ended with a few housekeeping details, telephone numbers and the name of the small consulting firm that would identify itself if I called. "Don't be surprised if the girl answers as Company X," he said, "That's the name we use." They didn't use e-mail, for security reasons. He would pass the details of our conversation along to his principals and see if there was still any interest:

> In the meantime, I'll send you a security form we ask all our applicants to fill out. You should have it by the middle of next week. Call me if you have any questions. You can send it back priority mail if you want, but because of our procedures it won't reach us for a couple of weeks. Oh, and please don't mention our name. Incidentally, we are NOT talking about Iraq or Afghanistan.

This was interesting but I wasn't going to hold my breath. They were probably looking for native-born Egyptians or Syrians or Iranians to return to their countries of birth and report on what they found there. But the odd sense of *deja vu* lingered. Here I was, talking to a representative of *the* American intelligence agency who confessed to his ignorance of the geography of the western United States; didn't use e-mail; did use hidebound expressions like "Frisco;" and was dependent on paper documents that could take weeks to reach the recipients. When the form arrived, it was like the one I had filled out in the Navy for a top-secret security clearance. The only thing about this proposition that seemed to represent the twenty-first century was the desire to do it on the cheap: the job would be on a contract basis, with no benefits.

Several weeks later I spoke to the same man who thanked me for my effort. He understood how tough it was remembering the details of foreign travel over the past forty years. Actually, the most difficult part of the form, given my life overseas, had been with personal references: I couldn't think of anyone in the United States who knew me very well. But, as I expected, his principals were no longer interested. However, my documents were now circulating in the firm and he would advise me if there were any further developments.

The conversation was a brief, but interesting, glimpse into the intelligence world. There had even been the hint of a turf war in his remarks: Iraq and Afghanistan were administration fiascos, and the CIA didn't want to be tarred with that brush. However, I *had* been contacted earlier by a recruiter for a company involved in our latest war. The woman on the phone had seen my resume on the web and wanted to know if I would be interested in a job in Iraq. But she pronounced it "EYE-rack." That didn't make a very good first impression. If anything epitomized our misadventure there, it was that pronunciation. Pat Roberts, the Republican head of the Senate Intelligence Committee before the 2006 elections, regularly referred to "IZ-rul" and "EYE-rack."

As the woman described the position it sounded more familiar than the CIA job, with the usual benefits and a substantial country differential and danger uplift. It would be based in the Green Zone. If I was interested she would e-mail me the job description. She also gave me a web address where I could learn more about the project. After she hung up I recalled a proposal several years before for a university-link project between Iraq and the United States. It was in the early days after the invasion and an Egyptian-American acquaintance was bidding on the project, probably as a disadvantaged or minority firm. I had reluctantly allowed my name to go forward as project leader, detailing my experience in the Arab world, language skills, and knowledge of recent Iraqi history. The book on Niebuhr, who spent several months in the country in 1764, was evidence of my academic interest and credentials. Later, I imagined the snorts of derision that must have greeted the proposal in the CPA, even assuming it got that far: "He knows what? Something about Iraq? What is he, some sort of Arabist?"

When the job description arrived, it was for the Deputy Chief of Party (DCOP) on the "Iraq Strengthening Local and Provincial Governance Program." The program was funded by USAID, which accounted for the familiar terminology. But the job description was poorly written. The attributes were bulletized, but they were inconsistent: some began with verbs, some with gerundives and others were simple statements of fact. The DCOP, it said, would be responsible for managing all details of the program and would be "the alter ego" and "partner" to the Chief of Party (COP). That was fair enough, if quaintly expressed. There were the usual references to liaison with other parties, management of a multidisciplinary team, and maintenance of relations with the client and other organizations. But toward the end it stated that the DCOP would "bear responsibility for overall quality control and completion within our contracted budget." That seemed odd. What was the COP going to do? It was like saying that the executive officer bore ultimate responsibility for the safety of the ship. That was the captain's job.

The information on the website was even less reassuring. The program involved working with Iraqis to "establish and strengthen the conditions, institutions, capacity, and legal and policy framework for a coordinated democratic local governance system in Iraq." As usual with USAID it was a mouthful. But it seemed wildly optimistic in the Iraqi context. The project would be attached to the system of "Provincial Reconstruction Teams (PRTs)" consisting, in addition to the USAID component, of the U.S. Departments of Agriculture and Justice, the Army Corps of Engineers, and—ominously—"coalition military personnel." The military was needed to provide security, but there was a question of how much could be achieved in an atmosphere of rampant crime, corruption, and violence. The annual report for 2006 listed the program's accomplishments: it had held thirty-two conferences and workshops, sponsored 1,010 training events, provided 633 "counts" of technical assistance, developed eight new and enhanced training modules as well as thirty-seven supplementary training modules, produced twelve "papers," trained officials in all eighteen provinces, and "helped" PRTs in nine of them. But there wasn't a hard deliverable in any of it.

It was everything I had ever seen in a USAID program: vaulting ambition, poor project design, abdication of responsibility to the contractor, and absence of the tools necessary to make it happen. It was all responsibility and no authority, except that even authority probably wouldn't help in this context. Most of the "accomplishments" had to do with training. Training was like motherhood. You couldn't say anything bad about it. But it was one of the softer disciplines. And as a metric it was all wrong. Give the Iraqis security, electricity, and clean water and local governance would take care of itself. Those were the real metrics, and they were beyond the ability of a contractor to deliver. Even more troubling was the part about "grants management" I had been responsible for financial controls in the Afghan program in Pakistan, dealing with millions of rupees in cash in wild places like Peshawar and Quetta. But that had been a picnic by comparison with Iraq. How could you ensure financial accountability in a country without a banking system that worked, a vicious ongoing insurgency, everyone on the take, and local mafias competing for control?

There were other concerns as well. How would you deal with the regional problems, with separate Sunni, Shiite, and Kurdish councils? How would you ensure security in the regional training venues? What about the legislation necessary to empower the regional councils, as yet not passed? What systems of control, if any, were currently in place? Who was the departing DCOP and what was his take on the above issues? By the time we spoke again I had prepared a list of questions, but we agreed that the woman wasn't equipped to answer them. She would discuss the matter with management and get back to me if there was interest in the next step, which would be an interview.

I can't really say that I was tempted. The job promised to be part of another well-intentioned but impossible effort, with the added element of lethality. The only upside seemed to be the salary which, with the uplifts and tax exclusion, would be in the substantial six figures. But I didn't have to decide because the woman never called back.

16

The Renegades

IN THE OFTEN-HEATED EXCHANGES that have characterized the Western discourse on the Middle East, three expatriates from the region have added their voices to the din. I have called them renegades not because they were disloyal or went over to the other side, but because they left their countries of birth, worked and wrote primarily in English, and often flouted the conventions that might have been expected of them. Their opinions are valued in their adopted, not their original milieus. A Baghdadi Jew, a Palestinian Christian, and a Lebanese Shiite, they are of interest partly because they reflected important confessional divisions in the region, although religion seemed to be of little importance to them. Incidentally, they came from places very much in the news today: Iraq, Palestine, and southern Lebanon. All three represented minorities, although they did not necessarily represent those minority views. There is no Sunni Muslim among them, and that may be because Sunni Muslim voices are mostly heard over *there*, not over here. There is, of course, no shortage of Sunni Muslim opinion on issues that concern the Arab World, but it generally finds expression in Arabic. It is a lamentable fact that the two sides—one in the West, the other in the Arab World—talk past one another, one in English and the other in Arabic. It is a divide that neither side seems able to understand, much less to bridge. The writers in English have a preponderance of credibility, at least in the West, just as the West has a preponderance of military and economic power.

Although their native language was Arabic, all three of our subjects were very competent writers of English, and appear to have come to the conclusion that the world worth cultivating is an English-speaking one. It is an unfortunate fact that there are probably millions of native Arabic speakers who can read and write English, while the number of native English speakers who can be understood, much less write a PhD thesis, in Arabic, is limited to the specialists.

The primary contribution of the renegades is that to their careful reasoning and facility in English, they added first-hand experience. They have *been there* and presumably know better than the rest of us what they are talking about. This first-hand knowledge means that they are less dependent on what has been written and more on actual experience of life in the Middle East. As a result of their experiences they bring strongly felt opinions to the debate. This doesn't mean that they are more objective than others, but the experience lends authority to their prejudices. It has sometimes allowed them to be used by others with agendas, although they have not necessarily been party to the abuse. What also makes them interesting is that they are not always predictable. And their Arabic gave them a facility, some lesser and some greater, to bridge the cultural divide, although that language, too, is often put to tendentious uses. It has even been suggested that Arabic *itself* is a part of the problem in that it does not promote the kind of rational discussion that we in the West, not always with justice, arrogate to ourselves. Unfortunately, the belief among writers in that language that they are a beleaguered minority in the debate only reinforces the tendency to irrationality and bombast.

ELIE KEDOURIE (1926–1992)

The first of our subjects, Elie Kedourie, was a Baghdadi Jew who spent most of his adult life in the United Kingdom, eventually becoming a professor and specialist in the history of the Middle East at the London School of Economics (LSE). Born in 1926, he was educated in primary and secondary schools in Baghdad where the language of instruction was first French and then English. After high-school he left Iraq to attend the LSE and then Oxford where his graduate thesis attracted attention for its acidulous account of the post-Ottoman Middle East. The thesis was eventually published in 1956 as *England and the Middle East*. It earned him the reputation of being, simultaneously, a conservative and a dissident. Both labels appear to have been deserved. His overall approach to the region found its most expansive statement in *The Chatham House*

Version and Other Middle Eastern Studies, published in 1969. His attitudes surely had to do with the unique place Iraqi Jewry occupied in the region and the larger Jewish World.

When the British under General Maude arrived in Baghdad in March of 1917 they found tens of thousands of Jews there, after Sunni Arabs its largest single confessional group in the city. They were an ancient Mizrahi, or Oriental, community dating, some said, to the Babylonian captivity. So, they did not fit easily into the Sephardic and Ashkenazi categories recognized in the West since the Middle Ages, although there was some overlap between the *Mizrahim* and *Sephardim*. As such, they had avoided the fate of their Palestinian coreligionists who were dispersed to the west after the revolt and destruction of the Temple in 70 AD. While there may have been later contacts with Spain (*Sepharad*) and Germany (*Ashkenaz*), that is, with Oriental and European Jewry, Babylonian Jewry claimed pride of place as probably the oldest continuously-existing Jewish community in the world and could boast of a family that traced its pedigree to King David. Indeed, Babylonia became a second homeland for the Jews and when the Persians permitted a remnant to return to Jerusalem in the sixth century BC, only a small number took up the offer. The majority, particularly those who were wealthy and established, chose to remain in their adopted home "by the rivers of Babylon." Baghdad eventually became the political and intellectual center of the Jewish World with its Gaonate and Talmudical academies at Sura and Pumbaditha. At the time of the Muslim conquest in the mid-seventh century AD it was estimated that there were as many as a million Jews in Iraq. They bore their fate under the Muslims with their customary fortitude as subjects of, first Arab, then Central Asian, then Ottoman rulers, just as they had previously under Assyrians, Parthians, Medes, Persians, and Sassanides. They not only survived but thrived, and by 1917 they virtually controlled the commerce of Baghdad.

Where their coreligionists looked to the west, Iraqi Jews traditionally looked east and Baghdadi Jewish merchants established trading colonies in India, particularly in Bombay and Surat, the Straits Colony (later Singapore), and China. There were fortunes to be made and at least one Iraqi Jewish family, the Sassoons, owed their millions to the opium trade. In the nineteenth century, Great Britain fought two opium wars with the Chinese, ensuring that this profitable commodity would continue to be admitted into China to replace the specie that had once been required to pay for imports of Chinese tea. It was an extraordinary act of statecraft—when one considers how many Chinese lives were ruined by opium addiction—and unthinkable today, the equivalent of waging war on a third-world country to force the importation of Columbian cocaine. The Indian Sassoons were beneficiaries of the war and the trade, and they used their millions to purchase estates and entry into the British upper class. Siegfried Sassoon's first literary effort had been *Memoirs of a Fox Hunting Man*, before he served as an officer on the Western Front and became one of the most celebrated poets of the First World War. The only surprise was how seamlessly he had been assimilated into the upper class before a serious wound and convalescence convinced him of the futility of the war. Another serving officer, T. E. Lawrence, found in Sassoon a bit of a soul mate, although Lawrence was decidedly of the middle class. Another, unrelated, Sassoon served in the first Iraqi government after the war as Minister of Finance.

On the arrival of the British, representatives of the Baghdadi Jewish community approached General Maude and asked that they be made citizens of the British Empire. It was an extraordinary request. But the times required extraordinary measures. With the unleashing of nationalist passions after the collapse of the Ottoman Empire, Jews were in danger of losing their position in a system governed by *millets*, or communities. It was not only Iraqi or Arab nationalism that threatened, however. The Jews of Salonika—who constituted 40 percent of the population of that city—watched with dismay as tens of thousands of Greek refugees from Izmir streamed into the city in 1921–22, replacing the tens of thousands of Muslims who streamed out to western Anatolia in probably the first internationally-sanctioned transfer of populations in history. The newcomers were penniless, utterly unknown, and prone to Hellenistic zealotry, unlike the Muslims among whom the Jews had lived on familiar terms since their arrival in the fifteenth century. The conundrum illustrated a truism that today is difficult to understand: to be called "a Jew" in Europe, even in the more enlightened West, was a reminder of one's difference, a source of anxiety and, ultimately, of alarm. British, French, and German Jews labored steadily to assimilate themselves into their societies, assuring all concerned that they were Englishmen, Frenchmen, and Germans first, and followers of a particular religion second.

In Eastern Europe it was different, and millions of Jews in Poland, Lithuania, White Russia, the Ukraine, and Russia itself were subject to repression, and periodic pogroms, even after their restriction to the Pale of Settlement had ended. But all European Jews, western and eastern alike, were ultimately at risk, as future generations would learn. Europe's treatment of its Jews had traditionally been a long-standing attempt at conversion followed, when that didn't work, by expulsion. Luther's fulminations against the Jews in the sixteenth century were not based on their ethnicity. He firmly believed they would flock to his new dispensation once the corruption and excesses of Rome had been rooted out. Only afterwards, when they did not, did he call for their expulsion from Germany. But almost all European nations had expelled their Jews at one time or another, and by the early twentieth-century schemes had been proposed with the ultimate aim of exporting Europe's intractable Jewish problem to some other locale. In 1903 the British offered Uganda to the Zionists, who declined, electing to hold out for Palestine. The Balfour Declaration in 1917 was in some respects a common European initiative—even the notoriously anti-Semitic Russians signed on—and the Germans produced their own version, which proved to be too little too late. Later, Stalin would establish the Jewish Autonomous Oblast in Siberia as part of his nationality policy, and the Nazis considered shipping European Jewry to Vichy Madagascar. The final option, extermination, was yet to come.

It was different in the Ottoman World. In the last throes of their empire the Ottoman Turks may have been corrupt and venal, and there is no question that the other nationalities in the Empire—particularly the largest, the Arabs—suffered under their rule. Arabs refer to *al 'asr al-jahili,* or the age of ignorance, as the time that preceded the coming of Islam. But they also speak of *'asr al-inhitat,* or the age of decay, to describe the 400 years under Turkish rule. However, if the minorities stayed out of trouble, they were allowed to practice their religion, regulate their affairs according to their own laws and share in economic activity and such wealth as thereby accrued. Iraqi Jews in 1917 were an example of that relative tolerance. In fact, to be called a Jew under the Ottomans was not a source of anxiety but, it could be argued, of reassurance: it was what defined one's place in the greater scheme of things, as well as one's rights and obligations. But it was predictable that the Ottomans would have rebuffed the proposal by the Zionists to settle large numbers of European Jews in Palestine, even with their offer of help to control the unruly Arabs. The Ottoman system was breaking down at the beginning of the twentieth century, and the Europeans in Rumelia and the minorities— the Armenians in particular—were growing increasingly restive. The last thing the Turks needed was another European minority in the Empire, particularly a stiff-necked one.

The Zionists were, of course, Europeans and primarily eastern Europeans. Assimilationist Jews in the West regarded them with disdain, as representatives of woolly-headed Russians, socialists, and revolutionaries. Tarring them with the Zionist brush would have threatened everything that Jews in the West had worked so hard to achieve. In 1917 five and-a-half million Jews lived in the old Pale, consisting of western Poland, eastern Ukraine, White Russia and Lithuania. They had drifted east over the centuries from their temporary abodes in the west, under the combined pressures of expulsion, persecution, and the prospect of opportunity in the wide-open spaces of eastern Europe. There had even been a "go east young man" impulse to some of the activity. They were called *Ashkenazi* as a result of their passage through Germany, and they brought with them their Germanized names and language, Yiddish or corrupt German. In the south and east, where the Austro-Hungarian Empire came into contact with the Ottomans, they mixed with Sephardic Jews, those who had been expelled from Spain and Portugal at the end of the fifteenth century. But most of the *Sephardim* had retreated with the Ottomans when the latter were checked and then thrown back in their annual campaigns against Vienna.

There had been a certain degree of intermarriage with gentiles over the centuries, and even examples of conversion to Judaism by Christians during the religious wars of the sixteenth century when Catholics and Protestants were enthusiastically burning each other at the stake. So, it was difficult to say what the Jews represented ethnically, but they were clearly a mixture, with some looking as Slavic as their gentile neighbors. In fact, some have argued that they represented a European people with a right to nationhood every bit as legitimate as that of other Europeans. They occupied an area larger than that of any European nation-state; they were more numerous than the Danes in Denmark, Fins in Finland, Norwegians in Norway, Swedes in Sweden, Belgians in Belgium, Dutch in the Netherlands, Portuguese in Portugal, and Swiss in Switzerland. They spoke a European language that was the source of a lively culture, with a literature, theater, and their own newspapers. And they had been in Europe for nearly two millennia. Surely, a place could be found for them in the European comity of nations.

This lengthy preface is necessary since the two factors—the request by Iraqi Jews to shelter against the new nationalism under the aegis of the British Empire, and the essential foreignness of European Jews to their old home—formed critical parts of Elie Kedourie's approach to the

Middle East. In fact, he would spend a lifetime fulminating against two forces let loose in the region by the British after the end of the First World War, Arab nationalism and Zionism. Neither, in his opinion, was a native growth and both were profoundly antipathetic to the Middle East in which he had grown to maturity. They were the source of both his conservatism and his dissidence. Briefly, in his opinion the logical successor to the Ottoman Empire in Iraq was the British Empire, with firm central rule and guaranteed rights for minorities, but now administered fairly. It was surely a conservative, not to say reactionary, approach to the phenomenon of the newly energized forces that attended the collapse of empires, not only in the Middle East but in Europe as well.

In Kedourie's view, it was only the weakness of British statesmen, and their misguided efforts to accommodate the demands of Arab nationalists, that prevented the imposition of strong imperial rule. There were two schools of thought in Iraq in the immediate aftermath of the War: the Lawrencian and the Wilsonian and they offered stark contrasts in their approach to the problem. T. E. Lawrence was an advocate of meeting Arab aspirations half way, for which he earned Kedourie's everlasting enmity. Wilson was not President Wilson with his Fourteen Points, but Arnold Wilson, the British pro-consul in Iraq, who advocated a strong hand. Lawrence won, although the approach might better be identified with Gertrude Bell. It became official orthodoxy, and from it Kedourie became a lifelong dissident.

The Iraq into which Kedourie was born in 1926 had already suffered through several years of occupation and insurgency, followed by relative calm with the withdrawal of British forces to air bases, rights to which they had negotiated by treaty. But the British withdrew not because of the failure of nerve, or because they saw the ultimate end of empire. Churchill would attempt to maintain the British hold on India after the even greater cost in blood and treasure of the Second World War. And the first tentative steps into Iraq in 1915 had been to protect imperial interests, the oil fields and refineries at the head of the Gulf. The Royal Navy had recently converted from coal to oil, and the supply was critical to the war effort. The Mesopotamia campaign was initially waged by an Indian army and run by the India Office until their effort to do it on the cheap led to a scandal nearly as great as that of the Crimea, sixty years before. The died-from-wounds rate was horrific, and the ensuing outcry combined with strategic blunders led the War Office to take over direction of the campaign. The initial British successes had led them to believe that an Indian army was as good as a Turkish army until they discovered that they had been fighting Arabs whose heart really wasn't in it. This was followed by a check at Ctesiphon, when Anatolian troops were thrown into the battle for the first time. Retreat and the long agony of investiture and surrender at Kut followed. It was a disaster that, coupled with the withdrawal from Gallipoli, administered a severe shock to British reputation in the region.

But the India Office retained an interest in Iraq, and even after the war looked to repay the cost of the campaign by making Iraq to India what India was to Great Britain—a colony—and schemes were mooted to introduce Indian Muslim settlers into the agricultural land between Tigris and Euphrates. So, empire was alive and well, and it was not a sudden conversion to the notion of independence for subject peoples that led to the tactical withdrawal in Iraq. Rather, in 1921 the British were being drained financially and couldn't afford to take on new imperial responsibilities, or even continue as an occupying power. They decided to use the new arm of air power to enforce the peace at a fraction of the cost of boots on the ground. Their forces withdrew to airbases from which they could intervene as necessary. And, as with the initial Indian effort, it would be done on the cheap.

The cobbling together of the Ottoman *vilayets* of Basra, Baghdad, and Mosul into the nation called Iraq was not as artificial as it may seem today, with Sunnis, Shias and Kurds fighting for control of their parts of the country. Iraq was not an invention of the British, and the three provinces were widely known as "Turkish Iraq" in the centuries before the war. They were contiguous and shared a common history, albeit one of exploitation. It could be argued that Mosul, with its large Kurdish population, was an exception and, in fact, the *vilayet* had originally been apportioned to France under the Sykes-Picot agreement. But Clemenceau surrendered Mosul and French interests in Palestine in return for oil rights in the north and a free hand in Syria. However, making Mosul French would not have been a solution. Creating an autonomous or independent Kurdistan surely was, and one of the tragedies of the post–war period was the failure of the Allies to do so.

At the end of the war there were several minorities in the region who clamored for redress of real or imagined wrongs—the Armenians, the Anatolian Greeks, the Maronites, the Kurds, and the Zionists, although the Zionists weren't really *in* the region. Only the Maronites and the Zionists were rewarded at the Peace Conference, since only they had great-power sponsors. After the agony of 1915, the Armenians were abandoned to the tender mercies of, first, the resurgent Turks and then the Soviets when they were driven into the rump state they occupy today. The Anatolian Greeks were massacred and the remnants driven out, although it was the foolhardiness of Greek statesmen and the blood lust of the Greek army that precipitated their downfall. The Kurds were left to nurse their grievances and national aspirations, spread across four countries: newly aggressive Turkey, Shiite Iran, French Syria, and British Iraq.

The Iraq godfathered by the British in the 1920s was probably as enlightened as could be expected under the circumstances, lying as it did at the confluence of imperial interests and Wilsonian (this time, Woodrow, not Arnold) principles. Gertrude Bell was as responsible as anyone for the trajectory of events. She was no stranger to Iraq and combined fluency in Arabic with knowledge of its leading personalities, based on pre-war travels in the area. She saw immediately that the local leading light, Sayyed Taleb, would be a very uncertain tool in British hands, if he could be controlled at all. Expanded empire may not have been an option, but British control definitely was. Taleb's power base was in Basra, a Shia stronghold, although he himself was Sunni. He was invited to tea, on the way to which he was seized and exiled to Ceylon. Her initial doubts about the fitness of the Iraqis to rule themselves were assuaged by the impossibility of any real alternative, and Miss Bell became the enemy of Arnold Wilson, for whom she technically worked. She used her contacts, which reached to the highest levels in the British government, to undermine Wilson, and he never saw what hit him. He would have put off indefinitely anything so silly as Iraqi self-government.

If mistakes were made in Iraq they had more to do with the failure to recognize the importance of Islam, and Shiism, in the affairs of the country, although the criticism is probably a case of being wise after the fact. What the British engineered was a hastily-built secular regime headed by the Hejazi Amir Feisal, leader of the Arab Revolt and deposed King of Syria, along with his Sunni Arab friends and fellow soldiers, particularly Nuri Sa'id, a Baghdadi, and Ja'afar al-Askari, a Mosuli. Ja'afar was assassinated in 1926, an indication of the Iraqi propensity for violence that other Arabs say is endemic. The bloody persecution of the Assyrians in the north after the British pulled out—they had been used as gendarmes by the occupiers—was another sign of things to come. But Faisal and his colleagues were known quantities and, as military men, spoke the same language as the practical British, who were not prepared to turn over control of the country to obscurantist Shia divines with ties to Persia, northern India, and southern Lebanon.

The Shia, authors of the revolt in 1920 and in the same approximate majority that they enjoy today, made it easier by largely abstaining from political participation, presaging the same mistake made by the Sunnis eighty years later. But even allowing for the gross Shia under-representation, an effort was made to make the government inclusive, with six seats in Parliament reserved for Christians and six for Jews. That provision lasted until 1948. The first minister of finance was a Sassoon, and certain portfolios—education, for example—were traditionally reserved for Shias. It was a parliamentary system of sorts, although the constitution strongly favored the executive over the legislative branch. Between 1921 and the revolution in 1958 there were 13 elections, the life of the average parliament only slightly shorter than the mandated four years. But it took a strong man to rule over the fractious elements, with the tribes, sects, and the military all jockeying for position. Nuri repeatedly served as prime minister, during which periods he cracked heads when necessary.

The military was nearly synonymous with the government and the parliamentary period was punctuated by coups and attempted coups. The most notorious was that led by Rashid 'Ali Gailani in 1941, an Axis sympathizer who courted Italian and German aerial assistance. It was not enough to prevent the British from mounting a rescue operation from Jordan, led by Glubb Pasha. A would-be T. E. Lawrence, Somerset de Chair, left an account of the campaign, *The Golden Carpet*, complete with dedicatory poem and an impressive bronze of himself as the frontispiece. It was during the unrest attending the coup that the *farhud*, or pogrom against Baghhdadi Jews, took place. It made a profound impression on Kedourie, confirming in his eyes the incurable propensity for violence of Arab regimes. Events outside the country were now drawing Iraqi Jews into the vortex. The final act in Iraqi parliamentary democracy was the *coup* administered by disaffected officers in 1958. They killed the king, Feisal II, and all the members of the royal family they could lay their hands on. When the Egyptians deposed King Farouk in 1952 they had escorted him, complete with bullion, down to his royal yacht in Alexandria before sending him off to Naples. That wasn't the Iraqi way. The perpetrators found Nuri trying to escape wearing a burka, and hacked him to pieces. The Ba'ath, more violence and eventually Saddam Hussein followed.

It was into this Iraq that Elie Kedourie was born and came to maturity. He was not a Zionist, seeing the Balfour Declaration, even with its qualifier—". . . nothing shall be done which may prejudice . . . the political status of Jews in any other country . . ."—as potentially compromising to the interests of Iraqi Jewry. To Kedourie, Zionism was another of those regrettable western influences introduced into the region after the collapse of the Ottoman Empire. Anti-Semitism, he believed, was a European phenomenon, although it had found Middle Eastern resonance under the impact of war and the introduction of increasing numbers of European Jews—never enough for the Jewish Agency and always too many for the Arabs—into Palestine. When the early Zionist pioneers arrived they were, according to Kedourie, profoundly ignorant and equally contemptuous, of the Palestinian Arabs whose lands they had come to take. Subsequent events have shown that it was not just the Arabs, but also the Middle Eastern Jews, who were the objects of European prejudice. Kedourie even suggests that the Zionists may have been behind terrorist attacks on Jews in Baghdad after 1948. They had secured their country and there was now pressure to fill it with pioneers. Middle Eastern Jews were "encouraged" to emigrate to Israel, just as Palestinian Arabs were "encouraged" to leave. To Kedourie Palestine was not a promising place to plant the Zionist dream. It was homogeneous, 95 percent Sunni Arab, and so not susceptible to the divide-and-rule tactics used by colonial regimes elsewhere. The holocaust, the establishment of Israel and subsequent Arab-Israeli hostility may have modified, but did not fundamentally change, these early views of Kedourie. They represent, needless to say, a part of his body of writings on the Middle East that is not emphasized.

If he had reservations about Zionism, Kedourie reserved his particular scorn for Arab nationalism, and he unleashed his highly developed vocabulary of invective on the fools and knaves among British officialdom who pandered to it. Basil Liddell-Hart makes the cogent observation that at least part of the hostility to T. E. Lawrence was really hostility to the political aspirations of the Arabs, the cause that Lawrence, in some minds, represented. Kedourie detested both the phenomenon and the man with his "meretricious flamboyance," "hysterical mendacity," and "disoriented fanaticism." He attacked the entire idea of Arab nationalism, in its historical, legal, and practical aspects. If there was anything more dangerous than the phenomenon itself, in Kedourie's view, it was its metastasized form, pan-Arabism. Historically, the tracing of the nineteenth-century origins of the Arab national movement by writers like George Antonius was only an attempt to put a twentieth-century gloss on a late, and externally developed, movement.

Antonius is the author of *The Arab Awakening*, and Kedourie grudgingly admits that he has put the case ably and eloquently. But, in his opinion, the account is overblown and the Arabs remained inert well into the twentieth century, most particularly during the war. This view was important in the development of the position, shared by others, that the Arabs didn't do enough to "earn" their freedom from the Turks. It is true that the Levantine Arabs, decimated by famine and Jemal's brutal rule, were largely spectators during the Arab Revolt, although subsequent developments suggest that their misgivings (always excepting those of the Maronites) about trading a Turkish master for a French one proved to be justified. Kedourie's later studies of two of the leading lights of movement, Jamal al-Din al-Afghani and Mohammed Abduh, paint both in an unflattering light. Not content with debunking the movement he resorts to character assassination as well, the accounts spiced with suggestions of sexual impropriety. It was a tactic he would also use with Feisal in Iraq, suggesting, with slender supporting-evidence, that Feisal was a womanizer.

To Kedourie the Christian missionaries who founded the Protestant colleges that later became the American Universities in Cairo and Beirut, were the real authors of "the Arab Awakening," and they were ultimately to blame for the disasters that followed. It was also the mischief caused by American missionaries that brought the Armenians to grief. The missionaries, in the process of converting large numbers of Orthodox Christians to Protestantism (Muslims were off-limits), introduced to their proselytes American notions of democracy and accountability that were unsuited to the region. It should be noted that, in so doing, they were early precursors of the Zionists who, holding oriental Jewries in contempt, sought to bring them into the light from their allegedly primitive, feudal, and unprogressive existence. The Turks naturally suspected them all, especially the Armenians, of disloyalty, particularly in northeastern Anatolia where the Russian and Turkish armies moved back and forth, exchanging atrocities over a ravaged landscape. There were enough incidents of revolutionary activity, and outrages, to compromise the entire community. The Armenian agony followed and Turkish apologists today continue to refer to the disloyalty of the Armenians as the root cause of the massacres. They refuse to call them genocide.

Kedourie's version of the course of the Arab Revolt also reflects his deep conservatism. In rebelling the Arabs were, quite simply, in violation of legal obligations to their Ottoman suzerain, in effect abandoning the Turks in the hour of their greatest need and going over to the enemy. The Ottoman response, including Jemal's hanging of prominent Arabs in Damascus and Beirut, not to mention the enforced famine that killed hundreds of thousands in Syria and Palestine, was entirely justified. The Arabs were led astray by meddlesome amateurs like Ronald Storrs, the chief interlocutor between Henry McMahon, the High Commissioner in Cairo, and Sharif Hussein in Mecca. McMahon, an Indian civil servant and a weak man, was persuaded by his local advisors to promise to the Arabs more than he was authorized to offer by London, and more than the British were in fact able to deliver. In this account, Kedourie puts his considerable forensic skills to work, in English, French, and Arabic. There is no question that the McMahon correspondence was characterized by all the vices of amateurism in the worst sense of the word, and the record of the three-year correspondence between Cairo and Hussein constitutes a mother lode for an observer with a sharp wit and a sharp pen. Kedourie had both. Storrs, an inveterate name-dropper, had studied Arabic at Cambridge under Johnnie "Persian" Browne but, as Antonius observed, he knew a little of the language and had a talent for making a little go a long way. The real author of the correspondence, written in a tiny crabbed Arabic hand, was a factotum by the name of Ruhi whose first language was Farsi. It was so full of flowery circumlocutions that Hussein was annoyed to the point of vexation.

The lengthy and detailed review of the correspondence by Kedourie in *In the Anglo-Arab Labyrinth* includes reference to the opinions of officials in the India Office who were, needless to say, intensely hostile to any notion of Arab independence. They feared the impact among Indian Muslims of the rebellion against the Sultan-Caliph, although during the war British-Indian Muslim units fought the Turks in Sinai and Palestine largely without incident. They also believed, rightly in this case, that McMahon's vague and sweeping promises might later expose the British to the charge of bad faith. But more importantly, and unbowed by the mess they had made of "Mespot," Indian officials still nursed postwar imperial ambitions in Iraq and were, to a man, incredulous at McMahon's undertakings. Needless to say, their objections to the actions of Cairo found favor with Kedourie.

But there is a mixed message in his analysis and Kedourie seems to be saying, simultaneously, that McMahon exceeded his brief but, in the end, was so careful in his wording that he really didn't promise the Arabs anything at all. It is here that the value of the entire exercise can be called into question. The potential for misunderstanding in a correspondence carried on by a British civil servant and a crafty and suspicious Hejazi autocrat, in two languages—the Arabic of Hussein's letters being reviewed in translation and the British responses drafted first in English and then translated into Arabic by Ruhi—was very great. Kedourie's correction of Hubert Young's exegesis of the Arabic of one of the letters only illustrates the point. It is clear that Hussein thought that he had been promised a great deal and Kedourie's attempt to show that he had been cleverly hoodwinked by the British only redounded to their discredit.

The subsequent attempts to clarify what McMahon had, or had not, promised—the communication to Hussein by the British Government in February of 1918, the Anglo-French Declaration, and the Declaration to the Seven—only further muddied the waters. But they suggest that there was a serious issue in question. In fact, there were probably as many reasons for encouraging the revolt of Hussein as there were British officials in Cairo to make the case. There was little unity among Kitchener, Wingate, McMahon, Storrs, Hogarth, Clayton, Wilson, Lawrence and the rest, nor were they naïve. Lawrence probably put it best when he said that they responded positively to the approach of Hussein because his rebellion would aid their victory in the East, and it was better that they should have won and broken their word than lost. Rather than naiveté they should be accused of thoroughgoing cynicism. They seemed to have believed that, whatever they said, their words had no consequence. And there was a profound misunderstanding of Hussein's motivations by the British. Lawrence referred to him as a "religious fanatic" whose main objection to the Young Turks, and ultimately the reason he sought British assistance, was because of their notorious irreligion. This is not to say that Hussein didn't have his own self-serving reasons for seeking British aid, and was capable of double-dealing himself. And no one—not the British, the French or the other Arabs themselves—was prepared to recognize him as "King of the Arabs," authorized to speak for them all.

But it is clear that he trusted in the word of the British, as he understood it, and felt badly let down. The British, on the other hand, although they found him an impossible negotiating partner, felt that they had faithfully discharged their obligation to him, as they understood it.

Between these two "understandings" lay a world of difference. As a result of his refusal to recognize the postwar arrangements in Syria, Palestine, and Iraq, Hussein was left to deal with the much stronger Ibn Sa'ud on his own. After a brief period of Hashemite rule in the Hejaz, characterized by inefficiency, extortion, and corruption, the whole rotten edifice was swept away in 1925 by the *Ikhwan*. In the end, the Hejaz mattered little. The British were interested in the corn and oil of Mesopotamia and were prepared to give France a free hand in Syria in exchange for relative freedom in Iraq. A friendly Palestine ensured strategic depth for Egypt and the Suez Canal, still the lifeline to India. These were important issues, and the notion that the British and French, having waged the war, would abandon their interests in the area to independent Arab regimes would have been naïve. Jewish settlement in Palestine was an afterthought, and was pursued with tepid enthusiasm (some called it outright obstructionism) by the mandatory authorities.

Kedourie's practical critique of Arab nationalism has cogency and his review of the experience of the Iraqi monarchy, with its constant refrain of Shiite grievances, Sunni manipulation, and Kurdish disaffection, punctuated by military coups, makes grim reading. But the experience of four hundred years of increasingly brutal and corrupt Ottoman rule, division into communities by ethnic grouping, tribe, religious affiliation and sect within religious affiliation made the Middle East in 1918, as it remains today, an unlikely place for the early blossoming of western notions of democracy. The authoritarian proclivities of the regimes in the region, their intolerance and repressive impulses, are a matter of record. The minorities—Jews in nearly every Arab country, Arabs in Israel, Christians in Palestine and Iraq, Shiites in majority-Sunni areas—have suffered as a consequence. But Kedourie's notion that the British Empire should simply have stepped in when the Ottomans left the stage (the only hope for reform in the Ottoman dominions, he believed, was if it was administered directly by a European government) was a non-starter, if only because the British could not afford to play the role, even had they wanted to.

So, we have the odd spectacle of an Iraqi Jew chastising the British establishment for their lack of spirit, their fecklessness in the face of difficulties, their misplaced guilt. It represented nothing less than a failure of imperial will. Kedourie knew the Arabs first-hand, and he knew that their pretensions were ridiculous and their threats were hollow. But this approach only seems an attempt to turn back the tides of history. "The proper objects of British policy," Kedourie wrote, "were the safeguard of imperial interests and of British predominance." But if the history of the twentieth century has taught us anything it is the futility of such views. The Arabs would have their independence and the only question was the forms it would take. If an historian is a visionary looking backward rather than forward, Kedourie fails the test. He is a very skilled practitioner of forensic historiography, capable of fine reasoning and careful analysis and comfortable in the languages that matter in the Middle East. But the vision is lacking. He stood firm to the last—a reactionary—true to his outdated vision of empire but—a dissident—defying the tides to rise.

EDWARD SA'ID (1935-2003)

The second of our subjects was a Palestinian Christian whose peregrinations throughout the region led his critics to suggest that he really wasn't a Palestinian at all. Born in Jerusalem in 1935 into a Protestant family, Edward Sa'id was for years the most articulate voice in the United States arguing against the dispossession of the Palestinian people. His American connection was a function of the fact that his father had emigrated from Palestine to the United States in the early part of the twentieth century and served with the American Expeditionary Force in France during the First World War. The young Edward would qualify for American citizenship (although he carried an American passport throughout his childhood) only if he spent five continuous years in the country prior to his twenty-first birthday. The family discovered this just in time and he was sent at the age of sixteen to a New England boarding school. It was followed by Princeton and Harvard where he earned degrees in English and comparative literature. He eventually became a professor of comparative literature at Columbia where his specialty was Joseph Conrad.

During the thirties of his childhood Palestine was not a comfortable place, wracked as it was by Arab-Jewish tension and violence. His father, moreover, found Jerusalem drab and depressing after life in the United States, and he moved the family to Cairo where he established a profitable stationary business in the downtown, or foreign, section of the city. He was a kind of successor to an earlier, *Shami* invasion of Cairo when Syrian Melchites were brought in to break the back of the Jewish and Sunni elites who dominated Egypt in the middle of the eighteenth century. The local representative of Royal typewriters and Sheaffer pens, among other products, Wadie Sa'id was born to the business of business and, when the shop was burned down by the Cairo mob during the riots of 1952, he simply rebuilt and became even more successful. Business was not what interested his sensitive and artistic son, who combined his literary interests with near-concert ability as a pianist. The family was well-to-do and they escaped the hot Cairo summers to a village associated with his mother's family in the Jebel Lebanon. After western Jerusalem, where the home of the extended family lay, was captured by the Israelis in the War of Independence, the connection with Palestine was severed. Combined with his later American schooling this early history led some to conclude—accuse would be a better word—that Sa'id wasn't really a Palestinian at all and fraudulently presumed to speak for them.

His youth, as detailed in his autobiography *Out of Place* includes a fascinating snapshot of the Cairo of the middle of the twentieth century, before revolution and a population explosion changed it forever. Published in 1999 as Sa'id was struggling with leukemia, the memoir tells the story of his growing up mainly in Cairo, but with summers in Lebanon and less-frequent visits to Palestine. He was enrolled in, first, British and then American schools before attending Victoria College, that avatar of Arab privilege, where anyone who was anyone in the Middle East seemingly went to school. Victoria College was to Egypt what Baghdad College—taught in English by the Jesuits—was to Iraq. But it was in the Shubra and then Ma'adi neighborhoods of Cairo where Sa'id matriculated, not the Alexandria of its more famous campus. School was not a happy experience and Sa'id used the memoir to settle old scores, including his detestation of the head boy at Shubra, Michael Shalhoub, later known as Omar Sharif. Victoria, called Victory College after the revolution, was followed by boarding school in Massachusetts, then Princeton and Harvard.

The memoir ends with completion of his graduate studies at Harvard. That is, it represents the retrospective view by the adult Sa'id of his childhood, adolescence, and college years with an almost photographic recall of the anxieties endured, slights suffered, resentments nursed, and sexual yearnings repressed of a sensitive child growing to adulthood in a coarse and uncomprehending world. The adult Sa'id rarely appears, except as commentator, and the message of the book seems to be "If you want to know why I turned out the way I did, here are the reasons." But the person that emerges seems more out of sorts than out of place. His relationships with others (with the exception of his mother, to whom he was devoted)—his father, teachers, siblings and school acquaintances—always seem problematic and the picture he paints of himself is that of a not very likeable person. His resentment of authority figures, acquired and then carefully nursed during years of exposure to his father, dismissive British teachers and administrators, and bumptious American educators, is a key to Sa'id's world view. Surely it lies at the root of his later championing of peoples who are on the receiving end in their relationships with the powerful.

But there is a genuine sense of dislocation in Sa'id and an intellectual honesty that will not allow him to be an unthinking Christian in Lebanon, Arab in Cairo or, for that matter, American in New York City where he lived for the last several decades of his life. The one identity he permits himself is that of a Palestinian. He was politically active as a member of the Palestinian National Council and a voice widely heard in its deliberations. But, even here, he was unwilling to give his support uncritically, and his writings are littered with criticisms of the stupidity, corruption, and blinkered vision of the PLO and then the Palestinian Authority. He is probably best known politically for his opposition to the Oslo accords which he saw as a betrayal of Madrid, requiring the PA to play the role of Israel's policeman in a few cantonments, in return for very little of substance answering Palestinian aspirations. It is hard to argue with the cogency of that view today, with Israeli settlement activity actually having accelerated after Oslo and perhaps reaching a point of no return. He was an enemy of the incrementalism that would, it was believed, somehow, at some future time, lead to a truncated, emasculated Palestinian state. He believed that a unitary state, open to both Arabs and Jews, was the only logical outcome of the dispute.

The American connection was fraught in that Sa'id labored throughout his life at the confluence of a nearly impossible set of contradictions: a Palestinian Christian, of all people, living and teaching in New York, of all places, in the second half of the twentieth century, of all periods. Europe's export of its Jewish problem to Arab Palestine is *the* issue that dominated the Middle East of the twentieth century and Sa'id, because of his origins, his experience, and his position at Columbia, seemed to be at the center of it all. At least one critic has suggested—a specious example of the even-handedness that is in such short supply in the debate—that the British in 1917 combined their naiveté about the Arabs with an equal naiveté about the Jews, and the notion that there was an "international Jewry" to whom they could appeal was flawed. But Lloyd George makes clear in his memoirs that political considerations were uppermost in the minds of the British government in the issuance of the Balfour Declaration. There has probably been no greater return on an investment in history than the Powers' postwar courting of American Jewry.

It was probably inevitable. With 80 percent of the Jews in the world today approximately evenly divided between Israel and the United States, ties between the two countries have always been strong, although Jews in Israel and the United States do not always agree in their approach to Israel's security. To its credit, Israel conducts a free and open political debate where the most contentious issues—institutional Arabophobia, ethnic cleansing in the '48 war, legality of the settlements, the future of Israeli democracy—are openly discussed. Official American Jewry, if the American Israel Public Affairs Committee can be considered the spokesman, clings to a sanitized version of events and reacts to any questioning of the orthodoxy with shrill accusations of anti-Semitism, blood-libel, and holocaust-denial. AIPAC has become an unassailable force in American politics, in the process creating a juggernaut that American politicians dare oppose only at the risk of political suicide. That five million American Jews—although AIPAC and American Jewry are not synonymous—feel strongly about the security of Israel should come as no surprise. That a lobbying organization should virtually dictate the position of American politicians on a foreign-policy matter as important as America's relations with the world's billion Muslims should be a source of shame, if not scandal.

Edward Sa'id was a Daniel cast into this den of lions. He had the temerity to be born a Palestinian Arab, although his nationalist credentials were denigrated. But his origins and the characteristics of his upbringing, particularly his middle-class background, relative privilege, and later expulsion from the home in Jerusalem, were precisely what made him legitimate. At least two powerful myths had grown up to justify the Zionist enterprise, and his experience gave the lie to both. The first was that there was no one in Palestine when the Zionists arrived. Sa'id was the embodiment of the fact that another people was there, and their presence was not insignificant. Balfour himself was more honest when he opined that Zionism was more important than the prejudices of 700,000 Palestinian Arabs.

A second myth was that if Arabs had been there, they were aborigines, little better than red Indians when the Zionist pioneers came to settle the country. It was unfortunate that they had to be moved off the land to achieve Israel's manifest destiny, but wasn't that what the Americans did with *their* red Indians? What right did Americans have to criticize the Israelis after their own history of dispossessing the Native Americans? Sa'id was also the embodiment of the fact that there had been a thriving, urbanized Palestinian society in cities like Jerusalem, Haifa, Jaffa, Gaza, and Hebron. They were literate and educated, with ties to the outside world, particularly to America, that had broadened their horizons. Much of that society had been swept away in the events of 1948 with large-scale ethnic cleansing, villages bulldozed, and their names forever erased from the map, if not from the memory of their occupants. Edward Sa'id was an inconvenient reminder of the profound injustice that had been visited on Palestine, with its Arab occupants being asked to pay the price of Europe's mistreatment of its Jews.

But Sa'id was more than the embodiment of a lost people or a reminder of a past injustice. He was also the most articulate voice in the West, protesting their treatment at the hands of not only the Zionists but also of a disinterested international community. He spent much of his time debunking the claims that surrounded the creation of Israel: how European Jews shared an equal claim to the land with its Palestinian occupants; how they, a tiny beleaguered minority, had fought to a standstill the combined forces of tens of millions of Arabs in 1948; how they were an outpost of democracy and rationality in a region characterized by autocracy and extremism; how it was only the perfidy of the Arabs that prevented any accommodation. Some of the founding myths had a basis in fact, but they were beside the point: settlers in a European colony in the Arab world would surely have been expected to behave like Europeans, people with whom we could identify, although Israel has made its own contribution to the irrationality that surrounds the issue.

But Sa'id expanded his critique of this particular colonial venture into a larger critique of colonialism in general. In this respect, he became a spokesman for the dispossessed throughout the world. He was a dissident from orthodoxy like Kedourie but, unlike Kedourie, his views probably earned him more enemies than friends. Kedourie may have paid an initial price for his outspoken views but he was criticizing a government, not a people, and the proper British role in postwar Iraq was not a matter to arouse the passions. In the end he became a respected, uncontroversial, expert in the history of the region. But the orthodoxy that Sa'id challenged roused the most violent passions, involving the Bible, the Chosen People, Judaism, Christianity, Islam, anti-Semitism, Zionism,

Jews in America, and the Holocaust, to name only the most obvious. It was inevitable that he would have been attacked, if not vilified, and attempts would be made to suppress his views, even by those presumably dedicated to academic freedom.

Sa'id's output of, broadly speaking, political and literary writing is roughly divided between the two. But it is for the political that he is best known, and *Orientalism* is probably his most controversial work. Published in 1978, Sa'id asserts that the mere *study* of the eastern regions by European experts served the purposes of colonial exploitation and control. He chronicles the process by which Europeans, particularly nineteenth-and early twentieth-century Frenchmen and Englishmen, distorted the image of the Arab and Muslim worlds in the West and contributed to its subjugation. The book is uneven, alternately turgid and inflammatory. The obsession of the "academy"—his word—with methodology is on full display. The "Orient" and the "Occident" are separate, fundamentally unequal entities, the latter approaching the former from an attitude of "flexible *positional* superiority." The discipline of Orientalism is simply a Western "style" for "dominating, restructuring, and having authority over the Orient." In the process of describing it the West has created an "Orient" that has little relation to reality. This is so because the region—inert, feminine, receptive—is unable to speak for itself. Authoritative westerners, or "Orientalists," are required to speak on its behalf. Such is the authority of this academic Orientalism that those who come into actual contact with the phenomenon of the East, and even those with the best of intentions, are unable to shake its prescriptive tyranny.

When Sa'id frees himself from methodological matters and personal animus (it is clear that he believes he is one of those Orientals who are deemed incapable of speaking for themselves), the book provides a valuable review of the history of French and British approaches to their Arab and Muslim colonial subjects in the nineteenth and twentieth centuries. This admittedly led to a great of nonsense, generalizations about the "Oriental" mind asserted as if they were truths etched in stone, rather than observations at a particular point in time by Europeans with a clear cultural bias. The real question is whether we have learned anything over time that would call into question these generalizations. Sa'id maintained that such is the congruence of academic, commercial, and governmental interests in maintaining the unequal relationship between East and West in the late twentieth-century that nothing fundamentally has changed. It is here that one can agree with almost everything Sa'id writes except his conclusions.

But it is important to recognize how narrow a focus Sa'id has chosen: he deals almost exclusively with the contributions of British and French scholars, travelers, government functionaries, and artists to an "Orient" defined as the Muslim Arab world in the nineteenth and twentieth centuries. He freely admits that he doesn't deal with the preeminent German scholarship of the nineteenth century or with the great German Orientalists: "Steinthal, Muller, Becker, Goldziher, Brockelmann, Noldeke," not to mention Niebuhr, von Hammer-Purgstall, Sprenger, von Wrede, Schlegel, Weil, Euting, and Wellhausen. It is a major shortcoming in a work that would presume to be comprehensive. The reproach that he delivers on himself for this shortcoming does not resolve the problem, and the simultaneous reproach he delivers on German Orientalism—that it shares with the British and French versions the "intellectual *authority*" over the Orient—suggests that it really doesn't affect his thesis.

Even within this limited frame of reference, and in his more cautious moments, he admits the problematic nature rather than the outright falsity of the Orientalist canon: the advances in knowledge we "objectively" take for granted are less true than "we often like to think." And while the work of dedicated scholars has produced "positivistically verifiable learning," it should be remembered that the truths it delivers, "like any truths delivered by language, are embodied in language and what is the truth of language." This would seem to be pretty thin gruel for someone looking for a revolutionary view of Europe's approach to eastern peoples. But that conclusion would be a mistake since Sa'id is not always so cautious. The relationship between Europe and the Orient always comes down to power. That power—military, administrative, intellectual, economic—is heavily weighted in favor of the Europeans. The reality of empire, in the case of the British a matter of fact, in the case of France a kind of intellectual and cultural imperium, dominates the exchange, and "every European, in what he could say about the Orient, was . . . a racist, an imperialist, and almost totally ethnocentric."

If only things were so simple. The suggestion that generations of gifted and courageous Frenchmen and Englishmen, pursuing their various demons in the East, were conscious, or even unconscious, enablers of colonial dominance unfairly indicts them all. And is Sa'id really saying anything more profound than that power perpetuates power? Is it any wonder that nineteenth-century Europe, in the midst of an unprecedented efflorescence of intellectual, scientific, industrial, and cultural achievement—and seduced by intellectual currents that suggested there was a scientific basis to its superiority—would have found itself superior to a supine East that was under its administrative control, and would have confidently asserted that superiority? By any measure Europeans were more advanced than other peoples, and it would have taken an act of the will to come to any other conclusion.

The unequal relationship was probably inevitable. Leaving aside the question of military strength, had "Oriental" countries developed a body of studies that could be termed "Occidentalist" the relationships might have been conducted on a more equal basis. But they did not, and a volume like Mirza Abul Hassan Khan's *A Persian at the Court of King George 1809–10* is as rare as it is fascinating glimpse into how *they* saw the West. Surely, part of this lack of Oriental interest in the Occident was the result of a tendency to despise Sa'id's "the Other." The old civilizations of China, Persia, India, and Islam found little to interest them in the crude and upstart West. By the time they awakened and saw the danger, it was too late. And eighteenth and nineteenth-century Englishmen and Frenchmen may have felt an instinctive superiority to the peoples they met in the East, but it had not always been so. Early European travelers were stunned by the architectural magnificence of cities like Delhi and Samarkand, which rivaled, if they didn't surpass, anything in contemporary Europe. And early British-Indian officials like Clive were frankly, and unashamedly, conniving and rapacious as they laid the foundations of later British rule. They had to be, since they were operating in an environment in which power still lay with the local rulers. It was this earlier view of a powerful, inscrutable Orient—the Turks were still threatening the heart of Europe in the late seventeenth century—that survived well into the later European period of ascendancy. Islam was a millennium-long trauma for the West and, in some minds, it remains so today.

For all the cogency of his indictment of nineteenth-century European attitudes towards colonial peoples, his contention that this was all part of a conscious pattern, that the "Orient" was little more than the *creation* of Western Orientalists, and that this artificial creation has become the reality, breaks down because of the sheer improbability that such a construct could withstand first-hand scrutiny in the field. If Sacy and Renan created this mythical Orient in their laboratories in France, generations of travelers and colonial administrators were forced to deal with the real Orient on the ground. They may have been guilty of insensitivity, but it was not because of the application of Orientalist principles, but because of the simple fact that power confers intellectual authority. The personal always lies close to the surface with Sa'id and, again, it is clear that he feels himself a representative of a people who were ignored by the authors of the Orientalist canon.

In the last chapter, "The Latest Phase," the theory is applied to the present. Inevitably Sa'id here stirred up even greater controversy, pointing out that Western anti-Semitism seamlessly transferred its animus from a Jewish (unacceptable) to an Arab (acceptable) target. An unthinking and culturally sanctioned Arabophobia, particularly in the United States, has been the result, allowing generalizations to be made about Arabs that would not be permitted with any other ethnic group. Orientalism has become an American phenomenon as the United States replaced Britain and France as the predominant foreign power in the Arab World. The American rise to prominence after the Second World War is roughly contemporaneous with the rise of Israel whose sympathizers would repair to the Orientalist canon—just as previous colonizers did—to justify the Zionist enterprise in Palestine.

In *The Question of Palestine* and *Covering Islam* (published in 1979 and 1981, respectively, and envisioned as constituting a trilogy with *Orientalism*), Sa'id elaborates these themes, minus much of the methodology. Here, there is no need to argue the question as to whether there is a real Orient or only an Orient created by Orientalists, or whether the dialectic between the canonically-accepted Orient and that of first-hand observers only reinforces the former. Instead, in *The Question of Palestine*, there is the brute fact of the displacement of Palestinian Arabs in their own land by frankly exclusionary and ethnocentric Zionist colonizers. The enterprise acquired legitimacy in the West partly through the same assumptions that justified earlier European colonial ventures, European superiority and Arab underdevelopment. To Sa'id it is beyond comprehension that liberal voices in Europe and America have been largely silent as this crude process plays itself out.

The disproportion between the two sides is striking, one an admittedly-accomplished people but also the beneficiary of an unprecedented level of support in the West, the other a subject people struggling under occupation and reduced to the sobriquet of "terrorists." The Zionist enterprise created three classes of Palestinians: those who remained in their original homes (the Arabs of Eretz Israel), those who left or were driven out in 1948, and those who came under Israeli military rule after 1967 as a result of the June War. All are, in differing ways, stateless. Arabs in Israel are, by definition, second-class citizens, and Israel admits no responsibility for the refugees. As for the inhabitants of the West Bank and Gaza, efforts by militant settlers and military authorities to suppress their rights and confine them to underdeveloped ghettos have largely been successful. The wonder is that the Palestinians, suppressed by Israel, manipulated by other Arabs, and largely ignored by the West have retained any sense of national cohesion. Yet they have, and Sa'id saw early promise in the PLO, although he was not optimistic about the prospect that the West would recognize the Palestinian right to self-determination. His final disenchantment with Palestinian leadership would follow its effective domestication by the Americans and Israelis.

In *Covering Islam* there are equally concrete facts: the Iranian revolution and the hostage crisis, exacerbated in the West by the old irrational fear of Islam. The recent claim by an American presidential contender that radical Islam presents the greatest threat to America in its history is an example of the apocalyptic rhetoric that, thirty years later, still prevails. Added to the Orientalist orthodoxy in the late twentieth-century is the rising power of the media to propagate the threat of terrorism and, more recently, the prospect of a nuclear-armed Iran. The media is characterized by "supercaution and self–imposed conformity . . ." in its treatment of Iran. The words were written in 1981 but the tendency prevails today, with few observers soberly and rationally asking themselves what threat a struggling, developing-world country with a widely unpopular government and a miniscule military budget can pose to the United States. Or, why Iranian initiatives to strike a grand bargain, with all issues on the table, have been consistently rebuffed by America.

The last collection of his political essays, *From Oslo to Iraq and the Road Map*, is vintage Sa'id and perhaps should stand as his legacy. The book consists of a series of articles written for the *Al-Ahram Weekly*, although a few were also published in *Al-Hayat*, the *London Review of Books*, *Le Monde*, *The Guardian* and *The Observer*. The Sa'id we have come to expect is on full display, alternately outraged, intemperate, sarcastic, condescending, deeply pessimistic, and defiantly optimistic about the fate of the Palestinians he has come to represent. There is nothing particularly eloquent about the essays, and the language is often commonplace. His facts are sometimes confused and often contradictory from essay to essay, but the inconsistencies are lost in the white heat of his narrative. Somehow these things don't matter and the lack of rhetorical flourishes lends credibility to the tale of abandonment by the world of a dispossessed people who have survived years of repression under the thumb of a colonial power. Over and over again, we are reminded of the targeted assassinations, civilian casualties and house demolitions, the cutting down of orchards, the land seizures, wanton destruction of infrastructure, checkpoints, and collective punishments that constitute the daily routine in the life of Palestinians in the West Bank and Gaza.

There is blame enough to go around for the disaster, from the disinterested Arabs, the brutal Israelis, the feeble Europeans, the Palestinians themselves, and the Americans who, when all is said and done, are the real villains of the piece since they, alone, have the power to bring Israel to heel. If, to use his words, to repeat a lie often enough is to believe it, he seems to hope that the reverse is also true: to repeat a truth often enough is to believe it. But he has chosen an odd vehicle if his message is to reach an American audience: an English-language Cairo periodical, appealing to a local readership that is probably committed to the American project in Egypt, and an expatriate community that is already sympathetic. Appearance in a few British and French newspapers doesn't help much. But he has probably given up on the Americans anyway, and the anguished cry for an intelligent resistance to occupation is really directed at the Palestinians themselves. The essays span the launching of the Iraq war, and events have proven accurate his pessimism about the potential outcome. Like many others he was deeply suspicious of the motives of the war's greatest enthusiasts, seeing in position papers written for Binyamin Netanyahu in the mid-1990s the real motives for the invasion. The attack on September eleventh merely provided the pretext.

Sa'id died of leukemia a few months after publication of the last of the essays, and it was probably not a happy man who breathed his last. His optimism that a new generation of Palestinian leaders, grassroots activists rather than paper-pushers and bureaucratic hacks, would rise up to challenge the corrupt leadership that has outdone itself in bowing to Israeli and American demands, seems hollow. The ringing words of defiance to a disinterested world in the June 26–July 2, 2003 piece seem forced. But he had a good run. He girded his loins, took on his enemies, made himself a force to be reckoned with in the debate, acquiring more enemies than friends in the process, and left behind a checkered legacy of scholarship and political commentary. His views on Palestine will probably be vindicated only in the very long term, when passions have cooled and the absurdity of a tiny, aggressive, and exclusionary Zionist entity in the heart of the Muslim Arab World will have become clear for all to see. Then, his vision of men of intelligence and moderation, Muslim, Jew, and Christian, coming together to create an inclusive and civilized polity in that little piece of land, might finally be realized.

FU'AD AJAMI (1945–2014)

The last of our subjects is Fu'ad Ajami, a Lebanese Shia of obvious Iranian extraction, who, like Kedourie and Sa'id, left his native country and spent his adulthood in the West. He earned advanced degrees from the University of Washington and lived for the past several decades as an intellectual émigré in the United States. He was a professor and then director of the Middle East Program at the School of Advanced International Studies at Johns Hopkins University in Baltimore and was later at the Hoover Institute at Stanford. He died of cancer in June of 2014. The name "Ajami" is the key to his origins, the classic Greek-barbarian, Jew-gentile distinctions being complemented by that between the Arabs and *ajam*. Technically, *ajami* means "non-Arab," but since the Persians were the foreigners most often seen in the early days of Islam, the term has come to mean more specifically Persian.

He was born in 1945 in the south of Lebanon—rural, feudal, inarticulate, poverty-stricken, a world apart from the heartland of the Maronites and the northern cities of the Sunnis—before coming to Beirut for schooling at a predominantly Sunni Muslim institution, where he imbibed the pan-Arab sentiments fashionable of the day. The Shiite background—his grandfather emigrated from Iran in the middle of the nineteenth century—was, he admits, unexplored. But it was also, one suspects, suppressed as a source of anxiety to one already set apart by ethnicity, geography, and social class from his more westernized and cosmopolitan Sunni classmates. If his early reaction was to embrace political and social orthodoxy and fly from everything Shiite, he later recovered and repaid the Sunnis many times over, in the process becoming their greatest rhetorical scourge.

Beginning with *The Arab Predicament*, published in 1981, Ajami chronicled the fate of the Nasser-inspired pan-Arabism that was dealt a deathblow in the Six-Day War. But, if the defeat in June of 1967 was the precipitating event, the difficulties of the Arab World in adjusting to late twentieth-century realities were his real subject and he brought to the discussion an impressive scholarship in English and, particularly, in Arabic. Much of the difficulty is chronicled by Arab writers themselves, whether Egyptians, Syrians, Palestinians, Lebanese, Sa'udis, or Algerians. Ajami's review of each of the various Arab polities is penetrating and insightful. But where Kedourie was a historian, Ajami, like Sa'id, is also a bit of a literary critic and, above all, a sociologist. His canvas is sometimes too broad and it is not clear what de Tocqueville, Clifford Geertz, Claude Levi-Strauss, Franz Kafka, and Joseph Conrad contribute to the discussion. He is unsparing in his treatment of the bombast, false nostalgia, unreality, and intellectual vapidity of the Arabs, as presumably only one born in the region can be. But the suspicion lingers that he is enjoying himself too much and that he harbors a fundamental lack of sympathy for his subject. He doesn't rub Arab noses in the catastrophe of 1967 in the same way that Raphael Patai does. But he makes the same questionable excursions into "the Arab mind" and there is something almost gleeful in his exposure of their disappointed dreams.

Ajami revisits the themes developed in *The Arab Predicament* in 1998 with *The Dream Palace of the Arabs*, the account of a generation's adjustment to failure. The title is a quote from T. E. Lawrence and the *Seven Pillars of Wisdom*. *The Dream Palace* is more literary and less sociological, and also less biting, with sensitive portraits of Arab thinkers and the American missionaries who had been instrumental in expanding their intellectual horizons. The portrait of the Lebanese poet Khalil Hawi is fine, but Hawi comes across in the end as petulant and self-indulgent. More sympathetic is the portrayal of three generations of Kerrs, from the original medical missionary with Near East Relief through the murdered president of the American University in Beirut, to the grandson who played in the NBA with the Chicago Bulls and now coaches the Golden State Warriors. The Kerrs epitomized an early, quintessentially American interest—one could almost call it disinterest—in the Near East with none of the political edge that it has today. It is odd that such sensitive treatment of what was, in the end, a proselytizing endeavor should have come not from an historian of the American missionary effort, but from a native-born Muslim. There is an equal affection for Egypt, for its essential stability, Mediterranean outlook, and sadly diminished status, with equal parts admiration for its once-outspoken intelligentsia and dismay at the sorry state to which they have been reduced today.

But interspersed with these sensitive portraits Ajami returns to the attack with a slashing treatment of the, by now, usual targets: the legacy of

Nasserism, Syrian meddling, Palestinian rejectionism, the demonization of Israel, and the refusal to come to terms with reality. There seems to be no concession to the idea that, for all the irrationality, there is a genuine grievance in the Sunni Arab world, the dispossession of the Palestinians not being an act of nature against which one might as well rail as against the course of a flood or the devastation of an earthquake. It is not the result of some ancient animus, but is rather a twentieth-century political problem created by twentieth-century political people. It was a profound injustice and until that is finally recognized by Israel, there will little hope of an accommodation between the sides.

There also seems to be no recognition by Ajami that the legacy of the Six Day War may be as fraught for the Israelis as for the Arabs, the difficulties just longer in manifesting themselves. The central myth of the smashing victory in 1967—that the Israelis were supermen—has been steadily eroded, first in 1973 and then in the long and unsuccessful occupation of Southern Lebanon. The final nail in the coffin may have been the assault on Lebanon in the summer of 2006 when draftees of the vaunted citizen army were chewed up by Shiite militiamen who had sophisticated arms, internal lines, and no fear of death. They had abandoned the quiescence and timidity of their elders, so skillfully drawn by Ajami, and defended themselves and their communities with every means at their disposal. Gone are the days, in Moshe Dayan's description of the Egyptian army, when Arab generals were too fat and privates were too thin. No longer could the supermen prevail over the forces of evil in lightening campaigns, and that is probably a healthy phenomenon.

In *The Vanished Imam*, Ajami's moving account of the career and disappearance of the Imam Musa al-Sadr, a Shiite cleric of outstanding human qualities, social awareness, and political acumen, the old bugbears are still there. But they are incorporated into a discussion of the fissiparous fabric of Lebanon, created when the French attached Sunni Tripoli and the Shiite south to the Maronite heartland around Beirut. The already fractious polity—and it is hard to understand how they thought the country would work in the first place—was complicated by the dispossession and expulsion of the Palestinians after wars with Israel in 1948 and 1967. This was followed by King Hussein's ruthless crushing of the state–within-a-state in Jordan in 1970, and their resettlement in Lebanon. The book is a work of some subtlety and nuance, although often repetitive and given to the same questionable marshalling of outside experts as in *The Arab Predicament*. But Ajami's use of Arabic sources is a valuable addition to our understanding of people and events. Overall the book is Ajami at his best, dealing with a subject he knows at first hand, the Shia of Lebanon. Despite the scholarly detachment, it is difficult to believe that he is not aware that he is speaking about his own people. There is even a hint of pride in the person of al-Sadr, for all of his ambivalence a man of "eloquence, spontaneity and gentleness," a worthy representative of Iranian clerics who were themselves the legatees of a Persian culture that, with its suppleness and ambiguity, dominated the medieval Muslim world.

There is also a sympathetic treatment throughout the book of the diffident, at first, then increasingly assertive claim by the dispossessed Shiites—once subject to the unfettered power of the *bey*—for their right to a place at the table in the power structure of Lebanon (the same sympathy, it should be mentioned, never seems to extend to the overwhelmingly Sunni Palestinians). There are valuable touches too numerous to mention, such as the diplomatic accident that shunted Lebanese Shiite emigration from the Americas to West Africa, providing context to those who have worked there and patronized Lebanese booksellers, restauranteurs, and stationers in Niamey and Abidjan. But everyone seems to be tainted or corrupted by their entry into the maelstrom of Lebanon: the Americans and their obsession with Nasserism (and, later, terrorism), the larger Arab World with its Israeli obsession, the Palestinians with their recklessness and bravado, the Israelis with their bloody and counterproductive response to attacks launched from the south, the Syrians with their meddling, and the Iranians with their opportunism. For once with Ajami there don't seem to be clear-cut good guys and bad guys. Even al-Sadr's ultimate fate, elimination at the hands of Qadafi's thugs, seems to be less a matter of right and wrong than the normal course of events when the status quo and the powers-that-be are challenged.

But there are also hard lessons to be learned in Lebanon. The velocity of events when the country began to unravel was terrifying, and sectarian divisions that had lain dormant for generations raised their heads when it all began to come apart. These were portents of the unraveling of Yugoslavia and, later, of Iraq. It was the Israeli invasion in 1982, led by men ignorant of the country's fabric and divisions, that ultimately empowered the Shiites in the south, an unintended consequence that continues to reverberate today. And the American intervention in the Lebanese civil war in 1983, without a clear mission and woefully ignorant of the ethnic and sectarian forces in the country, was an ominous portent for the misadventure in Iraq. Then, the Shiite pushback was followed by a precipitate American scuttle, with the United States apparently weighing in the balance the importance of its local clients and its larger strategic and regional interests. The larger interests prevailed then, and it is an open question as to whether it wasn't the better part of wisdom.

However, with *The Foreigner's Gift*, published in 2006, Ajami seems to have crossed a line. In spite of his best efforts, the picture he unwittingly paints is not a pretty one because he has moved from his earlier role as commentator and critic to, one suspects, that of enabler. All the decades of fulminating against the Sunni elites in the region finally came to a head with the opportunity to *do* something about them. There is strong suspicion that Ajami lent his blessing, that of a purported insider, to the invasion of Iraq. All the nuance and sensitivity of his approach to the region seem to have been put aside. One wonders if he was present at that September 19, 2001 meeting of the Pentagon Review Board during which another familiar actor, Bernard Lewis, was the featured speaker. Lewis reminded the audience, as if they needed reminding, that the only thing the Arabs understood was force. This helpful bit of advice would eventually percolate down into the force structure and one of Gen. Odierno's staff in Anbar would later be quoted as saying that "The only thing these sand-niggers understand is force, and I'm about to introduce them to it." In fact, the history of the past eighty years suggests that the one thing that the Arabs do *not* understand is force. But the spectacle of this eminent Orientalist offering a prescription for the taming of Sunni Iraq would seem to justify Edward Sa'id's debatable thesis.

In the introduction Ajami goes after the usual suspects, the Sunni chattering classes and their institutional enablers, and extrapolates from the score of Sa'udis, Emiratis and Lebanese to the guilt of the entire Arab World for 9/11 and a justification for George Bush's war. He laments the "undermining" of the effort by such inconvenient facts as the absence of weapons of mass destruction or of ties between Usama bin Laden and Saddam Hussein. That facile distinction is certainly not made in the "coffee houses" of the intellectuals or the "safe houses" of the terrorists. But the damage is done and Ajami does his best to summarize the unfortunate turn of events in the war, by then in its fourth year and hardly in need of another chronicler. The disaster is there for all to see. He gives the back of his hand to the Iraq Study Group which he sees less as a bipartisan group of distinguished Americans than a few innocents dominated by the ultimate fixer, James Baker, who so signally let the Iraqis down in 1991, and his effort to cobble together another short-term fix. What is needed is not another fix, but extirpation of the Sunni virus, root and branch. Oddly the American effort, which has profoundly destabilized the region, is justified in Ajami's eyes as part of a broader effort to bring stability to the Arab World.

The book actually appears to be two books. The first, consisting of the opening chapters, is painful to read, so redolent of nobility of purpose and a refusal to see the darker side that it recalls the willful ignorance of fellow-traveling visitors to the Soviet Union in the 1930s. The vices to which Ajami is occasionally prey are here magnified: the sensitivity bordering on sentimentality, the tendency to lionize and demonize, the distancing of himself from his roots, the loquaciousness that leaves the reader reeling, wondering how many different ways the same thing can be said. There are a few discordant elements as well: the curious references to "Araby," or the citing of the name of the young Iraqi officer "Abdul Sahib," to be repeated later in the book with "Abdul Hussein" and "Abdulameer." The names are theological absurdities, recognizable as such to anyone with a rudimentary knowledge of Islam. But, then, we earlier learned that Ajami is not only not a practicing Muslim, but he never learned to pray.

The race to Baghdad was carried out, Ajami purrs approvingly, with "breathtaking speed." This was surely predictable to anyone contemplating an attack by the most technologically-advanced armed force in history on the broken remnants of a third-world army that had no air cover, hadn't maneuvered in eleven years, and whose arms had been obsolete in the first Gulf War. The Americans, says Ajami worshipfully, were for him a breed apart since his days as a boy in Lebanon. Unfortunately, too many of these Americans, untrained in what to expect, were too quick on the trigger and countless innocent Iraqi lives were lost at checkpoints with soldiers screaming unprintable expletives at bewildered Iraqis before opening fire. Whole families were lost in these incidents. The hagiography of "the scholar-soldier Lieutenant General David H. Petraeus" proceeds apace, Ajami having succumbed to the old Arab proclivity for impressive-sounding titles. In expiation of the purposes of the American invasion we are exposed to the rarified language of the speechwriters of President George W. Bush. Bush's approach to Saddam was, in its own way, far more eloquent: "Fuck him. We're gonna take him out."

THE RENEGADES 313

Ajami marvels at the "earnestness and devotion" of the Americans in the Coalition Provisional Authority. Everyone appears to be "courteous and polite beyond his years," devoted to doing the right thing, and only later must learn to rein in his idealism. The unfortunate reality was that the CPA was too often staffed with children and political hacks, utterly out of their depth in Iraq. He speaks of young, idealistic Americans who have "mastered Arabic" in their twenties. Now, Richard Burton, responding to criticism of his translation of the *Thousand Nights and a Night*, allowed that after forty years he didn't know Arabic "and I don't know the man who does." In Kurdistan, Ajami meets with Barham Salih in "a sunlit library of exquisite design with books tumbling out of the shelves . . ." He encounters melodic Arabic, apparently gone from being that handmaid of bombast and unreality to a beautiful accompaniment of everyday life. In Halabja he meets with peasants and we learn that he "knew and loved those threshing floors from my childhood in Lebanon." Peasants wave from the fields and the gunners in the American helicopter that has transported him to and from this pastoral idyll wave back. Even the least cynical among us must eventually grow weary of this cloying portrait.

But the war in Iraq "was now folded into a wider campaign on behalf of liberty and freedom." He glides past the fact that a shallow president had hardly given a thought to freedom before it became the latest in a series of discredited justifications for the war. He leaves unexamined the role of the war's architects on whose careless watch the United States effectively abdicated its role as an occupying power to preserve order. The breakdown in authority and the looting of arms stockpiles in a country awash in weapons were the disastrous results. Instead, we are treated to more bombast: "In the shade of these palm trees in Mesopotamia, a vast American expedition was trying to bring order to a fractious land." But the Sunnis, those unreformed antediluvians, were doing everything in their power to thwart the new order. In Fallujah they would soon strike back, although no mention is made of the incident where a score of demonstrators were killed by trigger-happy American soldiers, that sparked the unrest.

The intellectual underpinnings of the war, such as they were, are revealed early in the second chapter and the dirty little secret is out: the politics of the Palestinians will be transformed by this display of American power. The Palestinians, we have come to understand, have no grievances, but are only in need of political shock therapy. The overturning of the old order in Iraq will provide the necessary shock. So, the linkage between Palestine and Iraq, so discredited by Ajami, really exists after all. It is *never* about the Palestinians, but then, it seems, it is *always* about the Palestinians. They, and the rest of the Arab World, are collectively to blame for 9/11. Our authoritarian friends are responsible for the freedom deficit in the Middle East, the real source of the region's problems. But we can't invade Egypt or Sa'udi Arabia, although both need something to shake them out of their torpor. So, Saddam, having drawn the short straw, has to go. Iraq, we thought, represented low hanging fruit. So what if the ostensible reasons for the war proved hollow? So what if the Iraqis, after twenty years of war and sanctions, were impoverished, brutalized, deeply religious, and riven by ethnic, sectarian, and tribal differences? With typical American, can-do spirit we will create a beacon of democracy in perhaps the least promising place for its flourishing on the planet.

Ajami regains his footing in the remainder of the book, chastened perhaps by the realities of Iraq. The old bugbears are still there, and some new ones as well: Arabic satellite channels and "Arabists in the imperial capital." But we have his usual knowledgeable treatment of Iraqi realities, particularly in the discussion of Iraqi Shiism and its leading lights. And he is relatively unsparing of the mistakes made in the early part of the occupation. But, surely, if he is able to articulate them so clearly afterwards, he should have been able to see the terrors of Iraq's history and the problems it would present to a foreign occupier. As an Iraqi acquaintance, a professional who had long-since fled the country, observed: "We are happy to be rid of Saddam, but any fool could have seen this coming." Ajami is no fool. One wonders if he had brought his intimate knowledge to the attention of the war's architects. Given what we have seen in the first part of the book, it does not appear that he did.

But it is as an author, not an ideologue, that Ajami ultimately comes up short. For all of his fluidity in English, in this book he succumbs to a fatal deficit of irony. How else could he inveigh against the influence of *Al-Jazeera* in the Arab World without an awareness of the baleful effect that cable news channels have had on the quality of political discourse in America. Because of their influence 40 percent of Americans believed that Saddam Hussein was responsible for 9/11.

Other examples abound. Ajami points to the corruption in the Oil-for-Food program, but, surely, he knew that it was American complicity that allowed Jordan to become the epicenter of the smuggling operation that kept Saddam's regime afloat. And, as we are learning on a daily basis, the corruption, fraud, and waste associated with the American occupation of Iraq make the Oil-for-Food effort seem like a model of transparency. He repeats, yet again, the failure of the region to accept responsibility for its own deeds in the context of Abu Ghraib, of all things, where the refusal of the Bush administration to recognize the scandal as anything but the work of a few bad apples on the night shift has forever tainted our reputation around the world.

He objects to an Egyptian sheikh assuming "the right to rule on Iraq's affairs" when an outside power has arrogated to itself the right to do just that through the application of massive violence. His boast of the arms distributed to Iraqis in the training effort, "172,000 AK-47 automatic rifles, 163,000 pistols . . ." would sound more convincing were it not for the fact that most of them are unaccounted for and may have wound up in the hands of insurgents. It is puzzling how Ajami could pen of an Iraqi cleric "The content of his oration was superficial, but his self-confidence was unnerving" without reflecting on the performance of George W. Bush. And it is astonishing that he can he excoriate the "sycophants posing as historians in the service of the ruler" after his own lamentable performance in the run-up to the war.

In fact, the reputation of everyone associated with the misadventure in Iraq has suffered and Ajami is no exception. Just as with terrorism, the enablers are as much at fault as the perpetrators. Here, the fall is particularly precipitous. The reasons have probably always been there, from the rejection of his early enthusiasm for pan-Arabism, the worshipful approach to his adopted country, the curious blindness to suffering if it wears the wrong political colors, perhaps even the vicarious desire to be a man of action after so many years on the sidelines. Whatever the reasons, in the end the recipient of the MacArthur Fellowship and National Humanities Medal, this man of exceptional talent in the arts, the interpreter of Arabs and Islam to the West, this admirer of Niebuhr and Burton, Burckhardt, and Palgrave, T. E. Lawrence and Gertrude Bell, will be primarily remembered for his rhetorical support for that catastrophic intervention.

The West Bank

17

Nablus

IT WOULD BE A first real trip outside Ramallah. I had driven to Jerusalem through the Qalandya checkpoint and down to Tel Aviv by the more direct, but longer, route through the little villages that dotted Israel in the west. But this would be a first experience in the occupied territories in 2009. It was a repeat of earlier visits to East Jerusalem, Bethlehem, and *Khalil*, or Hebron, in 1983. But people said that everything had changed since then. Now checkpoints were everywhere and the security presence was far more pervasive. Settlements had grown from a few isolated outposts to large residential communities and there were hundreds of thousands of Israelis now living among the Palestinians in what religious Jews called Judea and Samaria.

Jordan held the West Bank until the June War in 1967. When the war broke out King Hussein was warned by the Israelis to stay out. But, given a choice between the West Bank and his throne, he had come in and, predictably, lost the territories. There followed Israeli occupation during which things seemed to work, at least from the point of view of the public-sector entities we dealt with. Cooperation between the Palestinians and the Israelis had at first been the norm. But it broke down after 1995 and the creation of the Palestinian Authority. The lack of budget and a chaotic civil administration—all entities reported directly to Arafat—exacerbated by corruption and cronyism, brought matters to a halt. The outbreak of the second *intifada* in 2000 dealt cooperation a final blow. We would learn later in the day that the road repair unit in the Ministry of Public Works and Housing (MoPWH) would speak of a kind of BC and AD, that is, before and after 1995. Before 1995, things worked. Afterwards, they didn't.

We left at eight fifteen, allowing about an hour and-a-half to Nablus. There were three of us in the Chevrolet sedan: Bashar, the embedded advisor in the ministry, Bashara, the Christian driver, and I. We took the white-plated sedan rather than the yellow-plated Blazer since Bashar's documents meant that he couldn't ride in an Israeli-plated vehicle. He was a civil servant with only a rudimentary command of English, and there was concern that his inability to write a coherent report would limit his effectiveness. I was willing to give him a chance, seeing his problem as largely one of language, not an inability to think clearly. Bashara was a typical project driver, fluent in Arabic and Hebrew and with very passable English. He was probably a Latin, or Roman Catholic. He was also a kind of general factotum, and could tell you where to have your trousers hemmed, where to get wine and beer, where the best pharmacy in town was, and even where you could get pork from a Christian butcher in Jerusalem. As a native of Ramallah, he could make himself very useful to a foreigner living there, and he knew it. In the easy democracy of the Arab World he would sit in on our meeting at the ministry later in the day, and I didn't discourage him, given Bashar's limited English. Besides, our Afghan consultant might need his services later on.

At the first checkpoint an Israeli soldier with a large floppy bonnet covering his helmet waved us through without checking our documents. There was an unpredictability about the system that made the experience even more annoying to those who dealt with it on a daily basis. As far as the Palestinians were concerned security was *not* the primary objective of the checkpoints, and they maintained that the soldiers—most of them eighteen-year-old conscripts—were simply there to harass them. I had my American passport and a green card that identified me as working on an American project but I had not been asked for either at any of the checkpoints thus far. Maybe it was because of my age. At the airport in Tel Aviv I told the unsmiling woman at passport control that I was working on an American government project and my documents had been stamped without comment. But younger members of the project team—particularly if they looked foreign—were taken aside and interrogated. One young Pakistani girl—an American citizen but born and raised in Abu Dhabi—was detained at the airport for several hours and grilled on why she was helping "these people." The Palestinians had enough help already. Why had she made a personal decision to participate in this project?

The stories of strip searches and harassment at airports and border crossings were legion. Everyone seemed to have their own tale to tell. It seemed outrageous that citizens of the United States would be treated this way by the largest recipient of American foreign aid. But this was the least of the contradictions in our odd relationship with Israel. American pushback had been nonexistent and the Bush administration had conspicuously refused to engage in the peace process. But in spite of the rhetorical hostility to Palestinian aspirations, it was said that Coldoleeza Rice took a personal interest in development of the West Bank. And the yearly aid program for the West Bank and Gaza—it couldn't be called Palestine—had quietly grown in the past few years from next to nothing to over $500 million. It was now the sixth largest program in the USAID portfolio.

At the same time, we refused to confront Israel with *the* critical issue that stood between the two parties, Israeli settlements in the territories. As recently as Annapolis the Israelis had agreed to dismantle over 100 "illegal" settlements, but had done nothing. And we had done nothing to enforce the agreement. Among English language Israeli dailies *Haaretz* on the left opined that they were illegal, and that everyone *knew* they were illegal. The *Jerusalem Post* on the right was, predictably, more hawkish. The *Post* seemed to epitomize what one Israeli observer called the country's schizophrenia about the occupation: Israelis had intellectually come to the conclusion that it was untenable—Israel could not be a democratic and Jewish state and still keep the territories—but that they were unwilling to pay the political price of withdrawal. In a "partners" conference sponsored by USAID, it was the Israeli representatives from "Seeds of Peace" and "Friends of the Earth"—their more hawkish countrymen would refer to them as "the usual suspects"—who were outspoken on the need to end the settlements and the occupation. The Americans in the room sat mute, not even permitted to have the conversation. In private we all agreed that ending the occupation was one of the critical challenges for the next administration but the subject had not even been raised during the presidential campaign.

Typical West Bank Scrub

The topography of the West Bank, limestone hills with a thin covering of scrub and dotted with terraced olive trees, was on full display on the drive to Nablus. Occasionally the prospect would change when we dropped into a valley where the soil, reddish and strewn with stones, had been recently turned over in preparation for the seed. But it was the exception rather than the rule. The Israeli settlements, residential communities and camps, were surprisingly unobtrusive. They could be seen crowning the hilltops, along with the nearby security outposts—tall, medieval-looking conical towers with slits for observation—that protected them. They seemed Orwellian: we were being watched by an invisible, but omnipresent, authority.

The highway was well maintained. This was, after all, an area used by both Israelis and Palestinians. The sight of Israeli girls hitchhiking—the practice would be unthinkable in the Arab World—was another reminder that we were not alone in the territories. Yellow-plated Israeli cars drove as if they owned the road which, in a sense, they did. But when we left the main thoroughfare and passed through Palestinian villages the roads were in noticeably poorer condition. There were no large potholes, just a less comfortable ride over uneven surfaces. This was important information, since our work would be with the Nablus road repair unit, responsible for maintenance of the network outside the municipality itself. These smaller roads didn't look like they had been repaired in years, something we would confirm later that morning. Groups of students on their way to school, most of them veiled girls, competed for space on the narrow roads. Signs on the main arteries were in English, Hebrew, and Arabic, and the relationship between the two Semitic languages was on occasional display: the Hebrew word for apple was transliterated in English as *tapawah*, close to the Arabic *tufah*, the nonexistent "p" appearing in the Arabic sign as a "ba" with three dots as the diacritic.

About five minutes from the city limits of Nablus we came to an intersection, and a decision point. We could go on and try our luck at the Israeli checkpoint ahead, or go around and enter by the back door, which would add another thirty minutes to the trip. It was hard to predict what would happen at the checkpoint. We would be stopped and the car could be forbidden to enter, which meant that we would have to walk through the barrier and take a cab into the city. That was assuming we would all be allowed to go on at all, but there was a possibility that the Palestinians would not. That would defeat the purpose of the trip. Since it was only nine fifteen and our meeting was at ten o'clock we decided on the second option. It was surprising that so simple a stratagem would defeat Israeli security, but it worked. Half an-hour later we passed through an unmanned checkpoint to the east and entered the city.

Nablus snaked away to the west in a valley dominated by two very high and steep mountains, between which the heart of the city lay although residential communities covered the slopes on either side. The mountains were called *al-Kibli* and *Ebal* in Arabic. To the north, *Ebal* was surmounted by what looked like a temple. It had been built by Samaritans, a community in the area continuously since biblical times. They were reportedly poor and backward and Bashara's broken English captured their situation perfectly: "Most of them are not so good since they marry from each other." Like other small groups in the area intermarriage had reduced the gene pool and increased the incidence of damaging traits. We made our way for ten minutes along the floor of the valley, before reaching our destination: what appeared to be a large construction yard with heavy equipment in the back and an office building at the front.

Inside the building we were greeted and ushered into the office of the general manager who, it seemed, was away on the *Hajj* in Mecca. We would meet his deputy, who had been delayed in the morning commute, although we had seen little traffic outside. The first order of business was something to drink, followed by the usual sweets. After introductions—most of the men in the room were engineers—we began by explaining the objectives of the project and the purpose of our visit. They seemed to have been briefed and produced a nice brochure, in Arabic, showing the organization of the office, a list of staff, a plan of the grounds and color photos of the heavy equipment available to the maintenance unit.

Then the deputy, a jolly little man, arrived and we went over the same ground again before getting down to the real business of the visit, assessment of the state of the existing road-repair unit. It was then that we learned that it had effectively ceased to function after the Israeli withdrawal in 1995. The Palestinian Authority had taken over, but a lack of budget and administrative know-how had compromised the effectiveness of the unit. Most of the trained staff had long-since retired. There had been sporadic donor interest and the Europeans had provided some heavy equipment—two large steamrollers were donated by Spain and a bucket-loader by Germany—but this appeared to be a classic case of unsustainable development. There had been no provision for maintenance or the supply of spare parts. The maintenance shops were now closed or used as places to park excess staff.

We later saw a collection of open-end wrenches, some metric—some English-system, mounted like trophies on one wall, but none of them appeared to have been used recently. The heavy equipment—worth several million dollars new—sat idle and rusting in the yard. It didn't seem that the ignition in some of the pieces had been turned over in years. I later looked on the Internet to get a rough idea of the cost of the equipment and found a road grader, of about the size I had seen in the yard. It was offered for $159,000, used. Our procurement budget of just over $2 million would be rapidly depleted if we had to replace not only the equipment here in Nablus, but in the other units in Ramallah and Hebron as well.

That wasn't counting the new units we had proposed to create in the six other governorates. And road maintenance was only one of five projects the procurement budget was designed to cover. Clearly, we would have to scale back the effort to make the best use of our limited resources. Since Nablus was the maintenance hub for the other areas in the north, including Qalqiliya, Tubas, and Jenin, it might be a candidate for a larger effort. That would fulfill another of our objectives, to expand donor assistance to areas outside of Ramallah. But all of that remained to be seen. Clearly, sustainability was the key: we had to ensure that after we left this same situation didn't recur. The one positive note seemed to be that the engineer responsible for road maintenance was still there, a repository of knowledge that would help in staffing and equipping the new unit.

Afterwards we paid a visit to an asphalt plant—also donated by Spain, in 1999—a five-minute drive from the maintenance yard. It was the same story. The plant, where bitumen from Israel was to be added to aggregate from Nablus, had never been put into operation. It, too, sat idle and rusting, the conveyor and other moving parts having been exposed to the elements for the past nine years. It would take an expert to know how long it would take to repair this or any of the other equipment—or if any of it was repairable. In the worst case that it would all have to be scrapped. That would add unexpected costs to the project. How would you move equipment weighing tons, that hadn't been started in years? Fortunately, a large scrap yard with heavy equipment scattered over several acres was located halfway between the office and the asphalt plant. At least it wouldn't have to be moved very far. The visit had been anything but reassuring. We had expected to complement the existing road repair units by creating new ones. But they were all shells, without even staff to man the crews. And we would have to first deal with the old before we could begin building the new.

Before leaving for Ramallah we were given a guided tour of the old city by one of the engineers. He was a typical multi-lingual Palestinian, fluent in German, Hebrew, and Arabic but speaking very little English. Nablus was noted for having one of the oldest covered *suqs* in the Arab World.

New Construction

Engineer Bassam insisted that it was over a thousand years old, but had difficulty tracing the history much beyond the Ottoman period. We parked in a modern multistory parking garage, built by one of the city's oligarchs, before crossing the street to the *suq*. From the outside it was unimposing, looking neither very large nor very old, but once inside it was labyrinthine and the roofed sections and vaults gave it the look of the *Khan al-Khalili* in Cairo. Much of it had been razed by the Israeli army in 2002 during the *al-Aqsa Intifada*, but it was now back in business. Unlike bazaars in Cairo, Damascus and Istanbul, there was little in the way of brass and copper, carpets, or handicrafts. This market offered practical, everyday necessities: fruits and vegetables, meat, spices, nuts, olives and olive oil, clothing, shoes, cheap toys, everyday furniture. The produce seemed fresher and the prices lower than in Ramallah. We completed our tour in a *kunafa* shop where Bassam matter-of-factly produced four plates of the sweet—goat cheese with a sprinkling of corn meal and sugar and fried on a large griddle—and four glasses of water from a nearby tap. Nablus was famous for its *kunafa* and we tucked it away like Egyptians.

Departure from the city was a repeat of our entry, by the back door. But we took a circuitous route, climbing up the nearly sheer *al-Kibli* before creeping along the steep hillside to the east before reaching the abandoned checkpoint. There was a surprising amount of construction activity in the area, new apartment buildings in white limestone going up everywhere. That was another puzzle in the West Bank. All the Palestinians said things were much worse than before. But here, as in Ramallah, there was clearly money to be invested and people were taking the plunge. A prominent Jordanian had observed that "the Arabs are pretty good at turning money into stones. But they're not very good at turning stones into money." It may have been true and these investments would generate few jobs other than in the building trades. It was hard to say how much of the money was local and how much from the diaspora in the Gulf, Sa'udi Arabia, Canada, or America. But, whatever the source, the activity was reassuring evidence of confidence by some in the future of Nablus.

18

Christmas in Jerusalem

AT FIRST, I THOUGHT of Christmas in Bethlehem. There were a few advantages of being on the West Bank and the proximity of the holy places was one of them. Bethlehem was only half-an-hour away from Ramallah, although that was on a good day. The capriciousness of Israeli soldiers at the checkpoints could make the trip much longer. Everyone seemed to have a story of the inconveniences, not to mention the indignities, endured at the checkpoints. But, even so, it would be worth the trouble. What better place to celebrate Christmas than in Church of the Nativity?

I had last been there in 1983. Everyone on the West Bank said that things were now much worse. Palestinian Christians were under increasing pressure to leave and Bethlehem was largely a Christian town. The rise of Islamism in the region had taken its toll and the second *intifada* had supposedly administered a deathblow to West Bank tourism. Christians were already leaving in droves and those who remained were economically squeezed. In the brief period of euphoria after Madrid a developer had built a five-star hotel in Bethlehem, the Jacir Palace, within walking distance of the Church of the Nativity. It was in anticipation of the hordes of tourists who would flock to the city when peace came. But it hadn't worked out that way and the hotel supposedly sat empty almost most of the year. So, there didn't seem to be a reason to make advance reservations. A couple of days before Christmas I had the office manager call the Jacir Palace to check on availability but she reported that it was fully booked. She tried several other hotels in the city and they, too, were full. Bethlehem this Christmas season was booming. So much for the conventional wisdom.

If Bethlehem wasn't an option Jerusalem was the next best thing. It would be a chance to revisit the American Colony hotel in the eastern part of the city. It was originally built as a pasha's palace and I had stumbled on it during the visit in 1983. It was a jewel, although the rooms were less impressive than the common areas. It was still in business in 2008, now the favorite watering hole of American contractors. But it, too, was fully booked. So, I settled on the Ambassador near Mount Scopus, half a-mile from the American Colony and still within walking distance of the Old City. Although it had none of the amenities or history of the American Colony, it would do. I left on Christmas Eve, a Wednesday, and caught a ride with our Jerusalem-based driver on his commute home. We avoided the Qalandya checkpoint, always a bottleneck, and went through Baytuniya where there was generally less wait. The uniformed girl at the booth was officious, but Kanaan was fluent in Hebrew and gave as good as he got. We were soon through the checkpoint and entered the maze of side streets, uprooted pavement, unimproved roadway, concrete barriers, and the Wall that constituted the Palestinian entrance to Jerusalem. The locals said all this was designed to make their lives as difficult as possible and eventually drive them away.

Ten minutes later we exited the maze near Beit Hanina and merged onto the freeway that bisects the city and carries traffic to Tel Aviv. From then on it was clear sailing. At the Ambassador, the desk clerk was helpful and after selecting a room with a view to the south we traced out the most direct route to the Old City. Dinner that night was in the hotel dining room where the clientele were representatives of the middle-to upper-crust of Palestinian Christian society, or at least those of the Latin persuasion. The Orthodox had never accepted the Gregorian adjustment to the Julian Calendar and, over the years, the difference in timing of the feasts had grown to thirteen days. The Orthodox would celebrate Christmas on January seventh. But they looked the same the Middle East over, these local Christians, different from the Arabs who came in the seventh and the European Jews who came in the twentieth centuries. On this festive night the short men and stout matrons, all of them dark-eyed, were dressed to the teeth.

If it couldn't be Bethlehem, the Church of the Holy Sepulcher here in Jerusalem was a good second choice. Christmas day dawned cold and drizzling. We tend to think of the Middle East as dry and unpleasantly hot. But the latitude of Bethlehem was just under 32 degrees, about the same as that of Los Angeles. And the Levant was subject to the Mediterranean weather system of dry summers and rainy winters.

Amman Snowfall

Snow was not unheard of in December and January. To the east it was colder still and we had experienced snowfalls in Amman that were heavy enough to shut down the airport and bring the city to a halt. The snow and the evergreen Christmas trees of our Western tradition came from Germany, although Bethlehem may well have had both on that first Christmas day, with snow on the ground and stands of pine in the surrounding hills. But the question was probably moot since most scholars believe that Jesus wasn't born in December at all, if only because shepherds weren't tending their flocks in the fields during the winter. It would have been too cold in late December and, anyway, the animals would have been brought in after the first autumn rains.

I set out from the Ambassador in mid-morning and made my serpentine way down to Nablus Road. There were a couple of convenience stores nearby that would come in handy later in the day. In the shops in Ramallah there was only poor-quality Palestinian and worse Israeli wine and I was looking forward to a room-service Christmas dinner with decent wine. I passed the American Colony, looking farther from the road than I remembered it, and resolved to pay a visit on the way back. By the time I reached the junction with Salah al-Din Street the rain was falling more heavily and I stopped in a shop and bought a *shamsiyya* to ward off the downpour. Umbrellas in the Middle East typically protected you against the sun, hence the name in Arabic. But there was no sun on this, the Latin Christmas day.

Damascus Gate

After fifteen minutes, I reached the *Bab al-Amud*, otherwise known as the Damascus Gate, also looking different from twenty-five years before. I entered the Old City and headed southwest towards the Christian Quarter.

Now the cityscape became more familiar. The paths were narrow and slippery and I hugged the sixteenth-century Ottoman walls for what little protection they afforded against the slanting rain. I knew the general direction of the church, but the way was labyrinthine, steps up and then down and sudden turns that took me back the way I had come. So, after about ten unproductive minutes I began to ask directions. I wasn't sure of the Arabic of "the Church of the Holy Sepulcher" so I tried *kanisa kabira*, or "the large church," but since the Latin and Greek Orthodox patriarchates were nearby the question often drew a blank. Finally, a man pointed me in the right direction and I headed through a long, covered arcade with butcher shops featuring unappetizing-looking chicken parts, before several more questions, more arcades, and then a final turn into the large courtyard in front of the church. I had arrived. There were hundreds of people in the square and more in the church itself, most of them looking young and European. It was odd, this reverence for a Christian feast in a continent where church attendance had fallen precipitously.

But was Christmas really about church attendance? I had just read Simon Murray's *Legionnaire* and a description of the fervor with which Christmas was celebrated by the French Foreign Legion in Muslim Algeria in 1961. The legionnaires, many of them petty criminals or veterans of the *Wehrmacht* or the Polish resistance who couldn't adjust to life on the outside, were hardly exemplary Christians. And, it was true, Christmas Eve was just an excuse to get drunk. But, still, the Yuletide displays in the tents had been lavish and the Germans sang *Stille Nacht* as only the Germans could. It seemed that religion was as much a matter of culture as theology, in the case of the legionnaires, probably a defiant expression of identity in an utterly foreign setting. Much of the religious passion in the Middle East was an expression of the same cultural identity and solidarity.

Later in the day I would listen to the Bach's *Selig is der Mann* (Blessed is the Man) and the text of the cantata was a measure of the distance that separated the Europe of nearly 300 years ago from our own era. It had been written for the second day of Christmas in 1725 and the libretto of the second aria expressed a sentiment typical of the age:

> I would wish death upon myself, death,
> if You, my Jesus, did not love me.
> Indeed, when you trouble over me,
> I suffer more than the torments of Hell.

The words sounded strange, over the top, today. One of the reasons for the rapid loss of interest in the sacred cantatas—what John Eliot Gardiner has called the most consistently beautiful and varied body of music ever composed—is that the sentiments they expressed had passed out of fashion. Even the Bach sons found the music of their father dated, unlike the spirited operas, concertos, and symphonies of Haydn and Mozart. Comparison of the libretto of *Selig is der Mann* with something from the Ring Cycle a hundred and fifty years later was another measure of the distance Europe had come. Jettisoned was Christianity—that bastard offspring of Judaism and Europe—with its message of mildness and resignation, replaced by a celebration of the crude energy and strength of the pagan Nordic sagas. Europe threw out the baby with the bathwater and, with a little help from another anti-Christian creed it would soon enter a new Dark Ages. The pendulum had swung back the other way now, but I wondered who in the crowd outside the Church of the Holy Sepulcher today welcomed death or worried very much about hell?

This church, established on the site of Golgotha, the Place of the Skull where Jesus was supposed to have been crucified, was originally called the Church of the Anastasis or Resurrection. It was Crusaders who expanded the Emperor Constantine's fourth-century basilica and Constantine Monomarchus's eleventh-century rotunda into the eclectic Byzantine-Romanesque jumble that we saw today. It was also the Crusaders who began calling it the Holy Sepulcher. They did so by bringing all the shrines at the site—Calvary, Christ's tomb, and the resting place of the True Cross—under a single roof. The portion open to the public today appeared to represent only about a third of the complex, which also included dormitories, an infirmary, a kitchen, and a refectory. We entered through the left of the two arches in the facade into what appeared to be a warren, or a multi-storied series of warrens, with displays of every kind of liturgical decoration known to Christianity: gilt, paintings, icons, mosaics, candelabra, altars. The gross lineaments gave it the look of one of the massive Mamluk mosques in Cairo.

The focal point of the church should have been the Edicule, or the boxlike nineteenth-century shrine marking the tomb of Christ, which appeared from the floor plan to be located in the Rotunda that terminated the long axis of the church. But from the ground level there appeared to be no visible axis, nothing to draw the eye toward this point. There was too much else in the way, too many chapels and shrines catering to the many Christian sects to give the structure any semblance of architectural homogeneity. That was just as well because there wasn't much homogeneity in Christianity.

Such was the state of relations between Latin and Orthodox churches in the Holy City, and between sects within them, that Muslim authorities had traditionally been called upon to referee turf battles in the church. The Greeks jousted with the Latins, the Ethiopians with the Egyptians, and the Armenians, Syrians, Franciscans, and Capuchins all pursued their national or doctrinal interests. Each was confined to a particular part of the church, and woe betide the sect that trespassed on the preserve of another. When Ronald Storrs became the military governor of Jerusalem after the British took the city in 1917 he rigorously enforced General Allenby's doctrine of *Status Quo*: no innovations would be allowed to threaten the peace in this cockpit of sectarian animus. Storrs may have been a bit of a stuffed shirt, but it would be hard to imagine a more suitable governor for a place as eclectic as Jerusalem. He tells the story in *Orientations*, his account of, among other things, nine years of stewardship in the Holy City. With his fastidious culture, ecumenism, and catholicity of interests, he entered enthusiastically into the lists, technically as a referee but just as often tilting good-naturedly with all concerned.

The three "people of the book" all considered Jerusalem to be holy and Muslim-Christian or Muslim-Jewish or Christian-Jewish friction was to be expected. But the unseemly state of relations between Christian sects, and even within the sects themselves, was a regular feature of life in the city. Since neither the Orthodox nor the Latin community trusted the other—and the Protestants were, of course, beyond the Pale—the key to this venerable pile had traditionally been kept by a Sunni Muslim, and so it remained under the British. A minor—to some—incident illustrated the passions that could be aroused in this holiest church in Christianity. The Ethiopians had taken control of a small monastery on the roof of the church, which they previously disputed with the Egyptians. Both fell under the jurisdiction of the Coptic pope and the See of Alexandria. But given the general rule in sectarian discord—the closer the relationship the greater the animosity—the dispute led to physical confrontation and even bloodshed. Storrs had earlier been called on to rule whether electric lights could be introduced into the cells in the monastery. But electrification was considered an innovation and, so, in violation of the *Status Quo*. The Egyptians and the Ethiopians were free to carry on their feud but they would continue do so in an unenlightened state.

After a rapid circuit of the chapels and Calvary sites, we exited from the church through the same doors by which we had entered. It wasn't much of a spiritual experience. There was more to the city than this church, of course, and I missed the Armenian Quarter, the Muslim Quarter, the Jewish Quarter, and the Haram al-Sharif of the Muslims and the Temple Mount to the Jews. But it was the best I could do on this Christmas Day. Most of the shops in the vicinity of the church were open, featuring olivewood figurines, and crèches, Palestinian pottery, local handicrafts, brass and copperware, and oriental carpets. But after thirty years in the Middle East I had seen it all before. I left the Old City through the Jaffa Gate and made my way northwest to vicinity of the New Gate where the walls turned northeast towards the Damascus Gate. The rain was still falling steadily and the lower half of my trousers and my shoes were soaked through. At Nablus Road, I turned left and made for the American Colony. After ten minutes, it appeared on the right, inset from the road and protected by its own gate.

It had an interesting history. Founded in 1881 by a group of families from Chicago devoted to a communal Christian life, the "colony" maintained good relations with both its Jewish neighbors and the nearby Bedouins, in the process earning a reputation among all-concerned for fairness and generosity. More families followed, mainly Scandinavians from the United States, and they needed a larger space. So, they bought a nearby pasha's palace and, seeing the need for decent accommodations for westerners, they turned the palace into the hotel. After the British capture of Jerusalem many prominent figures, including Churchill and T. E. Lawrence, stayed at the hotel. In *Orientations* Storrs dryly observed that the families "came to do good and stayed to do well . . ." Although it was still called "the American Colony," by 1917 the majority of its members were Swedes or Norwegians. It continued as an outpost of Scandinavian evenhandedness over the next three-quarters of a century and, for that reason, was probably suspect to the Israelis after their capture of East Jerusalem in the Yom Kippur War. I recalled the disgust of the Swiss general manager in 1983 over the bribes she had to pay to the Israeli authorities to keep the place in operation.

Both the hotel shop and bookshop, across the courtyard from reception, were open, although the shop was unattended. It contained the usual collection of brass, copperware, and local artwork, including some nice David Roberts prints. At the bookshop, I bought Karen Armstrong's *A History of Jerusalem*. She was a bit of a phenomenon, a one-woman publishing house, a former Roman Catholic nun whose writings on the three "Abrahamic religions" made her a kind of Bernard Lewis without the agenda. At the main desk, I learned that the bar was closed for Christmas but that they served beer in the reception area and I started on *Jerusalem* while my pants dried. The mixed nuts were as good as they had been in 1983 and the traffic in and out was a repeat of the Ambassador the night before, nicely-dressed adults and little children in their holiday best. There was even a Santa Claus, not the roly-poly, pink-cheeked figure we saw in the West, but a thin, dark-eyed man whose costume seemed to envelop him. I finished my beer and moved on, back to the Ambassador with a stop at one of the stores I had seen that morning. There, the Christian shopkeeper had a good collection of wines in the fifty-shekel range and a bought a fifth of Cabernet for Christmas dinner.

It was now early in the afternoon and back in the room I flipped on the television and surfed through the channels. *Rai Uno*, the Italian channel, had departed from its usual fare of silly game shows and scantily-clad women and was showing a Christmas special. The music put me in the Christmas spirit, something that the morning in the Old City had not. Later, also on *Rai Uno*, came the Pope's *Urbi et Orbi* address, and it seemed fitting here, a mile from the Old City in Jerusalem. There he was, this frail little man on that stupendous balcony, in the skullcap that on someone else might look bizarre or vaguely threatening, with his scholarly bent and facility with languages, blessing "the City" and "the World" on the occasion of the birth of the Redeemer. For all of its insularity and resistance to change, this splendid, often corrupt, and thoroughly human institution had preached the same message for nearly two millennia. Dinner was roast beef in the room. I turned in early.

The next morning, December 26th, was getaway day. I made arrangements for a cab to Ramallah and the 200-shekel fare seemed reasonable. The cabbie—actually the owner of a transportation company—was, like most educated Palestinians, cynical about everything: the wall, the occupation, the Israelis, the Americans, and the Palestinians themselves.

On the news that morning appeared ominous signs that Israeli patience with Gaza was wearing thin. Or maybe it was just the political calculus. On Christmas Day, it had been reported that the IDF had completed preparations for a large-scale offensive. Before the day was out Olmert would issue another warning. The next day, Operation Cast Lead, the massive Israeli assault on Gaza, began.

19

Ramallah

Ramallah Real Estate

RAMALLAH WAS A TYPICAL West Bank city, laid out irregularly over the limestone hills that constituted most of the West Bank. It would be difficult to build anything geometrically over so uneven a surface. Actually, it appeared to be a series of separate cities that had radiated out from the old urban center. New neighborhoods seemed to be sprouting up everywhere, evidence of the building activity that seemed such an anomaly here. For a country under occupation with their every move under the watchful eye of the occupier, a surprising number of people were investing in new residential and commercial real estate. Everything was built of the white limestone that characterized the West Bank and the gleaming new surfaces gave parts of the city a tidy, even prosperous look. Some of the new apartments were very nice, large and tastefully appointed, and would not have been out of place in Jerusalem or west Amman. Our office was on Irsal Street in one of the new neighborhoods, next to the building where Hanan Ashrawi maintained an office. I sometimes saw her in the street, taking an evening constitutional. My apartment was a five-minute walk from the office. Both buildings were new. I didn't have a car, although the project Blazer was available on the weekends. But it would be difficult parking a big car in the narrow streets of the old city. That's where I did most of my weekly shopping. Besides, it gave me a chance to walk and that was always the best way to know a city.

Many shops were closed on Friday morning, the Muslim Sabbath, but the butchers, grocers, and greengrocers were open and those were the ones I patronized. The walk took me 500 meters up Irsal Street and past the office to al-Itha'a Street, the main drag into the city center. At nine o'clock there were few cars and fewer pedestrians in evidence, although the military and the police were already there, preparing for events later in the day. After another 500 meters, soldiers in green uniforms and red berets and carrying Kalashnikovs began to appear on the west side of the street, and they became more frequent as I approached the *Muqata'a*. That was the large compound and seat of the Palestinian Authority. It was also the site of Arafat's tomb, a tall rectangular structure with Arabic characters etched in the same white limestone that appeared in the rest of the city. The Israelis had worked over the compound in 2002, although it had no military value. But it was a symbol of Palestinian aspirations, always treated with contempt by the occupiers, and they razed it virtually to the ground, leaving Arafat to wash out his underwear in the single building that remained standing. The compound had since been rebuilt, probably with European money, and had the same clean look of the new neighborhoods. It was where the regular stream of dignitaries that came to Ramallah met Abu Mazen, or Mahmoud Abbas, the Palestinian president. The stream became more concentrated during the Israeli assault on Gaza. It also became a source of criticism of Abbas. Arafat would have been in Gaza with his people, at least rhetorically, but Abbas was in Ramallah sizing up the situation and weighing his options. Some Palestinians said he would never recover from the failure of leadership.

Ramallah Street Scene

The barking of the German Shepherds in the kennels inside the compound was the only sound that interrupted the quiet of the morning. After the *Muqata'a* the soldiers thinned out, to be replaced further on by armed figures in black, in the Arab world generally worn by the *mukhabarat*, or security services. The 700 meters from the *Muqata'a* to *al-Manara* square, a kind of city center, were increasingly commercial, with shopping centers, banks, parking lots and commercial buildings lining the east side of the street. But here the look of West Amman gave way to something closer to Cairo, and the warrens were decidedly Middle Eastern and Arab in appearance. Instead of the travel agencies and western name brands featured on Irsal Street there were little shops selling everyday needs, appliances, inexpensive clothes, and cheap cooking implements. On the west, aside from a narrow commercial strip, the land fell away steeply to the gorge below. There were a few new high-rises on the hills opposite but mostly it was barren, folds of limestone with a thin covering of scrub, rising and falling away into the distance. Tel Aviv lay only thirty miles or so away, and on a clear day you could see the city and, beyond it, the Mediterranean.

Judaean Hills

An earlier trip to Tel Aviv had been a lesson in geography and it showed why the early Jewish pioneers had avoided the West Bank. The sense of descending—literally—from the Judean hills to the plains of Galilee and Sharon was palpable. There was really nothing up here except hardscrabble limestone massifs dotted with the few things, mainly olive trees, that would grow in the terraces that had been wrested over the centuries from the niggardly soil. It was also easy to see why the olive was such an important part of the economy of Palestine, and how the uprooting of trees, not to mention the stoning by settler extremists of Palestinians during harvest time, was an assault on an entire way of life.

The early Zionist settlers had occupied the relatively fertile plains near the coast and in northern and central Galilee. It was a reversal of the situation in biblical times, when the Jews occupied the rocky hills and the Philistines and other people the flatland. In the 1948 war the Zionists had improved their positions from those laid out in the United Nations partition plan, largely by consolidating their hold on Galilee in the north and widening the corridor up to Jerusalem from the coast. But they left the West Bank alone, mainly because they might have provoked British intervention if they had taken on the Jordanian Arab Legion. Also, they wanted to preserve the international legitimacy that the United Nations had conferred on them with the partition plan. The plan called for 56 percent of the land be given to the Jews and 44 percent to the Arabs. Arab rejection meant that, by the time the armistice was brokered in 1949, the Jewish percentage had grown to 70 percent. Partition was a good deal for the Jews and the other 30 percent could be dealt with later. The Arabs had never been amenable to deals, having on their side *right*, that most seductive of advantages.

The British-officered Arab Legion had taken the West Bank and East Jerusalem during the war and, unlike the Iraqis, Egyptians, and the Syrians, the Jordanians had *not* threatened to throw the Jews into the sea. King Abdullah had limited objectives, essentially the same as those of the Zionists, which were to preserve the UN lines. He would take and hold only that area apportioned to an Arab entity in the partition plan. He also wanted that entity to be under Jordanian control, which it was until 1967 and the Six-day War. It was an exercise in *realpolitik* that made him suspect among extremist elements in his own country and he later paid for it with his life.

But the Jews could have taken the West Bank in 1948 had they wanted to. By the time the armistice was brokered in early 1949 they were in a much stronger position than the Arabs. They had internal lines and access to modern arms, mainly from Czechoslovakia, through black market connections they had developed over the years. International volunteers came from many countries in the West. The Israelis were better motivated, better led and, being largely European, were familiar with Western technology. And they were even more numerous, having combined Irgun and the Stern Gang with Hagganah into what later became the Israeli Defense Forces, or IDF. The integration was not without friction since the first two were terrorist organizations, guilty of widespread atrocities during the war.

But integrated they were, and the net effect was that by the end of 1948 the Arabs were outnumbered, outgunned, outgeneraled, and outmaneuvered. The notion that the tiny prospective Jewish state was assaulted by millions of hostile Arabs was largely a fiction. The armies of the front-line Arab states—Egypt, Syria, and Iraq—were weak, the British and French colonial regimes having done little to create strong militaries that could have challenged their rule. The Arabs invaded without plans, or even the rations necessary to sustain a prolonged campaign. Their most notable product was hot air and the armistice allowed them to withdraw from essentially untenable positions. It was not the last time they would be saved by international intervention, leaving the Israelis with an inveterate distrust of well-intentioned outsiders.

At *al-Manara*, so-called because of the statue of a minaret in the roundabout, the black figures gave way to the blue of the traffic police, and a Toyota pickup was generally parked there waiting for the morning temperature to rise. It was also a first stop, the newsstand where a Friday *International Herald Tribune* and English-language edition of *Haaretz* were available. The two came packaged together. The *Tribune* was essentially the *New York Times* minus the ads and the local sections, and you could get through it relatively quickly. But *Haaretz* required serious reading. The Friday edition included a section called "Week's End" and it was typically ten dense pages of op-ed pieces. The Israelis liked to talk and to write, and the pieces were long and sometime convoluted, full of deliberate Americanisms.

The generally leftist and pacifist editorial stance of *Haaretz* made it must-reading for anyone interested in exposure to the range of opinion of Israel. But it was honest enough to include opposing views, and was always an interesting read. To give Israel credit, there was a lively debate in the country about settlements, something that would be unthinkable in the United States. A recent Israeli study had shown that 40 percent of the settlements had been built on private Palestinian land for which no compensation had been paid. *Haaretz* opined that the fiction that there were "legal" and "illegal" settlements was just that, and everyone knew that they were *all* illegal. An Israeli acquaintance said that if I thought the English edition of *Haaretz* was outspoken I should read the Hebrew edition. The *Jerusalem Post* was also available but, by comparison with *Haaretz*, it was a bit of a rag, *USA Today* with an agenda.

Roundabout, Ramallah

By nine thirty people were beginning to appear in the center of the city and they were an interesting mix. There were a few older men wearing *kufiyas,* or head scarves, and occasionally an old woman in a Bedouin smock, but for the most part they were in nondescript western dress. Most of the women were veiled and in a random sample one day I counted 79 of the first 100 women I saw wearing the *hijab*. What I took to be Christian women were fashionably dressed and bareheaded, emphatically not veiled. In general, the men were darker and more hirsute than any Arab people I had ever seen. A barber earned his wage with the average Palestinian man, clipping the dense black hair on top, using a thread to remove facial hair above the line of the beard and electric clippers to remove the hair on the neck before it disappeared beneath the shirt. The men seemed more like the descendants of Assyrians, Medes, Persians, Hittites—whose beards, if the statuary was accurate, seemed to begin just below the eye—anything but the relatively smooth-cheeked Arabs of the peninsula. Surprisingly, they seemed different from the Jordanians, maybe because there were more Bedouins and Europeans in the Jordanian mix. I was used to seeing fair Palestinians, but these people were anything but fair. Could it be that they had avoided mixture with the Romans, Greeks, and Crusaders in the lowlands to the west and represented a relatively homogeneous remnant of an earlier, or even original, populace of upland Palestine?

After *al-Manara* it was on to *al-Mughtaribeen* square, or "Square of the Foreigners" if the dictionary was to be believed. Like *al-Manarah* it was not a square but a roundabout. Then it was 300 meters down Jaffa Street to the ATM across from the Royal Courts hotel where cash was available in dollars, shekels, and Jordanian dinars. By now the soldiers and police had disappeared. It was an area of restaurants that catered to the Palestinian upper crust and the expatriates who worked with them. Most served edible Italian food and drinkable Palestinian wine, although Darna was a bit of an anomaly, a large restaurant with a covered outdoor terrace that, like Tanoreen or Fakr al-Din in Amman, featured excellent mezzes and other local fare. In the evening, prominent lawyers or members of the Palestinian Authority—ministers or their deputies—could be seen eating, smoking, or just talking in the terrace. Strategically-placed charcoal braziers kept it warm in the winter. The area was also a kind of youth scene, and many of the restaurants featured live bands and the *shishas*, or water pipes, that were now a regular feature throughout the Arab World. Old men had always smoked *shishas*, but now everyone in Cairo, Amman, and Ramallah was a smoker.

After an infusion of shekels, it was northwest for 300 meters, past the restored Ramallah municipality building, where a plaque with the date 1908 presumably recorded its incorporation. Ramallah was not very old, having been settled by Christians in the nineteenth century, before the *nakba* changed its complexion forever. After the events of 1948 Muslim refugees streamed up from what was now Israel and by the end of the twentieth century many of the original Christian inhabitants were gone, having emigrated to the United States. Ramallah was now largely a Muslim city. But there were still Christian shops in the old city selling liquor—beer, wine, and hard stuff—although you had to go to Jerusalem to get pork.

The first stop was at the butcher, a Christian, where chicken at sixteen shekels a kilo (about two dollars a pound) and beef at forty-eight shekels were bargains. For some reason lamb, at sixty-five shekels, was much more expensive and I ate mainly chicken and beef stews in Ramallah. The butcher had relatives on both coasts of the United States and we always chatted in Arabic, although not about politics. Next, it was to the grocers where I bought a bottle of ʻarak, an anisette-like liqueur that, in ice and diluted with water, served as a kind of cocktail, and a couple of bottles of local wine. Then, for fruit and vegetables, it was up the street to the greengrocers, where the oranges were big and the bananas were small. All the ingredients for a good mixed salad were available, including radishes nearly the size of turnips. The selection was plentiful, clean, and beautifully displayed. There were even a few surprises, chestnuts from Turkey and avocados from Israel.

Down the street from the greengrocers was the pharmacy where I had gone when I had a parasite. In the Middle East, the first person you visited when you were sick was generally the pharmacist, and he or she often acted as physician as well. This man had listened to my symptoms and prescribed a cocktail that, after a week, had me feeling much better. He was a graduate of Cairo University and said he had been first in his class. I sometimes paid a visit just to chat. We spoke mostly in English about Arabic calligraphy or current events or, most often, about history. He was in his sixties and well-read, and particularly remembered the address of John Foster Dulles before the United Nations during the Suez crisis in 1956. The British, French, and Israelis had concocted a plan that would initiate action and then call for outside intervention, allegedly to separate the combatants. But the war was a transparent attempt by the British to punish Nasser and reestablish their hold on the canal. The French and the Israelis had different bones to pick, the French resenting Nasser's assistance to the FLN in Algeria and the Israelis his fostering of *fedayeen* attacks inside Israel. The invasion had been mounted without American complicity or even knowledge. Eisenhower was furious at being kept in the dark and Dulles had turned up the rhetorical heat on all three, threatening sanctions, most of them financial. They had caved. It was the first—and probably also the last—time that we had used our leverage over the Israelis in any meaningful way.

The pharmacist was a product of an Arab educational system that supposedly taught by rote and didn't encourage independent thinking. But this man was a reader and a thinker, old enough to remember a more evenhanded America, or at least one with a different set of prejudices. As with other educated Arabs, there were aspects of his experience and upbringing that we would never understand. With the passing of his generation the residue in the occupied territories would be one only of bitterness.

In the shops the news from Gaza on *Al-Jazeera*, was the constant backdrop, but no one—not even the occasional shopkeeper with the typical Sunni beard, unkempt but with the mustaches clipped—seemed particularly energized by the unfolding disaster. They had seen it all before, with the two *intifadas* and most recently the second Lebanon war in 2006. No one seemed to blame us, but we did bear some responsibility for the disaster, if only in our refusal to restrain the Israelis. It wasn't clear that we actually accelerated the delivery of smart weapons as we had done with Lebanon in 2006, but this was the second act in Condoleezza Rice's unfolding drama, "The birth pangs of the new Middle East."

It was waged allegedly to stop Palestinian rockets on Israeli cities, which was fair enough, but the timing and scale of the response made it clear that this was a political war. There was an upcoming Israeli election and Tzipi Livni and Ehud Barak were angling for electoral advantage. As it turned out, the real beneficiary was Bibi, waiting in the wings. This was democracy in the Middle East in action, although some would argue that elections and democracy were not the same thing. It was different from 2006 only in that, this time, there would be no Israeli casualties, although the wanton destruction of infrastructure and use of banned weapons were a repeat of the earlier action. In 2006, the Israelis had put a quarter of the population of Lebanon on the road, in the process destroying their homes, mosques, shops, schools, and hospitals. When they were finished, they strewed cluster bomblets over what little remained. In Gaza in 2008, there was nowhere to go, but the destruction was just as great. For the F-16's overhead it was like shooting fish in a barrel.

The local newspapers were full of grisly color pictures of the dead—generally children—but there seemed to be a lack of spirit in the people

I talked with. Of the three channels in English covering the events I preferred *Al-Jazeera*, not only for its nonstop coverage but, oddly enough, because it seemed the most balanced. The BBC was uneven, depending on the correspondent they had stationed outside the strip, and their man inside was alarmist and barely understandable in English. The events spoke for themselves and didn't need editorial emphasis. CNN was, well, just CNN, the same collection of news readers I remembered from Jordan in 2005, earnest in a particularly American way, although they may have originally been from Bulgaria, Australia, and Canada. That was another difference between Israel and the United States. They saw everything while we were fed a steady diet of Fox, CNN, and the tepid fare on local channels.

With three heavy plastic bags the mile and a-half back to the apartment would be by taxi and I would hail one near the greengrocer's. The Ministry of Transport had mandated the introduction of meters in the cabs, but by the time I left they still weren't working. Most cabbies didn't seem to think that things would change much from the informal system that already seemed fair. The cabs were typically new and clean and you always rode in the front seat next to the cabbie. That was the way it was in the Arab World. The back seat was where women rode. Seat belts were available but only the expatriates wore them in Ramallah. That wouldn't have been permitted in Israel and drivers buckled up on the outskirts of Jerusalem. They grudgingly praised the system in Israel, even if they had no use for the occupation. Our driver, fluent in Hebrew, would even argue with the soldiers at the checkpoints, smirking at them as we drove away. The occupation bred contempt on both sides of the divide. The cab took the back-way home, down Ein al-Mishbah Street into the gorge before climbing up the other side to Irsal Street. Some of the streets were so steep that they looked like they would be impassable in the winter and cabbies said that when it snowed nobody drove at all. The trip took about five minutes and cost ten shekels, or two and a-half dollars.

I was generally back in the apartment by eleven o'clock, well before the mosques emptied. Then, the streets that had been deserted would be thronged with tens of thousands of people, especially as the events in Gaza unfolded. It was then that we would hear about protests in Ramallah. They were generally peaceful, although the Palestinian police increasingly used batons and tear gas when things threatened to get out of hand. The Israeli military headquarters for the West Bank was in a suburb of Ramallah and, although I didn't see a soldier in four months in the city, the Palestinians said their presence could be sensed everywhere. It was at these times that I realized the futility of what we were trying to do, in effect making our own little contribution to democracy in the Middle East.

The Israelis had given Abu Mazen nothing that he could take to his people. So, the American projects were designed to resurrect his electoral fortunes and those of *Fatah*, widely perceived by the Palestinian people to be corrupt and out of touch. But the results to date had mainly to do with improved policing, admittedly a necessary if not sufficient condition for progress, and they were probably more reassuring to the Israelis than to the Palestinians. The real power to change the lives of the people lay not with the Americans or *Fatah,* or the Palestinian Authority, but with the occupying power. It was said that the Israelis had come to the intellectual realization that they couldn't hold the territories any longer, but politically they couldn't cut the ties. There it was, democracy—or was it politics—again, although some would argue that democracy and politics were not the same thing. But it was clear that if they wanted peace with the Palestinians the Israelis would eventually have to get off their land and get out of their lives.

www.ingramcontent.com/pod-product-compliance
Lightning Source LLC
Chambersburg PA
CBHW070226230426
43664CB00014B/2230